HISTORY OF INDIAN NATIONAL CONGRESS
(1885–2002)

HISTORY OF INDIAN NATIONAL CONGRESS (1885–2002)

Compiled and Edited by

Deep Chand Bandhu

KALPAZ

Published by

Kalpaz Publications
C-30, Satyawati Nagar,
Delhi – 110052
Ph.: 011-47034999, 9811692060
www.kalpazpublications.com
E-mail: kalpaz@hotmail.com

Distribution Network
gyanbooks.com
India, USA, Canada, UK, Australia, France

ISBN: 978-81-7835-090-5 (HB)

Reprint in India, 2024
First Published, 2003

Printed at: Gyan Press, Delhi.

History of Indian National Congress (18852002)
Editor: Deep Chand Bandhu

Dedicated

to

The People of India

Contents

PART–II

Preface

The foundation of Indian National Congress in 1885 is the most significant in the annals of the Indian sub-continent. It was spearheaded by top educated people of India who could attract the attention of millions of people living in the far flung areas. The anti-Raj stance under Gandhiji's leadership was successful as it was totally non-violent.

He emerged as a Congress leader in 1915 after the sudden demise of Gopal Krishna Gokhale and Pherozeshah Mehta. He took up the tremendous responsibility as he was advised by Gokhale his political *guru.* Indeed the period from the commencement of the first global war to the end of the second global war is most crucial in the annals of Indian sub-continent.

The theme has been comprehensively weaved into thirty chapters, giving each and every detail having deep bearing on political and socio-economic developments of more than a century. It covers emergence of Indian National Congress as a foremost political party on the stage of Indian sub-continent, the role of prominent leaders, Annie Besant's Home Rule Movement, role of Gokhale, Tilak, Gandhiji and Nehru, to Patel, Azad and Bose to generate the spirit of patriotism among the people, Congress and Anglo-Muhammedan Alliance, Reaction against Rowlatt Bills with the emergence of Mahatma Gandhi, Congress and Khilafat, the Non-Cooperation Movement, the role of Swaraj Party, Nehru as Congress President in 1929 at Lahore session, the Civil Disobedience Movement, Gandhi-Irwin Pact, elections after the Act of 1935 was passed, role of S.C. Bose, Quit India Movement, road to Partition, Congress under Nehru, Indo-China War, the regime of Shastriji, Congress and Indira Gandhi, role of Rajiv Gandhi, Congress and P.V. Narasimha Rao, Sita Ram Kesari and last but not the least the role of Sonia Gandhi as a disciplined parliamentarian in the Lok Sabha. Her speeches in Lok Sabha as well as in public are quite logical and based on the high principles of Indian National Congress. Whenever she tours any part of India, millions of people gather to listen to her. Thus she has gained remarkable love, respect and support from all sections of our society including men, women, students, peasants and weaker sections, labourers in the far flung regions. She always gives out her ideas for numerous socio-economic schemes meant for the weaker sections of our society. Indeed her love for India and the people is superb in every respect. With her disciplined policy, planning and efforts Congress has gained power in as many as fourteen states.

This work indeed would be useful for numerous categories of our society including teachers, researchers and students.

Deep Chand Bandhu

Introduction

This book is a chronological study on the journey of the Congress from its birth on 28 December 1885 in Bombay under the guidance of Allan Octavian Hume till 2001. During the early decades of twentieth century when the increasing tides of Congress might were felt across the nation, the Home Rule, a brainchild of Annie Besant, an Irish lady, bolstered the very essence of this nationalist movement. The advent of Annie Besant came at a time when India needed the services of a leader who could give practical lead to the nation. The launching of an All India Home Rule League in September 1915 was, indeed, the most eventful episode in her career which was largely based on result-oriented political activities.

In the meantime, the Congress began to have a rather peculiar experience, in the form of Muslim apathy towards it, both from progressive and conservative sections, which posed a considerable threat to its political prospects. To the conscious Muhammedans, the Congress had posed a problem, whether to join or not to join it. This difference continued to persist till the end of the *Raj,* despite Congress' attempts to avoid the likely consequences inherent in the acceptance of the two-nation theory by the Indian Muslims. This led to Muslim tilt towards the British and it resulted in the formation of Muslim League. Though the post-First World War brought about a brief spell of Hindu-Muslim harmony, in the long run, it failed to last due to political separatism which sealed the fate of a United India.

The emergence of Mahatma Gandhi into political horizon of India transformed the very essence of the nationalist movement. Soon after his return to India from South Africa in 1915, Gandhi asserted that India's salvation lay in the adoption of *satyagraha* as the basis of political action. This led to the launching of the Non-cooperation movement in the early 1920s, a fallback of severe social and economic unrest. Although the movement was by and large peaceful, an act of violence at Chauri Chaura in the United Provinces compelled Gandhi to call it off altogether. Meanwhile, another movement in the name of *Khilafat* emerged in the national political scenario which gave a splendid opportunity to strengthen Hindu-Muslim harmony. But like the Non-cooperation movement, *Khilafat* movement also failed to make much headway.

The next movement to emerge was Civil Disobedience Movement. The contribution of Jawaharlal Nehru to the growth of the national movement was no less significant compared to that of Mahatma Gandhi. In fact, Nehru's socialist vision provided a novel ideological poise to the national movement. This, in due course of time, helped the Congress lead India to political independence. One of the prominent features of the Civil Disobedience Movement was the breach of the salt tax law led by the Mahatma at Dandi on the western coast of India alongwith Congress volunteers. Despite numerous arrests and police brutality, the movement continued unabated till the Gandhi-Irwin Pact was signed.

The emergence of Subhas Chandra Bose added a new dimension to the freedom movement as well as to the stature of the Congress itself. In the words of Gandhiji, Bose was not only a great patriot, he was 'a patriot of patriots'. But differences with senior Congress leaders cropped up which led him to leave the party. Bose, however, led a different armed movement which made him a unifying and inspiring symbol of Indian nationalism.

The Quit India Movement commencing on August 9, 1942 gave a new impetus to freedom movement, which was in its final phase. It was the last major movement launched in order to oust the British rule. The outbreak of Second World War in which Britain was also involved, delayed India's freedom to a certain extent. Meanwhile, with the Congress outlawed and its leaders in prison, the political stage was clear for the Muslim League regarding its demand for a separate nation for Muslims. Muhammad Ali Jinnah gave a new lead to the League's demands, despite Gandhiji's repeated requests for a single nation. To save the nation from an impending civil war, the Congress agreed to the concept of Partition, and consequently two separate nations, viz., India and Pakistan were born. Once independence was attained, it was left to the Congress to take new steps in building a prosperous India. The success of the Congress as a ruling political party in the post-independence era, especially until 1964 can largely be attributed to the charismatic personality of Nehru—the first Prime Mnister of independent India.

Indira Gandhi established herself as a frontline leader of the country. Indira, in fact, later on went on to become a world leader. She, like her father had the capacity to get people behind her. The slogans like *Garibi Hatao* won her the 1971 elections and 'Government that Works' brought her back to the saddle of power again in 1980. The Congress party organisation and its parliamentary wing were complementary to each other. Together they shaped the socialist policy—a dream project of the Congress.

The 1960s saw a rise in violent activities in various corners of the country, especially in the north-eastern part. Lal Bahadur Shastri, the second Prime Minister, assumed office at such a critical juncture. He wholeheartedly was in favour of sympathy, understanding and perseverance to solve any violent movement or unrest in any part of the country. As a Home Minister, he supported the amendment of the constitution to confer Statehood for Nagaland.

Shastri's tragic death in Tashkent in 1966 paved the way for Indira Gandhi to rise to the saddle of power. Indira, in no time, became aware of the design of the 'Syndicate' and began to build up an image of her own among the masses and also a base for herself in the party. This gradually led to struggle for supremacy between the 'kingmaker' and the 'king' which revived the old conflict between the government and the organisation resulting in Congress split of 1969.

Indira Gandhi introduced three striking changes in the structure of the Congress in terms of a new decision-making hierarchy in which power of the party and government became centralised with the Prime Minister; reformation of the federal character of the party and government and attempt to change the support base of the Congress through new and arbitrary standards of recruitment. One of the prominent features of Indira's Prime Ministership was the commitment of the Congress in developing the Indian economy for the upliftment of the condition of the masses.

This trend followed during the tenure of Rajiv Gandhi, following Indira's assassination in October 31, 1984. The Rajiv-led new Congress government showed commitment to increase the economic resources and also to provide priority in handling of policy matters. Rajiv Gandhi was determined to make the Congress effective in playing its role to make India vibrant, strong and dynamic in all fronts. His concern had all along been about the time and speed to put the nation on the track of development. However, Rajiv failed to enjoy another stint as the Prime Minister. When it seemed likely that he would return to power, Rajiv was assassinated at an election rally in Tamil Nadu. At this juncture, elections were held and Congress formed the government with P.V. Narasimha Rao as the new Prime Minister. In the area of nation building, the two most controversial issues which confronted Narasimha Rao-led government were the issue of reservation to backward castes and the dispute over the Babri Masjid.

Following the end of Narasimha Rao's tenure in 1996, Sita Ram Kesari rose to the position of the Congress president. A little later Sonia Gandhi at last gave her consent to become Party President following mass support in her favour. Though it is no more in power at Centre, the presence of the Congress can hardly be ignored.

Editor meets Smt. Sonia Gandhi with All India Jat Sabha to afford OBC status to Jats.

Editor with Smt. Sonia Gandhi on X-mas Day with all Delhi Congress MLAs.

Editor congratulates the elected Delhi Chief Minister Sheila Dikshit.

Shri Jag Parvesh Chandra's felicitation to the Editor, elected Delhi Congress President, 1995.

PART—I

1

Emergence of the Indian National Congress

The course of nationalism in India and it's freedom movement are intrinsically related with the history of the Indian National Congress. Even if at its inception its real implication was not fully evident, yet with the regular holding of its annual sessions, the growing numbers of delegates and sympathisers who attended these conventions and the bourgeoning of the organisational network labelled the Congress as the dominant nationalist institution in the country. What happened in the following years merely reinforced its pre-eminence in Indian politics.

With the mobilisation of new social groups under Gandhi's leadership since 1920, the Congress assumed the aspects of a mass movement uniting the Indian society to launch a major assault upon the bastions of the British *Raj.* When the *Raj* gave in by making constitutional amendments which brought the executive under the control of elected legislatures, after the Government of India Act of 1935, the Congress donned the garb of a parliamentary party. The elections of 1937 saw comprehensive victories for the Congress in several regions of the subcontinent. A decade later, the Congress came to inherit political power in non-Muslim areas, thus bringing to a successful consummation of several decades of relentless struggle for the realisation of India's freedom.

Congress Gets a Footing

Although the Congress represented the first truly all-India political institution in the subcontinent, yet its establishment must be seen as the consummation of the work of the associations that had come into being since the 1850s. These associations inaugurated by the intelligentsia played an instrumental role in ushering in the Congress. None played so prominent a part as the Indian Association which during Lord Lytton's tenure organised national campaigns against government policies which were seen as adverse to India's welfare. It was the leadership of this association which saw itself as the nucleus of the emerging nationalist movement.

Recent studies have revealed the role of a relatively obscure and self-effacing retired British civilian—Allan Octavian Hume—in the foundation of the Congress.[1] While it is known that he had extensive contacts with the Indian intelligentsia prior to 1885, what puzzles us is that he had not taken into his confidence the leaders of the Indian Association nor actively involved them in his political campaigns. Hence, when the Congress came into being under the efforts of Hume and his allies in Bombay, the leaders of the Indian Association were playing host to a National Conference held in Calcutta.

The idea of an all-India collaboration had been mooted more than three decades prior to the emergence of the Congress. In 1850, when the issue of Lex Loci legislation had aroused Hindu fears of possible sedition of their established laws of inheritance, abortive discussions occurred between the leaders of Calcutta and Madras about the desirability of making nation-wide protest to the British authorities. Hindu leaders addressing a public meeting in Calcutta called for solidarity with fellow-Hindus in the districts and North-West Provinces. However, this appeal for unity ran into rough weather with Bombay and Poona forming their separate associations while Madras endured a brief and uneasy partnership with Bengal before going its own way.

These abortive attempts to develop inter-provincial cooperation, which in effect were failures of the bourgeoisie that inspired them, paved the way for the educated to demonstrate its commitment to national unity and thereby lay claim to political leadership of the country. Significantly the first-ever a near all-India level body was founded by Indian students in Britain in 1865, called the London Indian Society which failed to survive long, being soon absorbed into the newly-formed East Indian Association in 1866.

The East Indian Association represented a more ambitious endeavour on the part of the intelligentsia to develop all-India unity. A Bombay branch was established in 1869, and although it ran smoothly for several years, thanks mainly to Naoroji's efforts, nonetheless response from other Indian centres was poor as to make it a representative of an all-India institution.

It may be argued that the failure of the East Indian Association can be traced to its emigre status and influence of European element in its leadership. Close links with the Old India Hands further damaged the association's prospects. Naoroji and his Indian allies had hoped that the inclusion of Britishers would increase its effectiveness as a pressure group in Britain, but this advantage could only be bought by having an element which was not Indian and, what was more damaging, whose sympathy towards India was suspected in Indian quarters. Pleas for increased Indian representation in the committee of the association were heard in the 1870s, but when these went unheeded some Indian organs asserted that the body "does not represent the *people of India*". To add to woes, there was increasing suspicion amongst the Indian educated that the Old India Hands who conducted the East Indian Association were antagonistic towards Indian aspirations. Even the staunchest of the Indian supporters of the association, like Naoroji, had decided to part company with it, convinced that the contention between the Old India Hands and Indian intelligentsia made any further collaboration impossible.[2]

One group that had profited from these early experiences in all-India collaboration was the Bengali intelligentsia. The emigre organisations founded in the 1860s owed little to Bengali initiative. Whatever stimulus there was on the Indian side seemed to have emanated from Bombay, with which the Bengalis had few links.[3] While the intelligentsia in Bombay was busy with the London-based organisations, the educated Bengalis were taking the first steps towards discovering

India. Mainly through the Brahmo movement, with Keshub Chandra Sen as its leader, Bengalis in the 1860s began to roam the subcontinent, setting up Brahmo centres wherever they could enlist local support and bringing back to Bengal Brahmo recruits from other parts of India for training. Much of these efforts were part of the propagation of Brahmoism, but there were times when the Brahmos also donned the garb of political missionaries by boldly preaching the message of national unity and instigating the educated to come to the forefront. Sen's inciting speeches delivered throughout the country during the 1870s harped frequently on the theme of 'Young India' coming together to form 'one caste for all the educated natives of India' and then take in all other classes of the nature communities and unite them in a vast and mighty federation.[4]

In the choice of its name,[5] and in excluding Europeans from its ranks, the Indian Association tried to establish the pre-conditions for the inauguration of an all-India organisation which was followed by the setting up of branches all over the country, ties with local groups outside Bengal, and the utilisation of these ties to mount national campaigns. The controversial measures associated with Lytton's viceroyalty, notably the reduction of the age limit of entry into the covenanted service and the Vernacular Press Act, provided handy issues capable of rallying the intelligentsia throughout the country resentful of acts of colonial discrimination. Believing that personal contacts were needed to give a fillip to a common protest, the Indian Association deputed 'special delegates' to journey to important political centres in the country. Although these emissaries found themselves in the company of strangers, with whom they differed in all respects, yet when they addressed local audiences they found they were speaking the same language, voicing the same problems and articulating the same aspirations. This bolstered the confidence of the leaders of the Indian Association. As the *Bengalee* claimed in October 1879, the Indian Association "speaks and works for the millions and represents all sections of the community".[6]

The Poona Sarvajanik Sabha had come to improve ties with the Indian Association during the 1870s and had even entered into formal negotiations about the possibility of launching a nationwide movement. In January 1878, when a delegation of the Poona Sarvajanik Sabha visited Calcutta for talks with the Indian Association, both sides stressed on "the need for unity and inter-provincial co-operation".[7] In the South, politicians were also advocating such endeavours.

The failure of the Indian Association can be owed to its inability to comprehend the objective circumstances under which such ambitious schemes could be realised. Its leaders misread the significance of Lytton's policies as supplying the necessary catalyst to coalesce the fragmented political elites in the country under the banner of a common movement. It is hard to deny that rumblings and discontent did not exist in the country, or for that matter that emissaries of the Indian Association like S.N. Banerjea were unable to engender feelings of sympathy amongst leaders of other regions for the idea of a united Indian protest.

What also worked against the Indian Association's schemes was the technique through which such an ideal was to be realised. The Indian Association, since its inception, had projected itself as the central organisation at Calcutta. What the leaders of the Indian Association did not recognise was that the Indian intelligentsia, despite professions of being an all-India class and advocating for unity, formed a series of local elites jealous of preserving their freedom of action. It is noteworthy that in many centres, these cities had already founded their own associations which conferred on them considerable local influence and communication with the colonial authorities. When the Indian Association exerted pressure on these elites to open up branch associations, it gave rise to doubt that they were being called upon to surrender their autonomy for the benefit of national unity, which they were unwilling to make. Thus, as Professor Mehrotra argues, "the ideal of a central organisation in the metropolis of India, having branches all over the country and directing a national movement, was impracticable in the India of the nineteenth century."[8]

To add to woes, the visible manifestation of anti-Bengali sentiment in many parts of North India during the 1870s compounded the difficulties of the Indian Association. This was the legacy of the penetration of colonies of Bengalis in search of employment and livelihood. The migratory movement, which initially went quite unnoticed, had by then begun to draw resentments from local elites jealous of Bengali competitors for limited openings in the professions. The anti-Bengali feeling assumed gigantic proportions in the North-West Provinces and the Punjab thereby denting the prospects of the Indian Association which was hoping to stimulate goodwill to launch a nationalist movement under its belt.[9]

Another handicap which further diminished its prospects of leading an emerging nationalist movement stemmed from existence of regional and communal ideologies in Bengal which conflicted with the broad-based secular creed of nationalism that the body was trying to propagate. Communal and regional sentiment was not characteristic of Bengal alone. However, it was Bengal where such feelings had come to be articulated early and with great clarity and vigour. Even more powerful was the appeal of Bengali regionalism, founded upon unities endowed by common language, literary tradition and history. Intellectuals like Bankim Chandra Chattopadhyaya sought to give content and form to Bengal's sense of mission as well as develop appropriate imagery and symbols. Bankim Chandra decried the excessive westernisation of the Bengali intelligentsia, notably the neglect of Bengali language and the consequent alienation from the masses. He started a journal in 1872 to prove that Bengali was capable of becoming the medium of refined literary expression. He also exhorted Bengalis to write their own history so as to chronologise their past achievements and do honour to their immortal figures. Bankim, however, is best remembered for his famous, if controversial, novel *Ananda Math* published in 1882, where he portrays the story of a group of courageous Hindu holy men, called *sannyasis,* engaged in a religious war to liberate the country from the grasp of Muslim and British conquerors. Steeled by the courage infused by Goddess Kali (the Mother that the Bengalis worship), these *sannyasis* succeeded in re-establishing Hindu power and restoring the past greatness of the Bengali people.[10]

What followed was a political eruption of considerable duration and intensity. European discontent against the Viceroy finally burst into radical rhetoric and furious agitational activity. An Anglo-Indian Defence Association was formed in order to sustain the assault on the Ilbert Bill and carry the agitation to Britain itself. What came to be called as the 'White Mutiny,' the agitation was characterised by insults hurled at the Viceroy and the Indians, the attempt to drive a wedge between Ripon and his European advisors and organised efforts to undermine the confidence of the British public in the capacity of the Viceroy to govern the country. A beleaguered Viceroy, worn down by the intensity of the agitation, and apprehensive of the upshots of this campaign on his other schemes for reform, finally accepted a humiliating compromise in January 1884.[11] The Ilbert Bill announced that the European community held the power of veto over any progressive reform initiated by the government.

These circumstances troubled the Indian leaders because they witnessed the virtual disintegration of Ripon's viceroyalty in the months following the Ilbert Bill controversy. Assumptions about the mode of conducting political agitation held for a generation had now to be subjected to searching re-examination. Indian politicians, as Hume reported in sadness to Ripon in March 1884, were beginning to ask: "If, with such a Viceroy, things are to be thus, what hope is there for the future? . . . Who are we to look to?" As the Indians perceived the alignment of political forces ranged against them, they realised the enormity of the tussle that lay ahead of them. It was then that many begun to consider in earnestness whether their existing mode of conducting political work was indeed efficacious. The consensus that appeared was the need to endow Indian politics with a supraprovincial institution capable of mobilising the combined strength of the Indian people in furtherance of their rights.[12]

The *modus operandi* in transforming this aspiration into reality needed the services of someone having a flare for organisation as well as enjoying the confidence of the different factions in the provinces. Suspicions about Bengali dominance in Indian politics had not been stilled even in the wake of the recent crisis and nowhere was this more evident than in the absence of any enthusiasm for the Indian Association's schemes to sponsor the National Fund and the National Conference in 1883. Even the Poona Sarvajanik Sabha, which in the late 1870s had explored ways of alliance with the Indian Association, now showed a spirit of reticence to these new ventures of its Calcutta counterpart. However, Bengal's failure exposed Hume's opportunity, who now emerged from the shadow of retirement and relative obscurity to make his mark in the annals of the history of Indian nationalism.

Hume, however, did not envisage his role as merely an intermediary in the service of a beleaguered and beseeching Viceroy. Increasingly he saw himself at the centre of an immature all-India coalition. Precise information is lacking in the way that this all-India coalition was brought into existence. What is known is that by early 1883 a loose network of Indian caucuses, consisting of educated politicians who in recent years had achieved importance through newspapers and voluntary associations, had come to work under Hume's general direction. Hume cast a tight veil of secrecy over the identity of these caucuses or their members. However, in April, 1883, in a communication to the press, Hume identified as his friends the editors of *The Hindu, Hindoo Patriot, Indian Mirror, Indian Spectator, Amrita Bazaar Patrika* and *The Tribune.*[13] As these editors were known to be members of influential local elites in Madras, Calcutta, Bombay and Lahore, and their papers had become the mouthpiece of political activism in those places, it is apparent that Hume had built up lines of communication with allies of a potential all-India movement. In the early months of 1883, for example, the Indian politicians were concerned that the growing Anglo-Indian criticism of the Viceroy could undermine confidence in Ripon's administration. In order to counter any such impression, Hume and his allies organised public demonstrations throughout the country in which resolutions were passed expressing support in the Viceroy and his policies.

The extent to which an infant all-India coalition had taken shape was demonstrated during the closing days of Ripon's viceroyalty. In September 1884, the Simla correspondent of the *Indian Mirror,* in all probability Hume himself, issued a call for "a grand farewell demonstration to Lord Ripon for his large-hearted, liberal, and statesmanlike policy which he has tried to inaugurate in this country". For almost two months, the Indian press throughout the country carried a major publicity campaign in which the services of the departing Viceroy were highlighted. Ripon's farewell journey from Simla to Bombay, stretching over five weeks and linking the main towns in North India, witnessed large turnouts.

An important stage had been set in Indian political life when Hume and his allies were asked to give some concrete organisational form to the all-India coalition that they had developed in recent years. However, any decision on a matter of such importance required the prior nod of the Indian allies, a task which required Hume's delicate handling, given the disunited nature of Indian political life and the jealousy with which local elites looked upon their freedom of action. The initial consultations took place in Bombay during Ripon's departure in the presence of several front-rank Indian leaders provided a welcome opportunity for Hume to think about a more formal organisation. Encouraged by the response, Hume embarked upon a tour of the country in February 1885, visiting Poona, Madras, Calcutta, Allahabad, Agra, Delhi before finally reaching Simla in May. Soon afterwards, he sailed for England, hoping to enlist the blessings of Liberal politicians and the press to his projected political convention. On his return to India at the end of that year, it was formally announced that "a Congress of native gentlemen from different parts of India" would assemble in Poona after Christmas. It deserves mention that this event lacked minimum publicity. It may be, as Professor Mehrotra argues, that Hume and his associates intended the meeting to be solely "a private gathering of friends".[14] Thus was inaugurated the Indian National Congress which consummated the increasing demand for a national institution in the wake of the agitation unleashed by the European community against Ripon's liberal policies.

While the actual finishing touches to the formation of the Congress were mainly the handiwork of Hume, who can claim paternity to this organisation, yet it is important to recognise that at every step he relied on the support and assistance of his Indian allies. Influential factions which in recent years had come to form associations in Bombay, Poona, Madras, Allahabad and Calcutta were with Hume in giving practical shape to their desire for a nationalist institution. However, there was one faction which played little part in these events. The Indian Association, under the command of S.N. Banerjea, had not only sent delegates to the Congress but also organised at about the same time the second National Conference in Calcutta. It is clear that Hume had almost deliberately refused to take the leaders of the Indian Association into his confidence, neither consulting them on major issues nor informing them of his plans to hold the Congress. Whatever the reason, the anomaly of having two national assemblies working for almost identical aims could not last long. Hence, when the second convention of the Congress met in Calcutta in December 1886, the leaders of the Indian Association were compelled to dissolve the National Conference and join the Congress. At this point, Hume could claim rightly that the major Indian political factions had been brought under the umbrella of the Congress.

Congress in its Infancy

It is rather risky to generalise about the nature of a movement as complex as the Indian National Congress, with its slack organisational structure, its decentralised leadership and its undefined following.

The Congress in its initial years was almost synonymous with the annual convention that assembled every Christmas in one of the major cities of the subcontinent. Undoubtedly, this—the main event in the Congress calendar—received the widest publicity of all its activities and gave ample evidence of its claim to be an all-India endeavour. How important this event was can be measured from the amount of organisational and financial outlay that went into it. The selected city which would play host to the convention would form committees several months before the actual meeting preparing for the event which required the services of hundreds of people, most of them working on voluntary basis for long periods while some worked almost full time for several days before the convention met.

There were, however, voices raised against the importance assigned to the annual convention in achieving the objectives of the Congress. Doubts were raised as to whether the aim of political education of the people, the unification of all castes and communities under a single umbrella, or even impressing upon British rulers the need to grant concessions were to any significant extent facilitated by organising such extravagant conventions. Equally detrimental to the prestige of the Congress was the charge that the annual convention represented almost the entire activity of the movement. Even the inner circle of the Congress leadership admitted that the tempo of Congress activity slowed down markedly after the annual convention.

Such criticisms of the Congress, however, surely contain an element of exaggeration. The fact that the inaugural session of the Congress met in Bombay without much fanfare had led to criticism that the Congress was "a hole-and-corner Conference." The claim of the Congress to speak for all-India was ridiculed, the credentials of its delegates were put under scrutiny, and the resolutions were challenged as to how far they were reflective of the will of the country on a broader basis. The leaders of the Congress realised that they ought to take more active steps towards acquainting the country of their movement and enlisting public support for their cause. Another device in promoting Congress aims was the decision of the leadership to introduce a system of public election of delegates. It was felt that the practice that had obtained at the first convention, when representatives came as volunteers in the good cause should be replaced by a system of election where these delegates "ought to receive public authorisation from the bodies and communities (or leading members of the latter) whom they were to represent".

Modest activities also underlined the need for a separate organisational structure for the Congress. In the initial stage, the workload of the Congress was almost totally borne by the leading provincial associations in the country, like the Bombay Presidency Association, the Poona Sarvajanik Sabha, the Madras Mahajan Sabha and the Indian Association. It was these bodies which called meetings, nominated delegates and provided funds for the functioning. However, such an arrangement was considered to be responsible in depriving the Congress of its own independent machinery. Hence, when the second convention met at Calcutta in December 1886, it was decided to consecrate each province with its own Standing Congress Committee, comprising of influential members of every caste, class, community and language group.

In the 1890s, for instance, there were complaints in the Madras press that the Madras Mahajan Sabha was in a declining state for want of support from front-line leaders who were wholly involved in the work of the Congress. In the case of some local associations, like the British Indian Association, the leaders were clearly against the attempts of the Congress to acquire a separate machinery of its own. The other local associations were reluctant to go as far as this but attempted to work out in consultation with the Congress as to what constituted their domain of activity. The General Secretary acted as the link between the various Standing Congress Committees. The position was created at the inaugural meeting of the Congress and since 1888 it came to be occupied on the basis of election by delegates to the annual convention. Hume was the first holder of this esteemed post and indeed remained its only occupant until his retirement in 1906. As the founder of the Congress, commanding the trust and loyalty of the important factions in the country, Hume enjoyed a unique authority in the organisation that enabled him to discharge his manifold duties without any opposition or obstruction. He also undertook extensive political tours to the different corners of the country in a bid to raise funds for the Congress and to energise local committees that had relapsed into a state of inertia. Hume was also the medium of communication with the Government of India, having direct links with the Viceroy, explaining Congress position on important issues and making demands for concessions. As Hume's duties and responsibilities multiplied, the position of Joint General Secretary was created in 1889. Hume retired to Britain in 1893 and, although he maintained close contact with the Congress in India, yet many of his duties came to be increasingly shouldered by the Joint General Secretary.

In 1887, a Subjects Committee was set up. Care was taken that every important interest was represented in the Committee, notably the powerful provincial and communal factions. The Committee met secretly to consider items to be discussed at the open session. To avoid the danger of dissension, it was initially decided that the Congress as an all-India institution would only consider national issues, excluding those of provincial or local character. In reality, however, this rule became a device through which the Congress could escape the quicksands of provincial entanglements. Local Congress units, anxious to promote particular concerns, saw the Congress as an instrument to impart strength to their causes. Whether it be the sufferings endured by the Assam tea cultivators, about which the Bengali leaders were keen, or the Punjab Alienation of Land Act of 1900, about which Punjabi Congress interests nursed a deep sense of resentment, local factions exerted considerable pressures upon the Congress to seek remedies. However, by and large, the Congress managed to withstand such pressures, even if it meant at times courting displeasure of some of the provincial allies.

There were also several convincing reasons to exclude social issues from the Congress agenda. Hume had recognised from the start that social questions, because of their close identification with religious beliefs, were delicate issues which an institution like the Congress was ill-equipped to handle without arousing powerful emotions on all sides. When critics flayed the Congress that it was relinquishing social progress merely to acquire political power, the Congress leadership felt necessary to assert that separate institutions must be set up to cater for social reform. Dadabhai Naoroji, in his presidential address to the annual convention in December 1886, asserted that a National Congress must confine itself to questions which the entire nation has a direct participation and it must leave the adjustment of social reforms and other class questions to class Congresses. Even social activist like M.G. Ranade had to concede that a separate institution was needed for social reform, even if it be national in scope, and accordingly the National Social Conference was brought into existence in December 1887. However, as a measure of its sympathy towards social reform, the leaders of the Congress allowed the Social Conference to hold the latter's annual convention in the Congress pavilion.

The programme of the early Congress did not include the demand for an immediate independence for India. To its leaders, the question of political freedom required a long period of apprenticeship. Dadabhai Naoroji, for example, was sufficiently explicit in ruling out immediate Home Rule for India. Particular importance was accorded to the reform of the legislative councils and it was felt that these bodies would become the agency through which western democratic institutions could be set up on Indian soil. The successful incorporation of British parliamentary institutions was seen as *sine qua non* for India's gradual advance towards self-government. The ideology of the early Congress as a moderate movement working for self-government through gradual progress of democratic institutions reflected the political beliefs of the inner circle of its leadership. The early leaders of the Congress were mainly from the provincial associations that were instrumental in its formation. Prominent among those were Pherozeshah Mehta, Dadabhai Naoroji, K.T. Telang, Badruddin Tyabji and Dinshaw E. Wacha—all from the Bombay Presidency Association; M.G. Ranade, G.K. Gokhale and B.G. Tilak from the Poona Sarvajanik Sabha; and P. Ananda Charlu, G. Subramania Iyer, M. Viraraghava Chari, P. Rangiah Naidu and

C. Sankaran Nair from the Madras Mahajan Sabha. When the Indian Association merged with the Congress in 1886, S.N. Banerjea, Ananda Mohan Bose and Manmohan Ghose assumed the status of front-rank leaders. Some leaders, like W.C. Bonnerjee of Bengal, did not belong to any of the provincial associations but occupied prominent positions in the Congress on account of their close allegiance with Hume.[15]

The social background of the early Congress leadership also reflected the extent to which the intelligentsia exercised power inside the organisation. A majority of the front-ranking leaders were lawyers, either trained in England or had taken a law degree in India, and then proceeded to set themselves up in private practice. Next to lawyers came the editors of newspapers and teachers. Although neither of these groups enjoyed the income of its legal counterparts, their work nonetheless brought them closer with issues and groups essential in staking their claim for leadership. It enabled the leaders like Banerjea, G. Subramania Iyer, Tilak and Gokhale to obtain a degree of political eminence in the Congress that matched the influence of their lawyer colleagues like Mehta, Tyabji, Telang, Bonnerjee and Ananda Charlu.

The bourgeoisie was another group which was courted by the Congress since its inception and it was felt that some of its luminaries deserved place in Congress leadership. Amongst those who attained a degree of importance were Dinshaw Petit, the Parsi industrialist from Bombay, the Maharajah of Darbhanga and Rajendra Lal Mitter, the zamindar barons from Bengal, A. Sabapathy Mudaliar, the self-made textile industrialist from Madras and Raja Ramphal Singh, a substantial landlord from the United Provinces. However, it must be pointed out that their loyalty to the Congress was ambivalent and some, like Dinshaw Petit, threatened to pull out from the movement whenever they felt that their interests were being imperilled by the Congress.[16]

Although it will be correct to portray the leadership of the early Congress as an alliance of the educated and the bourgeoisie, in which the former exerted greater influence, it is also important to acknowledge the contribution of a small group of Britishers who had come to be associated with the movement since its inception. The Congress, despite claiming the movement to be of the Indian people, did also include Europeans domiciled in the country. Besides Hume, men like William Wedderburn, a covenanted civil servant, George Yule, a businessman in Bengal, Henry Cotton, another civil servant, William Wordsworth, principal of one of Bombay's premier colleges; and Eardley Norton, a barrister from Madras, had all served the Congress with distinction. These men represented the liberal tradition of the nineteenth century politics, ardent believers in the concept of true partnership between Britain and India, and looked confidently to the day when India would assimilate the values and institutions of the West and progress towards full nationhood. Their sincerity of conviction in equal partnership exercised a deep influence on the first generation of Congress leadership.

The second pillar of support for the early Congress was the bourgeoisie. Industrialists, merchants, bankers, moneylenders, petty shopkeepers, zamindars and landholders accounted for a sizeable section of the delegates who attended the annual convention of the Congress. According to Ghosh, 32 per cent of the delegates who attended the conventions between 1892–1909 were from the landed gentry and the commercial classes.[17] Prominent among them was the bourgeoisie from Bombay where Hindu, Parsi and Muslim shetias lent their support by attending the conventions and making financial contributions to the Congress coffers. A similar attitude was adopted by the bourgeoisie in Bengal where the zamindars entertained some doubts about the intentions of the Congress. Hume almost immediately recognised the delicacy of zamindars' position and assured that divisive issues like tenancy reform would not feature in the Congress deliberations. The zamindars were appeased and the British Indian Association agreed to nominate delegates to the annual convention, while individual zamindars, like the Maharajah of Darbhanga, made generous contributions to the organisation. In the South, merchants, industrialists and landholders were amongst the active adherents of the Congress since its inception. The absence of divisive issues, like the tenancy issue in Bengal, enabled the bourgeoisie in the Tamil and Telugu dominated areas to work in a spirited manner with the intelligentsia in building up the strength of the Congress.

Remaining outside the orbit of the Congress influence were elements of Indian society which managed to gain little from the beneficial changes wrought by British imperialism in India. The peasantry, the rural artisans, the working class employed in factories, plantations, mines and modern communications, minorities such as Muslims, and exploited castes such as the Harijans had all experienced the confusing effects of British policies but without enjoying any of its material benefits. The cultivators, artisans and urban craftsmen could claim displacement, either being robbed of their traditional tenurial rights to the soil or deprived of their customary vocation, and had gradually been reduced to a condition of pauper tenants or agricultural labourers. The condition of the small working class was only slightly better. Low wages, unsophisticated working conditions and lack of housing, medical and educational facilities had virtually condemned this class to a life of perpetual drudgery. To all these disadvantaged elements of society, the Congress in the early years offered little immediate relief. There were compelling reasons why the Congress leadership decided against mobilising groups which were in doldrums. A major constraint was the fear that such a strategy would offend the colonial authorities and could bring retaliatory action which in turn could even ruin the infant nationalist organisation. In that year, Hume and his allies in the Congress decided that only demands backed by the power of the people would yield the desired results. What followed was the preparation and distribution of thousands of pamphlets in Indian languages, the holding of public meetings in the districts and towns to awaken popular sympathies for the Congress and collect funds for the nationalist cause. The effects of these tactics were a intensified state of popular enthusiasm in the country, reflected in the willingness of even rural folk to attend political gatherings.[18]

The new Congress strategy and the co-existing excitement that it stirred up in certain parts of the country, alarmed British officials in India. Since the formation of the Congress, there had been a strong feeling of hostility amongst British officials towards the movement. They objected to the fact that a nationalist organisation had emerged to champion Indian interests and would represent the bureaucracy as the major hurdle towards the realisation of Indian aspirations. However, moderate British functionaries, like Viceroy Dufferin and Governor Auckland Colvin of North-West Provinces, had welcomed the formation of the Congress. However, the new strategy of Hume and allies alienated these liberal administrators as well who were apprehensive that such tactics could incite violence and give way to hatred between the rulers and the ruled. Colvin, who had studied the new Congress agitation in his province, alleged in a letter to Hume that such methods were premature and risky, partly because they aroused feelings of hatred towards the government and its officials and also because they had incited counter-agitation amongst groups hostile to the claims of the Congress. Viceroy Dufferin agreed with Colvin's speculation of the dangers of the new Congress strategy. In a public speech in Calcutta in November 1888, the Viceroy delivered a stinging rebuke upon the Congress leadership and warned that the colonial authorities noted these actions in a serious light and would call upon those responsible for them to face the consequences.[19]

Political mobilisation under the infant Congress thus failed to strike deep roots in Indian society. The fear of inducing an open confrontation with the British *Raj,* coupled with the necessity of developing nationalist unity cutting across the lines of class, had made the Congress into almost the exclusive property of the educated and the bourgeoisie. Although the early leadership of the Congress clearly admired the constraints imposed by the political environment in the country, it did not take long before rival factions came into existence which began to question their validity. The so-called 'Extremist Challenge' that first began to find expression in the 1890s attempted to refuse many of the cherished canons of Congress politics and in so doing it unleashed a powerful internal feud within the movement which culminated in an open split in 1907.

The Extremist Threat and the Surat Split

The second and third decades in the history of the Indian National Congress were witness to bitter internal feuds. The established leadership of the Congress found itself opposed by a more fundamentalist faction which had hitherto exercised little real influence in the conduct of the nationalist movement. The former, referred to as 'Moderates' were of a firm belief that the Congress should continue to adhere to the principles enunciated by the founding fathers in 1885. Their critics, called the 'Extremists,' commented that the Moderates had failed to give a proper definition of India's political goal, adopted ineffectful methods of agitation and had failed to enlist mass support as a basis to deal with the British from a position of strength. These criticisms of the Moderates were accompanied by allegations that the latter had established an absolute control over the Congress and thereby refused positions of leadership to other groups. The beginnings of extremism were hardly anticipated in the 1890s, but with the partition of Bengal in 1905 the rift within the Congress started to assume alarming proportions with a considerable threat to nationalist movement itself.

It is difficult to date with any precision when rift between the Extremists and the Moderates first came to light in the Congress. However, there is no doubt that the first authoritative exposition of the Extremist ideological position was penned down by Aurobindo Ghose. Born in 1872 into an anglicised Bengali *bhadralok* family, and given a near entirely western education in India and England, Aurobindo had intentionally flung his examinations for the covenanted service and returned to India in 1893 to take up a position with the Maharajah of Baroda. Within less than a year of returning, he contributed a series of articles to a Bombay newspaper under the title 'New Lamps for Old'. What these writings amounted to was an impassioned accusation of the way that the Moderates conducted the Congress. Aurobindo claimed that the Congress leadership was wasting Indian energies by seeking trivial reforms and was placing almost total reliance upon British goodwill and promises to realise its aims. In calling for a new strategy for the Congress, Aurobindo advised an unequivocal demand for Indian independence, the mobilisation of mass support and the adoption of the doctrine of change through revolutionary cataclysm.[20]

The immediate impact of Aurobindo's writings has not been ascertained, least of all on the Congress leadership. However, what is significant is that at least in one province, namely Maharashtra, the shape of politics was beginning to assume forms conducive to the strategy expounded by Aurobindo. In spearheading a Hindu resistance movement in the seventeenth century against the increasing tide of Mughal imperialism then sweeping West and South India, the Mahrattas under the leadership of Shivaji and a long line of Peshwas had staged a sustained and successful assault on Mughal bastions. The aim of founding a lasting Hindu *Raj* failed, for it was the British who inherited the mantle of power from the Mughals and in the process destroyed the last vestiges of Mahratta power in 1818. As late as 1879, a Maharashtrian Brahmin Vasudev Balvant Phadke raised the colours of revolt against the British, proclaiming himself as the minister to Maharaj Shivaji and promising freedom from alien oppression. The revolt though quickly suppressed, afforded British officials with enough evidence of the enduring strength of Maharashtrian national sentiment and its potential danger. That such apprehensions came in true colours were further attested by the fact that it was another Maharashtrian Brahmin, Bal Gangadhar Tilak, who came to express the spirit of radical Indian nationalism. It was Tilak, who more than anyone else fathered the Extremist movement, initially in Maharashtra during the 1890s, and subsequently by spreading similar ideological groups in other provinces.

An understanding of Tilak's espousal of extremism can only be gauged through his involvement in the political and social uprisings in Maharashtra in the 1880s. Although Tilak received modern education and had graduated with an arts degree from Bombay University, he had intentionally not followed the footsteps of many of his educated counterparts by entering government service. Instead, he joined the company of public-minded Maharashtrians like G.C. Agarkar and G.K. Gokhale in order to dedicate himself to the service of his nation and people. A private English school was founded in Poona by these Maharashtrians to inculcate in the coming generation the ideals of service and sacrifice to the nation, while two newspapers, one in English and the other in Marathi, were launched to shape the adult mindset. While Tilak and his supporters took absolute control of the newspapers, Agarkar and Gokhale inherited the educational institutions.

The Moderates were not the only hurdles that lay in the path of Tilak's ascent to nationalist leadership. Just as daunting, was the opposition presented by the colonial authorities in 1897, this was the year of grave social distress in Maharashtra inflicted in part by the widespread occurrence of famine and in part by the harrowing damage caused by bubonic plague in Poona and elsewhere. Tilak was appalled by the suffering that these events caused to the populace at large and called for massive public relief to control the suffering. On the issue of famine, Tilak urged the government to extend best possible relief to the affected peasantry, including the reduction of the land tax for the period of famine. When the local authorities refused to adopt such proposals, Tilak secured the support of the Poona Sarvajanik Sabha to send out agents to the countryside to collect information and to launch a no-tax compaign. These actions sent alarming signals to an embattled bureaucracy which retaliated by decreeing that the Sabha should cease to be considered as a body which has any claim to address the Government on question of public policy.

What brought things to a point of confrontation between Tilak and the colonial authorities in Bombay was the latter's handling of the plague operations. Amidst utter dismay all round, the Bombay government decided to set up a Plague Committee under a tough-minded W.C. Rand to take whatever measures necessary to combat the disease. Rand and his associates with the aid of British troops, entered homes and holy places to eradicate the disease, forcibly isolated plague victims, and even transported to distant places those suspected of the disease. Though well-intentioned, these measures aroused widespread resentment even amongst Moderates. Tilak who was himself involved in anti-plague relief work, flayed the attacks on Rand and the government. It was in this simmering tension between the plague officials and the people that Rand and Lieutenant Ayerst were assassinated by two Hindu youths involved in the *mela* movement. A conspiratorial group, which in recent years had functioned as the militant wing of Tilak's conservative crusade, had thus set the instance of the first act of political assassination in the name of Indian nationalism.

While the Extremist movement in Maharashtra was in disarray as a consequence of government retaliation, another province—the Punjab—began to assume the mantle of opposition to the Moderates in the Congress. Initial support here for the Congress had come mainly from the expatriate Bengali community staying in such cities as Lahore and Multan, while the Punjabi Hindu intelligentsia, especially the members of the Arya Samaj, called Aryas, were doubtful about this nationalist institution. Arya qualms about the Congress were founded on the role of Europeans in the movement, its preoccupation with western political and social institutions, and its trust upon British goodwill to achieve Indian upsurge. Almost in the lines of Aurobindo and Tilak, the Aryas proclaimed the doctrine that real national progress depended upon self-help and sacrifice of the masses, pursued through schemes of industrial development and mass education, and not by passing resolutions and making futile speeches. In the early 1890s, the Aryas began to adopt a more conciliatory attitude towards the Congress, founded on the belief that the institution could be converted into a more useful agency through their own constructive participation. The Aryas began to attend the provincial conferences with much enthusiasm and were also more regular participants of the annual conventions of the Congress. It was not long before the Aryas took over control of the Congress organisation in the Punjab, displacing the expatriate Bengalis, and then began to exert their influence so as to shape the movement according to their way of thinking.[21]

The adoption of a constitution by the Congress at its annual convention held in Lucknow in 1899 was a triumph for the Aryas. However, Arya satisfaction over the new departure was mitigated by the recognition that the distribution of seats in the Indian Congress Committee favoured the coastal presidencies. Hence, when the annual convention of the Congress met in Lahore in 1900, the Aryas used their numerical strength in the Subjects Committee to outnumber the representation of these presidencies and increase that of the Punjab and United Provinces. Not satisfied with this change, the Aryas also wanted the Congress to take practical measures for national regeneration. Two committees were also set up to formulate schemes for Indian advancement in these areas.

These changes sent alarming signals to the established leaders of the Congress. Many Moderates, like S.N. Banerjea, while willing to accept the constitution adopted at Lucknow warned those urging radical changes to choose between the path of reform and revolution. In deciding to retaliate with their warning went unnoticed, they chose the Indian Congress Committee as their principal target. Convinced that such a committee was both unnecessary and unworkable, the Moderates crippled it by absenting themselves from its meetings, Bengal did not send a single representative when the Committee met at Allahabad in September 1901. However, the more decisive salvo was fired when the annual convention met in Calcutta three months later. Moderate chiefs led by Mehta, Bonnerjee, Banerjea, Gokhale and Wacha, who were in absolute control of the proceedings, ignored the existence of the Indian Congress Committee altogether, refusing to consult it while choosing the president or in drafting the agenda.

It is clear that rift within the Congress had begun to develop along fairly well-defined ideological lines. The extent to which these ideological divisions were beginning to emerge is revealed in the writings of Lajpat Rai in 1902. An Arya activist, Lajpat Rai rebuked those politicians in the nationalist movement who linked politics with agitation. For Lajpat Rai, politics "concerns itself with building up the nation with a view to its future". This, he considered, was a more sublime struggle, almost "a religion, and a science, much higher, both in its conception and in its sphere, than mere political agitation". Such a cause obviously needed the services of politicians who could not only set a proper goal for India's future but would also labour for its realisation through sacrifice, dedication and even personal suffering. Lajpat Rai asserted that "no nation is worthy of any political status if it cannot distinguish between begging such rights and claiming them".[22]

The Moderate leadership faced these attacks by reasserting the correctness of its tried methods of political action. S.N. Banerjea, in his presidential address to the annual convention in 1902, contended that there was no reason for the Congress to feel a sense of disappointment over its past achievements. Lambasting the critics as the 'pessimist school', he claimed that the goal of securing India's just rights was a continuous process and could only be consummated "after prolonged preparations and laborious apprenticeship". Two years later, another Moderate stalwart was even more sanguine of the prospects of Indo-British collaboration. P.M. Mehta, inarguably the most powerful voice visible inside the Congress, defended the achievement of the Congress as "an honourable record which left no room for disappointment or despair". It was a strange twist of irony that at the very moment the Moderates were reposing their faith in the *Raj,* the very Viceroy, whom Mehta hoped would embrace the Congress, should have touched off a storm of controversy by splitting Bengal into two halves which not only gravely embarrassed the Moderates but also so nearly contributed to the capture of the Congress by the Extremists.

In order to comprehend the upheaval that followed the partition of Bengal, which is one of the turning points in the history of Indian nationalism, it is important to know something of the personality and policies of Lord Curzon. Curzon belonged to an age which marked the advancing tide of European imperialism in Asia and Africa. Like so many of his contemporaries, Curzon saw himself as "the representative of the race chosen by God for its loftier standards—administrative, cultural and moral..." in improving the efficiency of the government, setting new standards of justice and morality, and boosting the welfare of his subjects through education, irrigation, communications and tax reduction. While some of his reforms were welcomed, others met with general protest, notably the Calcutta Municipal Bill of 1899 which reduced Indian representation while increasing that of the European community.

However, a sizeable section of Bengali opposition to partition also stemmed from the possible repercussions that this measure would have on the employment and landholding interests of the Bengalis. A large avenue of Bengali employment under the British *Raj* had been the government, especially within the reclining Bengal Presidency itself. Business firms based in Calcutta echoed a fear because of competition from Dacca and Chittagong. The handling of the lucrative trade in tea, rice and jute, which in the past had profited Calcutta, was now expected to move to Chittagong.

The shock that spread through Bengal with the announcement of partition was sparked off mainly by *bhadralok* elements centred in Calcutta and the larger provincial towns. The Moderates and the Extremists, the educated and the landowners, the rich and the poor shared a similar view that the British *Raj* had inflicted a deep wound on the unity and greatness of Bengal. A signal of the changed mood of Bengal was reflected in the readiness of the zamindari aristocrats from the British Indian Association and the Moderate constitutionalists from the Indian Association to organise a mammoth mass meeting in Calcutta in August 1905. When partition finally came into effect in October 1905, the occasion was observed as a day of mourning, marked by fasting, the holding of special prayers in temples and even the markets pulled their shutters down for the day. By now, much of Bengal was in a state of frenzy, with public demonstrations held on regular basis, protest marches staged by students and other organisations and the singing of *Bande Mataram* as a show of patriotic defiance of the British *Raj.* In the wake of this clamour, new movements like boycott, swadeshi, and national education were also gaining popularity.

Of these movements, none engendered the kind of controversy as the boycott movement. It is not known how the idea of boycott actually inspired the Bengalis. Some believe that the Bengalis got inspiration from the Chinese boycott of American goods in 1904; while others assert that the idea had long been debated in India and had suggested itself to a people helpless in the face of British intransigence. Most of the Bengali exponents of boycott, including S.N. Banerjea, were of the view that this was a constitutional manoeuvre and was a temporary measure to draw the attention of the British people to the mistake made in Bengal. Affected by the boycott were such British imports as cotton goods, sugar, salt, tobacco and leather products. Prominent public figures like S.N. Banerjea took religious vows against using British goods until partition was revoked. Merchants, especially those who dealt in British goods, were the hardest hit, being denied the services of barbers, priests and washermen.

It was amidst such patriotic fervour that Bengal searched for explicit schemes of industrial enterprise. In the words of Sumit Sarkar, the air was full of swadeshi schemes—textile mills and imported handlooms, river transport concerns, match and soap factories, earthenwares and tanneries.[23] Action was taken on several fronts simultaneously. Some sought the revival of the cottage industry. Handlooms were started and traditional silk weaving was also encouraged. Besides boycott and swadeshi, the Bengalis also launched an active campaign on behalf of national education. Even before the partition of the province, the nature of education that the *Raj* had instituted in India received setback from many quarters. In 1893, for example, Rabindranath Tagore had flayed the educational system on account of its exclusive concern in training an elite in a foreign language. A decade later, he founded the Swadeshi Samaj which, among other things, hoped to impart popular education through the medium of Bengali language.

Aurobindo Ghose also spoke for many Bengalis when he claimed that national education was needed to give back to India "the long lost treasure of her race, the passion for self-knowledge" and combat the afflictions of westernisation "like industrialism, commercialism and imperialism".

The new movements in Bengal were also complemented by a redefinition of the goal of Indian nationalism itself. The faith in the ultimate achievement of self-government within the British Empire, as had been explained by the Moderate leadership in the Congress, was now abandoned in favour of full and complete freedom or Purna Swaraj. Radical elements in Bengal, like Aurobindo Ghose, wanted a total non-cooperation with the British *Raj* which would free the country from any form of subservience to an alien power.

However, the partition paved the way for a new kind of cooperation between the *bhadralok* and the labour force. Deepening labour unrest drew sympathy of *bhadralok* radicals who now became advisors of unions and helped to plan tactics of industrial action. In return, workers responded to *bhadralok* call for a joint protest against partition. For example, 16 October 1905 was observed by workers who staged strikes or forced the closure of mills for the day. Although one should not overstate the significance of this coalition between labour and the *bhadralok*, for this alliance was still fragile, yet it exposed a potential mode of mass mobilisation which held implications for the future nationalist struggle.[24]

The new movements that were embarked on in the wake of the partition and the relative success of the *bhadralok* in expanding its base of support, had effected a qualitative transformation in Bengal politics. Interestingly, the response of the Indian National Congress to this new situation was something to be noted. Many Bengalis voiced their demands that the Congress should wholeheartedly support their movements. It was also urged that the Congress should condemn partition and extend its blessings to the boycott, swadeshi and national education movements. Few in Bengal appeared to be seemingly bothered as to whether the established principles of the Congress sanctioned such actions.

What boosted the hopes of the Bengalis in making these demands was the expression of support originating from Extremist sources elsewhere. The latter were quick to recognise that partition had created a political atmosphere conducive to their ideology and could generate support so as to challenge the leadership of the Moderates. Tilak and his associates in Maharashtra condemned the partition of Bengal and urged the country to rally behind the Bengalis in their hour of need.

The Punjab was not lagging behind in its support for the new movements inaugurated in Bengal. Arya Samaj leaders like Lala Lajpat Rai were pleased that their call for self-reliance had finally found practical expression in the movements launched by the Bengalis. The Congress leadership was urged to follow the example set by Bengal by incorporating the new movements into the nationalist programme.

The Moderate leadership in the Congress experienced a crisis brought about by the dramatic turn of events that followed the partition. In the session held at Madras in December 1903, the Congress adopted a resolution which condemned the proposed scheme for the territorial adjustments of Bengal alongside other schemes which threatened the unity of existing provincial units. It is not known whether similar doubts perturbed the delegates who assembled a year later in the annual convention held in Bombay. At the annual convention held at Benares in December 1905, Bengali factions supported by Extremist voices from Maharashtra and the Punjab, were unrelenting that the Congress should not only condemn partition but should also extend its blessing to the new techniques adopted by the Bengalis, notably boycott and swadeshi. Gokhale as president of the session criticised the partition and its harmful consequences, praised "Bengal's heroic stand against the oppression of a harsh and uncontrolled bureaucracy", and hailed swadeshi as a constructive measure for India's regeneration. Extremists insisted on the Congress to declare the boycott movement in Bengal as a legitimate method to secure the revocation of partition. While Madan Mohan Malaviya, a Moderate, denied stoutly that boycott as a technique was being recommended to other provinces, Lajpat Rai favouring the Extremists hailed boycott as "the dawn of a new political era for India" in which Indians were urged to show to their rulers that the Indians are not beggars, and that they are subjects of an Empire where people are struggling to achieve that position which is their right by right or natural law.

The following months were witness to an intensified rivalry between the Moderates and Extremists. The former, despite controlling the organisation, were clearly alarmed that recent turn of events had lessened their credentials in the eyes of the Indian public. The Extremists, in contrast, concentrated their energies in building their strength in India. Continued British intransigence on partition, coupled with official curbs on the more extreme forms of Bengali agitation were able to fuel the boycott, swadeshi and national education movements. Sensing that the tide of Indian support was flowing in their favour, Extremists from Bengal, Maharashtra and elsewhere began to envisage a strategy to forge nationwide links and challenge the ascendancy of the Moderates.

The success of Tilak and his allies reached pinnacle in Naoroji's pronouncement of swaraj as India's birthright, thereby lending the seal of Congress approval to the Extremist slogan thus symbolising the nation's claim for freedom. Doubtless, an elated Tilak claimed after the convention that his faction was "able to carry out 3/4 of our programme in the Congress". Aurobindo, in a somewhat similar mood of euphoria, asserted that while the founding fathers of the Congress had done the spadework in preparing the ground for freedom, the responsibility for its realisation now lay with the younger leaders. The Extremist leadership, immensely boosted by the recent turn of events, was confident that the political mood favoured its capture of the nationalist movement. The Extremists christened themselves as the 'New Party' or 'Nationalist Party', declared that swaraj was their goal, and accepted every weapon in the armoury of political struggle except violence. These doctrines were spread across the country through organs edited by the Extremists, in the form of speeches at mass meetings and also by undertaking political tours to even areas relatively free from Extremist agitation. These campaigns aroused considerable mass excitement and Aurobindo claimed in April 1907 that his party had "in a few months absorbed Eastern Bengal, set Allahabad and the North on fire and is stirring Madras to its depths".

The Moderate leadership noticed that the moment had arrived to launch an offensive of its own to check any further erosion of its domination in the country. Moderate stalwarts like Mehta, Gokhale, Banerjea and Krishnaswamy Iyer had watched with alarm the expanding tide of Extremist influence. In an attempt to air the voice of moderation, Gokhale undertook in February 1907 an extensive tour of North India. In the United Provinces, Gokhale won over two of the most influential politicians to the Moderate cause namely Malaviya and Motilal Nehru. When he visited Punjab, Gokhale used his personal intimacy with Lajpat Rai to try and secure the neutrality of the Arya Samaj leaders in the ensuing confrontation with the Extremists. In Bengal, Banerjea and his old Moderate stalwarts had become disillusioned with the radical methods of Aurobindo and Bipin Chandra Pal, and had expressed his desire to return to the Moderate programme of the pre-partition days. In Madras Presidency, the Moderates were clearly enjoying supremacy and easily defeated an Extremist attempt to adopt more deep-seated platforms at the provincial conference held in August 1907. The Moderates had thus successfully piloted themselves into a position of strength in the major centres of provincial politics.

References

1. For instance see Mehrotra, *op. cit.,* chapters VI and VII; and B. Martin, *New India 1885,* Bombay, 1969, chapter III.

2. For more extended discussion of these London based bodies see A. Seal, *The Emergence of Indian Nationalism,* Cambridge, 1968, chapter VI; and Dobbin, *Urban Leadership in Western India,* London, 1972, chapters III and VIII.
3. Interestingly some Bengalis dubbed the East India Association as "a Bombay concern", indicating that Bengal would have no part of it.
4. S. Basu, *Life and Works of Brahmananda Keshar,* second edition, Calcutta, 1940, pp. 119-22.
5. In making their choice Banerjea and his colleagues rejected the alternative designation of "Bengal Association" as they wanted "an association which would become the centre of an all-India movement." See B.T. McCully, *English Education,* New York, 1940, pp. 301-02.
6. Cited in McCully, *op. cit.,* p. 314.
7. Mehrotra, *op. cit.,* p. 203.
8. *Ibid.,* p. 168.
9. On anti-Bengali sentiment in the Punjab see K.W. Jones, "The Bengali Elite in Post-Annexation Punjab", IESHR, III: 4, 1966, pp. 380-83.
10. The hymn *Bande Mataram* (Hail to Mother), which the Congress later adopted as the national anthem, was the song which the victorious *sannyasis* sang as they marched through the liberated country.
11. The only full-scale study of the Ilbert Bill and its ramifications is E. Hirschmann, *'White Mutiny' The Ilbert Bill Crisis in India and Genesis of the Indian National Congress,* Delhi, 1980.
12. A similar conclusion is reached by J.C. Masselos when he writes: "The antagonistic elements inherent in even embryo national movements were thus focussed against the bureaucracy in India, and, to a lesser extent, the Conservatives in England rather than against the might of the British Empire or against its chief symbol, the Viceroy." *Towards Nationalism: Group Affiliations and the Politics of Public Associations in Nineteenth Century Western India,* Bombay, 1974, p. 222.
13. Significantly, the editor of the *Bengalee* was not mentioned by Hume. It is evident that S.N. Banerjea and his allies in the Indian Association were working independently of Hume's caucuses.
14. Mehrotra, *op. cit.,* p. 408.
15. This relatively small circle supplied no less than 15 of the first 22 presidents of the Congress. See A.C. Majumdar, *The Indian National Evolution,* Madras, 1917, Appendix C.
16. R.P. Masani, *Dadabhai Naoroji: The Grand Old Man of India,* London, 1939, p. 317.
17. S. Ghosh, *op. cit.*
18. Wedderburn, *op. cit.,* pp. 60-66.
19. For text of Dufferin's speech see Grover, *op. cit.,* pp. 181-88.
20. Karan Singh, *Prophet of Indian Nationalism,* London, 1963, pp. 51-54.
21. The preceding discussion draws mainly from N.G. Barrier, "The Arya Samaj and Congress Politics in the Punjab, 1894-1908", *Journal of Asian Studies,* XXVI: 3, 1967; and K.W. Jones, *Arya Dharm: Hindu Consciousness in 19th-Century Punjab,* Delhi, 1976, pp. 241-52.
22. V.C. Joshi (Ed.), *Lala Lajpat Rai: Writings and Speeches;* Vol. I, *1888-1919,* Delhi, 1966, pp. 26-30.
23. The growth of swadeshi enterprises in Bengal is discussed in Sarkar, *op. cit.,* chapter III.
24. Sarkar, *op. cit.,* chapter V.

2

Tilak: The Great Patriot

Bal Gangadhar Tilak was born on 23 July, 1856 at Ratnagiri in Bombay Presidency. His father, Gangadhar Ramchandra Tilak, served as an Assistant Teacher at Ratnagiri and later on as an Assistant Deputy Education Inspector at Thana and Poona. Gangadhar was a renowned Mathematics Teacher of his time and was well-versed in Trigonometry and Grammar. Bal was hardly sixteen in 1872 when he lost his father. He pursued his studies and passed the Matriculation four months after his father's death. Thereafter he joined the Deccan College and passed the B.A. with honours in 1876. He further qualified in Law in 1879 from the Bombay University.

During his academic years, Tilak was not an ordinary student. He participated in several extra-curricular activities and gained much popularity among his fellow students. He was, however, dissatisfied with the existing educational system and, given time and opportunity, he made up his mind to suggest modifications for the same. While studying law, he developed friendship with Agarkar, who later on became Principal of the Fergusson College. Both of them deliberated upon the idea of opening a model institution. They also resolved not to accept government service, but to set up a private High School and College with a view to impart cheap and healthy education to the younger generation.[1]

In these efforts, they were assisted by Vishnu Krishna Chiplunkar, popularly known as Vishnu Shastri and M.B. Namjoshi. The former had resigned from government service as he could not continue with his supervisors and had shifted to Poona with a plan to start a private academic institution.[2] He was an outstanding Marathi prose writer of the time. So the four enthusiastic young men, Tilak, Agarkar, Chiplunkar and Namjoshi started the New English School in Poona for boys belonging to middle class families. It was indeed an innovative experiment in the field of education at a time when the development of educational system under the *Raj* was in infancy. It was a courageous step which was to lead the younger generation towards socio-economic progress in that region.

Tilak, however, did not want to confine his activity to the development of education. He had the desire to give vent to his feelings in the press with a sense of complete freedom. He disliked and opposed any kind of restraint on free-will, of course with a sense of responsibility. Realising that this could only be achieved if he had his own press, he started two newspapers, the *Mahratta* and the *Kesari* and alongwith Chiplunkar made a mark in the field of native journalism. Besides Chiplunkar established two printing presses, the *Arya-Bhushan* for the use of the two newspapers, and the *Chitrashala* for the purpose of encouraging fine arts. In no time, the New English School as well as the *Kesari* and the *Mahratta* became the leading institutions in the field of education and journalism in the Deccan. This kind of social encouragement afforded them academic motivation which prompted them to put in their extra efforts by burning mid-night oil.

Tilak joined the Congress in 1889 and he was a devoted follower of the Congress movement all through his life, although it is astonishing that he never became the president of the Congress. I remember the Calcutta Congress of 1917 clearly over which Dr. Besant presided, Tilak's speech supporting the resolution on self-government and also in the Amritsar Congress of 1919. Although he had opposed Dr. Besant in many particulars, he tried to be a harmonising factor.

Tilak's role now was in a wider field: as secretary of the Bombay Provincial Conference, he acted in a disciplined way. In 1893, when the communal riots broke out, Tilak offered his services and lambasted the policy of Divide and Rule adopted by the bureaucracy under the *Raj.* He was critical of the policy of Lord Dufferin. Indeed through the columns of the *Kesari,* he expressed his own comments of the existing affairs in the field of politics and the feelings of the masses which wanted nothing but justice to many causes having deep linkage with the constitutional reforms. His social activities made him a popular and respected leader and he was twice elected a member of the Legislative Council and the Fellow of the Bombay University.

Tilak also started a Law College with a view to prepare students for the High Court and District Pleadership examinations. Many students of the region were beneficiaries from this new academic experiment of Tilak. At this juncture, he took charge of the *Kesari* while Prof. Kelkar remained editor of the *Mahratta.* Soon after Kelkar left and Tilak started to manage both the papers. The *Kesari* specially flourished much and soon its circulation assumed enviable proportion in our sub-continent.

Tilak was well aware that the British Press in India was planning a mischief by labelling the Shivaji festival as a deliberate attempt on his part to stir up the Hindus against the Muslims. He warned his Muslim brethren not to fall into the Anglo-Indian trap. "The Shivaji festival" he proclaimed "is not celebrated to alienate or even to irritate the Mohammedans. Times have changed and the Mohammedans and the Hindu are in the same boat as far as the present political condition of the people is concerned." The people understood and followed him wholeheartedly.

Tilak's involvement in the Tai Maharaj Case is a tragic chapter of his career. His friend, Balia Maharaja, made him a trustee of his estate and he was also asked to take care of the interests of his wife after his death. Other trustees were G.S. Khaparde, Kumbhojkar and Nagpurkar. The document of the will had these words: "My wife is expecting a baby. If she gives birth to a daughter, or if a son is born but lives only a short time, then for the purpose of continuing the name of my family, with the *vichara* (consent and consultation) of the trustees, a boy shall be placed, as often as may be necessary, for adoption, on the lap of my life, in accordance with the *shastras* (religious practices), and the trustees shall, on behalf of that son, carry on the management of my moveable and fixed estate until he attains his majority".

After a few months, when Baba died, his wife gave birth to a son, who died two months later, Tilak was still in prison. On being released, he took up the complex problem of adoption by Tai Maharaj. The estate left by the Baba was in heavy debts and creditors were harassing for payment. He, however, suggested strict economy on several items of expenditure as he was dejected to see many resources being wasted away. The widow of the Baba did not like the economy measures suggested by Tilak. She was convinced by several hangers-on that her status would be reduced to that of a prisoner. She was also advised to get rid of these trustees and adopt a boy of her own choice.

Under these circumstances, Tilak and Khaparde took a different course of action. They in fact were pained to learn about such an adoption which, they would argue, ruin the economic status of the estate. They suggested to Tai Maharaj that she should adopt a boy from the Babre branch of the family of Aurangabad, in the Nizam's dominion. A boy named Jagannath, just seven years old, was found suitable for adoption. In a huge congregation of learned men who performed the religious rites and prominent citizens, the boy's father placed him in the lap of the widow and Jagannath was adopted in a formal way.

On returning to Poona, Tai Maharaj expressed her resentment against such adoption. She applied for revocation of the probate granted to Tilak and other trustees and the litigation started. The grounds of her application were: (a) that the grant of probate to Tilak and others had become void and inoperative through the birth (and subsequent death) of a son to Tai Maharaj and (b) that the executors had become unfit to act in the said trust, so necessitating the appointment of new trustees. Aston, the District Judge, decided in widow's favour, held the adoption disapproved and dissolved the probate. He committed Tilak to the City Magistrate to be dealt with according to the Criminal Law. He was convicted.

Tilak felt furious as his self-respect was outraged and his personal honour tarnished. He at once appealed to the Bombay High Court, and Aston's decision the matter of process was reversed. In the charge of perjury, Tilak was convicted and sentenced to eighteen months' rigorous imprisonment with a fine of Rs 1,000 which was relaxed to six months by the Sessions Judge. Later on, Tilak appealed to the High Court and he was freed from every charge. Meanwhile, Tai Maharaj passed away, but the case was continued in the name of her daughter, Shantabai. It was decided against Tilak who appealed to the Privy Council in London and finally won the case in 1915.

Speech on National Education

(Extract from the speech delivered in 1908, Barsi—Original in Marathi).

> I shall speak here this evening on national education. We are not accustomed to this term, hence it needs a little explanation. To be able to read and write alone is no education. These are simply the means of its attainment. That which gives us a knowledge of the experiences of our ancestors is called education. It may, however, be through books or through anything else. Every business needs education and every man has thus to give it to his children. There is no business indeed which does not require education. Our industries have been taken away by the other people, but we do not know it. A potter knows how to shape a pot of China-clay but does not know what this clay is made of; hence his industry is lost. Similarly is the necessity of religious education. How can a person be

proud of his religion if he is ignorant of it? The want of religious education is one of the causes that have brought the missionary influence all over our country. We did not think of it until very lately, whether we get the right sort of education or not. The tradesmen who are present here this evening send their sons very reluctantly to school and some of them do not send at all; because they do not get their education which they need. Besides their sons educated in the present-day system turn out fashionable. They wish to become clerks. They feel ashamed to sit on the *gaddi*[3] where their forefathers earned the whole of their estate. The reason of this is that the education which they receive is onesided. The Government wanted Engineers, Doctors and clerks. It therefore started such schools which could supply its need. The students therefore who came out of these schools at first were bent upon services. It was the state of things sometime back that after passing three or four classes in school one could easily get on in life, but it has now become absolutely difficult, even to live from hand to mouth. We have therefore become conscious. It has become now almost clear that it is not the fault on our part that even after getting so much education we remain unable to satisfy our bare necessities; but the fault goes direct to the education stood before us. If the Educational Department had been under our control we could have effected in it any necessary changes immediately. At first we asked the Government to transfer it to our control—the selection of the text-books for schools, for example. We feel now the necessity of such education which will prepare us to be good citizens. His excellency the Governor of Bombay also admits the necessity of reforms in the present system of education. But he says that the government is short of funds. I do not think this excuse reasonable, it may be true or otherwise. It is, however, true that the Government cannot think of religious education; and it is well that they are not doing it; because they are not our co-religionists. We are not given such education as may inspire patriotic sentiments amongst us. In America the Proclamation of Independence is taught in V or VI classes. In this way they train their children in politics. Some eighty or ninety years ago the industries of Germany declined on account of the rivalry between England and that country. But the German Government at once started scientific and mechanical education in that country. In this way Germany became so powerful in commerce that she has now become an object of dread to other countries. Properly speaking these things ought to be done by the Government itself. We pay taxes to the Government only that it may look after our welfare. But the Government wants to keep us lame. There is conflict between the commercial interests of England and India. The Government therefore cannot do anything in this matter.

There being no convenient schools in the villages, our villagers cannot train their children. We must therefore begin this work. There has been a good deal of discussion over this matter. And in the end we have come to the conclusion that for proper education national schools must be started on all sides. There are some of our private schools but owing to the fear of losing the grant-in-aid, the necessary education cannot be given there. We must start our own schools for this education. We must begin our work selflessly. Such efforts are being made all over the country. The Gurukul of

Hardwar stands on this footing. Berar and Madras have also begun to move in this direction. Our Maharashtra is a little backward. A few efforts are being made here also; but they need encouragement from you. Money is greatly needed for this work. I am sure, if you realise the necessity and importance of this subject, you would encourage the organisers generously. So far I have told you about the subject, now I turn to tell you what we shall do in these schools of national education.

Of the many things that we will do there *religious education will first and foremost engage our attention.* Secular education only is not enough to build up character. Religious education is necessary because the study of high principles keeps us away from evil pursuits. Religion reveals to us the form of the Almighty. Says our religion that a man by virtue of his action can become even a god. When we can become gods even by Virtue of our action, why may we not become wise and active by means of our action like the Europeans? Some say that religion begets quarrel. But I ask, "Where is it written in religion to pick up quarrels?" If there be any religion in the world which advocates toleration of other religious beliefs and instructs one to stick to one's own religion, it is the religion of the Hindus alone. Hinduism to the Hindus, Islamism to the Mussalmans will be taught in these schools. And it will also be taught there to forgive and forget the differences of other religions.

The second thing that we will do, will be to lighten the load of the study of the foreign languages. In spite of a long stay in India no European can speak for a couple of hours fluent Marathi, while our graduates are required as a rule to obtain proficiency in the English language. One who speaks and writes good English is said, in these days, to have been educated. But a mere knowledge of the language is no true education. Such a compulsion for the study of foreign languages does not exist anywhere except in India. We spend twenty or twenty-five years for the education which we can easily obtain in seven or eight years if we get it through the medium of our vernaculars. We cannot help learning English: but there is no reason why its study should be made compulsory. Under the Mohammedan rule we were required to learn Persian but we were not compelled to study it. To save unnecessary waste of time we have proposed to give education through our own vernaculars.

Industrial education will be the third factor. In no school this education is given. It will be given in these schools. It is an important thing. During the whole of this century we have not known how a match is prepared. In Sholapur matches are manufactured from straw; and straw is found abundantly in our country. If therefore this country is taken into our hands the importation of matches will largely decrease in India. It is the same with sugar industry. We can procure here as good sugarcane as is found in Mauritius. It is seen by scientific experiments that the sugarcane found in the suburbs of Poona can produce as much sugar as is found in the sugarcane of Mauritius. Six crores of rupees are drained out every year from this country only for sugar. Why should this be? Well, can we not get here sugarcane? or the machinery necessary for its manufacture? The reason is that we do not get here the education in this industry. It is not so in Germany. The Department of Industry investigates there as to which industry is decaying, and if perchance there be any, in a decaying state, substantial support at once comes forth from the Government for reviving it. The British Government, too does the same thing in England. But our Government does not do it here. It may be a mistake or the Government may be doing it knowingly, but it is clear that we must not sit silent if the Government is not doing it. We are intending to start a large mechanical and scientific laboratory for this purpose. Sugar produces *Rab* and from *Rab* is extracted liquor, but the Government does not permit us this extraction; hence we cannot get here cheap sugar. Mauritius imports to this country twenty thousand tons of sugar every year. All this is due to the policy of the Government, but we do not know it. The Government will be obliged to change it if we put pressure upon it. We have come to learn these things not earlier than twenty-five years after leaving the college. Our young men should know them in their prime of life.

Education in politics will be the fourth factor. We are not taught this subject in the Government schools. The student must understand that the Queen's Proclamation is the foundation of our rights. The Government is trying to shut our young men from these things. What has been proved by our revered Grand Old Man—Dadabhai Naoroji, after a careless exertion for over fifty years, should be understood by our students in their youth. Every year some thirty or forty crores of rupees are drained out of India without any return. We have, therefore, fallen to a wretched state of poverty. These things, if understood in the prime of life, can make such a lasting impression over the hearts of our young men, as it would be impossible in an advanced age. Therefore this education should be given in school. Educated men of the type of Prof. Vijapurkar, have come forth to devote their lives in the cause of this education. The educationists are helping with their learning and experience, and it now remains with the well-to-do to help them with money. It is a matter of common benefit, if the future generation come out good, able to earn their bread and be true citizens. We should have been glad if the Government had done it. If the Government cannot do it, we must do. The Government will not interfere with us and if at all it does so, we should not mind it. And the dawn of the Sun cannot be stopped so it is with this. Our poverty has not yet reached its zenith. In America such work is done by a single man. But if no one man can venture to do it here, let us do it unitedly, for we are thirty crores of people. A sum of five lacs of rupees goes out every year for liquor alone from Sholapur. Can you not therefore help us in this work? The will is wanted. Let the Government be displeased—we hope the Government will never deter us—we must do our duty. If the Government prohibits us from marriages, do we obey it? The same is the case with education. As men do not give up building houses for fear that rats would dig holes, so we should not give up our work for fear of Government displeasure. If perchance any difficulty arises our young men are to face it. To fear difficulties is to lose manliness. Difficulties do us immense good. They inspire in us courage and prepare us to bear them manly. A nation cannot progress if it meets no difficulties in the way. We do not get this sort of education for want of self-Government. We should not therefore await the coming of these rights, but we must get up and begin the work.[4]

The famine which broke out in Bombay in 1896 was thoughtfully viewed by Tilak. There was much loss of life and the sufferings of the people assumed serious proportion. The famine spread to Sholapur and other areas and seriously affected the socio-economic condition of the people. Tilak formulated a feasible scheme by which local committees were required to cooperate with the government in providing relief to the affected people. In spite of derogatory remarks by the government, Tilak acted fearlessly and went on pursuing the cause of the famine-stricken people.

In Poona, the plague took a heavy toll and thus posed a serious threat to the human life. Tilak at once came out as a champion of these hapless people, collected funds and set up a plague hospital. He organised a band of dedicated workers who could render selfless service to the suffering people. Indeed Tilak was critical of the upper class which began to leave Poona *en-masse* leaving their affected brethren in difficulty.

Tilak's public life had several ramifications due to which he suffered a lot. But nothing could deter him to relax his efforts in any sense. Rather it enthused him to be more determined towards new channels of solutions.

A serious incident took place on 22 June which involved Tilak, leading to his conviction. A group of unknown persons murdered Mr Rand and Lieutenant Ayerst which hurted the sentiments of the Anglo-Indian community of Poona and Bombay. The Government of Bombay gave orders for Tilak's arrest. Tilak pleaded for bail which was rejected by the High Court.

The case, however, took a serious turn in due course of time. On appeal, Mr Justice Strachey presided at the trial. The Jury had six Europeans, who returned a verdict of guilty while the other three of not guilty. As a result, Tilak was sentenced to eighteen months' rigorous imprisonment.

At this point of time, when all avenues of justice appeared closed for Tilak, Prof. Max Muller and Sir William Hunter sent a signed petition to the Queen on the plea that Tilak being a renowned scholar deserved to be released. Tilak was consequently released on 6 September 1898. This increased his popularity among masses to several notches and his reputation travelled in every nook and corner of the Presidency as well as in our subcontinent.

The Shivaji Festival[5]

(A speech delivered in Marathi, on the occasion of the Shivaji Coronation Festival, in Poona, on the 25th June, 1907).

> It is a pity the Government cannot yet understand that the object of festivals like these is not to create disturbances. Its mind is yet enveloped in undeserved suspicion. There are a dozen detectives and reporters at this very meeting. Now where is the need for all this suspicion and distrust? I am sorry that the District Magistrate himself did not take the trouble to attend. Why not take the golden opportunity to know firebrand what the advocates of the Shivaji festival have got really to say on these occasions? I, for one, am prepared to say every word that I now say even before His Excellency the Governor. I will say it before God Himself, for what I say I have honestly at heart. I will

proclaim it from the housetops if required. I will avow it if a detective come to me and ask for views. There is no occasion for expressing views by stealth or secrecy; and what need of it? Surely, Indian people are not robbers in their own country. They can certainly proclaim their aspirations and they really ought to. We do not fear a hearing, only we want a full and a fair hearing. I strongly condemn the mean attempt to lay the nets for a stray unguarded word to penalise and victimise the speaker. If Government wants to know the truth let it be prepared to hear the whole truth. Why spend two lacs on maintaining short-hand reporters and detectives, and such other men of the intelligence department? The money would be surely better spent on technical education. If we celebrate the Shivaji festival we do not do it for raising the standard of revolt. The idea will be foolish and absurd, as we all know that we have arms, no ammunition.

An educated man, an M.A., and an LL.B. may surely be given credit for knowing that the military strength of the Government is enormous and that a single machine-gun showering hundreds of bullets per minute will quite suffice for our largest public meetings. How can a detective find out things which never enter the perception of the educated classes? Those who are thus shadowed may however console themselves with the idea that the great God who sees everything is the people's detective upon kings and Governments, and that this divine detective must sooner or later bring the British Government to justice. The secret of all this mischief lies in the idea that the educated classes are the enemies of the Government. Mr Morley in fact said it in so many words, and he made much of the fact that every member of the proletariat did not often completely endorse what the educated man had to say—as if every savage or aborigine, every illiterate man of the masses, should be able to comprehend the depths of the political cunning of our bureaucracy. But what is it in the educated classes that leads Mr Morley to mistake them for enemies. Is it the knowledge in them that so leads him? Then surely Mr Morley himself is the enemy of knowledge. We all know that Adam, the original man, suffered because he ate the fruit of the tree of 'Knowledge' and the educated Indians are being treated similarly for the 'knowledge' which is bestowed upon them. Is the Government prepared to be classed with those who are the enemies of knowledge in this creation?[6]

To turn to the Shivaji festival, the knowledge we have, or the knowledge which we want to inculcate among the people in this connection, relates not to the actual use of the identical measures which Shivaji for instance took but to a proper appreciation of the spirit in which he resorted to the measures suitable to his time. Festivals like these prove an incentive to the legitimate ambitions of a people with a great historic past. They serve to impact courage, such courage as an appreciation of heroes securing their salvation against odds, can give. They are an antidote to vague despair. They serve like manure to the seeds of enthusiasm and the spirit of nationality. Malice or wickedness is never the keynote, or even the minor note, of those who come together on occasions like these. I wish that every word I say on this point should be faithfully reported, and I will gladly supply omissions if the report were submitted to me for correction. The time is surely not yet for lawlessness, for we have not yet exhausted all the possibilities of what may be claimed as legitimate and lawful action. But the pity of it all is that the Government is engaged in treating even this lawful action as unlawful. Lala Lajpat Rai, for instance, had done nothing that was not lawful and yet the whole official hierarchy conspired and acted like one man to deport him. I cannot imagine a clear sign that the greatness of the British Government is doomed, and that decay and demoralisation has set in. Mr Morley is a great 'Pandit', a learned man. There is no use denying the fact: but it was a pity that this excellent repository of learning, this great English 'Pandit', is no better after all than one of our own orthodox Pandits of Benares who are strangers to worldly wisdom. It is an irony of fate that the greater the scholarship, the less the statesmanship. Mr Morley ridicules the educated classes on the ground that they are poor. Has Mr Morley forgotten the old days when he himself enjoyed no better lot? The educated Indian may aspire to rise high office, but that is no more culpable in him than for this English Pandit to aspire for State Secretaryship. His analysis of the factors of the Indian population is very amusing. He claims the Princes and the Nobles on his side. Surely it is not a thing to be wondered at when we know that the Indian Princes are more puppets, whose tenure of life as Princes hangs on the breath of the British Government. The Viceroy proclaimed Ordinance I of 1907 as there were disturbances in Bengal and the Punjab; but the Maharaja of Kolhapore went one better though he had not the least excuse of any kind. Mr Morley claims the merchant class on his side. This is not true about the whole class and it must be remembered that merchants who are engaged in British trade and who depend on the means of enjoying the luxuries of life on that trade cannot be expected to come forward boldly to speak against Government. And, lastly, he claimed the lowest and the poorest classes, the illiterate *ryots,* as being on the side of Government. The Hon'ble Mr Logan echoed the same sentiment only the other day in the Bombay Legislative Council. But this is moonshine. The pretensions of this official friend of the *ryot* cannot be exposed and contradicted to his very face only because the *ryot* is illiterate and cannot know who presumed to pose as his friend. But surely these false pretensions will be deemed as soon as education is sufficiently extended, and I may perhaps say that, it is only for this reason that the Government is so cautious in extending it. The educated classes alone have the knowledge and the courage for agitation and naturally the State Secretary treats them as enemies. But I appeal to you that the educated classes need not feel despair over such a thing the educated classes are no doubt poor but they have one compensating advantage. They possess knowledge, and knowledge is not poor inasmuch as it possesses unlimited potentiality for wealth of every sort. They may also rely upon gradually bringing to their side those classes on whose support Government now thinks it may rely. History abounds in cases of kingdoms undone by the discontent of penniless beggars. No one could be more poor than the great Chanakya of mediaeval Indian History, and it is well-known how Chanakya, who had no stake in the world but the little knot of his hair, exterminated the whole race of the Nandas in return for the insult that was desperately given to him. Mr Morley of all persons should not have scorned the power of educated men because they were poor and had no earthly stake. But when thoughtful men like Mr Morley betray such evident signs of thoughtlessness, then surely the decline of the British *Raj* has begun. Mr Morley has however rendered one great service. He has disillusioned the over-credulous and optimistic souls among us, and literally proved that the greatest Radical after all is no better than the worst Conservative so far as India is concerned. The Old generation, to which I myself belong, is now nearly "hors de combat". The younger generation certainly does not share in this deluding optimism and that is a hopeful sign for India, and I look forward to their exerting themselves with courage and perseverance. Mr Paranjpe and another speaker had referred to the theory of social contract of Rosseau, and Mr Damale had constructed the Proclamation of 1858 as a contract. For my part I think that the word "contract" cannot be made applicable to relations existing between unequals, and it is dangerous for us to be deluded into a belief that the Proclamation is anything like a contract. No doubt it was a pledge solemnly given, but in its inception it was an utterance made in only a statesmanly spirit, because it was calculated to make for peace at the time. But the finger of the tactician is discernable in it. It is essentially an English idea that a political agitation is an attempt to enforce the terms of such an agreement. The Eastern idea is different; but it is a mistake to hold that it does not warrant an agitation by the subjects to control the power of the King. The idea is no doubt true that the King is part and parcel of the Godhead, and some foolish people have tried to fling it in the face of the Indian people to detract from their demand for popular institution. But the canons of interpretation of a text are not less important than the text itself, and the real mischief arises from not construing the text in this respect as it should be. The King or Sovereign is no doubt a part and parcel of the Godhead, but according to the Vedanta, so is every member of the subject people. For is not every soul a chip from the same block of Brahman? It is absurd to suppose that the Indian lawgivers of old regarded a King as absolved from all duties towards the subjects. Why? Many has distinctly laid down, for instance, that the King who punishes those whom he should not, or does not punish those whom he should, goes to hell.

Though downtrodden and neglected, you must be conscious of your power of making the administration impossible if you but choose to make it so. It is you who manage the rail-road and the telegraph, it is you who make settlements and collect revenues, it is in fact you who do everything for the administration though in a subordinate capacity. You must consider whether you cannot turn your hand to better use for your nation than drudging on in this fashion. Let your places be filled by Europeans on the splendid salary of eight annas a day if possible. You must seriously consider whether your present conduct is self-respectful to yourselves or useful to the nation. You must also consider what humiliation you have to suffer when foreigners openly express their wonder at the three hundred millions of Indians bearing their present ignominious lot without any effective protest. To say this, is not to violate the spirit of laws of any constitution.

Surely it does not violate the sense of God's justice as we understand it. It is but those who oppose the reasonable demands of the Indian people that offended against God's justice.

You must imitate your rulers only in one thing, namely, in maintaining an unfalling succession of public workers. If one Lala Lajpat Rai is sent abroad, another ought to be found to take his place as readily as a junior Collector steps into the shoes of a senior. It is vain to hope that your petitions will have the effect of releasing Lala, though it is well known that the Government do not mean to keep him a prisoner all his life. His deportation is intended not so much to penalise Lala Lajpat Rai as to terrorise those that would follow his example, and if their agitation stopped as soon as deportation took place, Government will run away with the idea that terrorism had triumphed. It is no use, in fact it is a wrong course, to declare your loyalty with the L. writ large, on an occasion like the present. Those proclaimers of loyalty may be loyal, but who is not? Government is too shrewd not to know the real sentiments of the people, how far loyal or how far disloyal. And just as they are likely to put down agitation under the deliberate presence of mistaking it for disloyalty, so also they are shrewd enough to know the real character of the loyalty that is so proclaimed by the placards, and by the beat of drums from the housetops. What you want is courage to declare that there is no disloyalty in agitating for constitutional rights and you will go on demanding them, though threatened that such demands will be treated as signs of disloyalty. What you want is bread for the masses and honourable rights for the masses as well as classes. That is not being disloyal, and I for one do not care that it is likely to be deliberately mistaken for disloyalty. The time has certainly come when you must be prepared to clearly formulate and persistently demand the more important rights and privileges. I say again to the reporters that every word that I am uttering. I am uttering deliberately and that a faithful report of those words will rather help than retard the cause I have at heart. With regard to Mr Kinckaid's lecture on the Peshwas I have to point out that on the whole he has taken a correct view of that period of the Mahratta history, though I differ from him in one respect. The rule of the Peshwas came to an end not because they were usurpers of the political power, but because in the very nature of things a single family or dynasty cannot produce an unbroken succession of men possessed of such incomparable valour, ability and statesmanship as the family of Balaji Vishvanath did. There would have been even in England the same collapse of dynastic rule if the British constitution did not afford the useful ballast of the Parliament in which the sovereign power is diffused among so many individuals. We, Indians, have learnt at our own cost the lesson of the importance of popular and representative Government, and that is exactly the reason why our aspirations seem to be diverted from the patent oriental ideal.[7]

References

1. N.C. Kelkar, Life and Times of Lokmanya Tilak, Delhi, 1987, pp. 1-17.
2. *Ibid.*
3. Throne.
4. Bal Gangadhar Tilak, *op. cit.*
5. *Ibid.*
6. *Ibid.*
7. *Ibid.*

3

Home Rule Movement

Its Birth and Expansion

The advent of Annie Besant on the political scene of India was a significant phenomenon at a point of time when the country needed a leader who could give a practical lead to the nation. With the death of Gopal Krishna Gokhale on 19 February 1915 followed by Pherozeshah Mehta in November the same year there was sudden and unexpected dearth of prominent leaders in India. D.E. Wacha was also fairly old and infirm. Surendranath Banerjea was not quite tuned with the new thought. Bal Gangadhar Tilak who was released in June 1914 was physically shattered and it was just not possible for him to take to tedious whirlwind tours of various regions in India. Lala Lajpat Rai was unhappy with the existing state of affairs. Gandhi had just arrived in India and it needed some time for him to introduce himself well to the Indian masses after the Lucknow session of the Indian National Congress in 1916.

The launching of an All India Home Rule League in September 1915 was the most significant episode in Anne Besant's career. Numerous sections of people including peasants and workers became active participants under her flag. India could never have been like it before—so one could say after witnessing such ferment and such passionate demonstration of active political life.[1] Thus, the year 1916 ushered in numerous significant developments which had deep linkage with the existing politics of the time. The country indeed was sans a leader with the untimely demise of Gokhale and Mehta. Tilak had as yet no place in the Congress, and he had to wait for another year to find his place in the party. He made himself deeply involved in the Home Rule activities. The same sort of efforts were made by no less a leader than Annie Besant.

The object of the Home Rule League, its definition and aims were explicitly explained thus.[2] The Home Rule has been established to carry out the following objects: To secure Home Rule for India through all law-abiding and constitutional activity; to maintain the connexion with Great Britain by becoming a free nation within the British Empire, under the Imperial Crown of His Majesty the King Emperor, George V and his successors; to support and strengthen the National Congress which has laboured for thirty years to lay the foundations of Indian self-government and to carry on a continuous educative propaganda on the necessity of Home Rule for India. In fact the Home Rule means the government of the people and by the people.

The call of Home Rule reached remotest corners of the country and Home Rule Leagues were established all over. In Mrs. Besant's hands the press assumed power in spite of repression under the Press Law. Another factor that largely contributed to the enviable success of the movement was that from its inception it recognised the integrity of language areas and in constituting the country, adopted the linguistic principle as determining the provincial delimitations.[3]

The first meeting of the Home Rule League of Annie Besant was held in Madras on 3 September 1915.[4] Around five hundred persons enrolled themselves as members of the League. Annie Besant was expectedly elected its president and G.S. Arundale as organising secretary. Besides C.P. Ramaswami Aiyar was one of the general secretaries and B.P. Wadia the treasurer.[5]

The Home Rule League consisted of two divisions—one in India and the other in England. While the function of the former was to educate Indians about the implications of the Home Rule Movement, the latter was entrusted to educate the English public opinion in relation to the political condition of India in the first two decades of the twentieth century.

The Lucknow session of the Indian National Congress in 1916 was presided over by Babu Ambika Charan Mazumdar. It was a unique congregation attended by 2301 delegates, besides a large number of visitors from several regions of India. It led to the fraternisation of the Hindus and Muslims as well as for the formulation of a scheme of self-government. But the reunion of the two wings of the Congress was equally important which experienced a split about a decade ago at the Surat session of the Congress. It in fact held a great political significance to have Tilak and Khaparde sitting by one another with other prominent leaders like Surendranath Banerjea and Rash Behari Ghose. The Congres-League scheme which was approved by the Congress received the immediate approval of the Muslim League.[6]

The resolution dealing with self-government for India declared that considering the ancient civilisation and the public spirit His Majesty the King-Emperor should be pleased to issue a manifesto announcing that it was the aim and target of British policy to grant self-government to India at an early date; that as a definite step in that direction the Congress-League scheme should be granted; and that in the reconstruction of the Empire, India should be elevated from the position of a dependency to that of an equal partner in the Empire with the self-Governing Dominions.[7]

Besides, the Lucknow Congress in a resolution, viewed with dismay the extensive use made of the Defence of India Act and the Bengal Regulation III of 1818, and appealed that in the application of the Defence of India Act, which was an emergency measure, the same principle should be practised as under the Defence of the Realm Act of the United Kingdom and the same procedure adopted in dealing with persons sought to be proceeded against under the Act, that a statement in writing of the charge should be given to an arrested person, and an explanation obtained from him placed before a lawyer judge of the High Court, a non-official practising lawyer, and a judge of the Indian Civil Service and no internment order before the same had been considered and the arrested persons provided proper facilities for legal assistance.[8]

In accordance with the terms of the resolution passed at the Lucknow Congress and under direction of All India Congress Committee, the Madras

Provincial Committee appointed a twenty-five member body to carry out educative and publicised work in connection with the scheme of self-government adopted by the Congress and by the Muslim League. Mrs. Besant, Arundale, Wadia and a few other leaders of the Home Rule movement were appointed to this body, and resolved among other things :[9]

1. to prepare a brief exposition of the scheme of reforms adopted by the Congress and the Muslim League with a view to translate the same into Tamil, Telugu, Hindustani, Kanarese and Malayalam, and spread it broadcast among the people, and
2. to send copies of the Congress scheme to all the non-official members of the Legislative Council, the members of the All India Congress Committee and leading citizens in the *muffassal*, requesting them to popularise the scheme by means of lectures in English and in the vernaculars.[10]

As Tilak was yet out of the fold of the Congress, he could act in an independent manner and could opine any political idea which might facilitate his political stability. It was not incumbent on him to seek the advice of the main body of the Congress before convening any meeting of like-minded persons. He came about to summon a conference of the nationalists representing Bombay, Central Provinces and Berar at Poona on 23-24 December 1915, i.e., just prior to the Bombay session of the Congress. As a result of deliberations in this conference, a fifteen-member committee was appointed which was to determine whether it was desirable to establish a League to obtain Home Rule for India and what steps should be taken with this aim in view. The Indian Home Rule League came into being on 28 April 1916 with Joseph Baptista as its president and N.C. Kelkar as secretary. The other prominent members were G.S. Khaparde, B.S. Moonje and R.P. Karandikar. It seems evident that Tilak did not accept any office in this organisation. There was a clear understanding that the Provincial Conference and the Indian Home Rule League would remain two distinct bodies.

Propagation of Ideologies

Annie Besant challenged British system of government in India, glorified Indian culture and heritage, demanded self-government for India, and came down heavily on the violent means used and advocated by extremists. It was a novel method of propagating the principles and ideologies of the Home Rule Movement. It was basically through the media of discussion amongst various groups, a series of lectures in district headquarters, launching of fund-raising campaigns amongst the financially affluent philanthropists and common people, publication of newspapers and pamphlets with main emphasis on *swarajya,* conduct of personal tours to different regions of India, by seeking the support of universities—authorities, teachers and students, and last but not the least, to send deputations to England with a view to mobilise British public opinion.

Besant was of the opinion that by understanding traditions of a rich Indian past, the future of India could be shaped. She, therefore, arranged her programme which had a social and religious background based on the preservation of India's ancient traditions and culture.

She had realised the magnitude of numerous movements in the domain of religion, education and political and social regeneration. During the course of a lecture 'The Birth of New India' delivered in 1910, Mrs Besant declared, "... I am a Punjabi; I am a Bengali; I am an upcountry man;" leave all that behind and teach your boys and girls to say, "I am an Indian". Out of the mouths of the children thus speaking shall be born the India of tomorrow . . . Hindus and Mussalmans must join hands, for both are Indians . . . If India is to be the spiritual light of the future, in her must be focussed the light that comes from every faith, until in the prism of India they are all united into the one light which shall flood with sunlight the world, and all lights shall blend in the Divine Wisdom. That is our work."

The outbreak of the war and the eagerness of the public for the latest news were partly responsible for the phenomenal growth of *New India* as an Anglo-Indian newspaper. Starting from nowhere in July 1914, it was printing five thousand copies in August, seventy-five hundred in September, and ten thousand in November.

Both the Indian and the Anglo-Indian press had mixed reaction about the writings of Annie Besant. Most of the Indian papers supported her cause, but the Anglo-Indian press demanded that she be asked to discontinue her activities. Where the *Times of India* criticised her writings, the *Englishman* stated that her demand for *Swaraj* was nonsense. The *Indian Mirror* from Calcutta, the *Indian Patriot* from Madras, the *Indu Parkash* and the *Gujarati* from Bombay—all were opposed to her ideas. Other papers supported her ideology and tone of her speeches and writings. This kind of critical assessment of her writings could not dampen her interest, courage and strength. Time and again she discussed about India's heritage, the urge for mass awakening and efforts for the development of educational system in order to prepare the mindset of the people for Home Rule Movement.

In the session of the Indian National Congress which met in Madras in 1914. Mrs. Besant gave vent to her feelings about the self-government for India ". . . Realise that you are asking now with a note of hope in your voice that, before you could hardly venture to have so made, that the time has come when India shall come to her birthright . . . she has suffered and through suffering she has learnt; she has endured, and through endurance she has grown strong; and in the patience of her waiting, comes her right to demand her freedom, and to be granted that self-government which alone can satisfy the longings of the Indian nation."

In a resolution on self-government for India passed in the session of the Indian National Congress held in Bombay the next year, she stated: "Oh! you are not fit for Self-Government. You are ignorant . . . It was the late Mr. Gopal Krishna Gokhale who tried to win free and compulsory education cautiously, carefully step by step, for he was not an impatient idealist in the world . . . It is only Home Rule that will enable us to defend ourselves . . ."

While levelling staunch criticism against British rule in India, Annie Besant unequivocally pointed out that it gave our country nothing but famines and poverty by cutting at the very roots of its indigenous economic system and imposing modern 'political economy'. She further explained, "To impose English political economy on India was a folly, but folly nonetheless to which India faced degradation and destruction of arts and manufactures."

In an address delivered to the Hindu College Boarders Debating Club at Banaras at its anniversary meeting, Mrs. Besant explained thus: "During the plastic years of boyhood it is best to mould and give to shape the character after its own type, to make the Mussalman boy a good Mussalman, the Hindu boy a good Hindu. Just as stones are given shapes and fitted and then built into their respective places in an edifice, so must these boys are shaped and fitted by their several religions to be built into the Indian nation."

In an article on 'India and the War' in the *Indian Review*, Mrs. Besant opined. ". . . . When all danger is over, when peace takes the place of war, and when the domestic concerns of each nation again assume their natural and rightful place in the minds of the people, then, of course, the questions now dropped will again be raised . . . We may, however, be sure that, when they come to be dealt with, they will be approached in a spirit very different from that of previous years."

The Acting Chief Secretary to the Government of Madras informed the Home Secretary, Government of India on 17 November, 1916, "The activities of the Home Rule League continue. Special Home Rule classes have been started and are to be held twice a week in the hall of the Young Men's Indian Association at Madras; the first meeting was taken by a number of the Theosophical Society under the presidency of Mrs. Besant herself, the attendance being variously reported at from 70 to 120. The influence of the Organising Secretary, Mr. Arundale, is undoubtedly on the increase and his name is mooted as possible political successor to Mrs. Besant . . . Attention is being concentrated on the student class . . . This is not matter for surprise seeing that students and school-boys read *New India* regularly, study Mrs. Besant's political pamphlets and attend home rule classes and lectures laying special stress on the great part which the youths of today will play in the future of India. The bad effect which this has on discipline extends outside Madras; it has been specially noticed at St. Joseph's College, Trichinopoly and in the College at Coimbatore where notices inviting the readers to 'kill the English' and to 'worship Mrs. Besant' were recently found pasted up on the College gates."

By 1st January 1917, Mrs. Besant and her lieutenant, Arundale, temporarily shifted their personal activities to Northern India, travelling to Lucknow by way of Calcutta and Bombay. '*New India* continues its praise of 'Professor' Ramamurti who on the 18th December, 1916 delivered a lecture of physical culture to a get-together of students "thus preparing" to quote from *New India* "in one particular field the way for young men for the priceless boon for Home Rule."

The same source opined thus, 'The *New India* has also held up to admiration Ramamurti, the Indian sandow, whose troupe has been giving recent exhibitions in Madras. Ramamurti who coquetted with Home Rule in Tanjore a few weeks ago, has been linkened in an editorial to Bhima, the hero of the *Mahabharata,* his feats of strength being attributed to his devout practice of breathing exercises, mind concentration and other forms of *yoga,* commended in the Hindu Shastras and appropriated by Theosophists as part of their cult. The line of argument was that it is incumbent on the youth of India to imitate Ramamurti if they wish to achieve Home Rule.'

On 28 June, 1917, the Home Secretary to the Government of India intimated the chief secretary, Madras government thus: "The effective control of Home Rule meetings raises a question of considerable difficulty. The utilisation of Rule 3 of the Defence of India Rules in order generally to prohibit organisers of any meeting from including in their agenda of business the subject of Home Rule would not, in the opinion of the Government of India, be legitimate. It was indeed to maintain that a meeting called to advocate the policy of self-government within the Empire in due course of time was in any way open to objection. The Government of India realise the great difficulties to which the local Governments are exposed in this matter. They think, however, that these difficulties would only be increased by a general prohibition of this character, and they are of opinion that the question of prohibiting organisers of meetings from including the subject of Home Rule in their agenda can only be decided with reference to the particular facts in each case."

References

1. Raj Kumar, *Annie Besant's Rise to Power in Indian Politics, 1914-1917,* Delhi, 1981, p. 134 and S.R. Bakshi, *Home Rule Movement,* Delhi.
2. See *Annie Besant: Builder of New India, Besant Spirit Series,* Adyar, 1942, pp. 269-73.
3. *New India,* 4 September, 1916.
4. *Ibid.*
5. See *Nation,* pp. 237-38.
6. See the proceedings of the Lucknow Session of the Indian National Congress, 1916.
7. *Ibid.*
8. *Ibid.*
9. Home Deptt. Pol. Dep., April 1917, File 60.
10. *Ibid.*

4

Congress and Anglo-Muhammedan Alliance

The tussle between the Indian National Congress and the British Parliament represented, in its abstract aspect, a struggle between the forces of indigenous nationalism and alien imperialism. The English people, though parted on the surface by well-demarcated political ideologies, were united in various matters of their national existence, especially, as far as the imperial interests were concerned. The story of the Indian nationalism, however, was not that ordinary as of British imperialism. In its subcontinental magnitude, India contained many races, religions, and languages. The forces of nationalism, therefore, had to cut across many boundaries to superimpose the essentials of national integration on this diversity. The process was, naturally, difficult and complex. Education, political awareness, patriotism, economic unrest, xenophobia and similar other factors brought the elite together to Indian nationality. But, to the vast majority of people, traditional socio-religious differences remained as clear as ever before. This was very much so in the 19th century.

No distinction was more deep and enduring in the annals of Indian history as between the Hindus and the Muslims as two separate communities from many fronts.

That distinction was primarily religious, and secondarily social, but rarely a political one. In the days of the great Mughals, Emperor Akbar and Rana Partap were engaged in bitter battles, but Akbar's general in the battles against the Rana was a Hindu, Man Singh. Even in the redoubtable Aurangazeb depended on his Hindu employees to administer his vast empire. His religious dogmatism did not affect his politico-administrative outlook. It was his Rajput generals who waged war against the Maratha, Sivaji. Kings fought kings with soldiers belonging to both the communities arrayed in their respective armies. In short, the Muslim theological state could not blacklist the Hindus either from the administrative services or from army, and the Hindus, in turn, tried to serve the Muslim state which employed them. The Deccanese Sultans regarded the Hindus as the major source of support to their political structure, though not in friendly terms with them on religious grounds.

Finally, in the days of the Mutiny of 1857 Hindus and Muslims stood shoulder to shoulder to fight and fall together. The trail-blazers of the Indian national movement hoped to develop political nationalism to secure political ends irrespective of contrasting religious beliefs. In an age of rationality, enlightenment, and socio-religious reform movements, they wanted to keep religion strictly at a personal level and separate from political principles. But history moved on its own uncertain course. The growth of nationalism came to be subjected to dialectical inevitability and attracted its antithesis in the form of communalism, the patrons of which made use of religion as an instrument of contemporary politics.

Within three years of the Rising of 1857, the most serious view regarding the future of the Indian Muslims was being paid by a Muslim leader who may be inagreeably regarded as the greatest Indian Muslim after Bahadur Shah II and before Muhammad Ali Jinnah. He was Sir Syed Ahmed Khan. It was the British abhorrence towards the Muslims which inspired him to evolve a new course of thought and action to defend the latter from further trouble. To Syed Ahmed, the really culprits were not his fellow religionists, but the Hindus. Neglected by Government and sinking into abject misery, the Indian Muslims at that time were indeed in a pitiable condition.

He was shocked to discover how the Muslims were described as corrupt, treacherous and contemptible. He condemned those Muslims who had behaved without a sense of duty and joined in the Rebellion. He labelled them as criminals and their conduct unpardonable. Thus, it paved the way for the beginning of a new religious approach to the Indian social scene, the drawing together of Muslims and Christians as partners in a noble cause against the Hindus.

The thesis which Syed Ahmed Khan worked out in 1860, narrating his community as the *Loyal Mohomedans of India,* was the foundation on which developed the future Anglo-Muhammedan rapport and rapprochement. He called upon his community to remain loyal to the British and take advantage of the many blessings of the British Rule.

While Hunter made an academic study of the condition of the Muhammedans, Syed Ahmed Khan carried out a practical approach to the mental isolationism of his community. He thought of an educational system which can suit the needs of the time and foster the educational growth of future generations. Through this new system, Sir Syed wanted to teach his fellow religionists to hanker after high positions in Government service, to enjoy a share in the management of the country, and to do good to their fellow men. His dreams were to come true in due course.

On 8 January, 1877, Lord Lytton, the then Governor General, laid the foundation stone of the Muhammedan Anglo-Oriental College at Aligarh. It is known that for the first time in the history of Indian Muslims a college like this owed its establishment to the combined wishes and the joint efforts of a whole community. The founders of the college hailed the British rule in India as 'the most wonderful phenomenon the world has ever seen' and wanted 'to reconcile oriental learning with Western literature and science; to inspire in the dreamy minds of the people of the East the practical energy which belongs to those of the West; to make the Mussalmans of India worthy and useful subjects of the British Crown; to inspire in them that loyalty which springs, not from servile submission to a foreign rule, but from genuine appreciation of the blessings of good government'.[1]

Aligarh gradually started to become not merely a place for Muhammedan

Anglo-Oriental learning, but also a centre of a new political ideology to promote Muhammedan interests. The leaders of the Aligarh school of thought, from the very beginning, projected their policies for safeguarding the interests of the Muslim community. For example, when the principle of local self-government dominated the mind of the politically conscious, Sir Syed Ahmed Khan slammed it with communal arguments. He warned the Government that the larger community would totally overrule the interests of the smaller community and the Government would be held responsible for the violent racial differences which would inevitably follow. The Muslim leaders drew the attention of the Government and showed how Hindus had ousted Muhammedans from the state employ in general, and prayed for state patronage. In brief, the highest quarters of Muhammedan aristocracy were getting suspicious about the rising Hindu influence in spheres of administration and education.

To the conscious Muhammedans, the Congress posed a genuine problem, whether to join or not to join it. Before the second session of the Congress in Calcutta in December 1886, Amir Ali, the honorary secretary of the Central National Muhammedan Association wrote a letter to the Secretaries to the National Congress narrating why the Association should stay away from participating in the proposed Congress.[2] It was the beginning of a parochial stand from the side of the largest religious minority of India towards a national organisation.

Apathy towards Congress

The National Congress made a Muslim, Budrudin Tyabji, its third President in Madras in 1887. It was a hint of the national character of the Congress organisation. Tyabji and the Congress adopted a practical line for national harmony by avoiding issues with socio-religious tinge.

Thus, within three years of the birth of the Congress, the Muslim opinion was polarised, one section seeking unity of the nation for a greater cause, while the other toying with the idea of two Indian nations, Hindu and Muslim. This difference continued to persist till the end of the *Raj* in spite of several attempts on the part of the Congress to avoid the likely consequences inherent in the acceptance of the two-nation theory by the Indian Mussalmans. For the British too, it was equally a development of considerable significance, to be utilised as per the needs of the time. Lord Dufferin was fully aware of the Muslim attitude towards the Congress. He did not want to exploit the racial differences. Before his departure from India, Dufferin expressed his views on this subject in the following manner:

> I confess I would rather see the Europeans, Hindus and Mahomedans united in criticising the Government than that the Hindus and the Mahomedans, the Europeans and the Natives, should become estranged from each other by unworthy prejudices, or animosities of race and religion. God forbid that the British Government should ever seek to maintain its rule in India by fomenting race hatreds amongst its subjects.[3]

The politics of India thus assumed a triangular shape with the three arms being the Congress, the British and the Muslims. In their triangular relations, as time went by, the Congress came to suspect the British for adopting a policy of *divide et impera,* and slammed the Muslim separatists for their nefarious designs. Pherozeshah Mehta drew the attention of the Congress regarding the utter disservice which Sir Syed was doing to the country by preaching a gospel of selfishness and isolation.[4]

At the popular level, the prospects of introduction of elective principles did not widen the rift between the Congress sympathisers and the Muslim leadership, but in the day to day life the two communities found themselves socially divided. And the most striking of those factors was the question of the food habit of the Muhammedans to which every Hindu appeared nauseus. To the common Hindu, cow-slaughter was religiously wrong, while to the educated Hindu it was economically harmful. But to every Muslim, the cow was merely a usual item of food. Though a non-political issue, this directly and indirectly influenced the political relations to a very large extent. Differences over cow-slaughter lead to communal bitterness in 1893, when a riot broke out in Bombay, and the Hindus agitated against cow-slaughter.

Lord Curzon, soon after his arrival in India, found it convenient to admit the greatness of Sir Syed Ahmed Khan and call upon the Muslims to follow his ideals. It is learnt that he bitterly hated the Bengali *babus* and by Bengali *babus* he meant the Bengali Hindus. Consequently, he developed a soft corner towards the Mussalmans in general and the Bengali Muslims in particular. The concept of putting the Muslims against the Hindus was not his original idea. It was an old concept. For example, a decade before Curzon's arrival, Sir John Strachey had written: 'The truth plainly is that the existence side by side of these hostile creeds is one of the strong points in our political position in India. The better classes of Mohammedans are already a source to us of strength and not of weakness, and a continuously wise policy might, I believe, make them strong and important supporters of our power. They constitute a small but energetic minority of the population, whose political interests are identical with ours, and who, under no conceivable circumstances, would prefer Hindu dominion to our own.'[5] Curzon decided to put that theory into practice. While looking at the Muslim population of Bengal in course of his tour in 1904, he announced at Dacca how his concept of a Muslim majority province 'would invest the Muhammedans in East Bengal with a unity which they have not enjoyed since the days of the old Mussalman Viceroys and Kings.'[6]

Partition of Bengal

Thus took place the partition of Bengal. The creation of a separate Muslim majority province was a bold step which only Curzon could have taken, of course, unmindful of the consequences. Unfortunately, he had to leave India before the consequences assumed an alarming proportion. It was left for Curzon's successor, Lord Minto, to face the situation.

It was during those earlier hectic days of Indian politics, when the *Swadeshi* movement flared up as a reaction to the partition that there hastily evolved between the British administrators and Muslim leaders an *entente cordiale* which, through ups and downs, continued till the partition of India. While the Congress and the nationalists aimed at winning the Muslim sympathy against partition, the Eastern

Bengal bureaucracy led by Fuller tried to persuade the Muslims to stand by the partition. As a result of the political rivalry, dangerous communal principles got mingled with economic issues of that poverty-stricken province. Muslim share-croppers took courage to protest against the needs of their Hindu land proprietors, and even refused to work for them.

Lord Minto, who had inherited the policies framed by Lord Curzon, looked upon the Muslim grievances against the Hindus and against the Congress-led *Swadeshi* movement as a source of help in strengthening the government policies against the nationalist agitation. The Congress agitation in favour of a boycott of the British goods was not wholeheartedly accepted by the Muslims in general, and the Bengal Muslims in particular. There were no doubt a sizeable section of Muslims who supported the anti-partition movement, but they were described in bureaucratic circles as people who were 'in the pay of the *Swadeshi* Party'.

In the larger interests of the British empire, Lord Minto decided to adopt a policy of active appeasement of the Indian Muslims. He was aware of a general dissatisfaction among the Muslims that they had not been given as much share in public employment as was their right or as they were qualified. Everywhere the Hindus dominated in government services, even in Muslim-dominated regions like East Bengal. For twenty years since 1885, there were instructions for proportionate representation to the Muhammedans in Government services, but due to Muslim apathy towards English education they were not able to compete with the Hindus in securing the Government jobs. But his successor, permission was sought from Viceroy's to issue a public circular about 'the great disproportion between Mohammedans and Hindus employed in public offices'. He also instructed his assistants to take necessary steps to correct the imbalance. With instruction from the Viceroy, the avenues of Government services we opened to the Muslims without making any official statement in that regard. Though the government policy of offering jobs to the Muslims met with staunch criticism from the Hindus, the Muslims, on the other hand, appreciated the Government stand. That the Viceroy wanted the Hindu-Muslim bitterness to grow was accepted as a patent fact. Fuller was doing his best to keep Muslims from Hindus politically separate. When he was expelled for his excesses, his Muhammedan supporters took it as a defeat of their cause.

Pro-Government Muslims in East Bengal started to take part in the politics of the new province with a communal stand towards every issue. They began to blame the Hindu leaders for spreading disloyalty in the country; they attached the Liberal Cabinet and particularly the Secretary of State for timid policy which helped the Hindu agitation while harming Muslim interests; and also lashed out at the Government of India for not being too firm against the agitation.

The Hindu nationalists on their part first tried to convince and then pressed upon the Muslims to join the anti-Government agitation. On being unsuccessful, the former identified the leading Muslim landlords of the area and began to boycott them socially. Similarly, the Muslim peasants who did not join the agitation actively faced various difficulties in the hands of their Hindu landlords.

This mutual hostility led to the inevitable result. In their bitterness towards each other, the Hindus and Muslims began to indulge in frequent communal clashes.

The Liberal Government in England, soon after assuming power, thought of pacifying Indian opinion by granting some constitutional concessions. The *Swadeshi* movement gave way to a crisis which was rather embarrassing for the entire nation. When Lord Morley began to think of the reforms, he certainly meant legislative institutions through election, while Lord Minto thought of consolidating the British power through constitutional reforms based on communal considerations.

It is in this perspective that took place two events of great future consequence. These were the Simla Deputation and the emergence of the All-India Muslim League. These were the concrete results of the improving Anglo-Muhammedan rapprochement at that time spearheaded by the Aligarh leaders and the conservative Viceroy Lord Minto.

The eagerness with which Minto took up the Muslim cause reflected his deep interest in the subject. And, the swiftness with which the Muslim Deputation was organised, reveals the actual motive of the parties concerned.

On 10 August 1906, Archbold received the green signal that 'His Excellency will agree to receive the Deputation'. On 15 August, the Viceroy wrote to the Secretary of State: "I have always had great hopes of the Mohammedan population . . . and now that they are becoming somewhat alarmed at what they consider Bengali successes, the justice of our safeguarding their interests will become all the more apparent, and ought to be of real assistance to us in dealing with much of the one-sided agitation we have to face."[7] When Mohsin-ul-Mulk got the document in Bombay he wrote back to Archbold on 18 August:

"Thanks for your letter of the 14th instant together with a draft of the formal application. I am sending it to a few of my friends, but I am sure nobody will like the opening phrases which give an assurance of a deliberate aloofness from political agitation in the future. Probably also they will not like me to represent their cause to Government without the means of a political association."[8] Archbold at once assured Mohsin-ul-Mulk that he had no objection to assimilating an indirect reference in the "Formal Request" for the need of a political association on behalf of the Muslims.

Archbold offered even to proceed to Eastern Bengal in connection with the proposed deputation. But the Viceroy did not think it necessary for him to take such 'heroic measures'. Instead, he sent all papers and copies of letters from Archbold and Moshin-ul-Mulk, etc., to L. Hare, the Lieutenant-Governor of East Bengal, and sought his opinion on the proposed Muslim deputation. Hare sent a long reply. He advised the Central Government to tell the deputation that the Government had no intention whatsoever of neglecting or overlooking Muhammedan interests. But he posed a question: "Whether the Government of India can accept the Mohammedans who address them . . . as representative of the feeling and opinions of the Mohammedans generally," and proceeded to describe his experience that it was only the political agitators who were recognised as people's representatives and not the loyal supporters of the Government. Hindus, in that sense, made themselves heard through opinions expressed in political meetings, while the Muslims went unheard because of their non-political character.

Hare was critical of the Liberals at home who gave undue importance to Congress agitators. "If," he wrote, "the Home Government will not accept the assurance that these representative Mohammedans do truly represent Mohammedan opinion, so far as any opinion has been formed at all, then I think the Mohammedans will decide that they must organise meetings to voice Mohammedan opinion. They can do it . . . Mr. Morley may ask, do these Mohammedan representatives really represent Mohammedan opinion? I answer most certainly they do. The Hindu papers may talk of the three Tailors of Tooley Street, and no doubt in East Bengal Mohammedan leaders of position and distinction are few; but unless these leaders go counter to the Moulavies, which would only be in some religious or quasi-religious question, the Mohammedans will follow their leaders without question, and to a man almost. As a matter of fact, all political agitation must be engineered.[9]

After the composition and character of the Muslim deputation had been ascertained, and the contents of their memorial known, the Viceroy intimated the Secretary of State on 10 September, 1906 that he was going to receive the deputation on 1 October. So, at last, on the heights of Simla, a great historical event took place. On 1 October 1906, at 11 A.M., a thirty-five member Muslim Deputation, led by His Highness the Aga Khan, met the Viceroy in the Viceregal Palace, and presented their Address.

"May it please Your Excellency," read the Aga Khan, "Availing ourselves of the permission accorded to us, we the undersigned Nobles, Jagirdars, Taluqdars, Lawyers, Zamindars, Merchants and others, representing a large body of the Mahomedan subjects of His Majesty the King-Emperor in different parts of India, beg most respectfully to approach Your Excellency with the following address for your favourable consideration."[10]

The Address referred to the many benefits conferred by British rule on brimming millions belonging to various races and religions, to the peace, safety, personal freedom and liberty of worship that the people enjoyed, and to the wise and enlightened character of the Government. It drew the attention of the Viceroy about the fact that the Muhammedans of India, according to the census of 1901, totalled more than sixty-two million, that was, between one-fifth and one-fourth of the total population.

Minto's reply was the 'most sympathetic'. As he delivered his speech, the Deputation applauded him again and again with shouts of 'hear, hear'. He declared his complete agreement with the view that any electoral system in India must acknowledge the various religious beliefs of the people.

The Muslims were greatly ecstatic. 'They were all nervous as to the reception they would meet with and the answer they would get.' But His Excellency's cordial manner as well as his impressive assurances aroused in them hopes of a purposive future. Simultaneously, Muslim satisfaction brought to the Viceroy a greater degree of hope.

The Indian nationalist Press also challenged the views of the British-owned Press like the *London Times,* the *Pioneer* and the *Englishman* that the Simla Deputation was a thoroughly representative association of the Indian Muslims. To act against this view, the composition of the Deputation was described elaborately. It was pointed out how most of the Indian provinces were either meagrely or not at all represented, how some of the front-rank and respectable Muslims did not like to identify themselves with the Deputation, and how the new generation of English educated Muslims were out of it. The Indian Papers said that Minto was not fond of speeches, and since his arrival ten months earlier, had not made any lengthy speech as such. Uncommunicative and taciturn by nature, the Viceroy generally chose to keep his opinion about various political matters strictly to himself. But his 'Moslem Address' was an exception. It touched on definite subjects and the political motivation behind it was crystal clear.

Finally, the Indian Press expressed its grave concern over the Viceroy's attitude towards the much expected representative institutions in India. John Morley had aroused hopes in Congress circles that constitutional concessions would soon be made. But Minto's way of approach appeared against the political aspirations of nationalist Indians.

Simla Deputation

While a section of the Press projected the Simla Deputation as the product of an Anglo-Muhammedan conspiracy, other sections of the Press considered the episode as a normal affair. For example, *The Indian Mirror* commented: "We are in entire sympathy with the aims and aspirations of our brethren. Hindus and Mahommedans are, after all, children of the same soil. Their interests are the same, and their hopes and yearnings must be the same."[11]

The immediate outcome of the Simla meeting was the tremendous encouragement which the Muslim leaders derived from the highly-placed authority for their future course of action.

Organisational activities almost followed the Simla meeting among the Muslim leaders which, both in purpose and essence, went contrary to the Congress movement. Within days, however, the Bengali sentiment against the partition of Bengal got a big jolt as the Muslims of East Bengal when proceeded to celebrate the partition itself. Pro-partition meetings were organised at many places with thousands of Muslims taking part. While the Hindus regarded those as government-sponsored, the Government circles described them as genuine, 'just as genuine as the Hindu opinions'.

Though he was not its creator, yet the gradually emerging Muslim political force became a source of strength to John Morley. In Parliament, the pro-Congress Members strongly opposed the partition and consistently pressed for a change in partition arrangement.

Coming to the Muslim leaders in India, the Simla Deputation appeared to them as the stepping stone towards a more vigorous political venture. The Aga Khan, by virtue of his position and religious status, as well as by the power of his financial affluence, came to be accepted both by the British and the Muslims as the champion of the cause of the biggest religious minority in British empire. The Viceroy reposed his full faith in Aga which became a source of strength to the latter for looking forward.

The Viceroy could not have disowned his blessings to a pro-British permanent Muslim organisation to counteract the anti-partition and *Swadeshi* movements. A class conflict which assumed a socio-economic character was slowly making its headway when a religious tint loaded to it became loaded with political potentialities. The only thing necessary to make use of that potentiality was a political organisation.

Formation of Muslim League

So at last, at Dacca, the All-India Muslim League was formed on 30 December 1906. The Nawab Salimullah of Dacca played the host to the gathering. The Aga Khan's most 'trustworthy man', Nawab Mohsin-ul-Mulk was the Chief Organiser. Defence and not defiance of the Government was asserted as the motto of the new organisation. It acknowledged the fact that the Government sympathy lay with the Muhammedans and that the cause of the Muhammedans was the cause of the British. The root of the idea for such a religious organisation was traced to the encouraging consequences for the Indian Muslims which emanated from the Viceroy's kind reception to the Simla Deputation.

The resolution which brought the All-India Muslim League into existence ran as follows:

> That this meeting, composed of Mussalmans from all parts of India assembled at Dacca, decides that a Political Association, styled the All-India Moslem League, be formed for the furtherance of the following objects: (a) to promote among the Mussalmans of India feelings of loyalty to the British Government and to remove any misconceptions that may arise as to the intentions of the Government with regard to any of its measures; (b) to protect and advance the political rights and interests of Mussalmans of India and respectfully to represent their needs and aspirations to Government; (c) to prevent the rise among Mussalmans of India of any feelings of hostility towards other communities without prejudice to the other objects of the League.[12]

The League, since its inception possessed alarming portents against the Congress in particular and the national aspirations in general. The Viceroy gained power on both fronts, namely, in facing the Congress while it claimed for representative institutions, and in facing the home authorities who gave due importance to nationalist demands. He could equally diminish the zeal of the Secretary of State in his proclaimed role as a reformer.

The role which the Muslim League considered to play was first to agitate against the *Swadeshi* movement, the next to stir for their exclusive rights in future frame of constitutional changes. The Nawab of Dacca, with the League and the Government after him, accelerated himself to play a decisive role in East Bengal politics. Simultaneously, he organised his dedicated followers to oppose the Congress supported movements against the partition of Bengal. In view of his role, a grateful Hare, the Lieutenant-Governor of East Bengal, decided to save the Nawab from his economic quandary and financial bankruptcy in order to elevate his political status.

The Anglo-Muhammedan rapprochement and the birth of the Muslim League came at a serious juncture of modern Indian history. The National Congress was no longer confined within the limits of annual meeting places for expression of loyalty and for passing of formal resolutions. The followers and supporters of that organisation came to the streets to agitate and disobey, to burn the British goods and encourage rebellious attitude among the masses.

It was amid these complexities and intricacies—imperialism, nationalism, and communalism trying to outdo each other in cross purposes—that the famous Morley-Minto Reforms or the Act of 1909 shaped itself. This Reform therefore was certain to assume a character of its own, at once progressive and regressive, workable towards democratic objectives, but harmful for national unity.

The Congress was worried for representative institutions wherein elected members, or even non-official members, would discuss all administrative matters including finance. The Liberal Ministry, particularly the Secretary of State John Morley raised their hopes that something by way of a constitution was surely to come.

The influence of Gokhale on Morley was quite noticeable. To keep the Congress on lines of moderation, constitutional reforms were the only safe method. The Indian problems were submitted to the Liberals in a vivid manner and the Secretary of State wrote to the Viceroy in June 1906: "I wonder whether we could now make a good start in the way of reform in the popular direction. If we don't, is it not certain that the demands will widen and extend into 'National' regions, where I at least look with a very doubting and suspicious eye? Why should you not now consider as practical and immediate things, the extension of the Native element in your Legislative Council, instead of four or five skimpy hours; right of moving amendments. (Of course officials would remain a majority)."[13]

The Viceroy's mind understood what indeed the Congress or the progressive Indians wanted. Morley wanted to present some pretended form of representative Councils. Once the Viceroy took up the cause of the Muslims, the nature of the approaching reforms appeared to him as not too dangerous to the imperial interests. Constitutional proposals were made to safeguard the interests of the Muslim community.

In January 1909, some of the Muslim leaders appeared before Morley to oppose the appointment of a Hindu in the Viceroy's Council. The unhappy Secretary of State described them in the following manner: "Amir Ali, the head of them, is a vain creature, with a certain gift of length, and I believe that I could convert him from the Crescent to the Cross, if I would only make him a K.C.S.I. His troop, I am told, represented the Aligarh breed of Mussalman."[14] They came to express their resentment of the presence of a Hindu at the highest place of authority. Others demanded for a second Native Member, a Muslim by all means. The Secretary of State, however, did not commit himself to a promise of that sort.

When the talk on the Indian reforms, particularly about expansion of legislatures had taken some shape, Lord Curzon in the House of Lords subjected such considerations to three conditions. "The first is," he explained in June 1908, 'that they have not the appearance of being wrung from him (the Secretary of State) by fear. Let them be measures which, agitation or no agitation, he will be prepared to justify on the ground of their conformity with the best and permanent interests of India. The second condition is, I think, that British rule, which needs as much strengthening and support as we can give it, should not be weakened by them. To enlarge the Legislative Councils in India to a point at which the risk might be incurred of placing the British Government—which is the only possible Government in that country and to which no alternative is capable of being suggested—in a position where they might conceivably find themselves in a minority, would be an act of almost suicidal folly. It would not placate the enemies of the Government, it would eliminate the friends of the Government, and it would embarrass the Executive to a dangerous and fatal degree. The third condition is that the concessions should be preceded by a resolute vindication of the authority of the Government, by the stern repression of those vile incitements to outrage and disorder of which I have been speaking, and by the encouragement of all the loyal forces in India which are waiting for the signal to come forward so soon as they can feel confident that the Government are strong and will not be afraid."[15]

Such sentiments of the British statesmen at home were natural and relevant. But, something much deeper was being achieved in India by Lord Minto. Ever since he assured the Muslims at Simla that in any system of representation in which electoral organisations would be introduced, "the Muhammedan Community should be represented as a community," he made his determined efforts to twist the constitutional proposals to suit his commitment. The Muslims, in fact, wanted sufficient number of seats for them in legislative institutions or any other elective bodies. But Minto designed and perfected the idea of complete secession of Muslims from Hindus in electoral systems and representative institutions. When this theory showed its potency, the Muslim secured of it and considered it as their supreme constitutional safeguard.[16]

The National Congress, meeting at Madras on 28–30 December, 1908, congratulated the authorities on their Reform proposals. It passed a resolution stating that "this Congress desires to give expression to the deep and general satisfaction with which the Reform proposals formulated in Lord Morley's Despatch have been received throughout the country; it places on record its sense of high statesmanship which has dictated the action of the Government in the matter, and it tenders to Lord Morley and Lord Minto its most sincere and grateful thanks for their proposals."[17] Muhammed Ali Jinnah, a veteran nationalist then and an antagonist of Aligarh communalists, thanked the Government for the concession it wanted to sanction and called upon the Muslims to approve of the mixed electoral system.

"It is a well-known thing," asserted Jinnah at the Madras Congress, "that responsibility brings with it sobriety, and unless you throw a certain amount of responsibility upon an individual or a nation you are likely to allow that individual or nation to drift astray and I have no doubt that now that this responsibility is thrown on our shoulders we shall show to the world and to England that we are competent and capable of receiving these reforms and a great deal more in future. From the Muhammedan point of view, speaking for myself, I think and I feel that there are many other Muhammedans, who ought to join cordially with our Hindu brothers."[18] Unfortunately for the Congress and Muhammed Ali Jinnah, the day after the Madras Congress came to an end, Lord Minto went on to destroy the concept of a joint or mixed electorate.

Morley-Minto Reforms

In the opinion of the Muslim League Lord Minto was their 'struggle for self-preservation and self-defence against an aggressive majority'. The delegation of the League headed by Amir Ali was on its way to England. A disturbed Secretary of State wrote to the Viceroy: "I have agreed to receive the sons of the Crescent . . . . I wish the Prophet himself were coming!! There are not many historic figures whom I should be better pleased to summon up from Paradise, or wherever he now abides. Your language to the Islamites about their 'just claim to something more than numerical strength' was perhaps a trifle less guarded than it might have been, if you will allow me to say so."[19]

The Muslim Deputation met Morley on 27 January 1909. The result was a foregone conclusion. Compelled by His Majesty the King, the Conservatives, the Viceroy and the Indian bureaucracy, and the Muslim League, the Secretary of State yielded ground and consented to give up proposal for mixed electoral college. The sole substitute was the acceptance of the idea of Separate or Communal Electorate, or as it was termed, exclusive Muhammedan Electoral College.

Time was nearing for the Secretary of State to conduct the Second Reading of the Indian Councils Bill in Parliament. The Congress was late in realising the secret arrangements that were continuing between the authorities and the Muslim League, and its leaders had little time to initiate a counter move.

Morley's Muslim policy was, on the whole, welcomed by the Liberals and Conservatives alike with satisfaction. But on other matters, such as, expansion of legislative councils, privilege of questions, etc., the Conservative leaders flayed the Government from every understandable ground of fear. On the concluding day of the discussion Lord Ripon criticised those who were 'filled with a dread of these reforms' by saying: "The late Sir Robert Peel, after the passing of the Reform Bill, once in the House of Commons alluded to the difficulty of carrying on government under an ancient monarchy, a proud aristocracy, and a reformed House of Commons. I venture to say that the difficulty of carrying on Government in India in face of the democratic movement today is at least as great, and that the dangers connected with it are at least as serious; and it is because I believe that my noble friend (Morley) has done something to meet these difficulties and to avert those dangers that I give to this Bill my heartiest support."[20] The Bill was passed in the Lords and was then sent to the Commons.

Surprisingly enough, the reaction in the Indian nationalist quarters was not as severe as could have been expected. Voices were heard that the separate electorate would 'divide the people and destroy hope of Indian nationality as a political unit'. But the general mood was one of caution and moderation in anticipation of the entire deal of reforms. Moreover, the bureaucracy pointed it out that if Hindus would defy concessions granted to Muslims, the latter would oppose to the appointment of a Hindu to the Executive Council of the Viceroy. The Congress moderates, in fact, were at the peak of their moderation on the eve of the Reforms.

On 1 April 1909, the Indian Councils Bill was moved in the House of Commons by the Under Secretary of State for India, Mr. Buchanan. The House was needed only to reemphasise the need for Separate Electorate with more demanding reasons to show how Hindus and Muslims differed from each other. "If you start from our democratic theories of representative Government," said the Under Secretary of State, 'of course, all such special representation is an anomaly, but we have to deal with the practical problem which is before us—the best practical solution which is available. And more than that, particularly with regard to the Mahommedans, they have a special and overwhelming claim upon us, namely, the solemn promises, given by those who are entitled with full responsibility to speak for us."[21]

Till that time, it was claimed, British administration maintained a great tradition, the tradition of equality by treating all races, all religions, and all creeds, considering them as equal. The partition of Bengal shattered that principle by favouring the Muslims of Eastern Bengal. The Separate Electorate was the next vigorous step to suspend that principle by favouring Muslims in general and rousing thereby 'the fanaticism of the Hindu and of India'.

The Leader of the Opposition, A.J. Balfour, condemned the opinion of the English radicals and strongly pleaded to establish the value of Separate Electorate. To him: "The religious distinctions of India are very different to those with which we are familiar in the country. There they cut far deeper than here into the social fabric, and divide far more fundamentally man from man, family from family, and even village from village."[22]

Challenging Balfour's theory that Hindus and Muslims are world apart from each other, Henry Cotton argued: "I have lived among them more than 30 years, and in portions of Bengal where I served you cannot tell the difference between a Hindu and a Mahommedan by his language, his conversation, or his manner of life. Even the very names are identical in many cases, and their interests, it goes without saying, are identical also, and to assume that people of this class require separate representation and separate organisation of electorate is to presume upon fundamental ignorance of the actual facts of the case. All this Mahommedan agitation of which we have heard so much in England is really not a representative agitation at all . . . Even His Highness the Agha Khan is the last man in the world to claim to be a representative Indian Mahommedan. His followers exist for the most part in East Africa, and he himself is a Persian, whose grandfather migrated from Persia to Bombay. There is a growing feeling in India among the Mahommedans, a feeling which is growing everyday, that it is the real interest of the Mahommedans to identify themselves with the Hindus as one people."[23]

After the tedious debates, a humiliated Morley wrote to the Viceroy whose cause had then been the cause of the entire Parliament: "Irreconcilable inconsistencies between what you said, and what I said, once upon a time and what we say today—all this was very easy to demonstrate . . . I am sure that I console myself by remembering that it was you who set the troublesome ball rolling in a famous speech which I have heard so often quoted in debate—but I know every word of it by heart, and so with less than my usual compunction, I can only ask you to make what you can of the Sphinx's riddle."[24]

When the Separate Electorate became a settled fact, Minto emerged from the acid test of politics as the saviour of the Indian Mussalmans. "The hearts of the Mahommedans of India were filled with deep gratitude to the Government, and they saw that, in the new Councils, not only would their interests be safeguarded owing to the presence on them of a sufficient number of their own real representatives, but that the state of things thus created would secure the stability of the British Government, which they look upon as their very own, and would prevent the Hindu dream of *Swaraj* from being realised," wrote Muhammed Shafi.[25]

With Reforms finally announced, and elections to the reformed Councils round the corner, many among the ruling circles became aware of the Government's undue favour to the Muslims. Some of them were happy for it, but some others became apprehensive, too. The author of the safeguards, however, himself became fearful of his own doings. "I am afraid," wrote Minto, "when the position is clearer we may fairly be accused of having neglected the even-handed justice to which we owe so much in India . . . I should say that, if the Government of India was biased in any direction, it was towards Mahommedan interest."[26]

The Indian National Congress took the whole episode of the Anglo-Muslim politics rather in a impassive mood. When the Congress met at Lahore in 1909 in its twenty-fourth session, Madan Mohan Malaviya, its President, said: "I have faith in the future of my country. I have no doubt that the policy of the preferential treatment of one community over another and all other obstacles which keep the great communities of India from acting together, will shortly be steadily disappear."[27] This was a mild comment. To Surendra Nath Bannerjea: "It is no exaggeration to say that the Rules and Regulations have practically wrecked the Reform scheme as originally conceived with a beneficence of purpose and a statesmanlike grasp that did not honour to all that are associated with it . . . Who wrecked the scheme? Who converted that promising experiment into a dismal failure? The responsibility rests upon the shoulders of the bureaucracy."[28] It took more than a year for the Congress to realise the evil effects of the Separate Communal Electorate, but when the harm was realised, it was too late to change the course of constitutional history.

The Morley-Minto era thus ended with a new twist in Indian political scene. Within the next few years the First World War and its aftermath although brought about a brief spell of Hindu-Muslim harmony, but in the long run it was their political separatism which sealed the fate of a united India.

References

1. SD, 183-84, see Muslim Address to Lord Lytton, 8 January, 1877.
2. The letter of Amir Ali was dated 12 December, 1886.
3. DC, Mss. Eur. F 130/11 A, Reply of Earl Dufferin to Addresses, 23 March, 1888.
4. BML, 8023 aa 45, Sixth Congress, Address of Pherozeshah Mehta, 1890.
5. Sir John Strachey, *India,* London, 1888, 225.
6. P. Mukherji, *All about Partition,* Curzon's Speech at Dacca, 18 February, 1904.
7. MRP, Minto to Morley, Vol. III, 15 August, 1906.
8. MTP, Correspondence, Vol. II, No. 50, see Archbold to Dunlop Smith, 20 August, 1906.
9. MRP, Minto to Morley, Vol. III, Enclosures, Hare to Dunlop Smith, 1 September, 1906.
10. MRP, Minto to Morley, Vol. III, The Muslim Deputation and Address, 1 October, 1906.
11. *The Indian Mirror,* 4 October, 1906.
12. Muslim Resolution at Dacca, see *Pioneer,* 2 January, 1907.
13. MRP, Morley to Minto, Vol. I, 15 June, 1906.

14. MRP, Morley to Minto, Vol. IV, 28 January, 1909.
15. PP, Lords, Lord Curzon, 30 June, 1908.
16. Soon after the Simla Deputation, Mohsin-ul-Mulk wrote to the Viceroy: "Both on the Supreme and Provincial Councils an adequate number of seats should be reserved exclusively for the Muhammedans. The present system of election applicable to the general body of the people need not be interfered with and it should remain open as hitherto, to all communities." (See Minto Papers, Correspondence, Vol. II, no. 108, Letter from Mohsin-ul-Mulk, 7 October, 1906.) The Viceroy's opinion was that "The only representation for which India is at present fitted is a representation of communities as I said in my reply to the Muhammedan Deputation." (See Morley Papers, Minto to Morley, Vol. V, 23 January, 1907).
17. INC, Resolution II, 1908.
18. CC, Speech of M.A. Jinnah, Madras Congress, December, 1908.
19. MRP, Morley to Minto, Vol. IV, 21 January, 1909.
20. PP, Lords, Lord Ripon, 11 March, 1909.
21. PP, Commons, Discussions on Indian Councils Bill, 1 April, 1909.
22. PP, Commons, A.J. Balfour, 1 April, 1909.
23. PP, Commons, Henry Cotton, 1 April, 1909.
24. MRP, Morley to Minto, Vol. IV, 28 April, 1909.
25. MTP, L&T, 1909, Vol. I, no. 157, Muhammad Shafi to Dunlop Smith, 30 April, 1909.
26. *The Times,* 16 November, 1909.
27. CC, Madan Mohan Malaviya's speech at Lahore Congress, December, 1909.
28. *Ibid,* Speech of Surendra Nath Bannerjea, December, 1909.

5

Reaction Against Rowlatt Act

When the First World War ceased, the people were eyeing for the repeal of the Defence of India Act. They had developed an abhorence for this Act, because contrary to the government's declaration, it was used by Michael O'Dwyer to punish people of the Punjab and suppress their political aspirations.

The Rowlatt Bills came as a surprise as they were issued upon an indignant, angry and frustrated people. These Bills took their popular name from the president of the Sedition Committee. This Committee was appointed by the Government of India on 10 December 1917 with Mr. Justice Rowlatt as president to report on what were termed as 'criminal conspiracies connected with revolutionary movements in India', and suggestion about legislation to deal with them. The committee was required to sit in camera. Its report was presented on 15 April 1918.

After a thorough survey of the existing political situation, the committee recommended special legislation which sought to curtail the liberty and legal rights of the people in a very drastic manner. Consequently, two Bills were prepared on the basis of these recommendations. The one that actually passed into law, was the Anarchical and Revolutionary Crimes Act, 1919. It made provision for quick trial of offences by a Special Court, consisting of three High Court judges. The public were unaware of the nature of the evidence given before the committee or even the names of those who gave it. In spite of the passionate protest, the Bill was rushed through, and during each crucial stages of the voting, no Indian member of the Legislative Council voted in its favour barring one member of the Executive Council and he, too, was to resign soon afterwards having witnessed the consequences in Punjab. The Bill was eventually passed on 18 March 1918, and three important members of the Imperial Legislative Council, M.M. Malaviya, M.A. Jinnah and Mazarul Haque resigned.

Jinnah, the chairman of the Muslim League, cautioned the government in his Assembly speech, "I do not wish to state it by way of threat or intimidation to government, but I wish to state it because it is my duty to tell you that, if these measures are passed, you will create in the country from one end to the other a discontent and agitation, the like of which you have not witnessed, and it will have, believe me, a most disastrous effect on the good relations that have existed between the Government and people."[1] In his letter of resignation to the Viceroy, he wrote: "The Government of India and your Excellency have thought it fit to place on the Statute Book a measure admittedly obnoxious and decidedly coercive at a time of peace and thereby substituted the Executive for the Judicial. Besides, by passing this Bill Your Excellency's government have actively negatived every argument they advanced but a year ago, when they appealed to India for help at the War Conference and ruthlessly trampled upon the principles for which Great Britain avowedly fought the war. The fundamental principles of justice have been uprooted and the constitutional rights of the people have been violated at a time when there is no real danger to the state... In my opinion a Government that passes or sanctions such a law in times of peace forfeits its claim to be called a civilised Government."[2]

Several Indian newspapers levelled serious criticism against this Bill. The *Bombay Chronicle* called it as 'repression in excelsis'.[3] The *Hindu* wrote, ". . . The Indian public would read the proposed provisions with shame, indignation and disgust."[4] The *Amrita Bazar Patrika* termed it a "gigantic blunder which would arose the worst passions of a peaceful law-abiding people".[5] The *Panjabee* regarded it as "a bare-faced attempt on the part of a bureaucracy which has been demoralised by the exercise of unrestrained power to interfere with liberty."[6] The *New India* described it as 'monstrous'."[7]

On 8 February 1919, Gandhi informed Madan Mohan Malaviya of his reaction regarding the Rowlatt Bills. 'The Viceroy's speech is disappointing. Under the circumstances I, at any rate, hope that all the Indian members will leave the Select Committee or, if necessary, even the Council, and launch a countrywide agitation. You and other members have said that if the Rowlatt Bills are passed a massive agitation would be launched the like of which has not been seen in India . . . . I have not yet fully decided but I feel that when the Government bring in an obnoxious law the people will be entitled to defy their other laws as well. If we do not show the strength of the people, even the reforms we are to get will be useless. In my opinion you should all make it clear to the Government that so long as the Rowlatt Bills are there you will pay no taxes and will advise the people also not to pay them. I know that to give such advice is to assume a great responsibility. But unless we do something really big they will not feel any respect for us. And we cannot hope to get anything from people who do not respect us.[8]

The next day, Gandhi communicated to V.S. Srinivasa Sastri that he could no longer keep eyes on the progress of the Rowlatt Bills as they were the aggravated symptoms of the deep-rooted disease. He considered the Bills as an open challenge to us and if "we succumb we are done for." Gandhi felt assured that the resignations of Indian members would rattle the British government's confidence in its ability to disregard public sentiment and thus would be an education of immense value to the people of India.'[9]

J.B. Kripalani reacted thus :

> It was during these days that the World War ended. The allies were victorious. However, there was no evidence of any change in Britain's attitude towards India. In fact, it looked as though with the end of their pre-occupation with the war, they had decided to turn their attention to the danger of an awakened India. The Defence of India Act was still on the statute book. Even then the Rowlatt Committee was appointed to enquire into the nature of Indian unrest and suggest measures to meet its threat to the Empire.[10]

But events were moving fast. Harrowing reports of the wanton violence that the Government was using on peaceful demonstrators were pouring in from all parts of the country, more especially from the Punjab. The repression evoked further demonstrations. In some places, these took a violent turn. Some British and Indian officers were killed. There were reports of rioting in Ahmedabad and other parts of Gujarat and in the Punjab. Gandhiji rushed to Ahmedabad. When he learned that his followers, who had pledged themselves to non-violence, had yielded to the provocation given by the authorities, he was greatly distressed. *Satyagraha* required strict adherence to non-violence even under the severest provocation. Gandhiji felt that people had not grasped the full meaning of his message. They were not yet ready to use the new weapon of non-violence. He, therefore, called off the movement and admitted that he had made 'a Himalayan miscalculation' in as much as he had overrated the patience of the people and their capacity for disciplined action.[11]

In spite, however, of the serious protest, the motion that the Bill be referred to a Select Committee, was carried, and the amendment, that its consideration be adjourned till six months after the term of office of the Legislative Council, was defeated on 6 February 1919; 22 voted in favour of the amendment and 35 against it.

Jawaharlal Nehru opined thus: "It was proposed in the initial stages that this Act, when passed, was to be a permanent measure, but an amendment was accepted in the select committee limiting its continuance to three years from the termination of the war . . . . the British Government, in the teeth of unanimous public opinion, pushed through a law which they themselves never used afterwards, and thus invited an upheaval. One might almost think that the object of the measure was to bring trouble".[12]

The response to Gandhi's call for *satyagraha* was spontaneous and incredible. His message for the people of India reached everywhere even though the Congress organisation had not become so strong and widespread. On 24 February 1919, a *Satyagraha Pledge*[13] signed by Gandhi, Vallabhbhai Patel, Chandulal Manilal Desai, Anasuyabai Sarabhai and others was issued as a mark of protest against the Bills.

On the same day, Gandhi sent a telegram to the Private Secretary to the Viceroy in which he asserted his sentiments about the Rowlatt Bills. "Ever since publication Rowlatt Bills have been considering my position regarding them. Have been conferring with friends. In my opinion bad in themselves Bills are but symptom of deep-seated disease among the ruling class, coming as they do on eve reforms Bills augur ill for their success. Those who have been associated with me in public work and other friends met today and after the greatest deliberation have decided to offer *satyagraha* and commit civil disobedience of such laws as committee to be formed from ourselves may decide. After Sir George Lowndes' speech it is necessary to demonstrate to government that even a Government the most autocratic finally owes its power to the will of the governed. Without recognition of this principle and consequently withdrawal of Bills many of us consider reforms valueless. I wish to make an humble but strong appeal to His Excellency to reconsider

Government's decision to proceed with Bills, and reluctantly add that in event of unfavourable reply the pledge must be published and the signatures must invite additions. I am aware of seriousness of the proposed step. It is, however, much better that people say openly what they think in their hearts and without fear of consequences enforce the dictates of their own conscience. May I expect early reply?'[14]

On 26 February, the Congress leadership issued instructions to the *satyagraha* volunteers to be followed by them while seeking support of the people for the national cause. Volunteers were told to read and explain the *Satyagraha Pledge* to every intending signatory before taking his signature to the vow for the national cause. The pledge was in three parts. The first part laid down the aims and objects of the pledge. It declared that the signatories considered the Rowlatt Bills were unjust, inflammatory to the principle of liberty and justice, and destructive of the elementary rights of individuals. In order to be able to make this statement one must fully perceive the Rowlatt Bills, hence it was up to the volunteers to explain the Bills clearly to the intending signatory.[15]

Volunteers were to accept the signatures of the persons under eighteen and also students. And even in the case of those over eighteen, he must make sure that the signatory had decided after careful consideration. But volunteers must not impel others to sign, upon whose earnings their families were solely dependent for their maintenance.[16]

On 11 March, Gandhi again reminded the Viceroy of the serious consequences the passage of Rowlatt Bills would lead to in the country. In a telegram to him, Gandhi explained, "Even at this eleventh hour I respectfully ask His Excellency and his Government to pause and consider before passing Rowlatt Bills. Whether justified or not, there is no mistaking the strength of public opinion on the measures. I am sure Government do not intend intensifying existing bitterness. Government will risk nothing by delay, but by expressly bowing to public opinion will smooth down feeling and enhance real prestige. I am proceeding to Bombay tomorrow by Jubbulpore Mail."[17]

The passing of the Act through the Legislative Council met with staunch criticism from vernacular presses of Delhi and there had been meetings in Delhi condemning the Act. On 30th March, rioting which was the outcome of the *hartal* and so-called passive resistance, took place. The crowds in the city were disorderly—mainly in Chandni Chowk and Hauz Kazi and people were being prevented from riding in *tongas* by the mob.

The outcome was that crowd became more and more berserk and excited, and went on to attack the forces present with sticks and stones. Mr. Currie ordered fire being opened, both police and troops firing a few rounds. As soon as the crowd began to pull back, the order to ceasefire was issued. Two rioters were killed inside the Queen's Gardens, and many more were wounded.[18]

Initially, 30th March, 1919 was fixed as a day of national protest, but the date was changed to 6th April. It was a simple, yet unique programme of mass agitation—24 hour fast as an essential discipline, the stopping of all work, the closing of all markets and business places and holding of public meetings.[19]

On 7 April, 1919, Gandhi launched a daily entitled *Satyagrahi* despite the Indian Press Act. The paper had not been registered in accordance with the law. Gandhi explained to the subscribers 'So there can be no annual subscription. Nor can it be guaranteed that the paper will be published without interruption. The editor (M.K. Gandhi) is liable at any moment to be arrested by the Government and it is impossible to ensure continuity of publication until India is in the happy position of supplying editors enough to take the place of those arrested. We shall leave no stone unturned to secure a ceaseless succession of editors. It is not our intention to break for all time the law governing publication of newspapers. This paper will, therefore, exist so long only as the Rowlatt legislation is not withdrawn.[20]

In fact, *Satyagrahi* had emerged for the sake of ensuring withdrawal of the Rowlatt legislation. Its sole motive, therefore, was to let the people know the ways and means of bringing about such withdrawal in accordance with the principles of *Satyagraha Pledge* directed the signatories to court imprisonment by offering civil disobedience by committing a civil breach of certain laws. This publication can, therefore, show the best remedy which was by committing civil disobedience in the very act of publishing this journal. Thus, the method of *Satyagraha* was unique. A final guideline was issued by the *Satyagraha Sabha* to the *Satyagraha* volunteers on 7 April 1919 along with a list of prohibited literature. This prohibited literature was as follows.[21]

1. *Hind Swaraj* by M.K. Gandhi
2. *Sarvodaya or Universal Dawn* by M.K. Gandhi
3. *The Story of a Satyagrahi* by M.K. Gandhi
4. *The life and Address of Mustafa Kamal Pasha*

In selecting this list, the *Satyagraha Sabha* had a few relevant considerations in view. The *Satyagrahis* were advised to receive copies of banned literature for distribution amongst the people from the secretaries of the *Satyagraha Sabha.* A innovative feature of such a distribution was that it was to be done not in a secret way. *Satyagrahis* were, therefore, required to write their names and addresses as sellers, so that they might be traced without any difficulty.

Another unique feature of the *satyagraha* was that it was to be as independent of financial support as far as possible.[22] Moreover, when the copies of the banned literature were seized by the government, *satyagrahis* were required to make more copies themselves or by securing the assistance of 'willing friends' and to make use of it until it was again confiscated by giving readings to the people from it.[23] When all the copies would finish by dissemination or confiscation, *satyagrahis* might continue civil disobedience by writing out and distributing extracts from accessible books.[24]

Undoubtedly, the *satyagraha* was organised, guided and planned by Gandhi at higher level, but it was impressively supported by the local leaders with the local support. At times, the sentiments of the mobs crossed the non-violent limits and resorted to assault, arson, looting and killing. As a result, the government machinery acted swiftly but callously and thus numerous shootings followed at places, the worst and the most pathetic being in Jallianwala Bagh at a non-violent and unarmed assembly of people.

Jallianwala Bagh Carnage

In the Punjab, Amritsar was second in importance to Lahore. In some respects, it was more important even than the former. Being the prominent commercial centre in the Punjab, it attracted travellers and visitors from various corners of the province and even from outside. Besides, it was one of the important centres of the Congress organisation in the province.

The Jallianwala Bagh, where the gruesome tragedy took place on 13 April 1919, is situated almost in the heart of the city. The word *Bagh* is rather a misnomer. 'Jalle' is the caste name of original owner, 'wala' is the genitive termination; and the *Bagh* means a garden, is, in fact, an open area of waste land surrounded by houses.

The Punjab government reported about political condition in Amritsar thus: 'Orders having been received for the arrest and deportation of Dr. Kitchlew and Satyapal, the Deputy Commissioner sent for them on the morning of April 10th to his house from where they left in motors for Dharmsala at about 10–30 A.M. with an escort, in charge of Mr. Rehill, Superintendent of Police. By about 11 A.M. the news of the arrests became known in the city, and ardent followers of the deportees went round urging the people to close their shops and assemble in the Aitchison Park, with the intention of proceeding to the Deputy Commissioner's House and demanding their release.

As it was expected that the arrests of Drs. Kitchlew and Satyapal would cause a certain amount of excitement, it had been previously arranged that the Officer Commanding the Station would have a force of British infantry and some mounted men from the ammunition column in the Rambagh with which he was to hold the railway foot-bridge, the railway over-bridge and the hospital level-crossing while the Police Lines level crossing was to be held by the police. There was also an armed police reserve of 75 men at the City Kotwali.

It was Sunday and the day of Baisakhi. In the Punjab, the harvest festival of Baisakhi is celebrated with much pomp as the day which marks the end of the period of long and arduous labour. For the Sikhs it is the day on which the Khalsa came into being.

General Dyer marched through the city with the civil officials and got the following official order announced at many places. "It is hereby proclaimed to all whom it may concern that no person residing in the city is permitted or allowed to leave the city in his own private or hired conveyance or on foot without a pass from one of the following officers . . . . No person residing in Amritsar city is permitted to leave his house after 8.00 P.M. Any person found in the streets after 8.00 P.M. is liable to be shot. No procession of any kind is permitted to parade the streets in the city or any part of the city or outside of it at any time. Any such processions or any gathering of four men will be looked upon and treated as an unlawful assembly and dispersed by force of arms if necessary."

According to the available source, prior to General Dyer's arrival, the audience estimated at 20,000. Hans Raj and a few others were standing on platform. An aeroplane was hovering over the meeting before the arrival of the troops. Hans Raj assured the audience not to be afraid. A few minutes before the sunset, Dyer with the company of young officers, Briggs and Anderson, fifty riflemen, forty

Gurkhas marched towards the Jallianwala Bagh intending to teach the severest lesson of life to the assembly of the people. The organisers of this meeting showed deep concern about the earlier happenings in the city when a few persons were killed as a result of promulgation of the Rowlatt Act.

Dyer had a minute glimpse of the assembly before ordering his sepoys to adopt kneeling position, a usual posture for a soldier to fire. The firing order was given and the numerous volley of shots began to pierce into the bodies of the people assembled there. It continued for nearly ten minutes till the ammunition was exhausted. Apalled by the incident, the panicked crowd ran pell mell in all directions. In a moment, men were falling dead and wounded on the ground.

There had been no agreement on the exact figures of those killed in this ghastly tragedy. Dyer estimated between 200 and 300 while official figures were 379 killed and over 1200 wounded. It is however probable that when 1650 rounds were fired, the loss of lives must have been nearly a few hundreds and a much bigger number must have been wounded.

This gruesome tragedy inflicted on a few hundred persons was indeed an unparalleled phenomenon in the history of India. This was carried out by a senior army official who gave little thought to his inhuman action which he undertook to satisfy his personal whims and fancies. There had been firing on meetings, processions and mobs on earlier occasions by the British bureaucracy in India, but this kind of mass massacre was never heard of. The justification for firing explained by General Dyer does not satisfy an impartial observer of the events at Amritsar.

It is unfortunate to learn Dyer saying that the assembly of people in the Jallianwala Bagh consisted of defiant characters and of criminal revolutionaries who were bent upon damaging human life and property. From all evidence available it was a non-violent assembly of the citizens of Amritsar and innocent people from the *mofussil*. To expect any kind of violent behaviour from them after the dispersal of such a meeting was only a mistaken notion in Dyer's mind.

The Government of India passed the following order on 13th April 1919. "Whereas the Governor-General-in-Council is satisfied that a state of open rebellion against the authority of the Government exists in the districts of Lahore and Amritsar in the Province of the Punjab.

Now, therefore, in exercise of the powers conferred by section 2 of the Bengal State Offences Regulation, 1804, the Governor-General-in-Council is hereby pleased to suspend the functions of the ordinary Criminal Courts within those Districts in so far as the trial of persons of the classes referred to in the said Regulation taken in arms in open hostility to the British Government or in the act of opposing by force of arms the authority of the same, or in the actual commission of any overt act of rebellion against the State or in the act of openly aiding and abetting the enemies of the British Government within the said Districts, is concerned, and to establish Martial Law within the said Districts.

The Governor-General-in-Council is also pleased to direct the immediate trial by courts-martial of all persons owing allegiance to the British Government, either in consequence of their having born, or of their residents within its territories and under its protection, who shall be taken in arms in open hostility to the British

Government, or in the act of opposing by force of arms the authority of the same or in the actual commission or any overt act of rebellion against the State, or in the act of openly aiding and abetting the enemies of the British Government within any part of the said Districts.' Similar orders were issued by the Government of India in connection with Gujranwala, Lyallpur and other areas in the Punjab.[25]

Girdhari Lal, a prominent local Congressman, happened to watch the scene from a house overlooking the *Bagh.* He saw hundreds of persons killed on the spot. The worst part of the whole thing was that firing was directed towards the gates through which the people were turning out. There were small outlets, four or five in all, and bullets actually rained over the people at all these gates. Many persons got trampled under the feet of rushing crowds and thus lost their lives. Besides, blood was pouring in profusion. Even those who lay flat on the ground were shot. There were heaps of dead bodies scattered in different directions. The dead bodies were of grown up people and young boys also. Some of them had their heads cut open, others had eyes shot, and nose, chest, arms or legs shattered. "I think there must have been over 1,000 dead bodies in the garden then . . . I saw people were hurrying up and many had to leave them dead and wounded, because they were afraid of being fired upon again after 8 P.M."

A proclamation was made in Amritsar and its surrounding villages inviting persons who had any information regarding the names of those who had met with deaths. Instructions were issued to the local authorities there to encourage local people to come forward with information. "Every possible step was taken in that direction. The result of the enquiry was that the total number of casualties amounted to 291, and any further number suggested by anybody must be taken with great discretion".[26]

The promulgation of martial law in various districts of the Punjab was disliked and criticised by the national leadership. By Article 2 of the Bengal Regulation 10 of 1804 the Governor-General-in-Council was given the power to direct any public authority or officer to order the suspension, wholly or partially, of the functions of ordinary criminal courts of judicature.

The powers of area officers as regards punishment were under the proclamations, limited to sentencing an offender to two years' rigorous imprisonment or fine not exceeding Rs. 1,000 or both, and to whipping in addition to or in lieu of any other punishment.[27]

In the first half of April, 1919, the government of Punjab reported, "The *Satyagraha* agitation and the Delhi riots have latterly monopolised attention. Violence and misrepresentation had reached such a pitch that Government has been constrained to take stringent action . . . . The extraordinary virulence and intemperate attacks on Government which have characterised almost the whole Indian Press for some time past are, as is becoming increasingly apparent, largely responsible for the present state of the country."[28]

On 19 April 1919, General Beynon issued a martial law proclamation containing certain regulations that were to be enforced within the limits of the 16th Indian Division in all places to which martial law had been or might be extended. This document defined as martial law offences the act of being in arms against the State or inciting others to be in arms; assisting or harbouring rebels; failure to report gatherings of rebels. Use of language or issuing proclamations likely to foment rebellion or promote hostility between different classes of His Majesty's subjects; interference with railways, canals or telegraphs; possession of a motor vehicle without permit; departure from or entry to a proclaimed area save under conditions to be prescribed; convening or attending a meeting of more than five persons, etc.

While the proclamation of martial law was made at Gujranwala, the General Officer Commanding, 2nd Rawalpindi Division, issued a proclamation on 20 April almost in the same tune to that issued by General Beynon.[29] The administration of martial law was managed by the General Officer Commanding, Sialkot Brigade who shifted his headquarters to Wazirabad. Besides the Deputy Commissioner of Gujranwala was announced as area officer for Gujranwala; an officer of Major's rank as area officer for Wazirabad, the Joint Deputy Commissioner for the Sheikhupura area as well as an officer of Captain's rank for Hafizabad. Gujrat and Lyallpur both came under the general Rawalpindi proclamation. Besides on 24 May, 1919, orders were issued by the Punjab government directing the precensorship of the same newspapers, viz., *Congress, Vijaya, Qaum* and *Inqilab*.[30]

The Aftermath of the Massacre

The government officials tried ways and methods of extortion which indeed left much discontent amongst the people. The Punjab was greatly hurt and was simmering with dissatisfaction, anger and discontent. The unmitigated force and unethical methods used, naturally, when became unbearable, came in for staunch criticism by one and all, and the Congress leadership did not hesitate to take steps in a non-violent way, such steps which should be an eye-opener for the British administration in the province.

Many of the orders passed during the period of martial law invariably caused general inconvenience to extreme proportions. Some of these were the promulgation of curfew order, restriction on railway travelling and prohibition against people assembling in greater numbers than ten.

The martial law regime had crossed all 'limits of decency' and the honour of any person in the province was perilous. Besides numerous rules and regulations were applied haphazardly and innocent persons had to bear the brunt of the hasty and illegal actions of the martial law administration. No profession was safe.

Michael O'Dwyer, General Dyer, Colonel Johnson and other British officials, 'exhibited no sense of shame or remorse' in relating their 'misdeeds' in the form of brutal atrocities meted out on innocent people of the Punjab and instead gave bold and fearless statements before the commission of enquiry. But it clearly appeared that all the British officials were in connivance with one another. Affliction was thus thrust upon a major portion of the population of the Punjab who were cowed down to the utmost.

The pledge of Gandhi for the inauguration of *satyagraha* received wide acceptance. It also proved instrumental for fraternisation of Hindus and Muslims, the Hindu leaders being asked to address the people even in mosques. Here was a unique and innovative method of political action by a leader of the largest political party in India who had charisma amongst the masses of the country. Undoubtedly, Gandhi's call for *satyagraha* was carbonated with all seriousness by the machinery of the government. It was in the Punjab, however, that this movement endured vehement opposition from the government and a crisis of immense magnitude was in evidence.

Judged by the appalling and gruesome happenings of April and May in various parts of the Punjab, we get a clear inkling from the contemporary rumour that it was definitely General Dyer's intention to raze Amritsar to the ground as a fitting punishment for the horrors of the 10th April committed by the local populace.

The political prisoners fell into two classes—the educated and the uneducated. The educated persons, to a great extent, enjoyed the privilege of separate cells; for the most part, they were persons who could afford to pay for special diet, a privilege which is provided to undertrial prisoners under the rules. They were not allowed to have cooked food brought from outside, but they could obtain fresh fruit, biscuits and books from outside and also had their own bedding. A few had their own camp beds and hospital beds were also given to some of them.

It is indeed curious to note about the candid statement which Dyer gave before the Hunter Committee. He not only admitted all the gruesome facts connected with the episode of 13th April, but he defended his achievements and sought to justify them in the best possible way. To him it was a 'merciful act' to fire without warning an unobtrusive crowd because it might have ridiculed him if he had refrained from doing so.

The findings of the Hunter Committee reveal the fact that there was hardly any justification for the launching of martial law with a view to have full command over the existing situation which had not worsened as it was thought to be. The Committee admitted, "The wisdom of continuing Martial Law for the whole length of time it remained effective in the Punjab is more open to the objection than the original declaration".

Dyer indeed gave an unconvincing plea before the Disorders Inquiry Committee that the crowd in the Jallianwala Bagh were in such large numbers that "if a determined rush had been made at any time, arms or no arms, my small force must instantly have been overpowered and consequently I was very careful of not giving the mob a chance of organising."

He also admitted that he had no idea of the exact geography of the *Bagh* and he was also unaware of the exits of its campus, "While standing on the raised platform, he could see the whole *Bagh* and . . . if the object was that the crowd should disperse then there was no justification for firing towards any other exit."

It may be possible to establish Dyer's motive in connection with the kind of action he had executed on 13th April. When he took charge of the whole situation, he was empowered with full authority to establish law and order. Even Miles Irving and Kitchin were not clear to what extent they had abdicated their authority and responsibility. But under the army control, the civil authorities including the police played a subordinate role even during the days when martial law was clamped in Amritsar. Under these circumstances, Dyer lost his contact with the civil authorities and did not bother to take their help, advice and support of any kind at the most crucial time. The stern action taken independently by a single individual was the result of the feeling of wielding unlimited power. Had he cared to consult the local officials, the disaster perpetrated by the firing on peaceful, non-violent and unarmed assembly would have been averted.

During the next year when the clouds of the first Non-Cooperation made its mark on the political horizon of India, Gandhi had decided to part with the Kaiser-i-Hind gold medal and the Zulu War medals conferred on him by the British government for his meritorious services. In a letter to the Viceroy written on 2 August, 1920, he appeared much critical of the British policy in India, particularly its light-hearted treatment towards General Dyer and Michael O' Dwyer.

Even O'Dwyer firmly believed that India could only be ruled by an iron hand and he had displayed the working of his mind when he had vanquished the Ghadr Movement, a few years earlier, by taking very stern action against the revolutionaries. He always showed aversion for 'educated Indians' as he called them trouble-makers. So far so that he even lebelled Gandhi as 'an unctuous hypocrite with his ascetic pose'.

References

1. *See* M.A. Jinnah's Legislative Assembly Debates on the Rowlatt Bill, 7 February, 1919.
2. Montagu Papers, M.A. Jinnah to Chelmsford, dated 28 March, 1919.
3. *The Bombay Chronicle,* 25 January, 1919.
4. *The Hindu,* 22 January, 1919.
5. *Amrit Bazar Patrika,* 13 January, 1919.
6. *Punjabee,* 21 January, 1919.
7. *New India,* 11 January, 1919.
8. D.P. Mishra, *The History of Freedom Movement in Madhya Pradesh,* Nagpur, 1956, pp. 278-79.
9. *The Collected Works of Mahatma Gandhi,* Vol. XV, August 1918—July 1919, p. 86.
10. *The Collected Works of Mahatma Gandhi, op. cit.,* p. 87.
11. J.B. Kripalani, *Gandhi: His Life and Thought,* Delhi, 1970, p. 18.
12. Jawaharlal Nehru, *An Autobiography,* Delhi, 1962, p. 41.
13. The pledge was drafted on 24 February 1919 and signed by those present at a meeting held at the Sabarmati Ashram.
14. Home Pol. A., March 1919, File 250.
15. *Young India,* 12 March, 1919.
16. *Ibid.*
17. Home Pol. A., March 1919, File 250.
18. *Ibid.,* File 452-53.
19. Publications Division, Government of India, *Jallianwala Bagh,* Delhi, 1969, p. 2. and S.R. Bakshi, *Jallianwala Bagh Tragedy,* Delhi.
20. *The Bombay Chronicle,* 9 April 1919.
21. *The Bombay Chronicle,* 8 April, 1919.
22. *Ibid.*
23. *Ibid.*
24. *Ibid.*
25. Home Pol. A., May 1919, File 74-108.
26. Home Pol. Deposit, October 1919, File 31.
27. Area Officers sitting as Summary Courts dealt with cases against 543 persons of whom 386 were convicted.
28. Home Pol. Deposit, July 1919, File 46.
29. Home Pol. Deposit, June 1919, File 26.
30. *Ibid.*

6

Mahatma Gandhi, the Congress and the Transformation of the Freedom Movement

The Indian National Congress was by no means a party capable of drawing different classes and communities in India, particularly the poor in the cities and villages under a single umbrella in the form of a nationwide movement against British imperialism. The leadership of the Congress was, during the early 1920s, drawn from the educated classes, mostly members of the legal profession, though journalists, educationists and men of business were not absent from its ranks.

The movement against the partition of Bengal, for instance, had spread substantially into the rural districts of the province and instigated the landed gentry and the petty zamindari classes into an agitation marked by widespread antipathy towards the alien rulers of the land. Similarly, on several occasions the industrial workers, the peasants, and tribal communities had expressed their repugnance of British imperialism in movements characterised by very substantial popular participation. Yet none of these movements, barring the *Swadeshi* Movement of Bengal, were initiated or controlled by the leaders of the Congress.

The political objectives of the Indian National Congress, prior to the First World War, were of a piece with its middle-class character. The organisation did not challenge the overall legitimacy of British rule over India. The Congress argued for a growth of the franchise base and an extension of the powers and prerogatives of these councils. Moreover, a number of other national issues were taken up by the Congress, including the progressive Indianisation of the civil services and the army; the dissemination of mass literacy, and the expansion of *swadeshi* industry. Perhaps the character of the Congress in the early 1920s is best summed up in a description by Jawaharlal Nehru of one of its annual sessions. "I visited, as a delegate, the Bankipore Congress during Christmas 1912," he states in his *Autobiography.* "It was very much an English-knowing upper class affair where morning coats and well-pressed trousers were greatly in evidence. Essentially it was a social gathering with no political excitement or tension."

The Rise of Mahatma Gandhi

Whatever be the constraints of the Congress in the second decade of the 20th century, it was nevertheless a national organisation which had already established strong roots in the soil of India. It was also clear that, despite its restrained support base and its limited political and constitutional objectives, the Congress was capable of being transformed into a mass organisation which would provide a firm sense of purpose to the people of India in their struggle for freedom.

It was left to a political actor of a truely epic stature, namely. Mohandas Karamchand Gandhi, to bring about a dramatic transformation in the dialogue between nationalism and imperialism in India. The life of Gandhi, who was heading to acquire the mantle of a Mahatma, is too famous to be spelt out at any length in the present context. When Gandhi went to South Africa in 1893 as a lawyer, he discovered that the Indian community there was subject to a number of exploitation. The humiliation of his countrymen, rich and poor alike, affected him deeply. While he was still in South Africa, Gandhi developed an innovative technique of political agitation which he called *satyagraha* or moral suasion through which he sought to persuade the alien rulers of the country, by militant yet non-violent means, to extend their Indian subjects a status of dignity in society. Gandhi agreed to the view that the religious impulse in man was the noblest impulse in his being. He further compared this impulse with the eternal search for truth, on the one hand, and the adoption of *ahimsa,* or non-violence, as the basis of individual and collective social relations, on the other. Turning to the sphere of politics, Gandhi believed that the 'weapon' of *satyagraha* could persuade exploiters and evil-doers to undergo a change of heart and redress the wrongs, moral and material which they were perpetrating upon others. Since *satyagraha* was based on non-violence, and since it aimed at conjuring into existence the 'good society' through a change of heart rather than through the application of mindless force, Gandhi was of the view that his technique of political action was not only entirely different from that of others, but that it also created a bond of sympathy and understanding between the exploiters and the exploited, the rulers and the ruled, and also resolved social and political problems. Finally, as he put it in *Hind Swaraj,* the most assimilated expression of his social vision, *satyagraha* as a case of social and political action was particularly relevant to the problems which crippled India in the opening decades of the 20th century.

Gandhi's assertion that India's salvation lay in the adoption of *satyagraha* as the basis of political action was put to a hard test soon after his return to India. On the evidence of the distinguished nationalist, G.K. Gokhale, whom he considered as his political mentor, Gandhi spent a full year travelling in different parts of the country after his return from South Africa, engaging himself in a series of dialogue with the urban classes (particularly the intelligentsia). The path suggested by Gandhi, the path of consummating a marriage between religion and politics, of adopting non-violence as the foundation of political action, seemed to offer interesting possibilities.

It would be true to say that Gandhi, initially, was no more conscious of the political frenzy prevalent among the popular masses in the cities and villages than the existing leadership of the Congress. The initiative in bridging this gap and transforming the social character of the struggle for freedom came from the peasantry of a remote district in Bihar, which reached out to Gandhi in 1916 in order to lighten their burden of misery. Champaran, the volatile district, had for long been dominated by European planters of indigo, who forced the peasants of the region to cultivate the land on a meagre payment.

The unrest in Champaran was also reflected in the mood of the industrial and the rural classes in western India. At the very doorsteps of his *ashram* on the banks of the Sabarmati, Gandhi ran full tilt into the agitation of the textile workers of Ahmedabad, who were convinced that the factory owners of the city were depriving them of a fair share of the profits of industry in the form of equitable wage. Here again, Gandhi was able to persuade the textile workers to mount a struggle resting on the principles of *satyagraha*. Finally, the peasant proprietors of Kheda in Gujarat, the so-called Patidars, were greatly grieved at the rise in their tax obligations arising out of a new revenue assessment of the district by the Government of Bombay. The leaders of the Patidars, too, turned to Gandhi for guidance in their quandary. Once again Gandhi was able to project *satyagraha* as weapon best suited to waging a militant struggle against the British Government. He enjoyed similar success in Kheda, Champaran and Ahmedabad.

The Rowlatt *Satyagraha* of 1919

The possibility of mounting a nationwide agitation based on non-violent means came sooner than Gandhi or his rapidly growing number of followers had anticipated. The liberal mask of imperialism was reflected in the Declaration of 1917, which stated that 'the Policy of His Majesty's Government . . . is that of . . . gradual development of self-governing institutions with a view to the progressive realisation of responsible government in India as an integral part of the British Empire. To corroborate this declaration a parliamentary committee was set up with a view to drafting a new constitution which would give a measure of autonomy to India.

While proposals for constitutional reform was being thrashed out by Montagu, conservative civilians within the Government of India were engaged in preparing the ground for the enactment of legislation which would greatly enhance the despotic authority vested in the hands of the British administration. The initiative for such legislation was taken by Sir Reginald Craddock, the Home Member of the Viceroy's Executive Council, who was one of the most conservative members of the Indian Civil Service. Craddock believed that the values as well as the institutions of liberal democracy were totally irrelevant to India, and he argued that the Government of India should at no stages, loosen its grip over the levers of political power.

Conservatives like Craddock could not stem the tide of constitutional progress in India despite the wide support of the British community. The Rowlatt Committee, which came into existence as a result of pressures coming from the British community in order to set up a commission to assess the strength of revolutionary groups committed to violent policies explored the genesis and the expansion of revolutionary movement in India and recommended the adoption of legislation.

The passage of the Rowlatt Bills in the Imperial Legislative Council was opposed by nationalists. Members with radically different views—loyalists, moderates or extremists—were appalled at the insensitivity of a government which sought to arm itself with such extraordinary powers of coercion at a time when it was seeking to win over nationalist opinion through constitutional reforms. Gandhi, in particular, was distressed at the immorality of the whole proceedings.

Gandhi had even prior to 1919 led with conspicuous success non-violent agitations both in South Africa and in India. Yet the scale of the Rowlatt Satyagraha was qualitatively different from the scale of the earlier agitations. In the spring of 1919, Gandhi appealed to an entire nation of 400 million to launch an onslaught upon the British Government of India through a unique technique of political warfare. Nevertheless, he was agreeably astonished at the enthusiasm of the people of India who responded to his call for a *satyagraha* against the Rowlatt Act. All over the country, irrespective of Hindus and Muslims, the rich and the poor, businessmen and professionals, industrialists and workers, and artisans and lumpen elements, rose in a protest against the British government. Broadly speaking, the agitation was confined mainly in the cities and in the larger towns than in the rural areas; though it reached out to the smaller towns, and even villages in Gujarat and in the Punjab; and to a lesser extent, in the United Provinces and in western Maharashtra. In Bombay, the *satyagraha* was mainly the middle and lower middle classes belonging to the Gujarati and the Muslim communities. In Ahmedabad, the mercantile and the professional classes, as well as the workers, Hindus and Muslims rallied to support in great numbers. Calcutta was comparatively quite despite its reputation for being one of the liveliest centres of nationalist politics in India. However, the southern cities like Madras witnessed numerous demonstrations of support for the *satyagraha*. But it was the cities of northern India like Delhi, Lahore and Amritsar and the numerous district towns of the region which witnessed the most crowded, the most vocal and the most enthusiastic demonstrations for the repeal of the Rowlatt Act.

The agitation launched by Gandhi in April 1919 was unparalleled in nationalist history in two respects. First, it was essentially subcontinental in character; and secondly, it drew classes and communities in the cities and towns which had hitherto refrained from participating in nationalist agitation. That the agitation took a violent turn, more particularly in the cities of the north, was largely due to attempt of the local British administrators to suppress popular demonstrations. The most ghastly incident in the course of the Rowlatt Satyagraha took place in Amritsar where, on 13 April 1919, the army fired upon a peaceful crowd of 20,000 citizens, killing 397 and wounding 1,143 of them. However, the extent to which people participated in the Rowlatt Satyagraha clearly symbolised the transfer of 'moral authority' over the country from the authority of the British Government into the hands of the nationalist leadership. Indeed, this 'moral authority' was now entrusted upon the person of Gandhi, who was very soon to assume formal leadership over the Indian National Congress.

The Non-cooperation Movement

While the social and economic unrests which affected different classes and communities in India during the early 1920s provided the backdrop to nationalist agitation against the British *Raj*, it would be a gross mistake to assume that such discontents in themselves provide a full explanation of demonstrations of popular will like the Rowlatt *Satyagraha.* The people of India, the elites and the popular classes, were convinced that their liberation from British rule would enable them to initiate a moral revolution.

The leadership of the Muslim community in India, at this stage, lay in the hands of clerical figures like Maulana Abul Kalam Azad and Maulana Abdul Bari; and secular personalities like Mohamed Ali and Shaukat Ali. The outbreak of war in 1914 reinforced Pan-Islamic sentiment in India. However, it was the defeat of Turkey (along with Germany) in 1918 that invoked a qualitative change in the temper of Muslim politics in India. There was now a growing alarm among the Muslims that the Ottoman Empire would be disjointed, as part of the post-war settlement, with grave consequences for the position of Islam in the world community.

Gandhi was acutely aware of the sentiments abroad in the Muslim community. He was also aware of the opportunity which these sentiments afforded for a great Hindu-Muslim entente against the British *Raj*. The two communities had already formed a united front at the annual session of the Congress in 1916. But this had barely affected classes other than the educated and the professionals. The *Khilafat* issue, however, had made a deep impact upon the poor Muslim classes like the artisans, the industrial workers and the peasantry. Gandhi was very sensitive to the religious sentiments of the people and his vision of the good society encouraged him to look favourably upon the inference of religious grievances for political purposes.

The crucial step before the leadership of the Congress at the annual session of 1919 was the attitude to be adopted to the constitutional reforms which had been announced before the session commenced. C.R. Das, the great Bengali leader, moved a resolution which defined the Reforms Act as 'inadequate, unsatisfactory and disappointing'. It was also stated that 'This Congress further urges that Parliament should take early steps to establish full responsible government in India in accordance with the principles of self-determination.'

Despite the moderation of the Congress leaders at Amritsar in December 1919, the events which followed in the next few months made it clear that the British Government was set upon a collision course with nationalist sentiment in India. The Muslim community was particularly excited over the *Khilafat* issue and Gandhi, who had close contacts with the Muslim leaders put before them the idea of an agitation resting on the principles of non-violence to redress the wrongs suffered by their followers.

Despite the support which Gandhi received from the Muslim community, the Congress session at Calcutta, where the proposal to adopt non-cooperation was to be discussed, proved to be a very stormy affair. Lajpat Rai, a veteran leader of the Punjab and the president of the Calcutta session, was opposed to the Gandhian programme, though he did not voice his views in his presidential address. However, when Gandhi formally decided in committing the Congress to non-cooperation, a number of leaders from Bengal, Maharashtra, the Central Provinces, the United Provinces, and the south, like B.C. Pal, C.R. Das, M.M. Malaviya, Joseph Baptista,

M.A. Jinnah and Satyamurti, stood against it. Indeed, Motilal Nehru was alone among the established leaders of the Congress in supporting Gandhi at this juncture.

The mass support in favour of Gandhi, for the attainment of *swaraj*, and for *satyagraha* as the weapon most likely to attain this objective, is vividly reflected in the proceedings of the annual session of the Congress held at Nagpur in December 1920. After the deliberations of September 1920 at Calcutta, the Congress leaders discovered the full extent to which Gandhi's moral authority reached out to different classes and communities in India and this persuaded them to support a *satyagraha* movement against the British Government. Even the educated classes of Bengal were passionately nationalistic, responded to the Mahatma's charisma in a manner which obliged their leader, C.R. Das, to reconsider his attitude towards non-cooperation. In Maharashtra, in the Punjab, in the Central Provinces, in the provinces of the south, throughout the length and breadth of India, nationalist leaders discovered that the message of *swaraj* had made a great impression upon the popular psyche and had transformed Gandhi into a truly national figure. The annual session of the Congress at Nagpur, therefore, witnessed an overwhelming support for the Mahatma.

The manner in which the people of India, irrespective of caste, creed, religion and social status fought British imperialism under the leadership of the Mahatma Gandhi and the Indian National Congress has been described at length in the historiography of the National movement. Unlike the uprising of 1857, however, non-cooperation rested upon a modern concept of nationalism and the movement was characterized by a spatial distribution and a social depth absent in the events in the middle of the 19th century. For these reasons in general, and Gandhi's moral influence in particular, and the prospect of *swaraj* reached out to the common people of India, the non-cooperation movement posed problems for the British Government.

The grand conflict between nationalism and imperialism at this stage was best reflected in the reception accorded to the Prince of Wales when he visited India towards the end of 1921. The visit was organised by the British Government with a view to undermine the increasing tide of nationalist struggle. Symbolically, amid high drama, precisely when the Prince of Wales landed at Bombay harbour on 17 November 1921, the Mahatma was addressing a mammoth gathering of 60,000 at a meeting in the heart of the industrial suburbs in the city, where he also applied the torch to a huge pile of foreign cloth specifically for this purpose.

As the movement to wrest *swaraj* from the grasp of the British Government gained momentum, Gandhi and the Congress leaders faced difficult questions of control and management of their followers. The mobilisation of the people of the subcontinent was a truly stupendous undertaking. Moreover, the cleavages of class, community and religion within Indian society could assume a menacing proportion and erupt into sectarian or communal conflict, the violence was accepted as a legitimate instrument of the anti-imperialist struggle. Indeed, in the city of Bombay, the demonstrations against the Prince of Wales soon led to violence between Hindus and Muslims, on the one hand, and Parsis and Christians on the other. Even more serious was the Moplah uprising of Kerala, where a Muslim peasantry, agitated over the issue of *Khilafat*, attacked the British Government at the same time as it went berserk against the superior Hindu rural classes in the region.

The possibility of violence against the British Government or between different classes and communities within Indian society haunted Gandhi because he was considering, at that time, the use of the most militant weapon available to a *satyagrahi*, namely refusal to pay taxes to a government which had lost the moral right to rule. To initiate this aspect of the movement, Gandhi had selected the taluka of Bardoli in Surat district. The *patidars*, the peasant proprietors of this region, had been organised for a peaceful struggle under the leadership of Vallabhbhai Patel, one of Gandhi's principal lieutenants, and the no-tax campaign at Bardoli was expected to rattle the edifice of the British *Raj* to its very foundations.

However, when the *patidars* of Bardoli were all set to denounce the British Government, an astonishing act of violence in the United Provinces persuaded the Mahatma to stop the movement for non-cooperation altogether. The occasion was provided by the peasants of a village called Chauri Chaura in Gorakhpur district, who, when filled upon by the policemen of a local outpost retaliated by setting fire on it and killing their oppressors. Gandhi saw in this ugly episode the symptoms of a deep-rooted malaise. The incident also revealed the extent to which violence had the very core of Indian society. From all over the country, where substantial Muslim communities, deeply agitated over the *Khilafat* issue, was located; the perceptions reaching out to the Mahatma revealed that an intensification of the struggle would lead to violent uprisings against the British *Raj*. Such upheaval would provide the authorities with the pretext to unleash a reign of terror, in which non-violent and legitimate forms of political protest would be suppressed with the same ruthlessness as violent and 'illegitimate' forms of political protest. For these reasons, the Congress Working Committee, at a meeting held in February 1922, at the personal initiative of Gandhi discontinued the non-cooperation movement and advised the people to a programme of constructive activity, having as its objective the regeneration of Indian society.

7

Congress and *Khilafat*

The anti-*Raj* stance gained momentum from various sections of the Muslim community mainly on account of the fact that Turkey and the Caliph, greatly insulted and humiliated due to the unbearable political conditions placed on their shoulders, must be saved at any cost, including physical and financial sacrifices. To achieve this end, the feasible step decided upon by them was the attainment of independence for India which had by this time become a popular slogan of the masses under the political leadership of Mahatma Gandhi.

The government sources feared a great danger to the existing political situation created by the *Khilafat* propaganda. On 17 October 1920, the *Khilafat* Day was observed throughout India and a movement was launched to boycott the peace celebrations of December. The *Khilafat* Committee which sat in Delhi on 23-24th October and was attended by Gandhi and other front-rank leaders passed 'violent' resolutions advocating total abstention from the peace celebrations, the gradual boycott of British goods, the abandonment of cooperation with the government as regards military and civil services, etc.

Gandhi commented in this *Autobiography* thus: "The Congress inquiry into Dyerism in the Punjab had just commenced, when I received a letter of invitation to be present at a joint conference of Hindus and Mussalmans that was to meet at Delhi to deliberate on the *Khilafat* question. Among the signatories to it were late Hakim Ajmal Khan Saheb and Mr. Asaf Ali. The Mussalmans adopted a very important resolution. If the peace terms are unfavourable to them—which may God forbid—they will stop all cooperation with Government. It is an inalienable right of the people thus to withhold cooperation. We are not bound to retain Government titles and honours, or to continue in Government services. If Government should betray us in a great cause like the *Khilafat*, we could not do otherwise than non-cooperate. We are, therefore, entitled to non-cooperate with Government in case of a betrayal."[1]

A New Resolution

In scheming the resolution Mahatma Gandhi said it divided itself into two parts. The first part dealt with the Karachi Resolution and was intended to be its confirmation from the national interest. He considered it their duty to state their position clearly and to inform the sepoy that it was wrong to help a Government which had forfeited the confidence of the country. One thing the resolution did not require the people to do, namely, to carry on secret propaganda. They had denied secrecy from their book of non-co-operation. They were ashamed to say in secret what they were not prepared to say in public.

The other part of the resolution pointed out to the soldier the way to a distinguished livelihood. It referred to *swadeshi*. The resolution told the soldier that he could earn his living by carding and weaving. He strongly believed with Maulana Mohamed Ali that they did not lead any gunpowder. Yarn balls were their lead and the spinning wheel was their gun.

He was sorry that he had not the power of convincing every lawyer that it was of no worth to practise before the courts which gave no justice. He knew that he had not been able to persuade every man and woman of Bombay that it was sinful to wear anything but *khaddar*. Nevertheless he adhered to his faith in the spinning wheel. He was sure that it alone could solve the problem of India's poverty. Its acceptance, to him, was a test of the reality of Hindu-Muslim unity and (of freedom) from violence. He wanted to see the men and women of Bombay to be dressed in *khaddar* only. He wanted to see the spinning wheel at work in every house in Bombay. He could not advise civil disobedience without *swadeshi*. He knew the science of civil disobedience. He knew its power and its risks as well. A completely non-violent atmosphere was a necessity and it could not be ensured unless the countrymen had recognised the power of the spinning wheel and settled down to it. He expected princely men to take to *charkha* and the mill-hands to take up the spinning-wheel. And once they had done that, they would safely go to individual soldier and openly ask him to give up his service.

In due course, Gandhi came to Simla at the request of Malaviya and Andrews and asked for an interview with the Viceroy which was instantly arranged. At the first interview, no mention was made of the proposed prosecutions. Upon the next occasion, the Viceroy stated that according to the government reports, responsible non-cooperators had made speeches instigating to violence contrary to the doctrine proposed by Gandhi. He indeed repudiated incitement to violence on the part of any of the responsible non-co-operators and said that if he was satisfied that any of them had incited to violence, he would publicly reject them and their teachings unless they withdrew their statements that amounted to incitement to violence.

It was at this juncture that the Viceroy said that it was proposed to initiate criminal proceedings against Shaukat Ali and Mahomed Ali in respect of these passages and that, if Gandhi showed him the statement and it satisfied him from the position of his government, he would use his influence to prevent the institution of indictment, for the Viceroy said, the object of the government would be attained if the making of speeches of a violent character was in future prevented.

During the whole discussion the Viceroy and Gandhi were activated by the desire to prevent any outward events as also to prevent speeches inciting to violence. The Viceroy informed Gandhi that he might not be able to check the commencement of proceedings if the statement was not published with the least possible delay. Gandhi agreed that the statement should be published without delay and after a brief gap telegraphed to the Viceroy that Shaukat Ali and Mahomed Ali had signed the statement with immaterial alteration and sent it to the press for publication.

After the publication of the statement an official communique was issued by the government. The terms of the communique were not properly settled until just before its issue and Gandhi never saw it although the substance of it as already indicated had been communicated to him. The main part of the interviews between the Viceroy and Gandhi included conversations which ranged over the several causes of discontent in India including the Punjab disturbances, the *Khilafat* agitation, The Treaty of Sevres and the general conditions of the people. Gandhi did not submit any scheme of *swaraj* to the Viceroy nor was a scheme of *swaraj* discussed at the interviews.

Jawaharlal Nehru commented thus:[2]

> Among the Muslims there was anger over the treatment of Turkey and the *Khilafat* question and an agitation growing. The treaty with Turkey had not been signed yet, but the whole situation was ominous. So, while they agitated, they waited. In India the *Khilafat* Committee came more and more under Gandhiji's influence and began to flirt with his ideas of non-violent, non-co-operation .... A *Khilafat* deputation was going to wait on the Viceroy, and Gandhiji was to join it. Before he reached Delhi, however, a draft of the proposed address was, according to custom, sent to the Viceroy. When Gandhiji arrived and read this draft, he strongly disapproved of it and even said that he could not be a party to the deputation, if this draft was not materially altered. His objection was that the draft was bague and wordy and there was no clear indication in it of the absolute minimum demands which the muslims must have. He said that this was not fair to the Viceroy and the British Government, or to the people, or to themselves. They must not make exaggerated demands which they were not going to press, but should state the minimum clearly and without possibility of doubt, and stand by it to the death. If they were serious, this was the only right and honourable course to adopt.
>
> This argument was a novel one in political or other circles in India. We were used to vague exaggerations and flowery language and always there was an idea of the bargain in our minds.

Lajpat Rai commented in *The Political Future of India* in 1919, "with 70 million Moslems India is the most important centre of Mohammedan sentiment. With Christians as their present rulers, the Hindus and Mohammedans of India are coming to realise that their best interests require a closing up of their ranks...The Hindus will stand by their Mohammedan countrymen in all their efforts to revive the glory of Islam, and to regain political independence for it. There is no fear of a Pan-Islamic movement if the new spirit of internationalism prevails. If, however, it does not, the Pan-Islamic movement might find a sympathetic hand in India..."[3]

Series of *Khilafat* Conferences

The series of *Khilafat* Conferences held at various places, from time to time, under the presidentship of prominent leaders, proved very effective in instilling *anti-Raj* feeling amongst Muslims and their supporters. Such a meeting was held at the Benarsi Krishna Theatre, Delhi on 19 April 1920. The prominent leaders who attended the meeting were Abdul Qayyum Haqqani, Maulvi Ahmed Said, Maulvi Muhammad Daud Ghaznavi of Amritsar, Maulvi Bashir Ahmed of Lahore, Tafazzul Hussain, Tajuddin, Abbas Hussain, Abdullah Churiwala, Arif Haswi, Manzoor Ahmad, Inder, Syed Ataulla Shah of Amritsar. Raziuddin Ahmed, Ghulam Muhammad Aziz of

8

Congress and Non-Cooperation Movement

Talking of the first great movement against the *Raj* which reached the zenith of a reaction engendered after a slavery of about two centuries, one could count reaction and opposition to the alien domination shown during 19th century. The great revolt of 1857, though a failure in its final review, regenerated a spirit of agitation deeply mingled with a patriotic fervour which was noticed both in the second half of 19th century and first decade of the 20th century. India governed by a number of Viceroys like Ripon, Curzon, Minto, Hardinge and Chelmsford witnessed several historic events, which showed way to a larger and more organised movement in 1920s. In fact, the foundation of the Indian National Congress, its initial manifesto and subsequent changes in it, the bureaucratic policies of Curzon, *Swadeshi* movement, the foundation of Muslim League, Minto-Morley, and the beginning of the global war in 1914—all had considerably affected the minds of those Indians who were to play a major role in the near future.

The Non-Cooperation Movement has deep bonds with the fundamental political problems of the time. Left with no hope of the grant of constitutional privileges at the end of the First World War, the Indian National Congress had also to encounter the serious implications of the Rowlatt Bills, the Jallianwala Bagh carnage and the *Khilafat* issue. The programme of boycott of various government institutions was placed before the nation with the promise of "*Swaraj* in one year". The movement, despite participation from all walks of life failed to last for a long time, rather it was suspended after one-and-half-a-year in February 1922 on account of a violent act at Chauri Chaura near Gorakhpur. The plea was taken that the creed of non-violence had been seriously violated by the *satyagrahis*.

The masses—the peasants and workers—joined the national movement primarily in the Gandhian era. This is perhaps the most important aspect of the growth of the national movement. Although it deserves mention that the capitalists as a clan also came into the movement, neither the Moderates nor the Extremists had been able to get the active support of this class since both the class and its contradiction with imperialism bloomed fully only during and after the First World War. Moreover, the Moderate and Extremist movements were not socially or politically prominent enough for the capitalist class to make a determined attempt to dominate them. Thus, to repeat the extension of the social base of the movement to the capitalist class was an important and a new side of the movement in its Gandhian phase as its extension to the workers and peasants.[1]

The special session of the Indian National Congress held in Calcutta on

4 September 1920 was a significant episode in the inauguration of the Non-Cooperation Movement. The presidential address delivered by Lala Lajpat Rai was historic and most remarkable in contents. It covered the political situation in India, particularly in the Punjab as an aftermath of the Jallianwala Bagh massacre and the clamping of martial law in the province, the Muslim grievances and their agitation for *Khilafat*, economic and social conditions of the country, the Reforms Scheme, and the line of action to be adopted by the people of India during the ensuing movement. He indeed explained these major points in a comprehensive way.

The happenings in the Punjab in 1919 during the administration of Michael O' Dwyer met with a staunch criticism by the Congress president. The Congress delegates, assembled from all over India, although well aware of the gruesome tragedy in the *Bagh*, were once again highlighted about severe measures taken by the British civilians and defence officials.

The *Khilafat* issue was dealt with in a comprehensive manner. In fact, the second question that had been referred to the special session of the Congress for consideration and decision was the question of the *Khilafat*.

Nagpur Congress Session and Thereafter

The thirty-fifth session of the Indian National Congress was held at Nagpur on December 26-31, 1920 under the presidentship of an eminent Congress leader, C. Vijiaraghavachariar.[2] The Chairman of the reception committee, Jamnalal Bajaj, reviewed the political situation in India in his inciting speech where he criticised the policies of the government in his reference about Defence of India Act, Rowlatt Act, administration of Michael O' Dwyer, the Jallianwala Bagh carnage and the *Khilafat*.[3]

The Working Committee of the Indian National Congress allowed the members of the provincial Congress committees to launch a civil disobedience in their respective areas. But certain conditions were put before them before they could execute their plans. These conditions were as follows: The Civil resister must discard foreign cloth and accept *Khaddar*; he must know spinning; he must be a believer in non-violence and an avid supporter of Hindu-Muslim unity and he must also undertake to work for the removal of untouchability for which Gandhi always showed deep concern and anxiety.[4]

Prominent Congress leaders like Mahatma Gandhi and Motilal Nehru attended this session and gave their approval of the resolutions passed therein. The following important resolutions were passed and thus a clear-cut programme was chalked out for the execution of the movement at all-India level.

> Resolved that whereas, in the opinion of the Congress, the existing Government of India has forfeited the confidence of the country; and
>
> Whereas the people of India are now determined to establish the *Swaraj*; and
>
> Whereas the methods adopted by the people of India prior to the last Special Session of the Indian National Congress have failed to secure due recognition of their rights and liberties and the redress of their many and grievous wrongs, more specially in reference to the *Khilafat* and the Punjab;

the widespread revolt. When the flames of revolt were doused, it was estimated by an official report that 2,288 Moplahs (affiliated with the Sunni sect and having deep religious involvements, they showed much respect towards the Sultan of Turkey) were killed, 1,630 wounded, 5,712 captured and 39,107 surrendered themselves voluntarily. The number of persons committed to the sessions was 1,704, those slapped two years' imprisonment were 2,985 and a few hundreds more were sentenced to varied period, from one month to one year.[10]

On 29 October, 1923, a republic was proclaimed in Turkey—Mustafa Kemal,[11] the saviour of Turkey's independence, who emphasised his country's Asiatic vistas and the desire to build a national life in Anatolia by changing the capital from Constantinople to Ankara, became the first President. His main aim was to liberate Turkey from foreign influence and domination and this he achieved by the Treaty of Lausanne.

A few Muslims of India had to accept the state of affairs in Turkey. Ansari and Ajmal Khan asserted that the selection of a new Caliph by the Turkish National Assembly[12] was a comeback to the great tradition of the elected Caliphs and such a change, they stated, would strengthen his position. At the annual meeting of the *Khilafat* Congress held in December 1922 under the presidentship of Ansari, a few resolutions were approved in connection with the *Khilafat*.

The Agha Khan and Sayyid Amir Ali showed concern over the decline in Caliph's authority and prestige. They wrote a letter to Ismet Pasha in November 1923 and highlighted that when the *Khilafat* had been in danger, Indian Muslims wholeheartedly supported the Turkish nationalists. Their letter, however, failed to receive any favourable response to the solution of the problem. Instead they were condemned as dissidents as both of them were Shias. Besides they were termed as agents of Britain with a motive to harm the republic by overthrowing it and restoring the Ottoman dynasty.[13]

The *Khilafat* Committee in India felt much dismayed about it. On 11 March, 1924 Shaukat Ali, president of the *Khilafat* Committee and Mufti Kafayatullah, president of the Jamiat al Ulma sent a telegram to Mustafa Kemal expressing grave concern for the political action taken by the new government in Turkey. They assured the president that they had no intention of any interference in Turkey[14] and pleaded not to take any crucial action and wait for the arrival of a delegation at Ankara. The new regime in Turkish did not enjoy this telegram and the delegation, therefore, could not get to Turkey.

Failure of Turkey

When the failure of Turkey with the systematic military assaults of the Allied Powers became a glaring phenomenon in the international arena, Mohammed Ali realised the fact that the freedom of India was an absolute necessity for the freedom of Islam. He started appealing to the Muslim masses to come forward for supreme sacrifices and made them realise the fact that "slave India will be of scant help to the Turks and the Khalifa". He was assisted in the propagation of this ideology by Maulvi Habibul Rahman, the president of the Jamaat-ul-Ulema-i-Hind, who emphatically explained the fact that "...as the betterment of Islam could be achieved only if India was autonomous, the Jamaat had placed above all the efforts at securing independence."

In fact, as early as 1914, Gandhi began to show deep concern about the future of

Caliphate, an issue which had greatly aroused the religious sentiments of Muslims. As was obvious, when Gandhi reached India during the next year, he did not involve himself with the controversial political events in the subcontinent during the war. He, however, fully equipped himself with the crucial issue having linkage with the division of the Turkish Empire thus greatly effecting the Caliphate. While offering his full support for their religious cause, he always cautioned them to be patient in putting forward their demands to the government and never to allow their workers to follow the path of violence.

The argument of Gandhi with Lord Chelmsford regarding a favourable solution of the problem did not bring forth any concrete result. This kind of reluctance of the Viceroy and the home government worsened the issue to the extent of changing Gandhi's views which made him adopt a line of political action in 1920 when the *Khilafat* was made an important link with the other scheme of things sponsored during the Non-Cooperation Movement.

The year 1924 opened with new issues on the Indian political horizon. In February, 1924 Gandhi found that the non-cooperating lawyers had resumed their practice; the students gone back to their schools and colleges and *charkha* and *khadi* had almost disappeared from the minds of the people. In fact, unable to withstand the physical, mental and financial strain of the mass movement, the educated class made the nationalist movement the 'militant wing' of the Congress and founded and organised the Swarajist Party with a regular programme of obstruction of government bills in the councils.

Under these circumstances, Gandhi devoted himself to three main objectives, i.e., to maintain Hindu-Muslim unity, removal of untouchability and spread of the doctrine of hand-spinning. Thus, his idea was to organise the people on one platform irrespective of caste, religion and creed and to bring about the economic stability of the masses in the villages. These measures were expected to fulfil his dream of the attainment of *swaraj*. He fully realised the fact that disintegration, strife and violence would bring about much damage to his cause.

During the period, Gandhi was a much worried leader. The problem of Hindu-Muslim unity was indeed a nightmare for him. There were riots in Amethi, Gulbarga, Sambhar, Kohat and numerous other places. To bring about peaceful atmosphere, Gandhi undertook a twenty-one day fast in Delhi in Mohammed Ali's house as a measure of "...warning to Hindus and Mussalmans who have professed to love me. If they have loved me truly and if I have been deserving of their love, they will do penance with me....The world is watching, some with glee and some with sorrow, the dog-fight that is proceeding in our minds."

The efforts for Hindu-Muslim unity, however, did not abate upto this point. A unity conference was convened in Delhi and was attended by prominent leaders like Pandit Madan Mohan Malaviya, Annie Besant, Mohamed Ali, Shaukat Ali, Swami Shraddhanand and about three hundred other delegates. All the leaders unequivocally agreed to affirm freedom of conscience and religion and resolutions were passed for generating goodwill and removal of mistrust and suspicion amongst Hindus and Muslims.

Even in the Belgaum Congress in 1924, Gandhi in his presidential address expressed strong dissatisfaction at the political atmosphere in India. At no cost could he afford to notice Hindu-Muslim unity being crushed under communal and sectional sentiments. He opined thus:

> Hindu-Muslim Unity...is the breath of our life...The *Khilafat* agitation in which Hindus made common cause with their Mussalman brethren and the non-cooperation that followed it caused an awakening among the hitherto slumbering masses. It has given a new consciousness to the classes as well as the masses. Interested persons who were disappointed during the palmy days of non-co-operation, now that it has lost the charm of novelty, have found their opportunity and are trading upon the religious bigotry or the selfishness of both the communities. The result is written in the history of the feuds of the past two years. Religion has been travestied. Trifles have been dignified by the name of religious tenets which, the fanatics claim, must be observed at any cost. Economic and political causes have been brought into play for the sake of fomenting trouble. The culminating point was reached in Kohat...Suffice it to say that the Hindu refugees fled for fear of their lives...The Mussalmans of Kohat may not rest satisfied till they have brought back to Kohat every one of the refugees.

The problem of Hindu-Muslim unity was seriously taken up by the Ali Brothers in early 1920s when the communal frenzy had engulfed two communities in various regions of the country. Both the brothers toured almost the whole of India and emphatically stressed upon the need of a joint political action by both the communities at an all-India level, and in one of his speeches Mohamed Ali stressed this point forcefully.[15] The *Young India* commented, "One thing is certain, and it is this, that neither can the Hindus exterminate the Mussalmans today nor can the Mussalmans get rid of the Hindus. If they cannot rid of one another, the only thing to do is to settle down to cooperate with one another... and while the Muslims must remove all doubts from the Hindu mind about their desire for *Swaraj* for its own sake and their readiness to resist all foreign aggression, the Hindus must similarly remove from the Muslim mind all apprehensions that the Hindu majority is synonymous with Muslim servitude."

In April, 1924, Gandhi asserted his feelings about *Khilafat* thus:[16]

> I have been asked to give my opinion on the *Khilafat* trouble. I have none to give. It were impertinence for me, an outsider, to thrust my views on my Muslim brethren. It is a question which the Mussalmans must settle for themselves. All that non-Muslims can do is to assure them of their deep sympathy in their affliction. The existence of the *Khilafat* is an essential part of their faith. Everyone who holds his own religion to be dear to himself is bound to express genuine sympathy with those of a different faith. The heart of every Hindu who values Muslim friendship must go out to the Mussalmans in their great sorrow. They have a more anxious time now than when the *Khilafat* was attacked from without. But now that the danger comes from within and several sections are contending for their own views, it must tax the utmost resources of those who are engaged in solving the problem in a manner that is consistent with the deep truths of their own faith and acceptable to all sections. This much is

> quite clear to me that the future of the *Khilafat*, indeed of Islam itself in so far as it can rest with man, lies in the hands of Indian Mussalmans. Theirs is the burden, theirs the privilege. May god grant them strength to follow it.
>
> The Hindus can live in the midst of an overwhelming Mussalman majority only if the latter are willing to receive and treat them as friends and equals, just as Mussalmans, if in a minority, must depend for honourable existence in the midst of a Hindu majority on the latter's friendliness... A *swaraj* government means a government established by the free joint will of Hindus, Mussalmans and others. Hindus and Mussalmans, if they desire *swaraj*, have perforce to settle their differences amicably.[17]

A special session of the Jamiat-ul-Ulema was convened on 11 January, 1925 at Moradabad. Maulvi Abdul Hafiz, chairman of the reception committee condemned non-Muslim interference in Muslim religious places and vehemently opposed Britain's policy in Hedjaz and Iraq. Unless British and other non-Muslim influences in Hedjaz and Iraq were eliminated, *Khilafat* question could not be said to have been satisfactorily solved.

References

1. M.K. Gandhi, *The Story of My Experiments with Truth,* Ahmedabad, 1981, pp. 363-65.
2. Jawaharlal Nehru, *An Autobiography,* Delhi, 1962, pp. 40 ff.
3. Lajpat Rai, *The Political Future of India,* New York, 1919, p. 207.
4. Home Department, Pol. Deposit, May 1920, File 12.
5. *Ibid.*
6. *Ibid.*
7. *Ibid.*
8. *Ibid.*
9. *The Collected Works of Mahatma Gandhi,* Vol. XXIII, March 1922—May 1924, pp. 368-69.
10. Jawaharlal Nehru, *An Autobiography,* Delhi, 1962, pp. 71-72.
11. Home Department, Political, File 241/1-B, 1922.
12. Kemal died in 1938 and was succeeded by General Ismet Inonu as President of Turkey.
13. In October 1923, The Grand National Assembly elected Mustafa Kemal as President and Ismet Pasha as Prime Minister.
14. Home Poll, File 197. II, 1923, On Ist March 1924, the Assembly banished all surviving members of the Ottoman house after deposing the Caliph.
15. Home Poll, File 167, 1924.
16. See for complete reference in *Young India,* 29th May 1924.
17. *Young India,* 3rd April 1924.

Amritsar, Sunder Singh of Amritsar, Bawa Amar Singh of Amritsar, Lal Khan of Gujranwala, Wazir Hussain of Muzaffarnagar, Nisar Ali of Ajmer and Ibrahim Khalil Arab.[4]

Maulvi Ahmed Said favoured the concept of boycotting English goods and advocated the use of *swadeshi* goods. He spoke in detail on the point of migration to Afghanistan and urged the people to take advantages of the Amir's offer and leave India. He accused the English of having arrested the *Sheikh-ul-Islam* of Turkey by treachery and pointed out that the English did everything by treachery.[5]

Similarly Maulvi Muhammad Daud Ghaznavi castigated the government for its exploitation and drew parallels between the Turkish massacres of Armenians and the Punjab disturbances.[6] He said that a nation with a black list of records against them such as the government had could not be called a proper nation.[7] He further stated that the Czar of Russia had learnt his lesson, but the British government would not take heed and would soon taste same result.

As a protest against the terms of the Treaty of Peace with Turkey, Hakim Ajmal Khan of Delhi, to whom the Kaisar-i-Hind Medal of the First Class was conferred on 1st January 1915 returned the medal to the Government of India on the occasion of the Coronation of His Majesty and that of the Coronation *Durbar* of 1912. Besides he apprised Gandhi of the relationship between Hindus and Muslims on 17 March 1922.

The similar sentiments were expressed by Gandhi in his discussion with M.A. Ansari.[8]

> Not a single day passes when I do not think of the Brothers and their sorrows. The *Khilafat* is dear to every Mussalman, but the Ali Brothers have made its prestige and honour their life-work. I can therefore understand how the decision of the Turkish Assembly must have shaken them...Mahomed Ali will bring me all the messages from Shaukat Ali and that would be quite sufficient to go on with. As far as I am concerned, there is not much really that I now want to know except the view of yourself and the Brothers and of a few others whose opinions I value. My mind is practically made up, and I am becoming impatient to deliver my soul.

An Assessment

The union of Congress and the *Khilafat* worked well for a cause taken up by both the organisations at national level. The motivation for this cause was national in its characteristics and it strengthened the liaison between the two communities at least for some time. Certain elements which inspired in creating misunderstanding between the two communities, included the Anglo-Indian press of the time which, however, failed to achieve its desired results in early 1920s, due to the fact that the nationalist forces functioning at that stage overpowered these elements which could not be smashed by a powerful bureaucratic machinery operating in various regions of the country.

Undoubtedly, the two movements—the Non-cooperation and the *Khilafat* movements—failed to make much headway as expected. The role of prominent Muslim leaders in the freedom struggle in 1920s was a remarkable episode in our history. Amongst these leaders, the names of Hakim Ajmal Khan, Maulana Abul Kalam Azad,

M.A. Ansari, T.A.K. Sherwani, Saifud Din Kitchlew, Syed Mahmud, Rafi Ahmad Kidwai and a few others deserve mention.

Religion was used as a tool for the first time as an anti-*Raj* stance. The speeches and writings of Ali Brothers and other Muslim leaders were tinted with the ideology propounded by Quran and Hadith. Owing to the importance given to the *Khilafat* movement in 1921, a large number of *Moulvis* and Muslim religious leaders took significant part in the political struggle. They gave a definite religious status to the movement and Muslims generally were greatly influenced by it. The influence and prestige of the *Moulvis* which had been gradually declining owing to new ideas and increasing tide of westernization, began to grow again and dominate the Muslim community. The Ali Brothers, themselves of a religious bent of mind, helped in this process and so did Gandhiji who paid the greatest regard to the *Moulvis* and the *Moulanas*.[9]

But it cannot be denied that certain tendencies had developed in the body politic of the movement when the hopes and aspirations of its leaders were shattered at the time of decisions not similar to their original religious stand. The *Raj* had its dominance at various levels and it could create a serious wedge between the two communities affording whole-hearted support to one against the other. As a result of such political model at higher level, certain elements had gone out of control of Gandhi in spite of the fact that he geared up the available resources to collect the scattered elements which perhaps thought of more advantages if they dissociate themselves for the main political organisations whose ideology they supported for a few years. The orgy of communal riots encompassed a major portion of the population and in spite of the best efforts on the part of the functionaries in *Shuddhi, Sanghathan, Tabligh,* and *Tanzeen*, the hopes for straightening and mitigating the relations were belied.

The financial crisis in one form or the other stood as a crucial factor in initiating serious difference of opinion amongst the prominent members of the *Khilafat*. The Central Committee wished to transfer one lakh to the *Khilafat* Fund and ten lakh to Angora. Chotani who was operating these funds refused to comply with the request of the Central Committee and soon it was discovered that there had been serious financial anomalies at various levels.

The *Khilafat* Committee, however, tried to justify the expenditure from public funds with the appeal that if the amount had been deposited in the bank, there could be a possibility of it being seized by the government. Some ledgers were maintained but they were taken away by the police during their raids. It defended the position of the president who had the absolute authority to spend money on various items concerning the party.

The future of the *Khilafat* appeared dusky after the decision made at the Paris Conference and this was taken a serious challenge by the Muslims with a wave of resentment, anger and discontent. The issue was raised in several meetings, public speeches and deputations. A few demands were, however, made and these were Turkish independence and autonomy, revival of Thrace, Smyrna, Adrianpole and other regions of Asia Minor.

At this juncture, the involvement of the government became an outrageous phenomenon. The official machinery used numerous oppressive measures to suppress

9

The *Swaraj*ist Interlude

When the nationalist leaders surveyed the political scenario following the suspension of non-cooperation in the spring of 1922, they discovered that the countrywide agitation initiated by Mahatma Gandhi in the autumn of 1920 had suddenly been reduced into a fragmented and disorganised force. That matters had come to such a pass was hardly surprising.

To suggest a way out of the predicament, the Congress created a committee, called the Civil Disobedience Enquiry Committee, to review the events of the past two years and to chalk out an appropriate line of action. Its members were unanimously of the view that it was inadvisable to launch a fresh civil disobedience movement in the existing circumstances. Some of the members of the committee, the so-called 'no-changers', were against entry into the legislatures. Others who were called 'pro-changers' considered that it was advisable, indeed, necessary to contest elections for entry into the legislatures, if only with the objective of wrecking them.

A New Nationalistic Strategy

C.R. Das, who, along with Motilal Nehru, spearheaded the step for a new nationalist strategy, put the case for council entry, forcefully in his presidential address before the Gaya session of the Indian National Congress in December 1922. Defining nationalism as a process "through which a nation expressed itself and finds itself", Das explained the freedom movement as the 'great purposeful unfolding' of the political destiny of India. That this 'purposeful unfolding' of the national destiny was to be achieved through peaceful non-cooperation, the novel weapon of struggle fashioned by the Mahatma, Das argued, was a matter on which no one had any doubts. The Constitutional Reforms of 1919 were designed with a view to frustrate the movement for *swaraj*. However, consistently with the principles of non-cooperation, it was incumbent upon all true nationalists to establish control over the legislatures through the electoral process, and then to destroy them.

Notwithstanding the communication skill with which C.R. Das and other *Swaraj*ists presented the case for a change in nationalist strategy at the Gaya Congress, they were unable to convince a majority of the leaders who had responded to the Mahatma's call for non-cooperation in 1920. In view of this, they formed a new organisation called the 'Congress Khilafat Swaraj Party', with C.R. Das as the president and Motilal Nehru as the general secretary. The Swaraj Party, as it was popularly known, announced its overall loyalty to the creed of the Mahatma. But instead of seeking freedom through boycott, it sought to sabotage the British *Raj* by obstructing the conduct of business in the new legislatures, which had come into being as a result of the Reforms of 1919.

Although C.R. Das was the president of the Swaraj Party, he was so deeply involved in the political goings-on of Bengal that the affairs of the party at the national level were largely left in the hands of Motilal Nehru. The election manifesto of the new party, which was issued in October 1923, projected the *Swarajists* as "a party within the Congress, and as such an integral part of the Congress". Instead of depending on the boycott of the institutions created by the British *Raj*, the *Swarajists* were prepared to carry the struggle into the enemy's camp by entering the councils. The dynamic campaign conducted by the *Swarajist* leaders in 1923, and the popularity of their stance with the electorate, were admirably reflected in the impressive support which they won in the elections.

The strength of the Nationalist Party in the Central Legislature made its presence felt at the very commencement of the new session. The constellation of political groups, which had been brought together by the skillful leadership of Motilal Nehru, embarked upon a well-organised campaign to wrest political control from the British Government. The opening salvo was fired by a private member who moved a resolution recommending the appointment of a Royal Commission to review the Constitution of 1919 in such a manner so as to secure for India the status of a self-governing dominion within the British Empire. As was to be expected, this demand was promptly rejected by Sir Malcom Hailey, the spokesman of the British Government in the Central Legislature, who argued that the Constitution of 1919 had provided for a machinery of review after a decade in 1929. Moreover, he opined that the Constitution of 1919, upon which Hailey had taken his stand, was a piece of legislation designed for the sole purpose of foiling the aspirations of the people for political liberty. But if it took an awkward position, then Motilal declared, 'we shall, like men, stand upon our rights and continue to be non-cooperators'.

With the victories which the Swaraj Party and its allies won over the British Government in the Central Legislative Assembly, the *Swarajist* stock held high esteem in nationalist circles. Consequently, C.R. Das and Motilal Nehru made a renewed attempt to win over the Mahatma to their viewpoint. However, for Gandhi, non-violence was a philosophical truth to which he was deeply devoted; and the strategy and tactics of non-cooperation were inextricably linked to his overall view of the human condition. Later in the year he reached an agreement with C.R. Das and Motilal Nehru, whereby their party became an integral constituent of the Indian National Congress. This agreement, which signified a closing of the nationalist ranks, was eventually sanctioned at the Belgaum session of the Indian National Congress in December 1924 which was held under the presidentship of Mahatma Gandhi.

The ideological differences between different constituents of the Nationalist Party were greatly heightened by the constitutional privileges enjoyed by the Viceroy and the provincial governors under the constitution of 1919.

What Mahatma Gandhi and the no-changers, who supported his stance, had apprehended in 1922, thus actually came to pass. Nationalists who had fought elections and entered the assemblies presumably in order to wreck them found the temptation functioning under the government. In a mass gathering at Trichinopoly on 17 August 1920, he said, "Law courts are one of the greatest symbols of power."[9] Gandhi made it clear further: "We shall promote arbitration courts and dispense justice, pure, simple home-made justice, *swadeshi* justice to our countrymen. That is what suspension of practice means."[10]

The power of government depends on its courts. Through courts it punishes the guilty and it is thro' them that civil disputes are settled, and in this way the government acquires control over the people.

Dr. Rajendra Prasad explains in his *Autobiography* that 'one of the principal items on our programme was the establishment of *panchayats*, which we fulfilled in a great measure. We set up a number of *panchayats* which began settling disputes effectively. At one place, the *panchayat* acquired so much authority that it worked almost like a regular court of law. People filed cases and paid court fees. Most of the decisions were accepted by the people and only in some cases did trouble arise. There were two difficulties. One was that the people began to bring in long-standing disputes to the *panchayats*. If the *panchayats* rejected them as being time-barred, the people bitterly criticised the *panchayats* as being no better than other courts. On the other hand, if the *panchayats* took up the disputes and gave their decision there was no means of enforcing it against the parties concerned. Another difficulty was that social boycott was resorted to as punishment, and, though we discouraged this, our directives were sometimes ignored and there were occasional clashes with the police."

Gandhi recorded his assessment in *Hind Swaraj* in 1908. "The lawyers have enslaved India, have accentuated Hindu-Muhammedan dissensions and have confirmed English authority. The law's delays and expenses in India were too well-known to need any elaboration." Motilal Nehru, one of the most successful lawyers in the land quoted a proverb to illustrate the ruinous effects of litigation, "*Adalat main jo jita so hara, jo hara, so mara*, success in the court is defeat, defeat is death."

In fact, during 1920-21, the Government of India viewed the movement with much seriousness as it expected troubles in some regions when it gained momentum after the Nagpur Congress. The Congress volunteers showed much enthusiasm and patriotic fervour and their respect for the authority manned by the *Raj* had vanished. In some areas when the situation went out of control and indiscipline had led to violent action, the authorities started to face numerous hazards. The movement posed serious political problems for the Viceroy and other functionaries. Lloyd George, the then Governor of Bombay, expressed concern about the Congress and its movement. About Gandhi he wrote: "He (Gandhi) gave us a scare. Gandhi's was the most colossal experiment in world history and it came within an inch of success." Lord Templewood expressed his anxiety thus: "It looked as if the Government of India would break down for want of the political support to direct it and manpower to work it."[11]

Undoubtedly, Gandhi enkindled the zeal of sacrifice and selfless service, amongst his associates and followers, without adopting any violent means. He made it clear that at a time when the movement touched its zenith. "Man must fill the jails. Men must prove to the Government that the awakening is not confined to a few men but it has permeated the masses, that the spirit of non-violence possesses not merely a select number but that it possesses the best part of India."[12]

The new spirit of nationalism engendered after the First World War was no more seriously concerned with the constitutional reforms, a demand put forward by the Indian National Congress during the first two decades of the twentieth century. It was now well-prepared for rejection of the *Raj*, considered as 'unwanted' foreign government.

The Congress leadership was quite confident of its strength, mobilisation of cooperation and also about unity of the people of India. It sought the support of teachers, lawyers, doctors, traders, women, students, various other functionaries in the villages, priests, *ulemas* and cultivators. In August 1920, Gandhi explained thus: "I believe and everybody must grant that no Government can exist for a single moment without the cooperation of the people, willing or forced, and if people suddenly withdrew their cooperation in every detail, the Government will come to a standstill."

The Indian National Congress firmly believed that its movement was not at all unconstitutional as it was planned as well as executed at various levels in a non-violent manner, without any secret motive behind it. The British government, on the other hand, faced much obstruction in the smooth functioning of the administrative machinery.

The organisation, operation and effectiveness of the Non-Cooperation Movement have met with critical assessment by prominent public figures and political leaders like Rabindranath Tagore, Annie Besant, Surendranath Banerjee, Narayan Chandavarkar and some liberal leaders. Tagore termed the movement as negative and destructive in nature and Banerjea and liberal leaders opined that it was subversive and engendered hatred towards the *Raj*. Annie Besant criticised it by saying that the movement aimed at paralysing the administrative machinery of the government.

The Non-Cooperation Movement generated a sense of new realisation in the minds of the British bureaucracy in India and the Home Government in London. As a result, doubts of varied nature began to trouble them. The results of their economic, cultural, educational as well as administrative policies began to be assailed. The Congress and its policies were highly complex problems which provoked debates at various levels. The political consciousness of the masses had nightmarish effect on the minds of the successive Viceroys in India.

Spoor, a prominent member of the House of Commons, pleaded in favour of the Non-Cooperation Movement thus:[13]

> . . . There was no attempt made, at all events in all that we have heard so far, to meet what some of us regard as the legitimate demands of the Indian people. It is extremely difficult for those of us who have been reared amid the purely materialistic philosophies of the West, to understand, even dimly, the reasoning of the Eastern mind... So it is that this non-cooperation movement is very largely misunderstood, by its Western critics, but we do not get over it by calling it fanatical. We certainly shall not suppress it by imprisoning a few thousands of its leaders. The prison has not yet been built that will enclose an idea for a very long; the gun is not forged yet that can destroy a will, however, it may manifest itself, that is really making for freedom. I know that some

> people imagine that it may be possible to raise a dam that will hold the current in check; but the higher you raise your dam the greater becomes the pressure that is behind it. The great danger is that some day the dam will burst, as certainly some day in India the gaol doors will have to be opened.
>
> You are dealing in India with a terrible force and almost superhuman. The policy of blood and iron can no more bring peace in India that it brought peace in Ireland. It has never brought peace in any country in the world yet. You cannot defeat non-cooperation by it. Personally, I should like to see it defeated, but not by the methods that are being employed by the Government of India, backed by the British Government in this country. You can defeat non-cooperation by preaching cooperation. When I say that, I mean the willing, ungrudging cooperation of British and India on absolutely equal terms in the maintenance of a commonwealth jointly enjoyed.
>
> I do ask Government really to make an attempt to face the real issue. Instead of trying to understand Gandhi we put him in jail. Gandhi rightly understood is far less an isolated leader than the incarnation of what is undoubtedly the popular will. Whether we agree with him or not does not concern my argument but through Gandhi the hope of millions of Indians are finding utterance. We may disagree with his ideas entirely, but it is a profound mistake to imagine that they are merely personal.
>
> Unless there is a rapid change in the whole temper of the relations of Britain and India, India will be lost to Britain and Britain will be lost to India, and one can possibly imagine the magnitude of such a disaster as that... I submit, further that the practical solution of this difficulty is not so terribly hard after all, India simply wants to be master in her own house, and until she is master in her own house there will be no peace.[14]

The observance of strict discipline and non-violent behaviour on the part of the millions of people of India in Northern, Southern, Western, Eastern and Central regions of the country were the preconditions of the typical Gandhian style of initiating an anti-*Raj* movement. This kind of model placed before the masses was like something demanding a very high price on the political plane for achieving the highest political aim for the nation. But this kind of model could not be maintained by the participants in the movement for obvious reasons. A huge country with its teeming millions professing different religions and creeds, engulfed with regional and local issues raised with the bureaucratic repression failed to give what Gandhi desired. Instead he expected that this kind of agitation, a model which he had built up with the cooperation of the masses of India, would definitely act as eye-opener for the *Raj* which would not fail to recognise the great force, strength and power which Gandhi had gained with the mobilisation of a huge following. The Congress leadership was not unaware of the hard fact that the British rulers very firmly embedded in the body politic of our country would not come to negotiation of any kind which would make them to leave the shores of India.

A Glimmer of Hope

The movement sprouted glimmers of hopes and instilled fire and zeal into the inert, passive and demoralised people and galvanised them to put up a brave fight for their political emancipation. It evoked a sense of self-sacrifice and suffering in the people who were hitherto largely 'politically apathetic'.

The aftermath of the movement witnessed a regular programme of social reforms in the society by the efforts of prominent leaders in various regions. The growth of village industry with the introduction of *charkha* and *khadi*, the anti-untouchability measures, anti-drink propaganda, opening of *vidyapiths* and many such measures under the scheme of constructive programme, greatly benefited the underprivileged Indian masses. The movement greatly intensified the spirit of awakening amongst the masses earlier engendered in their hearts by prominent leaders like Bal Gangadhar Tilak, Gopal Krishna Gokhale, Pherozeshah Mehta, Bipin Chandra Pal, Lajpat Rai and others. The national consciousness was thus pervaded in various sections of Indian society which unified them in order to prove themselves as an integrated force for political action in a few years. Evidently, the Non-Cooperation Movement shifted politics from the drawing rooms of the educated and the businessmen only to spread its influence in the countryside to the tillers of the soil.

It was the increasing unrest among the peasants and industrial workers which brought about a change in the Congress attitude of cooperation in 1919 to non-cooperation in 1920. But once the non-cooperation started it galvanised further the agrarian movement which received a boost from the spirit of general defiance unleashed by the non-cooperation campaign of 1920-22.

The idea of jail-going as a volunteer without any second thought in mind amongst the manners at the call of the Congress was an unparalleled phenomenon in this movement. Indeed, the hardships in jails were of no consequence to them and they made it a way of life to bear them with ease.

References

1. Bipin Chandra, *Nationalism and Colonialism in Modern India*, Delhi, 1979, p. 134.
2. See the presidential address delivered by C. Vijiaraghavacharia at Congress session held at Nagpur on 26-31 December, 1920.
3. *Ibid.*
4. *Ibid.*
5. *Ibid.*
6. *The Tribune*, 3 July 1920.
7. *Young India.*
8. *Debates, House of Commons, op. cit.* pp. 372-73.
9. *The Hindu*, 19 August, 1921.
10. *The Hindu*, 13 August, 1920.
11. Templewood, *Nine Troubled Years*, London, p. 42.
12. *Young India*, 15 December, 1921.
13. *Debates, House of Commons*, Vol. 155, June 1922, pp. 598ff.
14. *Ibid.*

Now, this Congress, while reaffirming the resolution on Non-violent Non-cooperation passed at the Special Session of the Congress at Calcutta, declare that the entire or any part or parts, of the scheme of Non-violent Non-cooperation, with the renunciation of voluntary association with the present Government at one end and the refusal to pay taxes at the other, should be put in force at a time to be determined by either the Congress or the AICC and that in the meanwhile, to prepare the country for, effective steps should continue to be taken in that behalf:[5]

(a) by calling upon the parents and guardians of school children (and not the children themselves under the age of 16 years) to make greater efforts for the purpose of withdrawing them from such schools as are owned, aided or in any way controlled by Government and concurrently to provide for their training in national schools or by such other means as may be within their power in the absence of such schools;

(b) by calling upon students of the age of 16 and over to withdraw without delay, irrespective of consequences, from institutions owned, aided or in any way controlled by Government, if they feel that it is against their conscience to continue in institutions which are dominated by a system of Government which the nation has solemnly resolved to bring to an end and advising such students whether to devote themselves to some special service in connection with the non-cooperation movement or to continue their education in national institutions;

(c) by calling upon trustees, managers and teachers of Government affiliated or aided schools and Municipalities and Local Boards to help to nationalise them;

(d) by calling upon lawyers to make greater efforts to suspend their practice and devote their attention to national service including boycott of law courts by litigants and fellow-lawyers and the settlement of disputes by private arbitration;

(e) in order to make India economically independent and self-contained by calling upon merchants and traders to carry out a gradual boycott of foreign trade relations, to encourage hand-spinning and hand-weaving and in that behalf by having a scheme of economic boycott planned and formulated by a committee of experts to be nominated by the All-India Congress Committee;

(f) and generally, inasmuch as self-sacrifice is essential to the success of non-cooperation, by calling upon every man and woman in the country to make utmost possible contribution of self-sacrifice to the national movement;

(g) by organising committees in each village or group of villages with a provincial central organisation in the principal cities of each province for the purpose of accelerating the progress of non-cooperation;

(h) by organising a band of national workers for a service to be called the Indian National Service; and

(i) by taking effective steps to raise a National Fund to be called the All-India Tilak Memorial Swarajya Fund for the purpose of financing the foregoing National Service and the Non-cooperation Movement in general.[6]

Lala Lajpat Rai expressed his unhappiness about the functioning of the council and the role being played by the Indian members whose cooperation in the passage of some Bills was harmful to the interests of the people of India. He criticised the role of Gokhale and Malaviya whose support helped the government in getting through the Press Act and the Defence of India Act. He asserted, "So far the Indian members have failed to influence the legislatures of the country in the fundamentals of Government policy.... Their cooperation has been more harmful than their absence in the Council could have been..."[7]

In *Young India* dated 10 November 1920, the staunch criticism was levelled against the Indian councils by C. Rajagopalachari. He slammed the ineffectiveness of councils to stop the recurrence of the *Khilafat* and Punjab wrongs, unrestrained interference of Indian troops in subjugating other nations, the prevention of the theme of *Swaraj* at all costs, the obstacle in the economic freedom of the people, and to oppose vehemently those elements who raised their voice for the freedom of India.

Councils Boycotted

The boycott of councils was one of the important happenings in the Non-Cooperation Movement. There was a widespread feeling in the Congress circles that the functioning of the councils in different provinces of India did not serve any useful purpose. Besides, the presence of Indian members elected in a complicated indirect political method did not make any headway what was expected of them, i.e., effective opposition to the *Raj*, a strong plea for some more constitutional reforms and inform the government of the inadequacy of the political concessions hitherto granted to the people of India with the passage of Minto-Morley Reforms and Montagu-Chelmsford Reforms.

The non-Brahmin Federation of Presidency passed a resolution in January 1921 "condemning the non-cooperation scheme of Mr Gandhi and the Indian National Congress as calculated to subvert all constitutional agitation and to bring the country to chaos and anarchy and calling on all patriotic Indians to oppose it... (and) six associations representing the depressed classes in the Bombay presidency... urging that non-cooperation aims at the destruction of constituted authority and the withdrawal of British rule to which the progress of the lower classes is entirely due."[8]

Apart from boycott of election to the Legislative Assembly and the provincial council, the boycott of law courts was another noteworthy item in the programme of the Non-Cooperation Movement. The Congress mandate for the boycott of courts was followed by about 1500 lawyers. The prominent members of the bar who boycotted the courts were Pandit Motilal Nehru, C.R. Das, Dr. Rajendra Prasad, Vallabhbhai Patel, Dr. Saifud Din Kitchlew, Pandit Rambhaj Dutt, Asaf Ali, M.R. Jayakar and others who surrendered their lucrative legal profession. The country was profoundly stirred and unprecedented wave of patriotic fervour ran through teeming millions.

Gandhi, himself a barrister, was well-aware of the boycott of the legal institutions of executive office irresistible. The *Swaraj*ists who remained true to their mandate thus found themselves on great risk indeed. However, with C.R. Das no more. Motilal Nehru was quick to see the writing on the wall. He immediately came to the decision that an orderly retreat was necessary. On 8 March 1926, therefore, he led the Swaraj Party out of the Central Legislative Assembly, in order to project that he and his followers would have nothing to do with an imperial government which was so unsympathetic to the popular desire for *swaraj*.

*Swaraj*ist Walk-out

The *Swaraj*ist walkout from the Central Legislative Assembly, in 1926, bears telling witness to the sensitivity of leaders like Motilal Nehru to the winds of change throughout the subcontinent. In 1922, after the gruesome Chauri Chaura incident and the suspension of non-cooperation, the social anger of the people and their desire for a showdown with the British Government called for a programme of action wherein popular sentiment could express itself through militant act. Indeed, it is difficult to resist the conclusion that the period 1922-26 was a sheer trying juncture for nationalists of different persuasions in India. Not only had the agitation started by the Mahatma come to an abrupt end in 1922, but cleavages between different religious communities as well as between different generations of nationalist leaders had become apparent in the body politic. The most alarming development of the period under review was the breakdown of the Hindu-Muslim entente which the Mahatma had so skilfully handled during the purposeful days of non-cooperation. Further it was realised that a new breed of nationalist leaders—represented best of all by radicals like Jawaharlal Nehru and Subhas Chandra Bose—were becoming increasingly vocal of their strategy and tactics. This generation of nationalists wanted to launch a frontal attack on the British Government for a *purna swaraj* or complete independence instead of Dominion Status. Moreover, this generation of political activists also wanted to transform nationalism from a purely political into a social and economic phenomenon. They believed that the resolution of India's political affinity, as well as of her poverty could only be achieved by reorganising the polity on socialist principles, whereby the wealth of the country would be collectively owned and the rewards of labour be distributed between different social classes.

At the same time as he appointed the Simon Commission, Lord Birkenhead, the Secretary of State for India, challenged the nationalist leadership to devise a constitution for India that would be acceptable to all classes and communities in the country. Behind this challenge lay the assumption that the nationalist leadership in India was drawn from an irresponsible body of men; that the people of the country had still to acquire the consciousness of nationhood; that the great religious minorities, the Muslims in particular, would not make common cause with the Hindus in presenting joint constitutional demands before the British Government and last, but not the least, that Princely India remained largely untouched by the forces that were at work in the provinces of British India.

10

Nehru as President

Jawaharlal Claiming Gandhi's Favour

As per existing practice, the election of the president of the Congress started from the middle of every year.[1] In the month of August, the local Congress committees put in their nominations for the presidentship for the Lahore session of the Congress. Mahatma Gandhi's name was recommended by ten committees, Vallabhbhai Patel by five while Jawaharlal Nehru was recommended by three committees.

On hearing from Congress sources about the proposal of his name as president, Jawaharlal Nehru did not appear elated at the decision of the Congress for entrusting him the presidentship of the organisation. On hearing the talk going on in various circles about him, he lost no time in writing to Gandhi on 9 July, 1929. "Regarding the Congress presidentship I think it would be better if you did not write or say anything in public for another month or so. There is no hurry. I am very nervous about the matter and do not like the idea at all. The situation in the country is changing and developing and another month might give us more data to go by."[2]

Vithalbhai Patel wrote to Motilal Nehru, "I have come to the conclusion that in the interest of the cause we all have at heart, it is necessary that Mahatma Gandhi should preside over the deliberations of the Congress. I am, therefore, of opinion that Jawaharlal and Vallabhbhai should retire and help to secure the unanimous election of Mahatma Gandhi."[3] Motilal replied, "As regards the Congress presidentship, there are reasons both for and against Gandhiji taking it up. I have had long talks with him on the subject and I expect he will agree to take it up."[4]

In an article entitled, 'Who Should Wear the Crown' in *Young India*, Gandhi clarified a few fundamental points which instigated him not to accept presidentship of the Indian National Congress. He realised that the occupation of the Congress chair was becoming more and more demanding year after year. This might have been due to the widespread political programme of the Congress and the appropriate dimensions of its relationship with the *Raj*. After the first Non-cooperation Movement, the political complexities had touched its zenith and the Congress had to revise its whole ideology taking into consideration the British policy towards India's national upsurge amongst revolutionaries, appointment of Simon Commission, Hindu-Muslim conflict and the Nehru Report.

Nehru sent a telegram to Gandhi on 21 August 1929, "Beg of you not to press my name for presidentship."[5]

Gandhi explained to Nehru thus on 22 August, 1929, ". . . I felt bound to express my opinion to the committee at Lahore in reply to their wire. It is enough for your self-respect that you do not want the crown. . . . I have simply pressed your name as of a principle. . . . If you are not to be the helmsman, the only alternative I can think of at this juncture is re-election of Father, or failing that, of Dr. Ansari. Can you think of any other name?"[6]

On 28 September 1929, the All India Congress Committee was held at the Ganga Prasad Verma Memorial Hall.[7] The principal item of the agenda was the election of the president at the Lahore Congress, Mahatma Gandhi who was elected, having declined to reconsider his decision in spite of repeated requests.[8] The previous afternoon, members of the AICC met informally at the residence of the Maharaja of Mahmudabad and held an elaborate discussion on the election of the president. Gandhi who took part in the informal discussion but held strongly to his previous decision not to accept the Congress chair. Thus, Pandit Jawaharlal Nehru's election was a foregone conclusion.[9]

Pandit Motilal Nehru next stated that the meeting was arranged specially to elect a president for the forthcoming Congress replacing Mahatma Gandhi who had expressed his unwillingness to accept the office.[10] Before asking the members to propose new names, he invited Mahatma Gandhi to give his reason for the refusal.[11]

Mahatma Gandhi addressing the meeting said that he had intimate discussions on the matter with several members of the AICC.[12] He, in fact, wanted to see if such private discussions could create such an impression on him as to make change him his mind. The discussions, however, brought nothing fresh to light. He would, therefore, adhere to his previous decision of refusing the kind offer.[13] He was well aware of the fact that he was disappointing many friends, well-wishers and supporters.[14] Indeed Pandit Madan Mohan Malaviya had specially come down to Simla to convince him to accept the Congress chair. He felt that his hands were too weak to hold the reins of the Congress.[15] His own view was that the step he was taking was in the supreme interest of the country.[16] He felt that he would serve the Congress more perfectly if he were out of the presidential chair.[17] He further asserted that it should never be mistaken that there would be any lack in his devotion to the cause of the Congress party.[18]

After such explanation from Mahatma Gandhi, proposals for new names were invited.

But only Pandit Jawaharlal Nehru's name was duly proposed and seconded. He was thus declared elected amidst loud cheers.[19]

It is interesting to note that in 1927, Jawaharlal's candidature for Congress presidentship was proposed in the higher circles of the party and it led to an extensive communication between Gandhi, Motilal Nehru and Jawaharlal Nehru. Ultimately, Dr. M.A. Ansari was declared the Congress president for the Madras session.

On 22 April 1927, Jawaharlal Nehru in a communication from London, with Mahatma Gandhi reacted thus: "I did not send you any cable last week as I could not hit upon a sentence short enough and intelligible enough to convey my meaning. With more thought I adhere to my opinion expressed last week that on the whole it will be better if I am not chosen President. This disinclination is perhaps not due to the reasons you mention. Whether I am President or not I do not suppose I shall keep apart from political activity when I return home. I have begun to feel strongly that a *laissez faire* attitude and trusting to providence to right matters is a very feeble way of combating evil. I do not of course imagine that any individual can do much, but if everyone decided to wait and see, nothing would be done. Here far away from India it is exceedingly difficult to appreciate fully the position at home and I cannot therefore say exactly what I ought to do on my return, although I have general ideas on the subject. Under the circumstances and for the reasons I mentioned briefly in my last letter I do not feel inclined to welcome the proposal about the Presidentship. You and others in India are likely to be better judges. Personally, I should have thought that Ansari would be the best choice."[20]

Gandhi told Motilal Nehru on 19 June 1927:[21] "Things, as they are shaping in the Congress, confirm the opinion that it is not yet time for Jawaharlal to shoulder the burden. He is too high-souled to stand the anarchy and hooliganism that seemed to be growing in the Congress and it would be cruel to expect him to evolve order all of a sudden out of chaos. I am confident, however, that the anarchy will spend itself before long and the hooligans will themselves want a disciplinarian. Jawaharlal will come in then. For the present, we should press Dr. Ansari to take the reins. He won't control the hooligans. He will let them have their way; but he may specialize in the Hindu-Muslim question and do something in the matter. It will be quite enough work for him in the coming year to solve the almost insoluble problem.'

In 1929, Mahatma Gandhi preferred Jawaharlal Nehru ahead of Sardar Vallabhbhai Patel, and by doing so, he strongly indicated in his writings that he had the best choice in doing so. Indeed, he saw in Nehru a hope for the future—a young man with leadership quality who could guide the Congress and the country in the best possible way. Gandhi explained in the AICC meeting held at Lucknow on 28 September 1929, when Jawaharlal Nehru was elected president of the ensuing Lahore session. "I know my name was proposed and elected by a majority of votes, but I find myself quite unfit for such a heavy responsibility, though it is a great honour. . . . I assure you that in every programme adopted by you at the Lahore Congress, I would be with you, I feel I can do more work by not becoming the president of this year's Congress and I assure the house that I am firm on my words of responsibility that I gave at Calcutta . . . . I am not to run away from the coming battle on the 1st January 1930. I shall willingly extend every help in formulating the programme and scheme for Congress work. What I wish from you is to discard this futile mentality that if Gandhi is not on the chair or Motilal not in the front, the Congress would collapse. You should stand boldly on your conviction of heart and push the work ahead."[22]

At another occasion, Gandhi praised Nehru's qualities thus: "He is undoubtedly an extremist thinking far ahead of his surroundings. But he is humble and practical enough not to force the pace to the breaking point. He is pure as crystal. He is truthful beyond suspicion. He is a knight *sans peur, sans reproche*. The nation is safe in his hands."

The choice for the presidential chair was Jawaharlal Nehru who was nearly the youngest President, the Congress ever had. Greatly impressed and influenced by the patriotic fervour of Mazzini, Cavour and Garibaldi, by the writings and speeches of George Bernard Shaw, Bertrand Russel and Keynes and by the worldwide political reverberations of the French Revolution and the Irish struggle for independence[23] he was at that time the President of the Indian Trade Union Congress, Secretary of the Independence of India League and was intimately involved with the youth movement.

After he was appointed General Secretary of the Indian National Congress at its session in Calcutta in 1928, Nehru started organising and strengthening the party at its all levels. This he did by inspecting the Congress provincial headquarters, he himself surveyed half a dozen provinces and extended his advice for their smooth and better functioning.[24] His contact with various sections of Indian communities and regular tours amongst peasants, workers and labourers enabled him to associate them with the Indian National Congress.

To Gandhi, Nehru was the rightful navigator of the Indian National Congress, and he, in fact, wanted to separate him from Subhas Chandra Bose, so that the young leaders who wanted to break away from Britain, could not dominate the decision at Lahore. Gandhi was deeply concerned at Nehru's drift to the far left, as the latter, being strongly attracted to Marxism, was then in his extremist phase. The logic behind such a momentous decision was that the future lay in the hands of the younger generation and in Jawaharlal Nehru, Gandhi found this hope for the future. Pushing aside the arguments of those who feared that this transfer of power from the old to the young might prove disastrous to the Congress, Gandhi asserted, "He (Nehru) is undoubtedly an extremist thinking far ahead of his surroundings. But he is humble and practical enough not to force the pace to the breaking point."[25]

Gandhi, therefore, saddled Nehru with responsibility. Moreover, ". . . it was worth having in the chair a figure of glamour and integrity who would keep active within the Congress, wide following among the students and the intelligentsia."[26] The Viceroy expressed his apprehension and soon informed the Secretary of State, "His selection in any case will give impetus to the left which it may be difficult to control. It would appear at first sight that the youngers have proved too strong for the older school."[27]

Subhas Chandra Bose commented on Gandhi's decision thus: "For the Mahatma, the choice was prudent one, but for the Congress Left Wing it proved to be unfortunate, because that event marked the beginning of a political rapprochement between the Mahatma and Pandit Jawaharlal Nehru and a consequent alienation between the latter and the Congress Left Wing . . . it was essential that he (Gandhi) should win over Pandit Jawaharlal Nehru if he wanted to beat down the Left Wing opposition and regain his former undisputed supremacy over the Congress."[28]

Nehru opined in his *Autobiography*, "I have seldom felt quite so annoyed and humiliated as I did at the election. It was not that I was not sensible of the honour, for it was a great honour, and I would have rejoiced if I had been elected in the ordinary way. But I did not come to it by the main entrance or even a side entrance; I appeared suddenly by a trap-door and bewildered the audience into acceptance. . . . My pride was hurt, and almost I felt like handing back the honour. Fortunately, I restrained myself from making an exhibition of myself, and stole away with a heavy heart."

"Probably the person who was happiest about this decision was my father. . . My election was indeed a great honour and a great responsibility for me."[29]

Regarding the reception of the Congress President at Lahore, *The Tribune* in its headlines reported, "Two Lakhs Join President's Procession: Hurling Sea Of Humanity: Muslims and Hindus Unite: Unbounded Enthusiasm."[30]

The opening of the forty-fourth session of the Indian National Congress was marked with unprecedented enthusiasm. On 29 December, from early morning in spite of the intense cold, scores of people began to congregate at Lajpat Nagar. A host of men worked the whole night to arrange seats to give the final touches to the pandal.[31]

In the middle of December 1929, there were rumours about the programme of saboteurs during the Lahore Congress.[32] This paved the way for every possibility of thinning down of the attendance.[33] The prominent leaders of the Punjab expressed grave concern over these rumours and tried their best to falsify such propaganda being made.[34] The following appeal over the signatures of Maulana Abdul Qadir, Lala Dunichand of Lahore, Dr. Mohammad Alam, Lala Girdhari Lal, Sardar Sardul Singh Caveeshar, Lala Dunichand of Ambala, Maulana Zafar Ali Khan, Dr. Satyapal, Sheikh Serajuddin Paracha, Dr. Kahn Chand Dev, Maulana Habibul Rahman, Lala Pindi Das, Maulana Daud Ghaznavi, Sardar Kishan Singh, Choudhary Afzal Huq, Dr. Parshu Ram Sharma, Mehta Anand Kishore, Nandlal of Jaranwala, Mohamed Abdullah of Ludhiana, Daulat Ram Khanna of Jullundur, Hayat Mohammad, Santram Seth of Amritsar, Haki Nurudin of Lyallpur, Chintram Thapar and Ghulam Mohiuddin.[35]

> We have learnt with deep pain and strong resentment that some of our kith and kin are, at the instigation of interested agencies and persons, spreading baseless and false rumours to scare away the people of the province from attending the forthcoming session of the Indian National Congress to be held at Lahore. Some to them say that machine-guns have been requisitioned and that the whole of Lajpat Rai Nagar will be blown up. Others say that the Congress *pandal* will be bombarded and everybody found in the vicinity will be put in chains. Another rumour is that reactionaries and anti-Congresswallas will smash the Congress *pandal* to pieces.
>
> We earnestly appeal to our countrymen that they should deem it a sacred duty, an urgent obligation and a noble task to attend the Congress session. Even if you have some difference with the Congress, do not stay away. Join the Congress and get those differences adjusted. The Congress is our national assembly. It is striving to win our freedom. It is our common platform, it is our common body. To help the Congress is to help the Motherland and to harm it is to ruin our future. We expect every Punjabi to do his duty. We are fully conscious of the heroic nationalism of our province and we are confident that notwithstanding the persistent efforts of the enemies of the Motherland to injure our cause, the whole of the Punjab will help the Congress with a devotion and zeal the like of which cannot be found anywhere.
>
> Our province is on its trial and we hope to acquit ourselves admirably. The fate of our country is being moulded. Our future is being shaped. Can the Punjab keep away at such a juncture? It is unimaginative that this land of heroes should be found wanting at this hour.
>
> It is needless to mention that we are earnestly working for the success of the session with a devoted heart. We have deemed it our sacred duty to place ourselves unreservedly at the disposal of the Reception Committee, and we all are doing what we can to ensure the success of the Congress. The Congress first and everything else afterwards. We would have been disloyal to our country if

we had permitted our difference to cloud our vision or to prevent us from doing our utmost. At this juncture we know of only one thing, and that is to make a united and combined effort to make the Congress session a brilliant success—a success which it would be difficult to equal, much less to excel.[36]

The Congress is today meeting in an atmosphere charged with momentous possibilities of the future. The long night of political domination and servitude through which the country has been passing stems to have reached its end and the first streaks of dawn are almost visible, heralding the birth of a new India for Indians. The Labour Party in pursuance of its settled and fixed programme of freedom for all has set on the course of its Indian policy with firm and resolute steps and through its responsible spokesman, Mr. Wedgwood Benn, whose name will certainly figure high in the role of that distinguished land of British statesmen whose ensign was human freedom, is sending messages of hope and comradeship that leave nothing to be desired.

Mangal Singh G.O.C. of Congress volunteers at the Lahore session recollected thus: "We recruited about 2,000 volunteers and gave them training. Dr. N.S. Hardiker came there. He sent his men. So we trained them. We had also a Girls' Volunteers Corps in which three Zutshi sisters and their mother, Mrs. Zutshi, took prominent part. Lajyawati and Zutshi were the Lady Commanders. At the Ravi camp, we had a tough time. . . . I was busy in the management affairs to control the situation. The main discussion was about the Independence resolution. At the end, at about 12 o'clock, the resolution was carried. There was a great excitement and joyous celebrations. After that, I requested Panditji to come out and hoist the national flag of Independence. At mid-night, we hoisted the national flag. From there he went to the volunteers' camp, and we had a dance there, Pathan dance particularly; for the whole night singing and dancing went on. Nehru also danced with us."[37]

The following is the province-wise break-up of delegates who attended the Lahore Congress.[38]

N.W.F.P.	40
London Branch of Congress	2
Punjab	400
Andhra	101
Maharashtra	86
South African representative	1
Karnataka	36
Ajmer	75
Delhi	61
Sind	76
Bombay	19
Gujarat	68
Representative from Japan Branch	1
UP	543
Bengal	77
Bihar	282

Utkal	14
Burma	43
Assam	8
Tamilnadu	148
C.P. Hindustani	55
C.P. Marathi	29
Kerala	8
Berar	25

References

1. The Congress session was mostly held in the month of December.
2. *Gandhi Papers:* GSS, Serial No. 15417.
3. *Motilal Nehru Papers*, V.J. Patel to Motilal, 20 July, 1929.
4. *Motilal Nehru Papers,* Motilal to V.J. Patel, 31 July, 1929.
5. *Gandhi Papers:* Serial No. 15496.
6. *The Collected Works of Mahatma Gandhi,* Vol. XLI, p. 314.
7. *The Tribune,* 30 September, 1929.
8. *Ibid.*
9. *Ibid.*
10. *Ibid.*
11. *Ibid.*
12. *Ibid.*
13. *Ibid.*
14. *Ibid.*
15. *Ibid.*
16. *Ibid.*
17. *Ibid.*
18. *Ibid.*
19. *Ibid.* Sherwani opined that Congress was greater than Mahatma Gandhi, and when he was offered the national Crown, he refused. 'The Congress Crown would never go abegging'.
20. See Gandhi-Nehru Correspondence, Gandhi Smarak Sangrahalaya, Serial No. 12752.
21. *The Collected Works of Mahatma Gandhi,* Vol. XXXIV, Delhi, 1969, pp. 30-31.
22. *The Collected Works of Mahatma Gandhi,* Vol. XLI, pp. 482-83.
23. Tiber Mande, *Conversations with Mr. Nehru,* London, 1956, p. 15.
24. *A.I.C.C. Papers:* File G-68, 1929.
25. E.M.S. Namboodiripad, *The Mahatma and the Ism,* Delhi, 1958, pp. 49-50.
26. S. Gopal, *Jawaharlal Nehru: A Biography,* Vol. I, 1889-1947, London, 1975, p. 137.
27. *Halifax Papers.* Viceroy to Secretary of State, 11 October, 1929.
28. Subhas Chandra Bose, *The Indian Struggle, 1920-42,* Bombay, 1967, p. 169.
29. Jawaharlal Nehru, *An Autobiography,* New Delhi, 1962, pp. 194-95.
30. For details see *The Tribune,* 27 December, 1929. It gives a complete description of the President's reception and the procession through the main bazaars of Lahore.
31. *The Tribune,* 31 December, 1929.
32. *The Tribune,* 18 December, 1929.
33. *Ibid.*
34. *Ibid.*
35. *Ibid.*
36. *Ibid.* For full details of the appeal see *The Tribune,* 18 December, 1929.
37. Transcript of interview with Mangal Singh in the Nehru Memorial Museum and Library, New Delhi.
38. *The Tribune,* 4 January, 1930. For more details see S.R. Bakshi, *Nehru and the Lahore Congress.*

11

The Civil Disobedience Movement

While Motilal Nehru and the senior Congress leaders who had rallied around Mahatma Gandhi put in all their efforts in order to devise a constitution for India which would resolve the communal problem, they were equally concerned about the climate of opinion which was forming around the younger generation of nationalists. This generation was not only reaching out to a new ideology as the basis of the struggle for freedom but it was also impatient of the comparatively moderate strategy and tactics to their seniors and sought to launch forthwith a frontal assault on the British Government in India.

Jawaharlal Nehru's attempt to formulate along novel lines the ideological promises of the freedom struggle in India came at an appropriate moment. As suggested earlier, the movement led by Gandhi during the years 1920-22 had attracted in great numbers the intelligentsia, as well as a sizeable section of the popular urban and rural classes to the cause of Indian freedom. The unique notion of militant non-violence, as advocated by Gandhi, had appealed enormously to the people of India. Yet the manner in which Gandhi suspended the non-cooperation movement in 1922 and the communal strife which showed up immediately afterwards, caused a good deal of resentment among the leaders as well as intelligentsia.

There were, needless to say, no easy answers to such questions. However, as a result of his explorations in socialist ideology, Jawaharlal Nehru was able to frame a number of propositions of crucial significance to the freedom struggle in India. He now realised the liberation movement in India as part of a wider struggle between the capitalist forces of Europe, on the one hand, and the subject societies of Asia and Africa, on the other. He also recognised an organic relationship between the capitalist mode of generating wealth, which characterised the countries of western Europe. Within India, British imperialism had conjured into existence a strong bond of interest with the feudal classes and with sections of the industrial and commercial bourgeoisie. The relationship of superordination and subordination between Britain and India provided the basis of the strategy and the tactics which the Congress could profitably follow in the anti-imperialist struggle. In the first instance, it was necessary for nationalists in India to establish links with other nationalists in Asia and Africa with a view to devise a common stance in the worldwide struggle against imperialism.

The mood of radical militancy in the younger generation of nationalists was reflected equally in the person of another rising star in the political horizon of India.

Subhas Chandra Bose came from a distinguished family of Bengal and after a brilliant career at Calcutta University, he proceeded to Britain for pursuing higher studies and competed successfully for the Indian Civil Service in 1920. However, due to the influence of Vivekananda, he was attracted towards the freedom struggle and in 1921, after quitting the Civil Service, he entered politics under the aegis of C.R. Das.

Bose's distinction as an intellectual, his electrifying presence and his superb organisational skills assured for him in a short span of time a very prominent position in the political scene in Bengal. Following the death of C.R. Das in 1925, Bose became a commanding figure in the Pradesh Congress Committee, devoting special care to the organisation of the youth as well as of the working class of Bengal. Towards the end of the 1920, he was one of the few young leaders with a reputation that had spread to the far flung areas of the subcontinent.

Although Bose did not share, in a formal sense, the radicalism of Jawaharlal Nehru, he fully endorsed the hostility of the latter towards the British Government. Indeed, as already emphasised, Jawaharlal Nehru and Subhas Chandra Bose articulated the sentiments of an entire generation of the intelligentsia in their stance towards imperialism and in their desire to seek battle with the British Government with the objective of liberating India. At the Madras session of the Indian National Congress held in 1927, Jwaharlal Nehru sponsored a resolution asserting that "The Congress declares the goal of the Indian people to be complete independence."[1]

The Struggle for *Purna Swaraj*

In view of the significant role which Motilal Nehru had played in preparing a constitutional blueprint for India, he was the obvious choice for the presidency of the Congress in 1928. As time approached for the annual session at Calcutta, Motilal sensed the opposition which had crystallised to the constitutional future which he dreamt for the country. Two important sections of society, the Muslim community and the younger generation of nationalists, appeared to have serious reservations about the political future held out in the Nehru Report. The prominent younger members of the Subjects Committee, Jawaharlal Nehru and Subhas Chandra Bose, were unrelenting in their demand for *purna swaraj*. As it was, what emerged in the Subjects Committee was in the nature of a compromise. The Nehru Report was entirely accepted but on Dominion Status, the Congress leadership decided that if the British Government had not conceded his demand within the span of a year, they would initiate a movement of civil disobedience to win *purna swaraj* for the country. The settlement adopted in the Subjects Committee was then approved in the open session of the Congress.

The developments within the national movement were followed with keen interest by the Viceroy, Lord Irwin, who was fully conscious of the winds of change that were blowing across India. However, as Irwin's perception of politics in India sharpened, he realised the extent to which the yearning for freedom had taken firm root in the country.

He came to the conclusion that it was necessary for the British Government to publicly declare that India would in due course, acquire a status comparable in all respects to the status of the self-governing dominions of the British Empire. Irwin grasped the opportunity offered by a vacation in Britain, in the middle of 1929, to place his views before the British Government. Following these deliberations, Irwin, on his return to India, declared that the British Government would soon arrange a Round Table Conference in order to discuss the political future of India; and further that 'the entire issue of India's constitutional progress' was 'the attainment of Dominion Status'.[2]

Irwin's declaration of 1929 came at an appropriate time. It obliged Mahatma Gandhi, Motilal Nehru and other heavyweights of the Congress to re-examine the decision of the Calcutta Congress, that if Dominion Status was not bestowed upon India by 1929, then an agitation for *purna swaraj* would be launched against the British Government. As a result of the conciliatory gesture by the Viceroy, a group of nationalist leaders assembled at Delhi. At this meeting, Mahatma Gandhi, Motilal Nehru and their peers differed from Jawaharlal Nehru and Subhas Chandra Bose, who demanded an outright rejection of the Irwin declaration. However, the Delhi Manifesto, which was drafted by the more moderate nationalists, supported the proposal for a Round Table Conference on the understanding that such a "conference is to meet not to discuss when Dominion Status is to be established, but to frame a scheme of Dominion Status."[3]

The annual session of the Indian National Congress, held in Lahore in December 1929, under the presidentship of Jawaharlal Nehru was mostly a vindication of the stance adopted by the radical nationalists vis-à-vis the liberation movement. Indian National Congress held out a socialist analysis of the world situation as well as of the Indian problem, before the assembled delegates.

The deliberations of the Lahore Congress thus placed huge responsibility upon the Mahatma. The decision to entrust the destiny of India at such a crucial juncture to Gandhi, the veteran of numerous non-violent struggles, also reflected the root of sentiment within the premier national organisation.

As the sole leader of a *satyagraha* reflecting the aspirations of a nation of 400 million, Gandhi selected his battleground and his tactics with utmost care. The decision to focus upon salt, a commonplace product of daily consumption, may at first blush appear quixotic in the extreme. Yet it was a product closely linked to the daily life of millions of peasants and workers, for whom the burdensome salt tax was a sum of considerable magnitude.

The civil disobedience movement which Gandhi started at Dandi on 6 April 1930 through the symbolic manufacture of salt from sea-water, was to some extent similar to the movement which he had organized a decade earlier. In 1920, the movement was articulated by the Indian National Congress through organised networks in cities, townships and *casbahs* in a substantial proportion. Moreover, Gandhi's moral authority and the grievances which affected the peasantry and tribal communities across the country where the Congress lacked a formal presence, simultaneously triggered off mass agitations which had very little to do with non-violence as a mode of political action. If industrial and commercial participation strengthened the nationalist movement, then the alienation of the Muslim leadership and the Muslim community, with the exception of Khan Abdul Ghaffar Khan and the Pathans, was a source of serious disquiet to Gandhi and his associates.

The widespread support which the civil disobedience movement received from different classes and communities across the subcontinent greatly undermined the authority of the British Government over India.

Notwithstanding the complexity of the nationalist struggle over which he presided, the Mahatma was able to reach an understanding with the Viceroy, which is generally known as the Gandhi-Irwin Pact. According to this settlement, the Congress was to suspend the civil disobedience movement. Moreover, the Congress was to participate, along with the representatives of other Indian political parties, in the scheme of constitutional reforms to be discussed at the Second Round Table Conference: "Of the scheme thus outlined federation is an essential point; so also are Indian responsibility and reservations or safeguards, in the interests of India, for such matters as, for instance, the defence; external affairs; the position of minorities; the financial credit of India; and the discharge of obligations.[4] The Mahatma had to concede several significant points to the Viceroy. Moreover, radical and young nationalists within the Congress or outside it looked upon the conduct of negotiations with the British Government as politically inexpedient.

Gandhi attended the Second Round Table Conference as the single representative of the Indian National Congress and the most outstanding leader from India. In a memorable speech before the Federal Structure Committee of the Round Table Conference, Gandhi spelt out the genuine issues facing the assembled delegates, British and Indian, in terms which admitted of little ambiguity. Narrating the sources of the populist strength of the Congress, he stated thus:

> The Congress is, if I am not mistaken, the oldest political organisation we have in India. It has had nearly fifty years of life.... it is what it means—national. It represents no particular community, no particular class, no particular interests. It claims to represent all Indian interests and classes....
>
> [Above] all, the Congress represents, in its essence, the dumb, semi-starved millions scattered over the length and breadth of the land, in its 70,000 villages, no matter whether they come from what is called British India or what is called Indian India. Every interest which, in the opinion of the Congress, is worthy of protection, has to subserve the interests of those dumb millions; and so you do find now and again apparently a clash of interests. But, if there is a genuine real clash, I have no hesitation in saying on behalf of the Congress, that the Congress will sacrifice every interest for the sake of the interest of these dumb millions. It is, therefore, essentially a peasant organisation, and it is becoming so progressively.[5]

The 'fast unto death' which Gandhi undertook in September 1932 to effect a cancellation of the Communal Award, as it concerned the Depressed Classes the very foundations of Hindu society. The leaders of the community were startled at the prospect of the Mahatma sacrificing his life in order to atone for the indignity and worse which the Hindus had heaped upon the Depressed Classes over the centuries. Prominent personalities like Tej Bahadur Sapru, Madan Mohan Malaviya, M.R. Jayakar and a host of others, representing orthodox or liberal opinion within Hinduism, immediately arranged a conference to seek a solution to the problem.

The Mahatma's fast unto death aroused the conscience of diverse sections of Hindu society. 'To find a parallel for [*sic*] the anguish of September, 1932 we have to go back to Athens twenty-three hundred years ago when the friends of Socrates surrounded him in a prison and urged him to escape',[6] observed authorities through a civil disobedience movement of national proportions. Gandhi was unequivocally supported by radical nationalists like Jawaharlal Nehru in his assessment of British imperial purpose and British constitutional design. Yet some of the Congress leaders opined that it would hold little importance to wage an endless struggle against British imperialism; and they wanted to utilise the possibilities thrown open by the constitutional system created in 1935. The prospect of autonomy within the provinces, these leaders argued, provided the Congress with an opportunity to promote national interests at the same time as it prepared itself for a final attack on the British Government.

References

1. Quoted in B. Pattabhi Sitaramayya, *The History of the Indian National Congress,* Vol. I (1885-1935).
2. Statement by Lord Irwin, 31 October 1929: *Speeches and Documents on the Indian Constitution 1911-47,* Vol. I, Selected by M. Guryer and A. Appadorai, Oxford, 1957, p. 225-7.
3. *Collected Works,* Vol. XLII, p. 81.
4. Pattabhi Sitaramayya, *op. cit.,* p. 436.
5. Speech by M.K. Gandhi before Federal Structure Committee, 15 September 1931: *Collected Works,* Vol. XLVIII, pp. 13-20.
6. Pyarelal, *op. cit.* p. vii.

12

Arrangements for *Satyagraha*

The Lahore session of the Indian National Congress concluded on 1 January 1930 with a well-planned political programme for its leaders to execute in the near future. The initial step for its execution was taken by Motilal Nehru who addressed letters to the Congress members of the central and provincial legislatures asking them to send their resignations to the Viceroy in obedience to the resolution passed at Lahore. Motilal Nehru himself soon resigned and other front rank leaders like Vithalbhai Patel, Seth Govind Das, D.P. Mishra, V.V. Jogiah. B.N. Chaudhury and Lala Bodh Raj also submitted their resignations.

Through his writings in *Young India*, Gandhi projected the technique of *satyagraha* and the immediate objective of his party. In his article, 'The Cult of the Bomb', in the issue of *Young India*, 2 January 1930, he asserted, "We are now entering upon a new era. Other immediate objective and not our distant goal is complete independence.... It is not enough that we drive out Englishmen by making their lives insecure through secret violence. That would lead not to independence but to utter confusion. We can establish independence only by adjusting our differences through the evolving organic unity amongst ourselves."

Gandhi put forth the programme to be observed by the people on 26 January 1930. He said that it was easy enough to pass the independence resolution at Lahore but it was not easy to achieve it even by 'peaceful and legitimate means'. The people should know, realise and appreciate the message of the Congress and they must know what independence meant and what it was likely to cost. He advised house to house visits with an aim to distributing leaflets and delivering the message of the Lahore Congress to the masses.

Meanwhile, a draft declaration for 26 January was announced stating the inalienable right of the people to be free as well as have the necessities of life so that they might have maximum opportunities of growth. If any government deprived them of these basic rights and oppressed them, they had the right to change it. It explained precisely that the British government in India had not only deprived the Indian people of their freedom but also exploited the masses and ruined India economically, politically, culturally and spiritually.

Economically, the revenue derived from the people was far more of all proportions. Village industry, such as hand spinning had been destroyed thus robbing the livelihood of peasants idle for at least four months in the year. Politically, India's stature had never been so reduced as under the British regime. Disarmament had made the people unmanly and the presence of an alien army of occupation, employed with deadly effect to suppress the people, the spirit of resistance, had made them think that they could not look after themselves or put up a defence against foreign aggression, or even defend their homes and families from thieves, robbers and miscreants.

". . . We will therefore prepare ourselves by withdrawing, so far as we can all voluntary association from the British Government and will prepare for civil disobedience, including non-payment of taxes. We are convinced that if we can but withdraw our voluntary help and stop payment of taxes without doing violence, even under provocation, the end of his inhuman rule is assured. We therefore hereby solemnly resolve to carry out the Congress instructions issued from time to time for the purpose of establishing *purna swaraj."*

With these ideas in mind, by hoisting the national flag the ceremony was performed and Independence Day celebrated throughout India on 26 January 1930 with unprecedented pomp and fervour. Lakhs of people resolved to attain complete independence.

In Lahore, thousands of people hoisted national flags over their houses and shops with unprecedented enthusiasm. At almost all college hostels including the hostels of the Government College, Hailey College and S.D. College, national flags were hoisted with due ceremony and the students made merry. Independence resolution was read out by Maulana Kasuri, Lala Dunichand, Maulana Zafar Ali Khan, Dr. Kahn Chand Dev, Dr. Paras Ram and Parvati Devi, daughter of Lala Lajpat Rai.

Calcutta celebrated Independence Day with the hoisting of flags in every park and ward of the city and over all national institutions. The impressive ceremony was the rally of the Bengal volunteers. Another impressive feature was the participation of a large number of ladies and girl students headed by Mrs. J.M. Sen Gupta, wife of the Mayor and Lotika Bose.

Enthusiastic scenes marked the observance of Independence Day at Chaupati in Bombay, where a day long programme started with the hoisting of the national flag at the Congress House by Kamaladevi Chattopadhayay. Top-notch local leaders like K.F. Nariman and Abbas Tyabji addressed the meeting. The celebration of Independence Day at Ahmedabad began with the unfurling of national flag on the grounds of the Gujarat Pradesh Congress Committee. The Gujarat leaders including Vallabhbhai Patel, addressed the masses to get ready, even to die for the honour of the national flag.

At Allahabad, Jawaharlal Nehru hoisted the national flag with much fervour in the Purshottamdas Park. While addressing the audience, he said. "The pledge has been taken. The flag of freedom has been hoisted. Let no one who had taken pledge forget it or weaken in his resolve and let no one do anything which may bring dishonour to the national flag. Let us work to redeem the pledge with a right goodwill."

Delhi was not lagging behind either. It celebrated the Independence Day by carrying out the programme of the AICC. Dr. Ansari unfurled the national flag in the Queen's Garden in the presence of a mamnoth gathering of about 50,000. Besides the observance of Independence Day in other important cities like Patna, Peshawar, Multan, Agra, Banaras, Nagpur; Hyderabad got special mention in the newspapers. Even the small towns and bigger villages all over the country reverberated with an unparalleled enthusiasm.

The Akali leader, Master Tara Singh exhorted the Sikh Councillors to resign their seats from the legislatures and gave an impetus to the increasing tide of national movement.

The celebrations in various parts of India reflected the enthusiasm and the keenness for *satyagraha* amongst the Congress leaders and the *en masse*. The people of towns and villages were greatly encouraged by the subsequent speeches and press statements of Gandhi who assumed the responsibility of leading the nation against the British *Raj* for the second time.

Lord Irwin's immediate reaction to the celebrations of the 26th January was diplomatically mild but firm. He tried to direct the attention of the nation to his attempt to bring about unity among the Indian leaders on the constitutional issue. Keeping this view in mind, he made a statement in the Legislative Assembly that leaders of different shades of opinion would be summoned in any case at an early date. He declared that its main object would be to harmonise opinion in the country. He made no reference to political prisoner and only asserted that the prosecutions would be confined to men preaching treason or men who challenged the British authority established by law.

A few leaders of national repute including Motilal Nehru, Jawaharlal Nehru, Sardar Patel and Jamnalal Bajaj held a special meeting with Gandhi at the Sabarmati Ashram where a strategy of approaching Viceroy to find a way out of the stalemate with government before launching Civil Disobedience was decided upon and a draft ultimatum to be sent to the Viceroy by Gandhi in the event of failure of talks was prepared.

In the Congress camp, according to its mandate, 172 members of the legislatures resigned by February 1930, the Central Assembly contributing 21 and the Council of States 9, Bengal Provincial Council 34, Bihar and Orissa 31, CP 20, Madras 20, UP 16, Assam 12, Bombay 6, Punjab 2 and Burma 1. Those who did not resign and appeared for re-election were asked to resign their party offices or face disciplinary action.

Taking the letter of Gandhi as a menacing singal for the British in India, the Viceroy immediately geared up the whole machinery of the government. In his telegram to the Secretary of States on 5 March, the Viceroy communicated to him the contents of his letter and stated that Gandhi "contemplates action which is clearly bound to invoke violation of law and grave danger to public peace."

The stage was thus set for salt *satyagraha* by Gandhi and the Viceroy's plan for conviction was unflinching in his resolve. He thus formulated his plan for the salt *satyagraha* by violating the 'obnoxious' salt law. According to this plan, salt was to be manufactured and government salt depots were to be picketed by the *satyagrahis* all over the country as a mark of wrath over the British administration.

The march on foot by Mahatma Gandhi followed by seventy-eight Congress volunteers was the most significant event in the history of the breach of salt law in our country. It was started in accordance with a fixed schedule to be carried on by them during the long journey ending at Dandi. Indeed, it was a disciplined company of non-violent *satyagrahis* who were to present a model of *satyagraha* which later on converted into a bigger movement at all-India level.

Out of twenty-five days which the journey took, the *satyagraha* group had walked for twenty-two days, excluding three days of Gandhi's silence. On his way, Gandhi passed by forty villages and towns and everywhere he addressed the audience. The entire countryside was awakened to the call of the Mahatma.

At least fifty thousand persons heard his inspiring message to the nation. His speeches were generally impassioned and always brave and there was a tone of pathos which had motivated the listeners. Despite all the fatigue and other adversities of the journey, he never allowed himself any comfort that was denied to the last man of his 'army'.

After Gandhi had addressed a meeting at Dandi on 6 April 1930, about two *tolas* of salt which was taken by him in the morning and also cleaned by him was auctioned for Rs. 525 to one Seth Ranchhodlal Shodhan, a mill-owner of Ahmedabad.

Gandhi's on-foot march from village to village through Gujarat where his influence was next to none aroused considerable interest and excitement. It had, in fact, appealed to the imagination of people who were emotionally swayed by the dramatic turn of events throughout the occasion. Thus, salt became the symbol of India's will to freedom.

North India

The Civil Disobedience Movement received wide response in regions like the North West Frontier Province, the Punjab, the United Provinces, Delhi, Ajmer and Central Provinces and Berar. In all these regions, the *satyagraha* activities of the Indian National Congress were well-planned, well-organised and they included breaking of the salt law, forest laws, picketing in front of liquor shops, foreign cloth shops, boycott of schools and colleges and non-payment of land revenue. Women's active participation was the glaring feature of this movement in Punjab, UP and Delhi. Despite numerous arrests and cases of police brutality, the movement continued unabated till the Gandhi-Irwin Pact was signed.

In the North West Frontier Province, the Civil Disobedience Movement materialised around the dynamic leadership of Abdul Ghaffar Khan who transformed the sturdy Pathans into soldiers of non-violence.[1] He was able to secure the support of the rural as well as urban population of the region and thus came to be known as *Fakhr-e Afghan, Gandhi-e-Sarhad* and *Badshah*—the uncrowned king of the Pathan masses.[2] His popularity or charisma became an important factor in all the national activities and developments in the province.

He visited every village in the province spreading the message of love and labour and bringing socio-political awareness among the masses. They were made aware that the British government was exploiting them and had ruined them politically, economically, socially and spiritually.[3] He flayed the step motherly attitude of the Khans and Nawabs towards their community and the colossal waste of money on garden parties to win the favour of the British masters.[4] In several mass meetings that he addressed anti-British slogans were raised amongst the audience with enthusiasm, gusto and war cry. He gave to his people the message of peaceful resistance and defiance of laws as defined by none other than Gandhi.[5]

Before Abdul Ghaffar Khan could reach Peshawar to give shape to the movement in the urban areas, he was arrested on 23rd April 1930 and brought to Charasada jail.

Meanwhile the agitation commenced in Peshawar. Processions were carried out and a meeting was held at Shahibagh. On the morning of 23rd April 1930, the Congress and *Khudai Khidmatgar* leaders were arrested resulting in a *hartal* in the city. When the mob followed two of the Congress leaders, who were being escorted by the police in Peshawar, the police resorted to *lathi* charge in the streets to disperse them. Seeing the crowd being adamant, the police opened fire to teach them a lesson, although they were strictly adhering to non-violent action. According to the government report, thirty persons were killed and thirty-three were injured.[6] In the opinion of Abdul Ghaffar Khan, however, 200 to 250 persons were massacred.

The Kissakhani Bazaar massacre was followed by organised and unrestrained acts of repression in all parts of the province. All frontline Congressmen were arrested. Schools were closed and educational facilities were withdrawn forthwith.

For a time, strict censorship was imposed. Even letters and telegrams were censored so that people outside the province could not know what was happening in the North West Frontier. Consequently, the split between the Indian and the British accounts on happenings in the region was serious. To alleviate public suspicion and alarm and prevent the situation from becoming anti-British in India, the government appointed the Sulaiman Enquiry Committee. The Congress, in turn, appointed the Peshawar Enquiry Committee headed by Vithalbhai Patel on 14 May 1930.

The Peshawar Enquiry Committee maintained that in the situation that had arisen at Peshawar on 23 April, firing by the armoured cars and the military was totally unjustifiable. The Deputy Commissioner without any warning and without any justification rushed the armoured cars through the unarmed, unresisting and peaceful crowd and thereby killed and wounded twelve to fourteen persons. Had he not done so, subsequent tragic events of the day would not have taken place. The responsibility for all this was entirely on the Deputy Commissioner who had himself created critical situation by his action.

The ruthless suppression of the non-violent movement in Peshawar made this movement more widespread in areas like Kohat, Bannu, Dera Ismail Khan and Mardan where *Khudai Khidmatgars* obeyed the directive of their leader in all sincerity of purpose and courted arrests.

On 1 August 1930, several volunteers were arrested in Turangzai and were sentenced to various terms of imprisonment. In spite of so many hindrances, the *Khudai Khidmatgars* were mustering in thousands from different villages. On 3 August, forty out of a hundred volunteers who had gone for picketing were arrested; beaten and released.

The Frontier people were thus cut off from rest of the world. Visits in and out of the province were prohibited and communications were strictly censored. Still peace could not be restored on the previous. Unrest continued to grow and the British authority became shaky. According to the government's own version, "Probably at no time since British influence was first extended to the Frontier have conditions given cause for such acute anxiety."

On his release, Abdul Ghaffar Khan described the Gandhi-Irwin Pact as a temporary truce and appealed to his people to prepare for conflict to free their land from the rule of *Firangis*.

In the Punjab the movement was launched at Gujranwala by Maulana Zafar Ali Khan, president-elect of the *satyagraha* conference on 6 April 1930. Among the top-notch leaders who attended the conference were Maulana Abdul Qadir, Lala Dunichand, Dr. Satyapal, Dr. Mohd. Alam Raizada, Hans Raj, K. Santhanam, Gopichand Bhargava, Master Tara Singh, Dr. Kahn Chand Dev, Chhabil Das, Lala Pindi Das and Maulana Ata Ullah Shah Bukhari.

On 10 April 1930, a mammoth gathering of the citizens of Lahore was held in the municipal gardens outside Moti Gate under the auspices of the City Congress Committee about the programme of Civil Disobedience that was to be started in Lahore the next day. At least 40,000 persons, including over 1,000 ladies were present in the meeting.

Meanwhile, Amritsar became one of the strongholds of the movement. The Executive Committee of the local Congress appointed a 'War Council' with Dr. Kitchlew as the president. Under his leadership, a very long procession was carried out. In accordance with a decision, all the members of the Bar Association, Amritsar, pledged to wear *swadeshi* clothes. Besides, the Shiromani Akali Dal extended its help to the local 'War Council' with men in matters of picketing. The Viceroy expressed grave concern at the seriousness of situation in Amritsar. In a telegram to the Secretary of State, he stated, "In Amritsar too the situation was threatening."

Similarly, salt was manufactured at Rawalpindi, Jullundur, Ludhiana, Hoshiarpur and other towns of the Punjab. Everywhere there was tremendous excitement and enthusiasm to defy British laws.

Meanwhile, prominent leaders like Dr. Mohammad Alam, Dr. Gopi Chand Bhargava, Dr. Satyapal, Dr. Saifud-Din Kitchlew, Dr. Kahn Chand Dev, Chaudhari Krishna Gopal Dutt, Lala Des Raj and Lala Ram Saran were arrested. Besides, the houses of Congress leaders were searched indiscriminately. But in a few days, when the news of Gandhi's incarceration spread like wild fire in the province, there were *hartals*, processions and protest meetings by Congress leaders and workers in big and small towns.

By the middle of October 1930, the intensity of the movement had slowed down in several districts largely due to the imprisonment of leaders, official oppression, fund crunch, fear of the government and want of direction. The unbearable brutality perpetrated by the police on non-violent *satyagraha* in various towns of the province were forcefully echoed in the Punjab Legislative Council on 25-26 July 1930 by the frontline nationalist leaders. Lala Mohan Lal complained, "The police is using more force in Simla than they ordinarily should: volunteers were beaten. A young boy was pushed down from stairs from Mall and he fell down rolling about 40 steps."

Meanwhile, numerous volunteers for *satyagraha* were recruited in Allahabad, Lucknow, Meerut, Agra, Rae Bareli, Kanpur, Banaras and other towns of UP. The salt *satyagraha* started at Rae Bareli on 8 April 1930. However, no arrest was made. There were loud chants of *Namak Kar Ka Satyagraha* at Tilak Bhavan in the presence of Motilal Nehru, Rafi Amad Kidwai and Mohanlal Saksena. A crowd of 6,000 people gathered on the scene.

Indeed, Jawaharlal Nehru was deeply involved with students, volunteers and provincial Congress Committees in connection with the proper direction, planning and organisation of the movement. He advised the students, "... When the country is in a state of war with the government and large number of leading men are in jail, should not the young men throw in their lot with those who are leading the campaign? ... The best thing would have been a general strike of the students for a period of say, six months or a year."

On 14 April, Nehru on his way to Raipur to preside over the CP Hindi Provincial Conference was arrested in the train at Cheoki, taken back to Allahabad, tried, and sentenced to six months' simple imprisonment under Section 9 of the Salt Act.

After a few weeks, Jawaharlal was released on completion of the term of imprisonment. He delivered a speech on 12 October 1930 at Purshottam Das Park in Allahabad in front of a mammoth gathering. He advised the people to carry on the programme of breaking salt law and picketing in front of liquor and foreign cloth shops. He was, therefore, again arrested and sentenced to two years' rigorous imprisonment.

By the middle of October 1930, the Congress changed its tactics. Realising that the incarceration of its leaders might lead to disorganisation of the movement, it was decided to keep key men out of prison, leaving the open defiance of laws mostly to women and children.

In Delhi, initiative to start the National Week, 6-13 April 1930 to inaugurate the Civil Disobedience Movement was taken by Madan Mohan Malaviya, Devadas Gandhi, Lala Deshbandhu Gupta, Faridul Ansari along with other high profile leaders. Their operations for breaking salt law started from Shahdara.

Meanwhile the news of Gandhi's arrest spread like wild fire in the city. Parties of Congress volunteers were despatched throughout the city at once to stage *hartal* which became almost universal. The rumour that a Sikh woman was killed while picketing the courts, led to a violent scuffle between the Sikhs and the police. The police opened fire and as a result a Muslim youth was killed.

By the last week of July 1930, the sale of foreign cloth had almost stopped in Delhi. All the Hindu foreign cloth dealers had either got their existing stock of foreign cloth sealed by the Congress Committee or had reached to an agreement with it not to sell for two months. Even after the expiry of that period, they had agreed not to sell any foreign cloth without its consent.

The police raided and searched the office of *The Hindustan Times*, but nothing incriminating could be found. Its editor J.N. Sahni was arrested and sentenced to six months' rigorous imprisonment and a fine of Rs. 500. Another newspaper that suffered was the *Qaumi Gazette,* the editor of which Shafi was arrested. A notice was served upon the Jamia Millia Press to deposit a security of Rs. 2,000 under the Press Act. The press suspended its work.

In Ajmer the movement was inaugurated by Devadas Gandhi. On 5 April, he came to Ajmer, addressed the local people and advised the volunteers to work wholeheartedly in the campaign. Pandit Haribhau Upadhyaya emerged as the 'Captain' of the Civil Disobedience Movement in this region-and also became the first provincial 'Dictator' in Rajasthan. He paid visits to a number of sub-urban villages and within a week collected Rs. 3,000 and enlisted about 50 volunteers.

With the assuming gigantic proportion, censorship was imposed on the press and other communication media. Telegraphic news both private and press, going out of Ajmer were censored. The Press Ordinance was promulgated. Despite all these precautions and preventive measures, the Civil Disobedience Movement went apace unchallenged. Nearly all the caste 'Panchayats' enjoyed upon their members to use only *swadeshi* cloth. Some young volunteers in Ajmer and Beawar, by dint of vigorous picketing, forced some temple authorities to allow entry only to the *swadeshi* wearers in their temple premises.

The Central India which included Central Provinces and Berar comprised a triangular region, mid-way between Bombay and Bengal. The Civil Disobedience Movement expanded throughout the region with headquarters in British districts. The campaign began in a historical setting. A largely attended political meeting was held under the presidentship of Seth Govind Das. After a few days amidst scene of unprecedented mass enthusiasm, the leaders, with a batch of five volunteers broke the salt law by manufacturing salt before a public gathering of 15,000. After that, the president auctioned the salt prepared by the volunteers and sold one *tola* of it for Rs. 111.

In Nagpur, the nerve-centre of the Central provinces, 'National Week' was celebrated under the auspices of the City Congress Committee. Public meetings addressed by the local leaders were held in various parts of this town. Processions with the national flags were also taken out. *Khadi* was hawked in the bazaars and streets, and appeals were made to enlist as volunteers in large numbers for the freedom movement. The members of the 'War Council' undertook their tours in various districts to enlist public support for the movement and make it broad-based.

The Provincial War Council at Jabalpur set up Hindustani Salt Factory and a Seditious Literature Publishing Company to intensify the political activities of the *satyagrahis*. Another organisation, Boycott of British Goods League, was formed with M.V. Deshmukh as its president to give an impetus to the constructive programme of the Congress and provide a source of livelihood to the poor rural masses.

Another notable feature of the freedom movement was the boycott of elections to the provincial legislative council. On 10 November, when polling was in progress, volunteers picked the polling centres. Among those arrested at the polling booths was Ansuyabai Kale who was picketing the Town Hall centre. The boycott of elections was success. Only 1,137 voters out of a total of about 25,000 in the city used franchise. Elsewhere also, the polling booths were picketed. Thus, polling was dull and it evinced clearly Congress influence on the voters. The government recklessly arrested volunteers without caring to see whether they actually took part in the picketing or not.

Another significant item in the boycott programme was the boycott of census. This was carried on by the 'War Council' under the presidentship of Vaidyaraj Shivbalak with assistance from the volunteers. Seven of them who prevented the people from giving information to the census collectors were arrested. Many people either did not give information to them or gave improper information. The census report of year 1931 is therefore incomplete, inaccurate and undependable.

The condition of political prisoners in the jails of the Central Provinces was like that of those in numerous other jails across the British Indian provinces. They were served half-cooked rotten food hardly suitable for human consumption. They were made to break stones and the amount forced on them was beyond their capacity. If they failed to finish it, they were given solitary confinement, flogging, caning or further tasks for disobedience of orders.

The medical facilities provided to them were horribly inadequate. The services of the physicians were refused to Seth Govind Das, Ravi Shankar Shukla, M.V. Abhyankar and D.P. Mishra, though they were suffering from multiple physical ailments. Not even the change of climate through transfers from one jail to another suitable for their health was allowed to them.

Under these hardships and in the midst of horrible repression, the movement continued unabated in the Central Provinces till the Gandhi-Irwin Pact was signed on 5 March 1931. The most conspicuous result of this movement was the spread of political awakening in the rural areas and Adivasi regions where forest *satyagraha* had taken roots. The freedom struggle received a mass base and popular support. In the urban areas, the movement for freedom was made much exhilarating by organising processions, holding meetings, hoisting of national flags, flouting salt law, picketing of liquor shops, and educational institutions, boycotting foreign cloth and foreign dress and popularising *khadi*.

During the peak of the movement, the people courted arrests peacefully, filled the jails, withstood all kinds of sufferings without any resistance. They showed remarkable discipline and spirit of cooperation to work under their leaders. An undying patriotic fervour was kindled in them. They could discriminate between what was beneficial to the country and what was harmful to it. Thus, they developed moral courage to front laws which were not in the best interest of the people. They became conscious of their right to liberty and freedom and developed confidence in the efficacy of the weapons they would use for its fulfilment.

West India

In West India, the Civil Disobedience Movement was launched with great enthusiasm. Impressive scenes were witnessed at Hajiali Point. Mahalaxmi on 7 April, when the first group of the Bombay civil resisters led by K.F. Nariman broke the salt law in the presence of 10,000 spectators.

Similarly, the sale of contraband salt was arranged in every part of Ahmedabad city. The volunteers sang in chorus, "We have broken the salt law which will wreck the Empire". When the magnitude of the movement started to spread, Muslims labourers and factory workers also joined it in large numbers. Muslims of eight different localities of the town decided to organise boycott of all persons who took liquor.

The adoption of the cult of *swadeshi* was insisted upon as vehemently as the defiance of salt law. On 4 May, Gandhi addressed a letter to the Viceroy informing him about his programme of setting out for Dharasana along with his companions and demanding possession of the salt works. The daily reports of police brutality on *satyagrahis* in Bengal, Bihar, Orissa, Uttar Pradesh, Bombay, Delhi, Madras, Peshawar and Karachi prompted him to state, "I had hoped that the Government would fight the civil resisters in a civilised manner.... Bones have been broken, private parts have been squeezed for the purpose of making volunteers give up, to the Government valueless, to the volunteers precious salt."

Under these circumstances, Gandhi's arrest had become imminent. The Viceroy knew that the arrest might soon have to be done but he was anxious to defer it as long as he could. Irwin was, however, aware of the fact that his action in not arresting Gandhi was 'very illogical' but at the same time he was sure that it had helped the government. He also thought that Gandhi's plans were 'at present' uncertain but it was clear that he did not intend to remain immobilised by the seashore.

Mass protest against Gandhi's arrest on 5 May was demonstrated by a peaceful *hartal* the very next day all over the country. All the mills were to work as usual on 7 May. However, the instructions of the Congress, the mill workers of the Sholapur Spinning and Weaving Mill left their mill on 7th May for a mass protest march. To have control over the situation, the government handed over the charge of the situation to the military authorities which was followed by the imposition of Martial Law.

The Viceroy showed much concern over the existing political happening during his inaugural speech in the Legislative Assembly on 9 July 1930, "In my judgement and in that of my Government, it is a deliberate attempt to coerce established authority by mass action and. . . . it must be regarded as unconstitutional and dangerously subversive."

Women were active participants throughout the movement in this Presidency. They played vital role in this crucial phase of national politics. In Bombay, ladies teamed up with men in producing and selling the contraband salt. A batch of ladies, including Kamaladevi Chattopadhayay, Nirmala Devi, Mrs. Mushruwala and Ratanben Mehta sold the contraband salt in the suburbs of Bombay.

The raid on Wadala Salt Works was successfully attempted on 1 June by about 1,500 volunteers as a challenge to the 'British anarchy', in accordance with the Bombay *Congress Bulletin* of 31 May. This raid was a logical follow up of the defiance of the salt law. The government reacted promptly and eleven women including Mrs. Lilavati Munshi, seven Sikhs, one Gujarati and two Deccani women were placed under arrest and detained at Wadala.

The position created by the arrest and imprisonment of Gandhi was distinctly and forcibly pressed upon government and was distinctly in terms of the resolutions adopted by the 14-member strong representative body at a meeting held in Bombay on 6 May 1930 under the presidentship of Walchand Hirachand. These institutions vociferously protested "against the arrest and internment, without any trial and without any term fixed, of Mahatma Gandhi in an arbitrary manner and under an absolute regulation."

On 23 May, the commercial community in Bombay took out a huge procession as a mark of protest against the arrest of Gandhi. The meeting viewed with repugnance the methods adopted by the police and the military against the unarmed and peaceful public of Sholapur, Dharasana and Wadala, and condemned declaration of martial law at Sholapur.

"The mill industry is faced with a grave economic peril, which may culminate into a great hardship if political atmosphere remains strained and conciliation of national demand is not effectively met with."

The front line advocates and solicitors of the presidency headed by Bhulabhai Desai pledged to support the cause of the movement. The Parsi community also resolved to work for the same. The Muslim support was by no means large. They hesitated between cooperation and non-cooperation with the movement. Due to confusing and controversial propaganda about the Civil Disobedience Movements every section of urban Muslim kept out of the movement, but they did not provide any support to the government.

In October 1939, the government declared the Congress illegal and arrested Morarji Desai within just 10 days of his assuming charge of the Provincial Congress Committee. He was tried for violating the law and was sentenced to three months' rigorous imprisonment with a fine of Rs. 300. He was kept in the Sabarmati Jail in Ahmedabad where the quality of food served to the prisoners left much to be desired.

The other focal point of the West India Civil Disobedience Movement was the peasants' refusal to pay land revenue in the Bardoli *taluka* of Gujarat, where the land assessment had been soared by 30 per cent in 1926. Against this heavy assessment, Sardar Patel had launched a no-tax campaign in 1928 as a result of which the increased assessment was reduced merely to 6 per cent. This, however, did not allay the agrarian unrest and resentment.

Overwhelming East India Support

In the eastern region of India, the Civil Disobedience Movement gained momentum following the termination of the Dandi March and Gandhi's call for the commencement of the *satyagraha*. The intensity of the movement in entire region depended largely upon the organisation of local leadership and the enthusiasm shown by the *satyagrahis* at various levels.

In Bengal, unprecedented response was visible everywhere.[7] To celebrate the first day of the National Week, a largely attended public meeting was held on 6 April, 1980 at the Sharddhanand Park in Calcutta presided over by Lalit Mohan Das, who made a fervent appeal to the people to join the national movement and make it a total success.[8] Another mammoth public meeting was held at Wellington Square under the chairmanship of J.M. Sen Gupa who exhorted the people to participate in the movement in large numbers and continue the fight in a non-violent way, till salt tax was abolished.

The salt *satyagraha* spread to other parts of the province in no time. In areas like Noakhali, Khulna, Barisal, Tamluk, Midnapore, Pichchabani in Contai, Mahisbathan in 24 Parganas and Chittagong salt law was broken.[9] In fact, in all the sea bordering districts preparation for breaking the salt law was in progress.

The Civil Disobedience Movement dominated the imagination of the people. Boycott of foreign goods reached new heights. Funds for the Congress were raised by street and house-to-house collection. Students and teachers of private schools and colleges came out in large numbers as aspiring volunteers.[10] Women picketers also came to the fore. The Calcutta Corporation became the virtual gold mine of the Congress.

The no-tax campaign was another important episode in the Civil Disobedience programme. Leaflets were printed, issued and systematically 'broadcasted' for the purpose. The affected areas were Contai and Tamluk in Midnapore, Arambag in Hooghly, Bishnupur in Bankura, Balurghat in Dinajpur, Nababganj and Vikrampur in Dacca, Maju in Howrah and Mahisbathan in 24 Parganas.[11]

On 1 July 1930, at an All Bengal Students Convention held in Calcutta, Mrs. C.R. Das called upon the students to suspend their studies and join the 'national war' of liberation. Consequently, many institutions were closed for indefinite period just after their reopening and others which remained open were picketed.

The Muslims did not stay away from the Civil Disobedience Movement. The Bengal Muslim Political Conference held at Chittagong on 21 April 1930, offered whole-hearted support to the brethren goal of independence for India and urged the Muslims to cooperate in every legitimate way possible for the attainment of *swaraj* and democratic freedom. This appeal drew response from upper and middle class Muslim men and women who were quite active in Noakhali, Tipperah, Tripura, Bagura, Senhatta, Gaibandha and a few other towns. The students of the Dacca University did not lag behind in their contribution in the struggle for independence. They illuminated their hostels on 26 January 1931, hoisted the national flag and paraded the streets chanting *Bande Mataram, Gandhiji ki Jai* and *Alhah-o-Akbar.*

Newspapers and periodicals also could not escape from the repressive policy. The publication of the *The Hindu Punch Satyagraha News, Swadhinata, Muktivani, Jagaran, Ananda Bazar Patrika, Liberty, Advance, Bangavani* and *Swatantra* was stopped and their editors and printers were prosecuted.[12]

In Bihar, the foundation for a widespread Civil Disobedience Movement was prepared by Rajendra Prasad, after the Lahore Congress, on his returning from Ahmedabad in February 1930. In the first week of April, about 5,000 volunteers joined in and subsequently, their numbers gradually increased manifold. The *Satyagrahi* reported, "the thrill of a new hope, the surge of a new aspiration,' the pursuit of noble idea and romance of a new sacrifice that surcharged the atmosphere."[13]

Champaran and Saran first came in the field to start salt *satyagraha.* In the former district, the first *jatha,* consisting of thirteen enthusiastic *Satyagrahis,* was led by Bepin Behari Varma, president, District Congress Committee and chairman, District Board. Salt Law was broken in several *thanas* like Jogapatti, Motihari, Dhaka, Sugauli, Govindganj, Raxaul and Bettiah.

In Patna, the salt *satyagraha* was inaugurated on 16 April 1930 at Nakhas Pind. A rally of *satyagrahis* led by Ambika Kant Sinha, secretary. District Congress Committee, protesting against the prohibitory order, was obstructed by the police and cane-charged by an European Sergeant.

In other districts also, the enthusiastic leaders and volunteers carried on the movement peacefully in accordance with the salt programme unperturbed by official reaction and arrests, atrocities, fines and imprisonments. On the arrest of Jawaharlal Nehru *hartals* were observed in most of the towns.

Charkha came in greater vogue. *Takli* was popularised and people in large numbers took to spinning with a view to promote the cause of *swadeshi.* Many cloth merchants agreed not to indent foreign cloth in future.

In fact, Rajendra Prasad was the guiding force behind movement all over Bihar. His arrest at Chapra on 5 July 1930 while on tour and imprisonment for six months in the Hazaribagh jail gave fresh momentum to the movement.

In Orissa, the Civil Disobedience Movement was launched under the able leadership of Gopalbandhu Chaudhuri and Acharya Harihar Das, who led 12,000 persons to Mahanadi river *ghat.* For a month, Inchudi became a place of pilgrimage where people from far flung areas came with foodstuff, rice, vegetables, *ghee* and other eatables for *satyagrahis.*

The no-tax campaign was another weapon in the armoury of the *satyagrahis.* The movement took the form of non-payment of the *chaukidari* tax. Volunteers were trained for the purpose and were posted at different centres under the overall charge of Nabha Krishna Chaudhary, acting secretary of the Utkal Provincial Congress Committee. This caused alarm in government circles. After a week of the declaration of the movement, the officials rounded up the *satyagraha ashrams* throughout the district and began arresting their inmates and the prominent leaders associated with them.

In Assam, the students contributed a great deal to the success of the *satyagraha.* They took part in large numbers in *hartals*, political demonstrations and the Congress propaganda. The government, therefore, proposed measures to tighten their hold over the educational institutions in order to suppress the movement and keep the students under control. As a protest against the official restriction imposed on the government educational institutions, a number of schools on the model of Kamrup Academy at Gauhati were started by the public at various places, such as Texur, Dibrugarh and Barpeta. They were filled up at once by a vast number of students who had refused to give undertaking in the government and government-aided schools. As a result, the circular was relaxed and it was made possible for the students to re-enter those schools. Tarun Ram Phukan, an MLA, and president of the Assam Youth League, greatly influenced the student community to obtain its participation in the movement for independence.

Women of this province also came out breaking shackles to participate in the movement. At Dhubri, members of several social organizations, such as the *Dhubri Mahila Samiti* and the *Chhatri Sangha,* i.e., the Lady Students Union met at a joint platform on 14 April 1930 to protest against the arrest of J.M. Sen Gupta in Bengal. Some prominent ladies like Chandraprova Saikiani and Durgaprova Bora also came forward to take part in the picketing before the Cotton College.

The number of political prisoners in the jails of Assam by 15 November 1930 was 415 including 4 Muslims. Out of them 413 were males, 2 females and 44 juveniles under seventeen.

Wholehearted Response from South India

No less enthusiasm to participate in the Civil Disobedience Movement for the cause of independence was witnessed in south India. The people of all the regions under British rule such as modern Tamil Nadu, Karnataka, the coastal belt of Andhra Pradesh and Kerala, which constituted the Madras presidency overwhelmingly responded to the call of Gandhi and joined the movement in April 1930.

The salt *satyagraha* campaign opened in Madras city on 13 April 1930 after informing about it to the government.[14] The beach meeting held on 15 April as a mark of protest against the arrest and conviction of Jawaharlal Nehru surpassed the previous meetings in point of number and enthusiasm. The rally was represented by people of all castes and communities and a large number of ladies many of whom offered their members for the *satyagraha* campaign at the end of the meeting.

Salt law was broken everywhere in the presidency, wherever it was possible to manufacture salt, even in a token form with tremendous enthusiasm. The government of Madras took some measures to subdue the activities of the *satyagrahis.*

Like Gandhi's march in the west India, C. Rajagopalachari undertook a protest march on foot from Trichy to Vedaranyam in Tanjore district to break the salt law in the coastal region. The march came to an end on 28th April, the 16th day. Rajagopalachari was arrested at Vedaranyam and sentenced to six months rigorous imprisonment and a fine of Rs. 200 or three months in lieu thereof.

In the Karnataka region, the movement was initiated by R.R. Diwakar, N.S. Hardikar, Gangadhar Rao Deshpande, Hanumantha Rao Kaujalgi, among others. The Karnataka Provincial Congress Committee formed a *satyagraha* committee to bring about awareness among the people and instigate them to the national effort. The committee issued pamphlets indicating its aims and non-violent methods to be used by the *satyagrahis* during the struggle. The response to this call was prompt. Young men came in large numbers to the *satyagraha* centres established at Hubli, Belgaum and Mangalore.

The movement was launched with full enthusiasm by the manufacture of salt at various places in the region. At Belgaum, Gangadhar Rao Deshpande manufactured salt before a mammoth gathering of volunteers on 6 April 1930, and later on, auctioned it at a fancy price. The government viewed activities with concern and arrested all the four leaders the next day. As a result, *hartals,* protest meetings and rallies followed in many towns of Karnataka.

The scope of *satyagraha* was, however, extended to the boycott of foreign cloth, picketing of liquor shops, disobeying the forest laws and non-payment of taxes. In the boycott of foreign cloth, women took a prominent part under the leadership of Smt. Yesodabai Shenai. The anti-liquor campaign went on successfully, Liquor and *toddy* shops were picketed everywhere. Though beaten by the police, hundreds came forward to take part in picketing and, as a result, *toddy* sales slumped considerably.

Then came the no-tax campaign which capped the climax. As it was more widespread, it entailed considerable hardship and sufferings. Leaders like R.R. Diwakar, D.P. Karmarkar and Krishnabai Panjikar toured the villages and called a conference of all the leading men of the villages at Surve. Volunteers began to pour in from all places.

The forest *satyagraha* was taken up in the *talukas* of Sirsi and Siddapur. Sardar K.A. Venkatramiah came to Sirsi in June and made necessary preparations for it. It was started on 4 August. The *sandal* trees were cut down; the wood was loaded in carts, and everyone carried branches of those trees; the return procession gave the appearance of a moving forest. The wood was brought to Sirsi and auctioned. Every village of the two *talukas* followed this example.

The government, however, could not allow people to flout the forest laws with immunity. The *satyagrahis* began to be arrested and were prevented from entering the forests. Despite these arrests and display of force by the police, the forest *satyagraha* continued as enthusiastic villagers were ready to break law even at the risk of arrest.

In the Telugu-dominated regions, the Andhra Provincial Congress Working Committee appointed Deshbhakta Konda Venkatappaya as the 'Dictator' of the movement. He founded a districtwise organization for the movement, each district having a 'Dictator' and a 'War Council' to assist him. People from all communities including Adi Andhras and Christians joined the movement and contributed voluntarily to the maintenance of camps set up for *satyagrahis*.

Raiding of salt depots was another glaring feature of the salt *satyagraha*. The raids were organised on the line of the Dharasana raid in the Bombay province. Once such attempt was made on 20 May 1930 and others on the following three days by several groups of volunteers on Naupada Depot in Ganjam. Even though their leaders were arrested just before the raid, they did not stay away from the movement.

In the Malayalam-speaking parts of the presidency, the Kerala Youvak Sangham played a vital role in intensifying the movement and carrying it to the remotest rural areas. Its members traversed on foot through the north Malabar region doing intensive propaganda work and breaking the salt law at several coastal stations they visited.

A *Swadeshi League* was formed with Kalappan Nair, the president of the Kerala Pradesh Congress Committee. Its main aim was to promote the use of *charkha* and *swadeshi* and discourage people to use foreign cloth. The president along with some members met the leading piecegoods merchants of Calicut and discussed with them the modalities of boycott of foreign goods. Besides, a committee consisting of purely lady volunteers was formed for the purpose of spreading the gospel of *swaraj* through *takli* and *charkha* to every home.

Besides, the picketing of foreign cloth shops was also intensified in this region. On the refusal of cloth dealers to stop the sale of foreign cloth, shops were picketed at Calicut and the *Khadi Prachara Sangham* was established which did much propaganda for *swadeshi*.

Other organisations which also contributed during the movement were *Kerala Vidyarthi Sangham, Desa Sewaka Sangham, Bal Bharatha Seva Sangham* and *Balika Bharatha Seva Sangham*. They sustained the movement and ameliorated the cause of freedom both in towns and villages.

Like other provinces, students in South India too did not lag behind in their contribution to the national struggle. The main centres of their activities were Dharwar, Guntur, Nellore, Madras and Trivandrum, where they staged peaceful protest rallies with national flags in their hands and shouting pro-independence slogans, highlighting the names of Gandhi and other leaders; hoisting national flags at school and college premises, staying away from attending classes as a mark of respect and devotion to the national leaders arrested during the movement; propagation of *swadeshi* by wearing *khadi* clothes and Gandhi caps and defiance of the orders of the educational authorities.

The growing nationalist fervour among the students alarmed the government. The Department of Education issued circulars warning the students that any active participation in the Congress activities would be dealt with punitive measures. But this did not yield any positive result. Their participation in the movement went on increasing and the salt *satyagraha* reached its zenith.

In the deltas the Congress managed financial support from the upper classes. Wealthy land holders and prominent traders, particularly those hit by the price fall, poured funds into the Congress coffers. The Rice Mill Owners Association of Guntur too financed local Congress movement, the Masulipatam Grain Merchants Association provided a free mess for Congress volunteers.

To discourage the increasing tide of *khadi* production, the Divisional

Superintendent of Railway issued instruction not to book *khadi* yarn for transport. To impose these and other prohibitory orders and warnings, the strength of the police force and the reserves at its command were considerably increased in all the coastal districts. The police started conducting house searches at all hours of the day and night and tore to pieces the photos of Gandhi and other national leaders. They burnt national flags in the presence of the public.

Generally speaking, there was much police brutality and high handedness at almost all the places in south India. Section 144 was clamped almost everywhere in urban areas.

By 15 November, 1930, the total number of *satyagrahi* prisoners in the Madras presidency jails assumed a large figure. The overwhelming majority of these political prisoners were kept in 'C' class where they had very hard times.

References

1. Foreword of Zakir Hussain in Pyarelal, *Thrown to the Wolves: Abdul Ghaffar Khan,* Calcutta, 1966.
2. Jawaharlal Nehru, *An Autobiography,* London, 1962, p. 278.
3. Home Pol. File 18/VII, 1930.
4. Home Pol. File 11/3, 1930; and Home Pol. File 18/3, 1930.
5. *Ibid.*
6. *Debates, Legislative Assembly,* 14 July 1930, Vol. IV, p. 237; Home Pol. File 30/3, 1931.
7. *AICC Papers:* File G-86 (KW) (1), 1930.
8. *The Amrita Bazar Patrika,* 7 April 1930.
9. *AICC Papers:* File C-86, 1930; and *Young India,* 1 May 1930.
10. Home Pol. File 201/40, 1930.
11. *Young India,* 26 June 1930.
12. Home Pol. File 173/11-V, 1930; and *Young India,* 8 May 1930.
13. *The Searchlight,* 9 April 1930.
14. *The Hindu,* 14 April 1930. For details see S.R. Bakshi, *Gandhi and Civil Disobedience Movement,* Delhi.

13

Gandhi-Irwin Pact and Repression

New Viceroy and Repression

Gandhi's six demands which were the absolute minimum for the peace negotiations to begin were general amnesty; immediate end to repression; restitution of all seized property; reinstatement of all government servants punished on political grounds; liberty to manufacture salt and enquiry into the excesses committed by the police. Five of these demands were subsequently consented by the Viceroy.

During his negotiations with Irwin, Gandhi, however, concentrated more on the salt issue than any other matter. He believed that the violation of the salt law was moral protest and that no settlement could be honourable that did not concede the right of the people to the use of this nature's gift.

Throughout his negotiations with the Viceroy, Gandhi seemed to be in a propitiatory mood. The response of the Viceroy, on the other hand, far exceeded his expectation. So settlement seemed to be in the horizon.

On 2 March 1931, the Viceroy informed the Governor of Bombay, "Mr. Gandhi was not very difficult on majority of the points at issue but on picketing, salt and police enquiries, we have had a long tussle which is not over yet." But overall, he became quite hopeful of the satisfactory conclusions of the agreement.

The Prime Minister of England expressed his heartiest congratulations on the result of conversations with the Viceroy and to Sapru, Jayakar, and other Indian friends of the Round Table Conference who had assisted him. The cabinet in England approved of all the clauses of the Gandhi-Irwin Pact and expressed heartiest congratulations to the Viceroy through the Secretary of State.

In terms of prestige, the Pact appeared to be a triumph for Gandhi. He had realised that at a time, when the enthusiasm and energy for the movement were fading, suffering of the people had reached its saturation point, and general exhaustion of Civil Disobedience Movement was perceptible, it would not be a bad strategy to have a break to recorder. Moreover, the settlement opened options for Gandhi to go to the second Round Table Conference to test the sincerity of British professions, and also to see if something constructive could be achieved for the Indian people, who had full faith in the Mahatma's leadership.

The Gandhi-Irwin Pact had conceded very little to the Congress so far as its fundamental demand for independence was concerned. Gandhi, however, praised the heroic efforts of the masses who had undergone untold sufferings and advised them, during the coming days, to wait, watch, pray and hope.

After about three weeks of the signing of the Pact, when the Indian National Congress held its annual session in Karachi under the presidentship of Vallabhbhai

Patel on 29 March 1931, there was a note of great outrage and deep resentment at the execution of Bhagat Singh and his colleagues, Raj Guru and Sukhdev and of grief by the news of Ganesh Shankar Vidyarthi's martyrdom at Kanpur.

The Congress adopted its twenty fundamental objects, including lowering of land revenue by 5 per cent and total relief to small owners. It vociferously agitated for the reduction of land revenue all over India and particularly in the United Provinces, North West Frontier Province and Gujarat.

However, the attitude of the British bureaucracy, towards India did not change even after the signing of the Gandhi-Irwin Pact which held much promise. The official machinery under the new Viceroy did not implement its terms. In the name of law and order, Section 144 was clamped and *lathi* charges to disperse people still continued. The Congress criticised pinpricks and even Gandhi regretted the lukewarm response of the government.

Nothing was done to improve the lot of the peasantry growing under severe economic depression. The grief-stricken peasantry voiced protest against heavy rent and their inability to pay it. Agitation appeared in several centres in some name or other, and the government used them as accessible pleas to resort to its usual methods in the name of law and order. Fresh ordinance were also promulgated and enforced and these activities of the government amounted to a clear breach of settlement.

Gandhi returned from the Round Table Conference to Bombay on 28 December 1931 disheartened and sullen. He was apprised of the new development in the country during his brief absence from India. In his long conversation, Bose explained to him the seriousness of the situation in Bengal and impressed upon Gandhi the necessity of a militant programme. He urged him to visit Bengal and see things himself.

In the United Provinces, the agricultural decline of 1929 and onwards had come as a climax to a steadily worsening situation by 1931. Explanation of cultivators by landlords had multiplied in number and *zamindars* oppressions increased. Rent went up so that the tenantry found itself placed on the verge of starvation.

To tackle the increasing problem, the government of UP, appointed a committee consisting of three officials and twelve non-officials to advise readjustment of rents and revenue based on the fall in prices of agricultural produce.

However, the Congress propaganda against the British revenue policy continued unabated. In October, Sunderalal circulated a novel scheme for a parallel government to be brought into force in the Bara Banki district by 15 November 1931. He asked the peasants to turn their women as the back-up leaders so that when men were arrested, they could lead the *kisan* movement.

On 1 February 1932, Mrs. Vijayalakshmi Pandit, Miss Krishna Nehru and Mrs. Norab Banerjee were tried for flouting prohibitory orders and participating in a meeting and rally on the 'Independence Day' and each one of them was sentenced to one year's rigorous imprisonment. Mrs. Pandit was also slapped a fine of Rs. 300.

The prominent Congress leaders were rounded up by the police under the guise of the new ordinances. Arrests were made in Allahabad, Kanpur, Lucknow, Banaras, Agra, Rae Bareli and other towns of the United Provinces. At Lucknow Congress, leaders like Gopinath Srivastava, Mrs. Suniti Mitter and Sri Krishna received sentence of three months rigorous imprisonment and to pay a fine of Rs. 200 each.

By February 1933, there was a lull in Congress activities. Besides, the Gandhi Day celebrations in the cities and towns on 4 February 1933, sporadic attempts to hold non-rent meetings in rural regions and reports of picketing in three or four districts particularly Allahabad, Kanpur and Agra, there was hardly any vigorous political activity in UP. There was also no much obstacle in the sale of foreign cloth where cloth dealers chose to stock it.

With the Civil Disobedience came a flood of nationalist pamphlets, leaflets and posters which earned the wrath of the government. The police took action against a number of presses for publishing objectionable material. The works of Marx and Lenin, biographies of De Valera and Mazzini and eulogies of Bhagat Singh, Raj Guru, Sukhdev and Chandrashekhar Azad inspired students. Besides, a large amount of literature was distributed in the rural areas as well. In Kanpur and Rae Bareli, the Congress distributed large number of leaflets for carrying on no-rent campaign.

In Punjab, the Civil Disobedience Movement was resumed with renewed enthusiasm in January 1932, following the arrest of Mahatma Gandhi and Sardar Patel. Before anything significant could be done by the Congress leadership and the volunteers at Lahore and elsewhere, the Punjab Government bolstered with the new ordinances by Lord Willingdon, declared the PPCC an unlawful political organisation.

In Delhi, the local Congress leaders carried out the programme of the Congress in their respective localities. They took out protest rallies, picketed foreign cloth shops, wine shops, banks, post offices; took out *prabhat pheris*, hawked *khadi;* encouraged people to spin and propagate *swadeshi*. The celebration of Gandhi Day, Independence Day and other days of national importance was observed by the local leaders. Women also participated in these programmes.

There were random arrests and *lathi* charges on non-violent volunteers by the police. Their condition in the local jail was deplorable on account of unpleasant atmosphere in it. Some women were also convicted, the prominent being Smt. Satyavati, grand-daughter of Swami Shradhanand.

In west India, the Civil Disobedience Movement was resumed following the arrests of Mahatma Gandhi and Sardar Patel. A series of simultaneous arrests were quickly made including V.J. Patel, K.F. Nariman, and Nagindas Master, Mrs. Avantika Bai Gokhale, Sardar Jamiat Singh, leader, Bombay Sikh Association, Pandit Mukund Malaviya, Syed Abdulla Brelvi, editor of *Bombay Chronicle*, K.M. Munshi, Lilavati Munshi, Jamnadas Dwarkadas, S.K. Patil and Mrs. Captain.

To douse the fire of the movement, the government also raided the Congress *ashrams* and arrested the inmates therein. The *Satyagraha Ashram* at Wardha was a witness to police raid and its inmates were arrested. The tri-colour flag found flying on the *ashram* was pulled down.

The Congress *satyagrahis* took out rallies, picketed foreign cloth shops and wine shops and disseminated the gospel of *swadeshi* amongst the people. They succeeded in getting the foreign cloth sealed in possession of the dealers at Hyderabad.

Following the arrest of Gandhi and other members of the Congress Committee, all Congress organisations including the youth wings were banned by the government in the Central Provinces. The government issued instructions to its officials for confiscation of the property and funds of all these organisations; infliction and realisation of fines on persons arrested for Civil Disobedience.

Protest meetings were held at many places to condemn the arrest of Gandhi and other leaders of repute. In Jabalpur, the movement began in a unique way. A public meeting was held at Tilak Maidan at which Seth Govind Das and D.P. Mishra were present. It was a 'speechless' meeting on account of a government ban on public speaking: instead the national flag was worshipped and funds were collected for the movement.

The forest *satyagraha* was another feature of the movement in the province. It was launched on 18 March 1932, in the Shahpur Pargana of Betul district under the leadership of Kunjilal, the 'Pargana Dictator'. He guided a party of 200 persons to the government forest and hardly had they cut a few trees when their leader and some of the volunteers were arrested.

In Bengal, towards the end of March 1931, the executions of Sardar Bhagat Singh, Sukhdev and Raj Guru led to a number of processions, *hartals* and meetings at which speeches supporting their deeds were delivered, revolutionary slogans were chanted and violence, bloodshed and revolution were advocated. The Corporation of Calcutta, a Congress-dominated body, adjourned its meeting of 25 March as a mark of protest against the executions. The Congress Press was flooded with tributes to the heroes and martyrs of Lahore.

The following newspapers temporarily stopped their publication when their editors, printers and publishers were charged with the publication of pro-independence items and were also asked to furnish fresh securities along with fines. These papers were *Swatantra, Lokmanya, Swadesh, Hindi, Hindu Punch, Sarbahara, Benu* and *Nayak*

Women were also equally active in the second phase of the movement. They participated in picketing of foreign cloth and wine shops; post offices; promoting the importance of *swadeshi* goods and taking out processions in Patna, Gaya and Monghyr. Some of the prominent ladies arrested amongst them were Smt. Sona Devi, Smt. Thakur Devi, Smt. Murti Devi, Smt. Yasoda Devi, Smt. Anup Devi and Smt. Sushila Devi.

The government not only slapped heavy fines on individuals but also collective and punitive fines on villages and areas which they considered to be recalcitrant. Further, non-payment of fines or other charges often met with confiscation of property, goods of other kinds, money orders and even deposit in the banks of individuals and organisations.

In fact, repression and coercion, in one form or another had been continuing since the truce days of March 1931 to December 1931, under one excuse or another. A reign of terror was unleashed and every conceivable variety of atrocity had been resorted to. There had been indiscriminate *lathi* charges, firing, caning, kicking and stripping naked.

The return of Gandhi from England without earning any political concession for India; the arrests of Jawaharlal Nehru and Abdul Ghaffar Khan; the suppression unleashed in the form of ordinances by Lord Willingdon and the indiscriminate arrests and convictions of Congress *satyagrahis* had their effect in the political firmanent of Assam as well.

Meanwhile, in Karnataka, the Gandhi-Irwin Pact did not materially alter the nature of the struggle. The people of the *taluks* of Sirsi and Siddapur in North Kanara, and Kirekerur in Dharwar district were unable to pay their land revenue on account of lack of rains. They aired their plight to the government and appealed for an exemption from tax payment. The government refused to grant any concession and as a result *satyagraha* was taken up in all the three *taluks*.

The part played by women in the *satyagraha* was remarkable. Their work was confined mostly to picketing, taking part in processions and *satyagraha* before the houses of those who bought confiscated property at government auctions. They were arrested and bore the police brutalities with courage and determination.

The release of the political prisoners in Kerala after the Gandhi-Irwin Pact gave a fresh impetus to the boycott movement and the peaceful picketing of liquor-shops in Travancore, Malabar and Cochin. As these activities were no longer unlawful anybody could picket peacefully without fear of arrest. The members of Yuwak Sangh carried on their activities at several places. These activities enthused even the illiterate masses to participate in picketing. Educated ladies belonging to well-to-do families in Malabar came to the forefront and picketed the foreign cloth shops.

The worst feature of the government treatment with the volunteers was the inhuman behaviour of policemen. The volunteers were brutally belaboured with *lathis*, canes, etc. Numerous arrests were made and it became apparent that in spite of camp jails and temporary jails remained open, the members that suffered themselves for arrest could not all be accommodated. More than 95 per cent of the persons convicted were placed in 'C' class.

People attending processions and meetings were dispersed by the police by *lathi* charges. There was hardly an important place in any province, where the movement did not experience these sort of brutalities.

The Movement Called Off

The Civil Disobedience Movement was executed, inspired and organised by Gandhi and his associates. On a broad scale, it remained non-violent and there was not any serious instance of violence on the part of the Congress *satyagrahis* as it was in the case of her Non-Cooperation Movement of 1920-22. It, however, failed to maintain its momentum after fifteen months during its second phase and was practically crushed by official repression.

Such a mass movement, though non-violent could hardly be sustained indefinitely at a high level. Nearly 78,000 Congressmen had experienced imprisonment; thousands had sacrificed their personal fortunes and wrecked their health and homes for the national cause. But in reality, the tide of patriotic fervour and moral idealism which had swept the entire country with the launching of the Civil Disobedience Movement on 12 March 1930 began to wither away with the passage of time.

Realising this, Gandhi, therefore, came to the conclusion that his message of non-violence had yielded little result and that the country needed further discipline in non-violence through the suspension of Civil Disobedience and its substitution by the constructive programme at national level.

On 17 June 1933, the Civil Disobedience Movement was suspended for another six weeks. After consulting Gandhi, Aney issued the following statement. "In view of the present state of health of Mahatma Gandhi and the doctors' opinion expressed in today's bulletin issued by the Medical Board, I hereby extend suspension of Civil Disobedience for a further period of six weeks, that is till the 31st of July 1933".

On 21st July 1933, Aney issued his statement regarding the future policy of the Congress. He said that the mass civil disobedience, no-tax and no-rent campaign should be stopped for the time being, while those willing to offer Individual Civil Disobedience might do so on their own responsibility. All Congress organisations should cease to exist but wherever possible. He called upon all Congressmen unable to offer the civil disobedience to continue the constructive activities of the Congress. He further said that those Congressmen who did not wish to offer civil resistance under the new scheme would engage themselves in the various constructive activities of the Congress such as *khadi* production, total prohibition, Harijan service, communal unity, encouragement of indigenous industries and other national building activities.

The Mahatma was, however, not prepared for the total surrender which the government demanded. "I would rather be reduced to dust than surrender', he said. Under these circumstances, he resolved to renew the struggle with the government in the revised form of Individual Civil Disobedience with effect from 1st August 1933.

Gandhi began to tour India in connection with the Harijan work. Projecting himself as a Harijan worker, he asked for quarter *anna* or half an *anna* or any amount one could spare for the Harijan cause. This was his main refrain throughout his tour of central and south India. He called upon the *savarna* Hindus to purify themselves by fraternising with Harijans and to remove their social, moral and economic disabilities under which they suffered.

The discussions with Congress leaders convinced Gandhi that the country was exhausted and the Congressmen were in no mood to continue Civil Disobedience in any form. On the contrary, a section of Congressmen keenly expected the revival of the Swaraj Party and re-entering the legislatures.

Gandhi's next move came with a dramatic suddenness on 7 April 1934, when he declared the final suspension of the Individual Civil Disobedience Movement because of the possibility of internal degeneration of the movement, partly due to its own limitations and partly due to the impracticable results of the imperfect people handling imperfect instruments.

Rabindranath Tagore appreciated Gandhi's decision which provided freedom of action to every worker in the service of the country. While the *Bombay Chronicle* attribute its suspension to its inability to touch the hearts of those for whom it was meant, the *Pioneer* stated that the decision of the Mahatma could not be grasped. *The Times of India* called it as the 'customary sublime egotism' of Mr. Gandhi.

The withdrawal of the Civil Disobedience Movement, the revival of the Swaraj Party and the council-entry programme were mostly hailed by the majority of the Congress block and the nationalist press. But among the influential opponents some resented Gandhi's somewhat disparaging references to the shortcomings of the 'warriors' in the Civil Disobedience 'battle'.

1935 : A New Turn

The year 1935 saw the completion of the existence of half a century of the Indian National Congress as one of the most remarkable political organisations in history.

Of these fifty years, fifteen had passed under the leadership of Gandhi when a resurgent India saw two great revolutions which rattled the very foundation of the

British Empire. In the year of the golden jubilee it was evident that the Congress had definitely entered into the culminating phases of its efforts for the liberation of the country.

It was the Government of India Act, 1935, which paved the way for this final struggle. It came in the wake of Gandhi's Civil Disobedience Movement in which more than seventy thousand men and women embraced imprisonment for symbolically breaking the law of an alien power.

Complete independence had been the Congress demand since December 1929 and Gandhi sent this message to the British in the Round Table Conference that a constitution which did not accept that basic principle would not be acceptable to India. As a matter of fact, just twelve years separated independence from the Act of 1935. And, these years formed an epoch of adversity ahead of the Congress and the country and a time of severe ordeal for Mahatma Gandhi.

The framers of the 1935 Act worked on the basis of a few constitutional principles for a political settlement in India. Their main aim, of course, was to subdue the Indian revolution. Secondly, they greatly stressed on having strong executives in the provinces while conceding parliamentary government. At the same time, should the responsible ministers and the legislators fail in their duty in a province, it was felt necessary to have an authority in India, with adequate powers in reserve, to intervene.

The framers of the Act boasted that the greatest gift which British rule had conferred on India was its integrity and expressed their apprehension that in transferring the powers of government to the Provinces, and in encouraging them to develop an independent political life of their own, we have been running the inevitable risk of weakening or even destroying that unity.

Laying maximum emphasis on the unity of the country, the policy-makers came to a conclusion that, unless the Indian States under the princes came into a constitutional relationship with British India, the issue of unity could hardly take shape. An all-India federation was thus thought of, with the hope that the ruling princes would become its willing members, giving strong support to a powerful central government in matters of common policies, particularly in respect of economic arrangements.

The authorities apprehended that if the reforms were confined only within the limits of the provinces, leaving the Centre untouched, the whole of political India could turn to opposition. It would appear unusual if popular governments were created in the provinces while the centre was left to function under an official and irresponsible executive. Moreover, if the Indian States were not persuaded to join the all-India federation, the constitution would remain incomplete and imperfect.

While the Conservatives wanted to spoil the reforms by disapproving even the limited concessions the Indians were likely to enjoy under the constitution, the Labour Party could read the signs of the ominous consequences the Act was about to initiate. The debates had revealed Conservative hostility towards the Indian Congress. It was not considered as a dominating factor in politics and certainly not as the most powerful force whose responsiveness alone could pave the way for the success of the constitutional scheme, but as a non-entity undeserving of any serious consideration. That it is deliberately framed so as to exclude as far as possible the Congress Party from effective power in the new Constitution. On many occasions provisions have been deliberately put forward with that end in view. This is done at the Centre by giving an undue weight to the princes. The princes are represented as a conservative element to keep left wing elements in check. Meanwhile Clement Attlee also objected to the bill and criticized it for the premium it set on communalism. Such features as indirect election together with communal electorate, and elected chambers divided on the issue communalism made the Bill one of the worst the British could have thought of.

In spite of doubts and criticism, the Bill finally became an Act on 2 August 1935. Two features of the Act were noticeable, an All-India Federation comprising Governor's Provinces, Chief Commissioners' Provinces, and the Federating Indian States; and Provincial Autonomy. Moreover, issues like foreign affairs, ecclesiastical affairs, and defence were excluded from the jurisdiction of the Indian legislatures and were kept in the jurisdiction of the governor-general, while the governor-general and the governors of the provinces were consecrated with special powers in respect of the subjects transferred to the control of responsible ministers.

When the Act finally came into existence, it came as a challenge to the Indian people and the Congress decided to face it as such. The Lucknow session of the Congress which commenced on 12 April 1936 proved eventful for the nation. Accompanied by seven of its ex-presidents including Mahatma Gandhi, the new president, Jawaharlal Nehru, started its proceedings amid elated enthusiasm and high expectations of the assembled delegates.

It was pointed out that the struggle for freedom was not merely for the liberation of the land from the foreign oppression but also for securing social and economic justice for the uplift of common man. Nehru turned to the immediate challenge which faced the country. Describing the new Act as 'a charter of slavery', he proclaimed: 'To this Act our attitude can be one of uncompromising hostility and a constant endeavour to end it.'

14

The Election and Thereafter

Since the Act of 1935 was scheduled to come into force on 1 April 1937 and since the fate of the federation as well as of the central government remained apparently indefinite, the main attention of the country was diverted towards the prospects of provincial autonomy. On one hand, every party was dissatisfied with the so-called autonomy, yet, on the other, most parties wanted to make the best use of the election in order to serve their respective purposes. For the Congress, the election was desirable for educating the people and after the victory for utilising the popular verdict for attaining higher objectives.

Congress Realising Muslim League Strategy

The Congress realised during the electioneering that the Muslim masses, confined as they were within communal electorates, could not be influenced through general contact to any alluring extent because of the politics the Muslim League played. Even if the League policy in respect of the new Act was near the Congress policy, in actual ideology the two organisations differed widely. The Congress tried to address its doctrines among the Muslim votes while campaigning for its own Muslim candidates, but that did not dismantle their communal outlook. Attempts were made to set up Congress Muslims to stand as League candidates and talks were in circulation for harmony between the two parties after the elections and before office acceptance. Jinnah, at this stage, was in favour of such cooperation, aware as he was of the weakness of the League as well as of his own shaky position in that otherwise unsteady organisation dominated by religious dogmatists.

Meanwhile, it was not in the Central Provinces alone, but almost everywhere in the country, that the same name worked since Gandhi was the icon of the nation-wide struggle for freedom, the election being only a minor event in the nation's march towards independence under his leadership. Added to the Mahatma's charismatic hold on popular imagination, the organising ability of the Congress High Command was seen at its best with stalwarts like Nehru, Patel, Azad and Rajendra Prasad with myriads of leaders and followers along.

The elections were over, the immediate issue before the Congress leadership was to decide whether to assume another office or not in the Congress-dominated provinces. Of late, Nehru had been in a more radical mood in looking at the 'slave constitution' which he wanted to go 'lock, stock and barrel' so that the way could be paved for a constituent assembly of the Indian people. Many others, however, did not share this view.

Viceroy Fails to Convince Gandhi

Gandhi could not be influenced by the Viceroy as regards his principles. He failed to move him even from his policy of forbidding official contact between Congressmen and the British. On this, Gandhi did not try to conceal his suspicion of imperialist hands in influencing the Congress. Linlithgow also met some other Congress leaders. When Jinnah met him, the Viceroy formed rather a faulty opinion of him and commented: "I do not frankly feel any deep confidence in him and I suspected that he is one of those political leaders who can play a personal hand but no other, and whose permanent control on the allegiance of the followers is frequently open to question."

Jinnah, meanwhile in his frantic attempt to establish his hold on his co-religionists, was searching for faults in the Congress in order to prevent the Muslim masses from going over to it in response to its principle of economic emancipation of the poor and the downtrodden. He was alarmed at what Nehru was about to do in uniting the Hindus and Muslims.

Jinnah's ego as a formidable former Congress leader was deeply hurt at what he regarded as neglect and disregard on the part of persons whom he regarded as his juniors in national politics and thus reacted in a furious manner. An earlier statement by Nehru that, "In the final analysis there are only two forces in India today—British imperialism and the Congress representing Indian nationalism", have an unpleasant effect on him as he began to read between the lines of Nehru's latest Muslim mass contact theory.

Some of the elected Muslim legislators in the UP Assembly, as elsewhere, were meanwhile thinking of joining the Congress because of its new approach to people's problems. To Jinnah, however, these trends appeared most dangerous. He warned such waverers not to betray the party. He urged his followers to have courage and faith and give up their defeatist mentality, to organise, consolidate, and establish solidarity and unity.

Rapidly Jinnah transformed himself into a spirited communal leader, having everything to say against the Congress ministries, against Hindi and *Bande Mataram*, the Congress flag and Hindu nationalism, even though his conception for separation was yet to take shape. His phenomenal upturn to greatness within the next few years was rather providential shaped by historical forces and factors which came to operate abruptly, such as the Second World War, when the British Empire was called upon to fight a life and death struggle; the open revolution of the Congress to end British rule; and, the desperate need of the British to maintain Muslim India as its most dependable support.

With the Congress in power in so many provinces, Gandhi's vision widened for future scheme of things. There was no other political party in the country to question the authority of the Congress. "So far, therefore," he said, "as I can see a vast opportunity is at the disposal of the Ministers in terms of the Congress objectives of complete Independence, if only they are honest, selfless, industrious, vigilant and solicitous for the true welfare of the starving millions."

The Haripura session of the Congress has the distinction of being the first session attended by ministers in charge of provinces who attended it as delegates or members of the AICC. There were deputations from South Africa and Ceylon as well. Thanks to the organising ability and efforts of Sardar Vallabhbhai Patel, this session saw so large an assemblage that it came to be described as the 'biggest session in the history of the Congress'. The leaders were fully aware of the existing difference between the right and the left in their own ranks, but were equally determined to put these aside and work as 'the one supreme organ of mass struggle'. The need of the hour was to bring the whole country under the Congress banner. The president made a plea to the leftist-groups 'to pool all their strength and their resources for democratising the Congress and reorganising it on the broadest anti-imperialist basis.'

"In conclusion," said an emotive Subhas Chandra Bose at the end of his presidential address, "I shall voice your feelings by saying that all India fervently hopes and prays that Mahatma Gandhi may be spared to our nation for many, many years to come. India cannot afford to lose him and certainly not at this hour. We need him to keep our struggle free from bitterness and hatred. We need him for the cause of Indian independence. What is more—we need him for the cause of humanity."

By the time of the Haripura session, the hostility of Jinnah and the Muslim League towards the Congress had assumed rather ugly proportions. To counteract the League's subversive propaganda, Nehru moved a resolution on 20 February 1938 that the Congress "regards it as its primary duty and fundamental policy to protect the religious, linguistic, cultural and other rights of the minorities in India and will give widest scope for their development and their participation in the fullest measure in the political, economic and cultural life of the nation." Nehru lambasted the League for its attacks on the Congress and said: "Today, Muslims, Sikhs, Christians and Parsis are joining the Congress in lakhs. Vested interests are therefore afraid of its growing power. They fear that their control over the masses will be removed. Therefore, they want to spread communal feelings among them. In order to establish their own leadership they adopt wrong means and spread communalism in the name of freedom."

The intractable policy of the League prompted Nehru to enquire from Jinnah what actually he was aiming at. The latter in his press statements was throwing out challenges, saying that he was fighting the Congress leadership which was hoodwinking the people. "I would beg Mr. Jinnah," said Nehru in a statement on New Year's Day, 1938, "to remember what the Congress is today. It was very different from what it was in the days when he was associated with it. During this period, it has grown remarkably and with thirty-one lakhs of members currently on its rolls, about a hundred thousand are Muslims." He wanted to know from Jinnha what exactly were the points in dispute which required consideration.

Jinnah's prime objective was purely political, tinged with something personal, even though he defended the superficial demands of his community as its leader. All that he wanted was the Muslim League needed to be recognised the only authoritative and representative political organisation of the Mussalmans of India, with, of course, himself as its undisputed leader. Defying Nehru's claim that there were only two parties in the country, namely the British Government and the Congress, Jinnah put forward his theory to President Bose that any future talks by Congress on Muslim aspirations or demands should be conducted only with the League.

It was impossible for the Congress to accept Jinnah's claim that the Muslim League was the sole representative of the Indian Muslims. Long-drawn-out talks between Congress leaders and Jinnah, which had gone on for long, for an amicable understanding regarding the future of the nation thus yielded no result.

The situation in the country, as a result of national and international developments, was getting more tense when the Congress met in its annual session at Tripuri in the Central Provinces in March 1939. Many in the Congress were dissatisfied with the functioning of the provincial Congress ministries who were finding it hard to proceed with constructive innovations in view of financial and administrative restraints. The European situation, rapidly getting worser caused no less concern in Congress circles. In case war came, it was only the Congress that could face the eventualities. It was necessary for the Congress High Command to face the growing problems as a homogeneous body and constantly keeping the eventual goals in view.

15

Subhas Bose's Role in Freedom Movement

Subhas Chandra Bose was born in Cuttack on 23 January 1897. He hailed from the famous Bose family. His father was Rao Bahadur Janakinath who was educated in Calcutta and Cuttack. He joined the Bar as an advocate at Cuttack in 1885, the year the Indian National Congress came into being. He became the first non-official Chairman of the Cuttack Municipality in 1901. In the year 1912, he was honoured with the title 'Rao Bahadur' in recognition of his dedicated services to the Government. He resigned his post in 1917 owing to his differences with the District Magistrate. He disowned later his title 'Rao Bahadur' in 1930 during the freedom movement.

During the Ravenshaw Collegiate School career (1908—1913) itself, Subhas felt an acute mental conflict as he was caught in a strange dilemma between worldly life and mystic life. Subhas was a born spiritualist. He inherited spiritualism from his parents. During the same period. (1908—1913), he came under the influence of the works of Swami Vivekananda. He had seen many saints who used to flock to Puri, popularly known as Jagannath Puri, the abode of God Jagannath. He practised Yoga and mysticism even in his early life, which he continued till the end of his life.

Subhas passed his Intermediate examination in the first division from the same college. He wanted to train the young Indians to be able to shoulder responsibilities. He rightly pointed out the weakness of Indians—in not taking part in debates. 'What I want is' said Bose, 'that our body should learn the art of thinking quickly. And then, the art of debate initiates one into the art of self-reliance which is surely a great gain,' 'We, Indians, are', Bose continued, 'too dependent on others—for action, views, initiative—everything'. A memorable incident, the real turning point in his life, happened to Bose in the Presidency College, Calcutta, in the year 1916. Subhas was elected as class representative for the year. He enjoyed an enviable popularity among his classmates because of his suave personality, a high command over English, being a good debator, a class representative and above all his aristocratic family background.

The Presidency College then was a prominent college of Bengal with famous professors on the staff, like Sir J.C. Bose, P.C. Ray and others. The Eden Hindu Hostel of the College was a centre of revolutionaries. Subhas, however, got involved in an incident in the college, only because he was a class-representative then.

Prof. E.F. Oaten of History, forcibly pushed away students, who were roaming about noisily in the corridor adjoining to the room where he was lecturing. Subhas, as a class representative, complained to the Principal against the professor. The Principal remained unmoved. The students of the college, therefore, went on general strike against the professor demanding an apology from him. Principal still unmoved, instead fined the students. The professor took advantage of this and manhandled a student of the college. The students took their revenge by beating the professor in which Subhas was caught as an eyewitness, though he was not a party to it. The college was closed following students agitation. An enquiry into the incident started.

Subhas appeared before the enquiry commission presided over by Sir Ashutosh Mukerji, former vice-chancellor of the Calcutta University and a Judge of the Calcutta High Court. The Principal suspended Subhas saying, 'To me, Bose, you are most troublesome man in the college. I suspend you.'

Subhas tried to seek admission in some other college in Calcutta to pursue his studies, but everywhere he was refused, as the Calcutta University did not permit him. He had no other way except to return to Cuttack. He joined the Scottish Church College, Calcutta, the last educational institution, he joined in India in July 1917. As a student of the college, he joined the University Training Corps the following year which was attached to the Indian Territorial Army. He enjoyed the military training camp of four months. He passed his B.A. Honours securing second rank in the University.

Subhas appeared for the ICS examination in July 1920. The result was announced later that year which indeed was a great surprise to him that he had passed the 'heaven born', 'strategic', ICS examination and that too in the fourth rank. It was a record, until then among the successful Indian ICS candidates. It is to be mentioned that Satyendranath Tagore was the first to pass the ICS, but Subhas was the first to have a rank at the ICS examination.

Joining the service was, to Subhas, a slavery. "The principle of serving an alien bureaucracy." He wrote to his brother in 1921, 'is one to which I cannot reconcile myself... The day I sign the covenant, I shall cease to be a free man.' It was a surprise to Subhas to know that not a single person has resigned from the service in the cause of the freedom of the nation."

Subhas expressed his feelings to Deshbandhu Chitta Ranjan Das in a letter to him, 'I have the feeling that on my return to my country I should be able to take up two kinds of work—teaching in college and writing for newspapers. I desire to give up the Indian Civil Service with clear-cut plans.' In another letter to Das, he (Subhas) had shown his willingness to serve even in the field of research for the Congress, adult education and social service as well.

An ardent patriotic fervour in Bose forced him ultimately to resign from the ICS in the cause of the nation. The day, 22 April 1921, on which he resigned from the ICS was a crucial turning point in his life. It was like resigning from the material world with a view to serve the nation.

The day Subhas Chandra Bose landed in Bombay, he met Gandhiji at the latter's residence. That was his first meeting with Gandhiji. Differences between the two cropped up even at the very beginning of their meeting. Subhas failed to clear his doubts before Gandhiji. He had his own reservations about the efficacy of the non-payment of taxes, the campaign started by the Congress during the Non-cooperation Movement whereas Gandhiji, on the other hand, had an idea that his campaign started by the efficacy of the non-payment of taxes could not drive the British out from India. But Gandhiji was of the view that civil disobedience movement would force the British to acknowledge Indian demands. Moreover, Gandhiji has promised his followers Swaraj and that too within one year, which, Subhas thought, was impossible.

His public life started during the non-cooperation movement. He was made the principal of the National College, founded by C.R. Das. He was also placed in charge of the Publicity Board of the Bengal Provincial Congress Committee. He was the head of the National Volunteer Corps as well.

The *Statesman* rightly remarked that the government lost a competent officer but correspondingly the Congress, the nation and the people gained the service of an able personality.

Subhas participated first in the meeting of the Bengal Pradesh Congress Committee in November 1921, as a Member, of which Shri C.R. Das was the president. This was his first political activity, as an office-bearer of the Congress, though earlier, he used to work as a Congress volunteer or as an *ex-officio* member.

The All India Swaraj Party was inaugurated officially on 11 January 1923 at Gaya with C.R. Das as the president and Pandit Motilal Nehru as its General Secretary. Subhas, Vithalbhai Patel, Rangaswamy Iyengar and N.C. Kelkar were some of the other prominent members of the Swaraj Party. Its first conference was held in March 1923 at Allahabad where its constitution was drafted.

The Swarajist administration in the Corporation under Das and Bose, launched *The Calcutta Municipal Gazette*, the weekly, the first journal in India, stopped addressing the Government officials; instead launched receptions to nationalist leader, along with other social and economic programmes.

The Swaraj Party, the idea of which generated in the Alipur Jail under the leadership of C.R Das and Motilal Nehru to enter the provincial legislatures and other bodies to fight against the imperialist government, proved worthy of its aim to offer "uniform, continuous and consistent opposition" to Government from within.

Bengal, especially Calcutta, was a strong political forum for political developments during the Swarajists' administration. The political scene changed following the murder of an European. Warrants under Regulation III of 1818 were ready in July 1924, but were executed on 25 October 1924. A large number of leaders were arrested including Subhas on 24 October 1924. Two Anglo-Indian papers of Calcutta made allegations to justify Subhas's arrest. Subhas though filed a defamatory suit against these papers, later withdrew the case.

Bose was kept for about a month in the Presidency Jail, Calcutta. He continued to function as the Chief Executive Officer of the Calcutta Municipal Corporation. Later, Bose was transferred to Berhampore Jail. Orders were received on 25 January 1925 for his transfer to Calcutta, but actually the voyage was for Mandalay Jail in Burma, after a night's halt at the Lalbazar police station lockup. From Rangoon he was taken by train to Mandalay. "We had a very large police escort and at every stop on our way," wrote Subhas, "they would line up on both sides of the train. From the fuss they made one would think that we were either high state officials or wild animals."

Bose probably was the first person in the annals of Indian history who was elected to a position from behind the bars. He was put as Congress candidate for the Bengal Legislative Council from a Calcutta constituency against J.N. Basu, leader of the Liberal Party in Bengal. The opponent had defeated a Swarajist in the previous election in 1923, even in the midst of the Swarajist wave. The Calcutta constituency elected Bose but could not get him released from the Mandalay Jail.

Orders were issued to transfer Bose to the Almora Jail in the United Provinces; he left the Insein Jail in May 1927 and sailed for Calcutta. Before arriving in Calcutta, he was examined by a Medical Board consisting of eminent physicians like Sir Nilratan Sirkar, Dr. B.C. Roy and Major Hingston, the Governor's physician. The Board urged strongly for his immediate release, without heading police pressures. There was no other way for the Government but to release Bose who was released on 16 May 1927 after two years, six months and twenty-one days of detention without trial.

Bose's escape from Bengal is a risky story of his life covered in several writings. Once out of Bengal, Subhas took the help of the old revolutionary party workers of Kirti Kisan Party who, in fact, knew the exact route from Peshawar to Kabul as well as to Russia. Earlier they smuggled several political workers through this difficult route.

Subhas wanted to go to Moscow and in this regard, he wrote a lengthy letter to the Russian Ambassador. But his letter could not be delivered. His stay in Germany was fruitful, but he made up his mind that he should make South East Asia as the military base for onward march to India with the help of INA and Japan. His journey in the sub-marine was more risky. But he reached his destination safely.

Bose's ideas, ideals and dreams still continue to inspire us and illuminate our path. Every Indian is proud of him. He has assumed the status of a legend with his great deeds in Germany and South-East Asia after his sensational escape from India. He has become, in short, an inspiring and unifying symbol of Indian nationalism.

According to Subhas "Freedom means life, and death in the pursuit of freedom means glory imperishable." He has no faith in the Congress programme to win freedom for India.

Bose opined, "It is the duty of the Indian Independence League in East Asia, supported by all patriotic Indians at home and abroad, to undertake this task—the task of setting up a provisional Government of Azad Hind and of conducting the last fight for freedom, with the help of the Army of Liberation (that is, Azad Hind Fauj or the Indian National Army) organised by the League. In the name of God, in the name of bygone generations who have welded the Indian people into one nation, and in the name of the dead heroes who have bequeathed to us a tradition of heroism and self-sacrifice, we call upon the Indian people to rally round our banner, and strike for Indian freedom. We call upon them to launch the final struggle against the British and their Allies in India and to prosecute the struggle with valour and perseverance and with full faith in final victory—until the enemy is expelled from Indian soil and the Indian people are once again a free Nation."

The Provisional Government declared war against Anglo-American forces which were advancing towards South-East Asia. Subhas was confident that his National Army, besides being patriotic, would be able to do well against the enemy. In fact, he felt his position strengthened when his government was recognised by Germany, Italy, Japan, Siam, Philippines and Nanking.

Besides, his meetings with Hitler and Tojo proved very effective because he could gain much assurance from Germany and Japan for his struggle of freedom.

In the course of his conversation with Bose on 29 May, 1942, Hitler promised that he would demonstrate in concrete terms, Germany's recognition of India as a free country, which he indeed had by establishing in August 1942 the Indo-German Society at Hamburg.

Tojo was greatly impressed by the towering personality of Bose and the sincerity of the cause for which he was fighting. He commented spontaneously after meeting Bose, "You may go ahead with the establishment of your Provisional Government. With regard to the routine and formalities or plans, coordinate your views with general Terauchi's command and also Tokyo Government."

The Provisional Government of Azad Hind Fauj comprised of several stalwarts like Subhas Bose, Capt. Mrs. Lakshmi, A.C. Chatterjee, Aziz Ahmed, J.K. Bhonsle, Gulzara Singh, M.Z. Kiani, A.D. Loganandan, Ehsai Badir, Shah Nawaz Khan, Rash Behari Bose, Karim Gani, Sardar Ishar Singh, A.N. Sarkar, among others.

Shah Nawaz Khan indeed had great respect for Bose. In his book *INA and Its Netaji,* he wrote several pages in praise of his leader, 'I was spell-bound; here was for the first time in my life that I had seen him... We felt that he was the leader who could be trusted to take up our cause and our goal. At home the man in him occurred dominate. At the front and in the midst of his troops, the soldier in him shone greatly and in counsels and conferences his breath-taking statesmanship made a profound impression on one and all of us."

Bose was quite aware of the odds which he and his associates would have to face. He explained thus: "... We have a grim fight ahead of us, for the enemy is powerful, unscrupulous and ruthless. In the final march to freedom you will have to face hunger and thirst, privation, forced marches and death. Only when you pass this test will freedom be yours. I am confident that you will do this and thereby bring freedom and prosperity to your enslaved and impoverished land."

He succeeded Rash Behari Bose as the President of the IIL (4 July 1943) in South-East Asia after coming from Germany on invitation. As the Supreme-Commander, he reorganised the INA with a separate Jhansi Rani Laxmibai Regiment of women soldiers under the Captaincy of Laxmi Swaminathan (Now Mrs. Sahgal). The INA was, undoubtedly, his greatest achievement and significant contribution to the cause of his mission.

He organised the Provisional Government of Free India (on 21 October 1943) and at its inaugural ceremony he swore: 'I swear by God that I will do my best to emanicipate India its 380 million people. I will abide by this oath until my death. I will make every possible effort to bring freedom to the Indian people. I also swear devote myself to the good of India even after its emanicipation.'

Bose's eyes were set on Delhi. He wanted his INA to march to Delhi via Imphal, the present capital of the state of Manipur. He shifted his Provisional Government to Rangoon to speed up the march to Delhi. He informed his intention to General Kawabe, the Japanese Commander-in-Chief in Burma: "The Indian National Army should be the spearhead of the whole advance into India. The first drip of blood to be shed on Indian soil be that of a member of the Indian National Army." Any liberation of India secured through Japanese sacrifice according to Bose 'is worse than slavery'.

The Imphal operation (from 15th March to 9th July 1944) was the decisive stage of the freedom struggle of Bose and his INA. It was a crucial juncture of the Second World War in Europe and Asia. The fate of Bose and his INA was depending on the Japanese military might in which Japan deployed three Divisions (15th, 31st and 33rd).

Had Imphal not fallen, Bose would have been successful in his mission and the history of modern India would have been different. "Had he (Bose) only been able to take Imphal," said Bhulabhai Desai the Chief Counsel, who defended the INA officers during their trial at the Red Fort, "the bulk of the Indian Army in India would have deserted the British and flocked to swell the ranks of the Indian National Army."

Bose's plan failed largely because of the failure of the Japanese army in Imphal operation. Generally, it was considered that Mutaguchi's plan of Blocking Imphal-Kohima road was the main reason for the failure. Otherwise, the British army in Imphal—would have retreated by the same road.

Besides the torrential rains which disrupted the communication and supply lines, were the other reasons for the failure of Indo-Japanese army in the Imphal operation. Without arms, ammunition, air cover, food and medical facilities, the INA suffered a lot. A Japanese Army along the Indo-Burma border under the handicap of shortages of all kinds of supplies should go down as a glorious chapter in the annals of the Indian independence movement.

Bose declined to accept that his mission had failed. In his Special Order of the day (15th August 1945) Bose addressed the INA,: "You may perhaps feel that you failed in your mission to liberate India, but let me tell you that this failure is only of a temporary nature." He surveyed the achievements of the INA: 'No setback and no defeat can undo your positive achievements of the past. Many of your comrades have laid down their lives on the battlefield and have become the immortal heroes of Azad Hind. This glorious sacrifice can never go in vain." Bose had firm faith in India's destiny. He said: "The roads to Delhi are many and Delhi still remains our goal. There is no power on earth that can keep India enslaved, India shall be free and before long."

Bose was a dynamic freedom fighter and politician. "There is no nationalist in India,' Bose rightly estimated himself on 9 July 1943, "who can claim to possess the many-sided experience that I have been able to acquire." There was not even a bit of exaggeration or boast in it. He was a statesman, diplomat, organiser, administrator, orator, visionary, writer, journalist and a feminist at the same time. He stood for freedom, equality, unity, democracy and socialism. He was for a Constituent Assembly after attaining national independence. 'The party,' said Bose, 'that is going to fight for freedom is the party that is entitled to draw up the constitution.' He wanted a strong central government run by a strong political party. He was for freedom of speech, press, expression and religion. He had a secular outlook. He wanted to allow exposure to students and the youth in every sphere of life—including politics. He was a man of action and destiny.

16

Quit India Movement
(A Report by Wickenden)

1. The task before me is to ascertain the cause of, and assess responsibility for, the unrest which commenced with the arrest of the Congress leaders on August 9, 1942. Looked at in another way, I have to examine those conclusions, consider whether they are justified and form any other conclusions which may appear to me to be established. It was stated in a pamphlet published by the Government that it was in possession of a great deal of other material which it was not desirable to make public at that stage and it is that withheld material which has been placed before me. I have completed a great deal of reading in order to get as much background as possible. As a result, I have compiled a supplementary file of further evidence partly of a secret and partly of an open character.

2. The objection which was of course repeatedly voiced in the press when the pamphlet on Congress Responsibility was published was that it was all one-sided and no more than a speech for the prosecution. It should be possible to extract from it fair conclusion and, if there is material available on the other side, it is significant that no effort, as far as I know, has been made to produce it. Most of the adverse criticism indeed had political 'smell', Britain being blamed because India's just demand for independence has been wrongfully refused. The fundamental point is whether the reason behind disturbances must be laid at the door of Congress or whether they were mass outburst following the precipitate action of Government in arresting the Congress leaders following the termination of the session of the All-India Congress Committee in Bombay in August 1942.

3. The secret evidence falls mainly into four classes, namely,

(a) Agents' reports;
(b) Police reports;
(c) Interceptions of correspondence; and
(d) Interrogations.

I have to accept statements from the police and various intelligence officers which they place upon a particular agent but for the most part the value of these reports dealing with a particular subject matter depends mostly on their number and their emanating from different parts of the country. There are exceptions, of course, and even with a single report or just one or two reports of the same kind, it may be possible to say that they are reliable.

4. In the arrangement of the discussion which follows, I have dwelt on ascertaining the course of events and the facts which show how the situation developed. I have referenced throughout and given first place to the most important material; an index for the references is prefixed to this report.

Summary of Events

5. For a comprehensive understanding of what follows, it is desirable briefly to capitulate events prior to the outbreak of the unrests and one may conveniently start with the Bardoli Session of the Working Committee of the All-India Congress in December 1941. By its Resolution, the Working Committee terminated the individual *satyagraha*[1] campaign. Gandhi undoubtedly accepted this Resolution as a rebuff and for the time being pulled himself out of political activities and devoted himself anew to his constructive programme as his writings in the *Harijan* show. There is no need to recite the bitter disappointment that followed the Cripps' Mission and I do not think it will be disputed that Gandhi's 'Quit India' movement was one of its fall-outs. Meanwhile by the end of June, Gandhi has succeeded in bringing the members who stood against him into general agreement with him. That agreements found expression in the Working Committee's Resolution of July 14th, which demanded immediate independence and threatened civil disobedience if it was not forthcoming. A session of the All India Congress Committee was fixed for August 7th, before which the resolution was to be submitted for approval. Mainly it took the form of speeches and meetings, both open and conceded with a view to preparing the public in general and Congress workers in particular. In due course the All-India Congress Committee met at Bombay on August 7th. The General Committee passed the Wardha resolution as verbally amended by the Working Committee at Bombay and sanctioned Civil Disobedience under jurisdiction of Mahatma Gandhi. As a result, most of the members of the Working Committee and many other Congress stalwarts were arrested in Bombay early on August 9th and similar local arrests were made throughout the country. The immediate reaction was protest rallies, meetings and attacks on public vehicles and on the police in Bombay City as well as in Poona and Ahmedabad. There were also meetings and demonstrations in certain other towns. They increased on the next day especially in Bombay, and became general and assumed a violent character which steadily intensified from the 11th onwards. I need not say anything more here of what followed.

Gandhi, the Creator and Driving Force

6. ***The Allahabad Resolution.*** I have mentioned the simultaneous launching by Gandhi of the idea that Britain should immediately withdraw from India in his article in the *Harijan* and in his resolution sent to the meeting of the Working Committee at Allahabad. The Resolution itself, with notes of the discussion which followed, and the compromise resolution of the Working Committee have been published in the pamphlet on Congress responsibility. There has been a certain amount of dispute after publication of these documents on the notes of discussion, but it has not, so far as I know, been challenged that Gandhi sent a resolution and the published one is correct.

The Working Committee Resolution was very much a compromise arrived at in Gandhi's absence and without the possibility of consultation with him. It did not meet with Gandhi's approval.

Gandhi further considered contemplated a very early meeting of the Working Committee to be held in June so that he could explain and assert himself in the position he had taken up. This appears in a source report from Calcutta dated 25th May 1942 and has corroboration of a letter from Vallabhbhai Patel to J.B. Kripalani,[2] General Secretary, All-India Congress Committee, dated 26th May 1942. The letter indicated that Gandhi had been persuaded that such an early meeting was not necessary or convenient and it may be presumed, I think, they satisfied him that discussion with various members of the Working Committee from time to time would serve the same purpose.

7. ***A Movement contemplated.*** Though Gandhi's Allahabad Resolution makes no mention of any means by which it might be made effective, it is natural to suppose that Gandhi would have that in mind from the beginning; this also is established from the same letter of Rajendra Prasad. The relevant part runs as follows:

> Gandhiji is of opinion that if the British go away we will have to devise some means. So we should tell the British Government frankly to go away and withdraw their army from India. This cannot be satisfied so long as the public opinion is not raised with one voice. We must be ready to face the worst which may arise out of it and that would bring out a new life to the country.

8. ***Will to go ahead.*** There is abundant material to show that Gandhi was determined to push through his project of making Britain withdraw from India whether he got support from the Congress or not. I have already mentioned his concern at the compromise resolution passed at Allahabad and his calling of leaders to Wardha in that connection. He was bent on bringing others round to his view. I do not think this need be dilated upon, because it will hardly be disputed and is apparent enough from his writings. I might, however, refer to another intercepted letter written by a certain Sharaf Athar Ali, a Communist worker in Bombay, to P.C. Joshi,[3] the Communist leader. He was present at an interview given by Gandhi to Congressmen of Bombay and Gujarat on May 15th during his stay in Bombay. The writer would seem to have taken copious notes, because the letter comprise almost entirely an account of the interview in the form of question and answer. The foot-note indicated that he must have gone there with that intent and the letter reads as a substantially true account of what must have taken place. That there was an interview where the discussion took the form of question and answer is corroborated by another letter written on 6th June 1942, by a certain D.H. Wandrekar to Dr. A.G. Tandulkar,[4] a detenu in the Nasik Road Prison. Wandrekar's letter is shorter but the substance is the same.

9. One most significant act of Gandhi in furtherance of his proposal was his sending out and relying upon his own men, that is to say those who were his immediate followers as a constructive non-violent leader of India, prepared to act, all of them, blindly in response to their faith in him. Two important names may be given and they show in addition preparation by Gandhi as to future action that he might take. First is Mira Ben,[5] perhaps his most devoted disciple, whom he sent to Orissa to form an opinion of the condition and morale of the people in that part of India. This was particularly important since it was widely anticipated that a Japanese invasion would take place on the Orissa coast, because it was completely undefended and, apart from

the coastline contiguous to Burma, the nearest approach. Hurried preparations were being made in Orissa carrying with them obvious demands upon the population. In the neighbouring Province of Bengal, Khurshed Ben had gone on a similar mission. She may be considered as fanatically devoted to Gandhi, though there are indications that she had become comparatively recently impatient of non-violence as a practical policy. Whether she had expressed this to Gandhi we do not know, but both she and Mira Ben were undoubtedly most zealous in carrying out anything aimed at attaining independence. I do not think it necessary to refer more to what was done in these visits and the touring of these two ladies. There are voluminous reports[6] of their activities and they cannot be denied.

Leaving them aside, however, the evidence is that Gandhi was prepared to use his own followers—those who were closest to him in his constructive work—whether he had other support or not. Perhaps most reliable is the letter dated 26th May 1942, from Mridula Sarabhai,[7] who is well-known as a Gujarat Congress worker, to Mrs. Sucheta Kripalani,[8] wife of the Congress General Secretary, wherein she writes :

> Since the difference of opinion that has taken place between the Congress and Bapu (Gandhi) it appears that two organisations are working in the country. Bapu sends his people and gets work done through them and the other work is done by the Congress.

Another important document is an intercepted message from Salivati (Salivati Eswaran), the Bombay correspondent of the *Hindu* Madras and the *Daily Herald* London, wherein he mentions that Gandhi has sent letters to his intimate followers all over India to get ready for a mass movement. A third reference, which I think may be relied upon, is notes given by a certain Kanji Dwarkadas[9] to Sir Frederick Stone of the E.D. Sassoon Mills, Bombay. Dwarkadas, who is a Labour Superintendent in the Mills, was at one time a Home Ruler and is in close contact with political circles. The notes, I understand, were a purely private arrangement connected with labour conditions in the mills and were not obtained for any other purpose. There appears good reason to trust both the writer and Sir Frederick Stone as reliable on a matter of this kind. The part of the notes which I refer to here is towards the close where, in giving his opinion on the merits of Gandhi's proposed movement, he states as a fact, which presumably he would be in a position to know, that to ensure enough response from the country Gandhi was throwing on the political market his 'capital investment' of 25,000 workers from the Gandhi Seva Sangh whom he had so far kept out of politics. In further direct corroboration it is not necessary to go beyond the *Harijan*[10] pages 210-211, which is an account by Mahadev Desai[11] of a talk given by Gandhi to members of the All-India Spinners Association who were holding their annual meeting at Wardha.

One final point which has a bearing on Gandhi's determination to act alone is an indication that at an early stage the position was so acute that resignation from the Working Committee of some of his firmest followers was contemplated in order that they might be freed to give their full support to Gandhi. In Vallabhbhai Patel's letter to J.B. Kripalani previously mentioned there is the sentence "Bapu also wrote to me that we should all be released from the Working Committee." Corroboration comes from an unconfirmed, but reported to be reliable, source from the U.P. dated 13th June,

1942, that Gandhi was unchanged in his decision and determination to launch a movement on his own initiative and his followers in the Working Committee might resign.

10. The difference between Gandhi and the opposition members of the Working Committee would appear to have been more or less resolved by the end of June. A source report presumably from Wardha, dated 17th June 1942, deals with the discussion which were going on between Gandhi and Congress leaders throughout June. The informant, who is said to be closely connected with Sevagram Congress circles, would be entitled to respect when he says that Gandhi enjoyed the upper hand throughout. He refers to the main points in dispute and notes the arguments on either side, but for the present purpose there is no need to go into details. That Gandhi at that stage was still far from success is revealed by a source report from Calcutta dated 20th June 1942, which asserts that Maulana Abul Kalam Azad in talks with Bengal Congress leaders did not advise their associating with the efforts of the Khadi Group in preparing the Province for Gandhi's proposed movement, because in his opinion the proposal would come to nothing. Next in order of time, I think, comes a source report from Lucknow dated 6th July 1942. The source is said to have contacted two important Congress workers who had recently returned back to latter part of June. The Director of the Intelligence Bureau has subsequently informed me that the two Congress workers referred to are Thakurdas of Benares and Lal Bahadur Shastri[12] of Allahabad, both of them very well-known in the UP. The launching of a movement is looked upon as certain and an important Congressman at Wardha is said to have asked Nehru what would happen if the Government arrested all prominent leaders. Nehru gave no reply and the source gives his opinion, evidently from this and the general trend of conversations, that the differences of opinion between Gandhi and Nehru had disappeared. This appears probably because Nehru addressed a big meeting at Gorakhpur on 1st July 1942, wherein he reminded his audience of what 'revolution' meant. The police report attributes him as saying the time had come when the people would have to face greater perils. Nehru could have hardly spoken in such terms unless he had joined hands with Gandhi in agreeing that a movement had to be started. I understand that reports of meetings in the UP are stenographically recorded and therefore reliance may be placed on the record.

There is one thing to note here. When referring to Gandhi's last speech, I take it as reported in the illegal publication of the AICC "Do or Die" by Mahatma Gandhi. The speech is printed in the first 32 pages and, as far as I have been able to ascertain, it is an accurate record and probably taken from the actually written speech, a copy of which would no doubt be in possession of those who carried on the movement in the name of Congress after the leaders were arrested. Newspaper reports are not so full nor are other reports I have seen, but they bear out the record in the above pamphlet; and published as it was, I think it may safely be relied upon. Summing up the discussion of the evidence leads to one conclusion only and that is that Gandhi from the beginning had made up his mind to launch a movement without delay for the attainment of independence and he was prepared to proceed with it despite all obstacles that might be encountered even from those who had worked closest with him. This movement was not the creation of Congress, which in the first place was hardly prepared to follow him at all, reluctantly fell in line and gradually developed a generally whole-hearted support. Gandhi and the Congress were separate in the beginning but they gradually merged into one, Congress putting itself under Gandhi's leadership so that there was a complete identification between them.

Nature of the Contemplated Movement

11. In this short chapter I only propose to deal with the broad outlines of the movement, leaving more detailed discussion to later on when I take up the question of the programme involved. No great discussion is necessary because these features are not open to dispute. In the first place, the movement was to be all-embracing and without conditions and thus in contrast to all previous movements; markedly so to the campaign of Individual *Satyagraha* which had closed with the Bardoli Resolution of December 1941. We may contrast it with the Delhi Resolution of November 1921 which sanctioned the first Civil Disobedience Campaign. It was made subject to four conditions on all those taking part in it, namely, the fulfilment of the *swadeshi* programme, being a believer in communal unity, being a believer in non-violence and conviction of the wrongfulness of untouchability. This change evidently impressed itself upon all who had anything to say about Gandhi's plans and it was emphasised that everybody would be entitled to join in it. Irrespective of belonging to Congress and views upon violence and non-violence and irrespective of condition, one of the earliest mentions comes in Asaf Ali's letter to Abul Kalam Azad dated 25th May 1942, wherein he said:

> There will be no restriction on the movement which Gandhi has contemplated. There will not be any rule, *khaddar, charkha,* etc., but it will only be a demand for complete independence.

12. Then the movement was to be a mass movement of a non-violent non-cooperative character. That is the kind of expression which was used by all speakers and Congress leaders in keeping with Gandhi's general policy of non-violence. What in practice that could mean I shall discuss later on. I do not think any proof is needed of the description used beyond calling in Gandhi himself in the *Harijan*[13] (p. 233), when in replying to a question as to what would be done if the Working Committee Resolution was adopted, he said:

> You may know that it will be a mass movement of a strictly non-violent character and then you can fill in the details. It will include all that a mass movement can include.

13. Another important feature which has been stressed in the pamphlet on Congress responsibility is the emphasis laid upon initiative and each man acting as leader according to his own lights; to use a slogan said to have originated from Yusuf Mehar Ali: "Every man, a Congressmen: every house, a Congress house." In the source report attributed to Shankar Rao Deo we find that individuals should decide their own line of action, the object being to paralyse the administration in very possible way. Gandhi in his final speech called upon all persons to consider themselves free at that moment to act as such and as if no longer under the heel of imperialism. Maulana Abul Kalam Azad in the concluding session of the Congress stated that with the passing

of the Resolution the job had just begun and it was for the people to make a successful end.

14. One more feature which is of importance is the intensity of the movement, which was expected to be short, swift and effective—to use the words of Jawaharlal Nehru as revealed in a police report from Jubbulpore. He stopped there on his way to the Bombay session and spoke to students who collected at the railway station. According to a police report dated 31st July 1942, from Agra, S.N. Chaturvedi, a well-known UP Congress worker who had returned from Wardha, told Congress workers at a private meeting that though the policy was still non-violent, it was necessary for the movement to be complete and effective. There are other instances, but Gandhi himself laid down the same thing in the *Harijan*[14] (p. 233) in response to a question whether imprisonment would be courted. He said it would not and that his "intention was to make the thing as short and swift as possible." It may be concluded then that the movement was to be an intense mass movement without restrictions on those who might join it, that it was to include everything which had been done before in Civil Disobedience campaigns and probably other things as well, though it was repeatedly laid down that it was to be of a non-violent character.

Gandhi and Non-violence

15. ***His writings.*** I enter upon this chapter with a full realisation of the difficulties involved and conscious in trying to arrive at logical conclusions from the writings of Mahatma Gandhi that, whatever view is expressed, room will always be left open for unending argument. I am considering non-violence first in relation to Gandhi and then in relation to the Congress. The Government pamphlet on Congress Responsibility discussed at some length Gandhi's open writing, mainly in the *Harijan*, and since my task is primarily towards the secret evidence I would have been glad to avoid going over that ground; but it is impossible to examine the evidence without relating it to Gandhi's public utterances and I felt bound to re-examine the latter to satisfy myself whether the conclusions drawn were correct. This was rendered more necessary because of the repeated statements in the criticisms of the pamphlet that the quotations therein have been rent from their contexts and do not give a true picture of what Gandhi intended to convey. That perhaps is an inevitable objection, especially from sources which start with a pre-conceived attitude in favour of Gandhi and his creed of non-violence. I have no doubt that in regard to the quotations I shall give the same objections will be raised, but I have quoted nothing without being satisfied that it stands up true in its context and has a clear meaning to the ordinary man.

Perhaps the most potent cause of the contradictions which appear in Gandhi's writings is the distinction he draws between the ideological and the practical, between creed and policy. Often these are so mixed up in his writing as to create confusion and it is usually possible to find an opposite to any assertion he has made. Gandhi has always claimed to be a student, if not a master, of psychology and that is a claim perhaps which no one will refute; but it carries with it the understanding he must have of the mind of the ordinary man, whether individually or in the mass, and reactions to events. Gandhi and the Congress have always been at pains to draw up their Resolutions, especially when of a compromise character, so as to cover on the face of it the points of acceptance, leaving obscurities of wording which permit of further negotiations. In recent years most of Gandhi's writings have been in the *Harijan* which is printed primarily in English but is published in a number of other languages. It is significant that rapid strides were taken before the disturbances to print the *Harijan* in languages into which it had not previously been translated so that the maximum number of persons in India would be able to read what Gandhi was writing, especially on his 'Quit India' movement. For the most part, the people who would read and who would pass on word of mouth what they had read would have comparatively little education and in turn would have to speak in even simpler terms to the ordinary illiterate peasantry. Such people see only that which is on the face of things obvious and Gandhi would be well aware of how his writings would be taken by them.

As an instance of Gandhi's ideological beliefs I think we are bound to hold that his creed of non-violence is for an ideal world and goes little further than the universal recognition that the settlement of disputes, whether between individuals or between nations or groups of nations, should be done by peaceful means and war as a medium should be abandoned. There are, it is true, some people who unfortunately have attained supreme power in certain parts of the world who do not believe that the abandonment of war is for the good of man, but I do not hesitate in my belief that they represent a minute portion of the world's population and few men desire anything more than a life ruled by law, peace and a feeling of security. There is a relevant quotation from Gandhi in the *Harijan* of 15th March 1942 (p. 76) in an article dealing with the possibility of evacuation from cities owing to war conditions.

So he recognises that even the existence of large towns with populations firmly believing in non-violence predicates the nation and indeed the world as a whole being non-violent. The existence of large bodies of men believing in, and ready to practise, non-violence and all that is to be implied by it is possible until man has attained a much higher moral standard than exists at present and is indeed possible only when men as a whole have got to that stage and non-violence has ceased to have any meaning. In fact, Gandhi's conception of large bodies of men in a nation or of a whole nation devoted to non-violence constitutes a contradiction to a warring world and a world of men as they exist today. So, while accepting that Gandhi has never abandoned his ideological belief in non-violence and he has worked for it all his life, as many others have done too, we can only relate this to theory and hold that it can have little bearing in practice, the more so when great issues and passions are concerned. I shall show later on that Gandhi has always been alive to the practical side of any question and, to anticipate a conclusion, the practical side dominated all his efforts in propagating his 'Quit India' movement.

Closely allied with Gandhi's belief in non-violence are his repeated averments of his love for all men and hatred of none. At various places in the *Harijan* he has said that there is in him neither hatred of the British nor love for the Japanese. The argument from the other side is that Gandhi in his love of man could not have wanted or contemplated doing anything that would involve injury. That is a sweeping statement and I find it difficult to escape the feeling that Gandhi's love and hate have too much of a negative character and mean little more than an absence of personal ill-will towards individuals. It has never prevented him from contemplating suffering and loss of life, as when he has contemplated "a Ganges full of blood' or having to "wade through a sea of blood" to attain independence. I am aware that these expressions may be read with the concept of sacrifice, but the question to be asked is—what meaning can this have to the ordinary man and what will he think of a theme which was developed with constant references to fighting, bloodshed, giving up everything and risking all in order to attain the desired end? I do not indeed think that these theoretical questions can have much part in the practical aspects of the campaign which Gandhi executed, unless there are clear indications that they were always kept in the foreground.

16. ***Violence inevitable.*** It is hardly necessary to do more than state that Gandhi recognised Congress and India as a whole was not inclined towards non-violence. Gandhi has never denied it, but I would quote two or three instances to show not only that India was not inclined towards non-violence, but that non-violence had but a small hold upon the population. In reply to a question during an interview to journalists about Muslim reactions to British withdrawal (*Harijan*, p. 187) he said:

> I have not asked the British to hand over India to the Congress or to the Hindus. Let them entrust India to God or, in modern parlance, to anarchy. Then all the parties will fight one another like dogs, or will, when real responsibility faces them, come to a reasonable agreement. I shall expect non-violence to arise out of that chaos.

Surely the emphasis here is upon civil strife and not upon the possibility of an immediate agreement.

He concluded an interview which is reported under 'Fire Raging in Me' with these words:

> I have no false notions of prestige, no personal considerations would make me take a step that I know is sure to plunge the country into a conflagration.

He is justifying the creation of what he describes as a conflagration on the general grounds of India's interest and excludes personal aggrandisement.

17. ***Anarchy and chaos.*** Gandhi in his writings repeatedly made reference to anarchy and chaos and here again there is no secret about his being prepared to accept chaos, in more than one of the quotations already given there is this reference to chaos and anarchy. The theme is succinctly expressed in his words (*Harijan*, p. 161)[15] addressed to the British:

> Leave India to God. If that is too much, then leave her to anarchy.

And its consequences find graphic expression in an interview to a representative of the London *News Chronicle* (*Harijan*, p. 166).[16] He was asked a question on the practicability of withdrawal and in the course of his reply he said:

> Under my proposal they have to leave India in God's hands—but in modern parlance to anarchy, may lead to internecine warfare for a time or to unrestrained dacoities. From these a true India will arise in the place of the false one we see.

In other words, whether there would be a voluntary or a forced withdrawal, anarchy would be the sure result unless there was an immediate full agreement which would provide a suitable Government in the country. Writings show—the earlier part of this interview is in point—that he did not anticipate this and indeed I would not spend time in dilating upon the likelihood of an immediate Provisional Government. It finds no mention in Gandhi's writings in the early stage of his campaign and he showed no anticipation of it; it appears later and is not an idea of his own, but one from the Congress President and others of the Working Committee to which he paid lip service. It emanated from the expressed readiness from Congress for Britain to hand over the country to anybody, even to the Muslim League. But that was qualified by the condition that the Muslim League or any other body would be a mere trustee for the country and the immediate formation of a democratic administration. One marvels that Congress leaders could wander in such a world of fancy unless, as I think, it is to give point to the dominant demand for independence at any price and under any circumstances.

What is the ordinary man going to understand by chaos and anarchy? Is Gandhi to be permitted to play with words and say that these terms do not necessarily imply violence? If so, that is to ignore the material upon which he was working, a matter which I have discussed at length. In practice, chaos and anarchy without violent manifestations are almost unheard of and the ordinary man in using such expressions thinks first and foremost of the strife and disorder that such a state connotes. In practice, therefore it is impossible to distinguish between violence and chaos as the result of withdrawal—whether voluntary or forced by a movement—and still less in the prosecution of a movement with intent to force a withdrawal. That is the only conclusion to be drawn from a complete consideration of Gandhi's writings from the time he initiated the 'Quit India' movement; and the contention that his writings show Gandhi at no time contemplated violence does not bear inspection for a moment. It is only true to the extent that he personally desired to avoid it—did not wish to be violent himself and did not specifically initiate the movement as a violent movement. But there is no difference in its results and responsibility when he knew that violence and chaos were necessary associates of his movement and he was ready to bear with them. The form of words means little, for it is the essential features that count and which would be grasped by his public.

18. Two small points before I leave Gandhi's writings. First is to draw attention to the campaign in the *Harijan* which started before the 'Quit India' movement, which could only be calculated to stir up hate against the British regime and therefore against Britishers, for they cannot be dissociated from it. There are numerous examples of brutality, oppression, racial discrimination and the like put forward without enquiry and as if established facts practised by the military are laid at British doors. They form an effective comment upon Gandhi's professions in respect of love and hate which I have already dealt with. So do his comments thereon all being incitement to resist or as furnishing cause for seeking independence. I am not going to credit Gandhi with such lack of intelligence as not to understand the effect of such writings on a subject race or upon anybody of persons suffering under grievances, apparent or real. Throughout all the ages there has been but one response and Gandhi could have expected no other in India.

The second point is Gandhi's reluctance to be specific on what his campaign involved. There was no attempt to define, as there had been in the past, nor to remind the people what non-violence meant. The expression 'non-violent non-cooperation' and references to non-violence were there, but surely it is dangerous to assume that everyone would know what they covered. Gandhi's reticence is illustrated in the quotation already given, where he stated that the movement would be a mass one of a strictly non-violent character 'and then you can fill in the details.' Why should he have so delayed telling the people what he expected from them and what is the effect when at the same time insistence is placed upon individual action and all persons being invited to join in the movement? In short, the whole of Gandhi's writings on what be expected the movement to be like leave 'non-violence' as an unobtrusive and hazy background with violence and anarchy in all their reality to the fore. It is no answer to say that through strife will come the desired peace and non-violence. That is nothing new and has been the way men have always thought.

19. ***Secret evidence.*** If my conclusions on Gandhi's writings are correct, we would expect the secret evidence to reflect them for two reasons, first because of the way his followers would interpret and understand them, and secondly because in private, especially when engaged in subversive activities, one speaks more freely than in public. To begin with the militant, often military, phraseology of the speakers strikes us most forcibly. The references to fighting, to revolution, to obtaining independence at all costs, to unheard of sacrifices and the like are so numerous and would not be open to challenge that it is not necessary to mention more than one or two. It is *possible* to use them all in connection with a contest between opposing interests without necessitating violence, but what is the view that is going to be taken by audiences addressed by Congress leaders? If the emphasis is on 'non-violence', then there will be no need to use terms of this kind and there would be no need to have kept the non-violent methods contemplated so obscure. What is likely to be the reaction to Gandhi's 'Do or Die' slogan which first finds place in the source report during the Working Committee proceedings at Wardha? It would be unnatural to expect it to be confined to mere passivity, something in the nature of strikes, or refraining from doing things without in any way being violent. Read these words of Pandit Govind Vallabh Pant to a big meeting at Naini Tal on August 1st, 1942.

> Today when millions and millions of people in the world are sacrificing their lives and getting themselves cut into pieces for the independence and freedom of their country, will you too, on listening to the call of a leader like Mahatma Gandhi, not be prepared to do your duty? I am confident that you will wholeheartedly participate in this struggle... We would not rest until freedom is achieved. We would surely fight for ourselves and our country.

Equally graphic was Pandit Jawaharlal Nehru a month earlier at Gorakhpur when he said:

> Time has come when we have to face greater perils. Only jail-going is not the only act of *satyagraha*. The world is militarised these days. Military tactics are being adopted. Every person has to risk his life and unless we risk our lives we cannot be free.

20. ***Meaning of Non-violence.*** I have suggested elsewhere that non-violence may have taken on a different meaning in the course of the campaign, and the meaning of which there is a good deal of evidence is that the limitation was not causing death or grievous harm. This may be largely a matter of interpretation, but its importance is that no details had been explained and his interpretation is not inconsistent. It first appears in the notes of Kanji Dwarkadas previously mentioned. As I have said, he is in close contact with political circles, and particularly with Sardar Vallabhbhai Patel whom he repeatedly mentions, and he attributes to the latter:

> Everything and anything short of physical violence should be done to make the Britisher realise that he was an outlaw in the country.

I have ascertained that Mr. R.S. Pandit remained underground till he was arrested in September and apparently he is thought to have been in Bombay until that time. There is no evidence, therefore, that his daughter had had any contact with him, though she may well have through the courier system which was in operation during the movement. Anyway she clearly had many opportunities of contact with Congressmen of position and there is no reason to suppose that they would have broken when such person went underground. The objection can be raised that she is young and therefore likely to be volatile, but it is no more proper to regard that as a reason for rejecting the letter than to accept it without further examination. It may be possible to find more information about this letter and of the girl's contacts with her father. Presumably she was writing according to her information and the letter cannot be ignored.

But there is other material of the same nature and it is mainly from statements of Congressmen arrested after the movement started. One of these is Ram Nandan Misra,[17] one of the most prominent Congress Socialist workers, who was arrested fairly early and managed to escape from Bhagalpur jail early in November, remaining free until February 1943. During the interval he was one of those mostly active in prosecuting the disturbances underground. He made a long statement, mainly I think after his second arrest, which is impressive in its frankness and connectedness, entitling it to be treated with respect. The second of this type is the statement of E. Narayanan, Assistant Editor of *The Hindustan Times*, who was arrested on 29th October 1942. He also made a long statement which must be given due weight and which has the corroboration of statements of other persons who had associated with him in his activities before arrest. He was constantly with Mrs. Asaf Ali—wife of Mr. Asaf Ali, Working Committee Member—who, as will be seen presently, was one of the group who directed operations from underground almost from the beginning and still continues to do so. She had expressed her view to him—she had been to Bombay for the session—that Gandhi left the question of sabotage to the decision of those who embarked upon or organised it. She had told him that the opinion of Congress circles in Bombay was that any loss of life in a train disaster would be interpreted by Gandhi as violence of the first order. A third statement comes from V.S. Dandekar, the CP Congress Socialist leader, who was arrested only two months back. He had attended the Bombay Session of the AICC, and almost immediately went underground, as the statement shows. He says that he had discussed the question of non-violence with

Gandhi beforehand, giving his own opinion that killing was justified in view of the great issues involved.

Fourthly, there is a source report from the Punjab which contains the substance of arguments of Congressmen in jail. They were agitating whether the movement could be reconciled with Gandhi's doctrines and some of them doubted, it is reported, if Gandhi could have intended all the violence that had occurred. One man, Kishan Gopal Dutt,[18] well-known in the Punjab, averred that Gandhi had left a last message with his nephew-valet, Kanubhai Gandhi, that all was non-violence except injury to the person. Krishan Gopal Dutt had been to Bombay for the August session and could have known if such a message had been left or Gandhi had said something of that kind to his nephew. These views on the meaning of non-violence come, therefore, from different parts of the country and from different sources. It is true most of them are after violence had taken complete hold on the movement and thus open to the argument that these people are trying to excuse themselves or throw the blame upon Gandhi.

There are yet other references which, though not as direct, imply the same attitude of Gandhi towards violence. The most striking perhaps comes from one Rajindra Nath[19] who, after his arrest on 15th October 1942 made a statement. He was a worker at Sewagram and accompanied Gandhi to Bombay, staying with him at Birla House. On 5th August 1942, there was an emergent meeting of the Standing Committee of the States Peoples Conference which was attended by Working Committee members and was addressed by Gandhi in Hindi.

Further point is given to the meaning of non-violence in a police report from Bombay where Shankar Rao Deo addressed a meeting on 25th July 1942. Being a report of a meeting in Bombay, we may accept its essential accuracy and it is important because Shankar Rao Deo was one of Gandhi's most enthusiastic supporters in his movement. In the course of the speech he said:

> This time it was not a moral pressure as in 1940, but it would be a sort of rebellion. Mahatma Gandhi would emerge as a *bagi* (i.e., rebel) on the day he launched the movement for the freedom of this country. He may even discard his principle of non-violence in this struggle because he knows that his principle cannot be preached unless India is a free country.

Even the very doubts among Congressmen indicate that violence was natural interpretation of what Gandhi had been writing and the leaders saying. I have referred to instances of doubt among those confined in jail after the movement; I will give but one more, coming at an early stage. It is in a source report from Calcutta, dated 9th June 1942, concerning the activities of Dr. Profulla Ghosh and other Congress leaders of Bengal who were during the Province in order to popularise Gandhi's 'Quit India' movement. To quote from the report:

> In secret Dr. Profulla Ghosh was challenged by some of the workers who contended that neither the Congress Working Committee nor Gandhi himself had authorised such a propaganda. Dr. Profulla Ghosh assured all that Gandhi had personally assured his confidants including himself (Dr. Profulla Ghosh), that he was going to launch a movement on that line after he had put it before the Working Committee.

The 'line' in question was a direction to the masses to resist those measures which were interfering with their normal life in the Province and obviously such resistance could not but be accompanied by force. I will leave this part of the problem (marginally noted are further appropriate references) of Congress responsibility and, if it appears rather overburdened, I justify it because it is the main ground of dispute between the Congress and the Government. There is bound to be overlapping, though it has been convenient to separate out various aspects of the contest between violence and non-violence as revealed by the evidence. The ideal of non-violence has to bow before the exigencies of the situation and that is why, although non-violence runs through all the writings and professions of those who interpret them, it failed to attain any prominence against the strength and militancy of practical demands.

21. ***Congress views.*** In considering Gandhi's views on non-violence and how he was interpreted by his followers, it was inevitable that the attitude of Congress would at the same time be more or less dealt with. Members of the Congress in interpreting Gandhi's meaning were unboundedly at the same time giving their own. First and foremost, however Congress, unlike Gandhi, has never been non-violent; where it has adopted non-violence, it has been, as Gandhi has insisted, as a policy suitable for the immediate purpose and not as a creed, the meaning it has for Gandhi. He and the Congress leaders have throughout the history of Congress been careful of Congress unity and to preserve it as a single body representing the nation, with the All-India Congress Committee as a perfect cross-section. That is why its constitution has always been loose and it has sought to retain within itself not only orthodox believer in non-violence, but Congress Socialist leaders with their belief in direct action, and even the Forward Bloc with its frankly revolutionary outlook. Gandhi has been more concerned than when there was danger of a split in Congress; and Congress had been able to continue as a single composite body. He was using Congress and even going outside Congress for his 'Quit India' movement, and therefore the talk of Congress following Gandhi in his movement non-violently is practically a contradiction in terms. Part might, it may be conceived, but the rest never; yet the whole was to participate and the responsibility could only be one. Gandhi's closest followers showed their devotion to him even more clearly in this movement and outstanding examples are Dr. Rajendra Prasad, Vallabhbhai Patel, H.K. Mehtab and Shankar Rao Deo. These all spoke in Gandhi's language and they could have been in no more doubt of what was likely to happen than Gandhi himself. Generally their views were clearer, perhaps because the latter expressed himself mainly in writing. I shall have something to say about principal leaders at a later stage, but I have already given many instances of their incitements to violence or interpretations tending towards violence. It is perhaps superfluous to add to them, but one or two further examples might be given. Outstanding is Yusuf Mehar Ali, the Mayor of Bombay. Though he is a Congress Socialist, he is still a Congressman and from the beginning, as a firm supporter of Gandhi's movement, he took a prominent part in preparing the way.

In the speeches at the Congress session in August the leaders did nothing to create a non-violent atmosphere. On the contrary, Miss Adrienne Moore in her *notes of the proceedings* at Bombay reveals clearly the vehemence of Nehru's speech on the last day and it is to be borne in mind that Nehru stands out, after Gandhi, as the personification of India, calling forth to a degree the response of the people. It is incredible that the audience which listened to him could have been other than roused to enthusiasm for the task that was pictured ahead. Miss Adrienne Moore is among other things an American journalist and, whatever criticisms there may be of her, it will not be denied that she would be an intelligent and accurate recorder of facts and of the general sense of the meeting. Vallabhbhai Petel, in describing the programme as including all that had ever been done before, left obscure the possibility of other things as well. And lastly there was Azad's injunction to Indians to take a timely step forward no matter what the cost and it was for the people themselves to make successful the resolution that had been passed. Read all this with what Gandhi himself said, that all were to consider themselves free and even though he trusted in non-violence he was prepared to go on even if he were proved wrong, and it would follow that an inspired audience could not but go forth ready to do anything, violent or non-violent, to bring about the independence that Gandhi and Congress were promising them. If Gandhi's attitude and activities were bound to lead to violence, even more true would this be of Congress.

22. ***Voluntury organisations.*** In one of Gandhi's earlier writings there was a reference to 'peace brigades', an expression used by him, and it is convenient here to refer shortly to the various volunteer organisations that came into existence apart from the ordinary Congress volunteers, which at the time of the Bardoli Resolution were more or less moribund. These other organisations were partly the outcome of Gandhi's renewed attention to his constructive programme and partly due to Japan's entry into the war and its approach to the borders of India. The idea was publicised in a press statement of January 22nd reproducing a circular letter issued by J.B. Kripalani, General Secretary of the Congress. The formation of Volunteers Corps was to be under the direction of Congress to secure effective and speedy working of the constructive programme—to use the words of the circular. Their object was described in the following words:

> They must be principally in rural areas for self-reliance, mutual co-operation and to face any emergency that may arise. Though a uniform and some sort of drill increases the efficiency of a volunteer corps, yet in the present circumstances, wherever there is any possibility of conflict with authorities or with rival organisations, such aid may be dispensed with... It is needless to remind you that non-violence must be the basic principle of our volunteer organisation.

It will be remembered how Gandhi dealt with the question of non-violence and explained how such a policy would operate in an emergency as the war situation worsened. A further circular on the same subject was issued on 25th March 1942, it being a matter of concern to Congress that the appeal for volunteers had met with a poor response. The new circular was more explicit and may we not say, more attractive.

Surely a comprehensive organisation of this kind could only protect and keep order if force were used. The Congress therefore brought into existence organisations which were bound to use force in spite of the limitation of peaceful means. We may remember here too Gandhi's interpretation of non-violence as lying in the motive and mentality of the men concerned rather than in the actual act.

Such volunteer organisation under the name of *Shanti Senas* became popular in Assam where the war was nearest India. In the same papers there is an inspection report by R.K.L. Nandkeolyar, an AICC inspector whose duty it was to tour the provinces and inspect Congress committees and allied organisations. He refers with approval to the *Shanti Senas* and the measures of the Assam Provincial Congress Committee to make them effective and was convinced of their value, not indeed as being able to do anything to resist invasion or even predatory attacks by hill-tribes, but in controlling unsocial elements and professional gangs of dacoits which would be likely to make their appearance in times of disorder.

I have found it of some value to go through the intelligence reports from the various provinces covering the point I am dealing with. The Central Provinces reports, in particular pay attention to the *Sanraksha Dals* or self-protection societies similar to the *Shanti Senas* of Assam, which had already begun to be formed in response to the appeals I have mentioned. They were not very successful, but much greater activity was evinced and a considerable measure of success attained from the time Gandhi started his 'Quit India' movement. A Punjab report is, however, interesting and relates to Dr. Gopi Chand,[20] a well-known Punjab Congressman, who had returned from Wardha where he had been taking part in the conversations which had ensued between Gandhi and Congressmen during the first half of June. He stated that Gandhi wanted his constructive programme to be inaugurated on a grand scale in the Punjab with two objects, namely, in furtherance of his constructive programme to make the villages self-sufficient, and in perfecting the villagers in the art of self-defence, for the people would have to rely on local volunteer corps for protection rather than on the police or military. Presumably the intention was to protect from local disorders in the same way as the Assam Shanti Senas, but here again Gandhi was out to create his own machine, and the indication is that it was not meant to be entirely non-violent. United Provinces reports of the same period also refer to Gandhi's desire greatly to strengthen the constructive programme and for the formation of self-defence groups. It was first regarded as rather curious, but subsequently an explanation was put forward of its fitting in with Gandhi's campaign and his call for support from his own workers.

Left-Wing Contacts

23. It is admitted that the more extreme political elements in the country were most active during the disturbances and indeed one of the arguments of orthodox Congressmen is that it was they who were responsible for what took place and Congress, with Gandhi at its head in its non-violent programme, could neither have organised nor intended the violence that occurred. They seek to put responsibility upon individuals and upon the extreme elements. It will therefore be of some interest to examine the extent to which Gandhi and the Congress worked with which had a fair strength in the Congress, was led by determined men, and which, though believing in direct action, was nearer orthodox Congress views than the so-called revolutionary parties. Now it is clear there are several factors tending towards association with those whose views did not preclude them from using violence as an official elements in their activities. First, there is Gandhi determined to press his movement through at all costs. Secondly, there is the lack of support from Congress especially at the beginning, which nevertheless did not deter him from devoting all his energies in furtherance of his

purpose. He was determined to go on despite Congress opposition; and even after the passing of the Wardha Resolution could not be sure that the support they were giving him would not be withdrawn. Thirdly, there is the all-inclusive character of the movement, both in its call to all classes and manner of people and it's absence of conditions.

Proof is hardly called for the whole-hearted support which would be certain from the Congress Socialist Party, the Kisan Subhas, the Forward Bloc and other even more advanced elements. It is sufficient if I confine myself to the three named, and in particular to the Congress Socialist Party which is most important.

A meeting of the All-India Kisan Sabha was held at Bidaul in Bihar in the first week of June, wherein Yusuf Mehar Ali moved a resolution, which was passed unanimously, extending full support to the Congress in the event of the launching of a mass struggle. This support was repeated, according to a Lucknow report, when the All-India Kisan Sabha held a session at Bombay on August 7th. Whole-hearted support to Gandhi's movement was promised and it was further resolved that all families of kisans having more than one male member should be asked to give one for the movement while others should be asked to afford financial support to the best of their ability. For the Forward Bloc we have a letter from its leader R.S. Ruikar[21] who forwarded to H.K. Bose[22] in Calcutta a letter containing a statement which he hoped to get into the press. In it he declared "Mahatma Gandhi and the Congress Working Committee are now following the footsteps of Subhas Chandra Bose and the All-India Forward Bloc." One of his proposed headings to his statement is as follows:

> Congress Working Committee's move welcomed. Mahatma Gandhi is today following Subhas Chandra Bose and the Forward Bloc.
>
> Forward Bloc has been declared unlawful but is re-born through the Congress Working Committee.

It is surely not going to be argued that Gandhi was unaware of the support from, what from his point of view, would ordinarily be deemed dangerous elements.

24. ***Co-operation of Congress and Socialist workers.*** There are a number of reports which indicate there was no question of a Socialist being excluded from participation and active help in the movement. The most illuminating document is an appeal said to have been drawn up at Belgaum on August 3rd, when there was a meeting of Congress leaders of the Karnataka. It would appear that the source must have seen the appeal and taken a copy of it and here again there should be no difficulty in collecting other information.

Of other reports there is one from Lucknow relating to the United Provinces leader Ganga Sahai Chaube, discussing the movement with Congress workers and others; among those whom he talked with was a certain Prem Dutt Paliwal,[23] a notorious revolutionary, to whom he is said to have made clear that, although Gandhi was sticking to his creed of non-violence, the volunteers organised for the movement would be prepared to commit all sorts of mischief against Government property using force and violence where necessary. Prem Dutt Paliwal is mentioned in another UP report where he and some of his associates were present at a private meeting of Congress workers.

Prem Dutt's friends offered themselves for any sort of work, including removing of railway lines, from Bombay. Govindrao Deshpande, the Secretary of the Maharashtra Provincial Congress Committee. He was touring in support of the Working Committee resolution and sought the co-operation of Communists: he is said to have assured them that the launching of the forthcoming struggle was a certainty and its scope would be unlimited. Deshpande was said to have been engaged in preparing underground machinery for the furtherance of the movement. Congress Socialists were effective speakers at Congress meetings and Purshotam Trikamdas, the General Secretary of the Congress Socialist Party, and Yusuf Mehar Ali made inflammatory speeches advocating Gandhi's movement. From Bihar comes a report which speaks of a secret meeting of Socialist and Congress workers held at Gaya at the end of July at which is was decided that every individual should be prepared to sacrifice his life for the Independence of India.

I draw attention in particular to two of the above references as indicative of Congressmen using a method of approach more calculated to appeal to those whose co-operation was being sought. One is Ganga Sahai Chaube, who would seem to have tempted Prem Dutta Paliwal and his group with the prospect of violence against Government property; and the second is Govindrao Deshpande, who dangled a similar bait to secure Communist assistance. It would be interesting if other instances of the same kind could be found. In short, the circumstances tended towards Gandhi relying upon left-wing support and the instances I have given are sufficient to show that he actually did so. Nevertheless it would be more satisfactory if certain aspects of it that I have suggested could be corroborated further. Ram Nandan Misra is correct too in saying that Congress Socialists held important Congress posts and that was true all over the country. Collection of information might produce rather surprising results.

25. ***General ideas.*** Nevertheless it would be surprising if the form of the movement was not a subject of frequent discussion leading to some sort of broad outline. In this connection I have to refer again to S.N. Sanyal's letter of 1st August 1942, which mentions among other things that Gandhi had three or four plans in his mind and he would decide after seeing the reaction. That information he is said to have got from Kripalani and Pandit Nehru and would be typical of Gandhi, who usually makes a close study of conditions before he acts. In connection with his new movement he had sent out his own men to find how the land lay. He had also been working up the people through his writings, his call for constructive work and formation of volunteer corps. He was surely watching 'events' and settling in his own mind what would best meet the situation as it came to ahead. An interesting report comes from the Central Provinces, dated 27th August 1943. It relates to talks among detenus in the Jubbulpore Jail; and Kaka Kalelkar,[24] a C.P. Congressman and intimate follower of Gandhi, who was in close touch with him throughout the whole of the preparatory period, is related to have said that the actual details of the movement were left half-discussed, as time was hoped to be gained during the anticipated Gandhi-Viceroy talks.

26. ***Developments in Bombay.*** Having progressed so far, the question arises whether in the last few days something more definite did not emerge from Gandhi and the Working Committee. Naturally the AICC as a whole could not be responsible, for

their business was to sit in judgment and review, as it were, upon schemes and ideas put forward by the executive body of Congress. In particular what is to be examined is the origin of the now familiar 12-point programme and its environment of sabotage, especially of communications. Before the session of the main body of the AICC there was a session of the Working Committee, but what is more important for my purpose is the suggestion of a secret meeting of the Working Committee right at the end of the proceedings, probably on the night of August 8th. There are several references to such a meeting and on the whole I am inclined to agree that it took place. One of the most specific comes from a statement on interrogation of Prem Krishna Khanna who was not arrested until 7th August 1943, and who took a prominent part in revolutionary activities in Northern Provinces. His name constantly appears in statements of other workers who were arrested at different times. He says there was a secret meeting of the Working Committee on the night of August 8th, apparently to consider the further programme, because Mr. Gandhi and the Congress leaders knew that arrests were going to be made. It is difficult to see why such a statement should be made by a man of Prem Krishna's character if it were not true. Another revolutionary, Giani Mehar Singh of Amritsar, who was arrested on 7th August 1942, soon after the disturbances started, also speaks of the secret meeting in his statement. His got his information from a certain Hakim Ahmad Hasan, who was first detained with him and with whom he had conversations before he gave the statement. Hasan got his information from a certain Kedar Nath Sahgal[25] whose name appears in other statements also. Then there are two reports—I think part of same report—from the Central Provinces dated 12th August 1942. They come from a CID Inspector of Police who was deputed to attend the session at Bombay. The first report speaks of a secret meeting of the Working Committee where Gandhi is supposed to have expressed satisfaction at the possibility of arrests of Congress members and urged those who were not arrested to fan the hostility which would undoubtedly show itself. The second report refers to the immediate distribution of instructions for the carrying on of *satyagraha,* which according to the source's information had been drawn up by Gandhi during the interval between the arrival of the police and his arrest. That information could not be correct if it had anything to do with the 12-point programme, which clearly must have taken a considerable time to prepare. On the other hand, having regard to liability of confusion even in the best of these reports the reference may be to some short instruction which Gandhi may have given in the aforesaid interval.

These three reports taken together suggest the holding of a secret meeting on the night of August 8th. As a third source of information, we turn again to the statement of Ram Nandan Misra. He describes events up to August 7th when he had accompanied the other Congress Socialists in their visit to Gandhi. There was to be a meeting of prominent Congress workers from all Provinces at 9 A.M. on August 9th, when it was anticipated that Gandhi would explain the programme of his movement. There is ample evidence from others to show that such a meeting was fixed. On August 10th Achyut Patwardhan and Dr. Lohia told him Gandhi had approved of the tearing up of railway tracks and cutting of telegraph wires, provided no loss of human life was involved. This could only have been done in some meeting between the two dates. Directly in point is the previously referred statement of Rajindra Nath. He says he had gone to

Birla House early on the morning of August 9th, when he heard that the leaders had been arrested, and he saw Gandhi's secretary, Pyarelal, who gave him a copy of the instructions issued by the AICC. He recounted the general lines of these instructions and they would correspond to the 12-point programme. Pyarelal is supposed also to have given him the information that the instructions had been drawn up by Gandhi and the Working Committee in the small hours of the morning when it was known that arrest was probable. Lastly, there is a source report from Calcutta which purports to give information obtained from Gopi Nath Bardoloi,[26] the ex-Congress Premier of Assam, when he stopped in Calcutta on his way back to Assam from Bombay. He is supposed to have said that after the AICC meeting on the 8th Gandhi had a brief consultation with the Working Committee members. During discussion Gandhi said he had nothing to add to a circular put up to him by Kripalani; he expected the masses would take care of the working out of the programme.

27. ***A specific programme.*** I deal briefly here with the 12-point programme. I accept without discussion the statement in the Congress Responsibility pamphlet that it had a widespead circulation within a very short time of the arrests of the leaders. I consider, however, that it is desirable to make a collection of information from the various Provinces as to when and with whom it was first found. The point is to establish that it was a definite programme, that it had emanated from Bombay and could only be attributed to the Working Committee. I am not going to emphasise its strong Gandhian flavour, which has been analysed in the Congress Responsibility pamphlet; orthodoxy runs through it. I am not at the moment concerned with the comprehensiveness and the question whether, even on professed non-violent principles, such a programme could in practice be carried out non-violently. Numerous other instructions issued subsequently from time to time, which might or might not have had an orthodox origin, but I think it safe to say that no other organisation, like the Congress Socialists Party, would be responsible for this programme, since it would convey nothing outside ordinary Congress principles.

It is a lengthy programme, well-drawn up, and must have been carefully considered and drafted. This disposes of any contention that it was hurriedly brought into existence. It must have been in print in Bombay not later than August 9th and this is conclusively proved from the fact that a printed copy of it on yellow paper was recovered from the possession of Haripada Sarkar, a member of the AICC, who was arrested in Calcutta on August 11th on his return from Bombay. The more evidence that can be obtained of similar other recoveries, the better. Now this itself—for I accept the truth of the information—proves that the programme was in print in Bombay on the 9th and must have been drawn up before that. It lends point to the information attributed to Gopi Nath Bardoloi when he was in Calcutta on his return, which must have been about the same time as the printed copy was seized from Haripada Sarkar.

There is no other mention of a circular drawn up by Kripalani, but he was the General Secretary of the Congress and the presumption would be that the circular was the 12-point programme. There is one thing further about the 12-point programme and that is it has often been found in conjunction with a second instruction.

Some little time prior to the movement he instituted a series of newsletters containing confidential information which he sent out to a restricted clientele. The information he gave is entitled to respect and the newsletter of August 7th is remarkable because it contains almost word for word the addition which found public appearance after the disturbances started. It is supposed to be Gandhi's general idea, as explained to the Working Committee, of how the movement was to start and what form it was to take. It goes definitely beyond the generality and guess work which had been prominent up till then. It is surprising perhaps that more information on this point is not forthcoming, but it is true of course that most of those best acquainted with it have not given, and would not be likely to give, any information. The decision incorporated in the addition to the 12-point programme must have been taken, I think, not later than August 6th. Surely some definite programme must have been drawn up and would have been submitted for Gandhi's final approval while the leaders were still free.

28. ***Violence, part of the programme.*** The 12-point programme is not violent in any of its clauses and, while assuming that it is possible to carry it out non-violently, I would deal with the more direct assertion that it was accepted that violence in some degree would have to be used. The addition to the 12-point programme, which I have dealt with, implies violence and strong evidence would be needed to displace the implication. I refer in particular to the sentence: "The next stage would lead to breaking of salt laws on a large scale, picketing of foreign cloth and liquor shops, promoting industrial strikes, holding up the railways and telegraphs, calling army to come out, non-payment of taxes and setting up the parallel Government." Surely the holding up of railways and telegraphs could only mean positive action to break those communications. There is a reference to industrial strikes, but it is to be noted that, as regards railways and telegraphs, it is not strike that are mentioned. It is obvious that railways and telegraphs can be held up effectively by strikes but why was it not so worded? This makes it all the more easy to accept reports which, generally in reference to the secret meeting on the 8th night, state that Gandhi approved of positive action to disrupt communication. The statement of Giani Mehr Singh, the Calcutta and Central Provinces reports, and Rajindra Nath's statement, all of which I have dealt with in connection with the Working Committee meeting, so that Gandhi accepted violence as a necessary part of his movement. Some reports go further than others, but this, I think must be accepted that Gandhi consented to positive action, which went beyond what non-violence had always been taken to mean. I must also refer again to the C.P. report dated 27th August 1943, detailing talks among detenus at Jabbulpore. Kaka Kalelkar was responsible for the opinion that the line of action and public programme were the same, but Gandhi wanted individual action and no loss of life. He approved of tampering with communication, but expected the doer to remain on the spot to give warning. Kalelkar was closely associated with Gandhi, while the whole report attributed to him has an air of genuineness about it. A very recent piece of evidence on this subject has come my way being a statement of a certain Subedar Ram Nath, who was an Assistant Storekeeper in the Jubbulpore Arsenal and was arrested in connection with misappropriation of stores.

M.S. Bhatt, named in the statement, is the Secretary of the General Provinces Congress Committee. It would be most difficult at this stage to dissociate Gandhi from the Working Committee and the measures taken.

The procedure of the remaining members of the AICC, of which there are reports, give some further support to violence being an accepted part of the movement. Here again the evidence might be a good deal better and one is struck by the paucity of reports, especially from Bombay. Whether there are not more available if Bombay chose to produce them, or whether the city police and authorities were so occupied with the disturbances that all other considerations were excluded, I do not know. It is unfortunate, however, that more is not known of the movements of those Congressmen who were not arrested especially as a considerable number of well-known persons was still at large. A source report from the United Provinces, a few days after the disturbance broke out, describes a meeting of the AICC rump numbering about 70 members in all. This followed the alleged handing over of a last message from Gandhi, which he had left with his wife, to Mr. Satyamurti.[27] He is said to have called the meeting of the remaining members, read out the message and, after discussions, drawn up a programme which included among other things, sabotage of telegraph communications and destruction of the larger bridges. The whole report suggests that the instructions which were drawn up were the 12-point instructions and cannot, therefore, be accepted for reasons I have given. Another point is that it is most improbable a meeting of so many members of the AICC rump was held in Bombay that day. There is no other report on the subject and Bombay have specifically reported they have no information. Much more convincing is the statement of Jagat Narayan Chopra who was arrested soon after the disturbances started. I have previously said that he has given a lengthy statement on which, I think, general reliance may be placed. He had gone to Birla House after he heard of arrests and found confusion there, as was only to be expected. A programme, which has already been drawn up, was being reproduced and he saw one later on which must have been the 12-point programme. He does not suggest anywhere in his statement that sabotage was part of the programme. A Calcutta report also refers to a meeting of the un-arrested AICC members, among whom Mrs. Kripalani is first named. A Lahore report states that the 12-point programme was drawn up by the members of the AICC at Bombay, but this I am afraid I cannot accept. It is as well that we have evidence previously discussed on the subject of the 12-point programme. I have mentioned before the statement of Mukandlal Sarkar, Secretary of the Forward Bloc, to the effect that no official programme had been given by the Working Committee or the AICC, the workers left behind possessing the authority to chalk and work out their own programme. This, however, does not get us any further as to positive action by the AICC. The subsequent report, which actually quotes the whole of the addition, was explained by the new messenger as having the authority of the AICC and Gandhi. It would be desirable to get the obscurity in these reports cleared up and more details obtained if available. However, this evidence as to the part played by the AICC amounts on the whole to very little. It seems to have been thought that the AICC rump was responsible for the 12-point programme. On the basis of the reports one can only negative this, which would be consistent with my finding that the 12-point programme must have come into existence earlier.

29. ***Immediate reaction.*** Important corroboration of the character the movement was to have, and which would strongly suggest that Congress as a whole, represented by the AICC, was responsible for, or made itself a party to, violence, is

afforded by activities of Congressmen immediately after the arrests. Even legally immediate reactions are accepted as reflecting truly an incident of which otherwise there might not be direct proof. We have numerous examples in the secret evidence, and outstanding among them is one already given, being Kala Venkatarao's letter in connection with the Andhra Programme. The instructions he gave correspond to those in what I have called the addition to the 12-point programme and afford further support for what I have already said in that connection. The letter reads as from a man who had been in contact with those most closely connected with the movement. Next I would refer to the statement of Annu Guruji who said that after the arrests Belgaum Congress workers met AICC leaders who had returned from Bombay and they decided to go underground and further a programme of cutting communications, derailing, burning of village records, railway stations, etc., disarming the police and looting of revenue centres and mail bags. I have tried to get further details of this statement but Annu Guruji I understand is not inclined to be more specific. Nevertheless corroboration is afforded by the pre-arrest activities of Belgaum workers, of which we have the instructions of August 3rd and Annu Guruji's further statement.

Gandhi expected every Indian to take part in the movement and Bihar Congress workers should start their work from the villages, capturing police stations, stopping the payment of revenue and establishing their own panchayats to run the administration. This, it will be remembered, would be in accordance with the instructions which were circulated in Bihar from August the 9th as Rajendra Prasad's instructions. Rajendra Prasad, it is said, could not be more explicit because of the presence of the police. Jai Chand Vidyalankar went to Benares to get into contact with other workers and speaks of instructions from Bombay being brought by Dr. Tungamma[28] and others about August 12th. The instructions would seem to have been the 12-point programme and he refers to further instructions being received a day or two later from Agra, purporting to be from AICC. These instructions *inter alia* advocated disruption of communications. They did, however, contain a warning that, before railway tracks were removed, red flags should be put up in order to avoid loss of life. Even before the movement, according to an Agra report dated 31st July 1942, at a meeting of Congress workers attended by S.N. Chaturdevi, there is the same mention of a red flag being put up as a warning when rails were removed.

Dr. Gairola who was most active in sabotage in the United Provinces also refers to the same Dr. Tungamma bringing instructions from Bombay as emanating from the AICC. There is no mention in his statement specifically of sabotage, but he says there was the instruction to cause the maximum of delay and harm to the war effort, and he graphically describes how this programme was 'successfully" followed in instances of sabotage which he helped to direct.

Deshbandhu Gupta actually returned from Bombay in August and he is known as a leading Congressman with no violent associations. There are other reports which mention him. Again, V.S. Dandekar in his statement refers to meeting several Congress leaders after the arrests and says that with one of them he saw a 10-point programme leaflet in manuscript which contained instructions for cutting telegraph and wires and removal of rails.

It is true that this is only a second-hand report, but the circumstances and persons involved give it a high degree of reliability and I do not think its importance can be exaggerated. In view of all this, should there be any difficulty in accepting the incident referred to in the Congress Responsibility pamphlet that Pandit Ravi Shankar Shukla, the former Congress Premier of the Central Provinces, told the police officer in whose custody he was that, if they had been given ten days time instead of being arrested on the way back from Bombay, every police station in the district would have been burnt down? I am given to understand that this statement was made to a Sub-Divisional Officer of Police and the want of such a responsible officer must count. Whether it would be sufficient if a criminal case were concerned is beside the point. As far as I am concerned, it is only one piece of evidence among many touching upon an aspect of the disturbances. I have seen one comment to the effect that, if the statement had been true, a prosecution would have resulted. I record as my opinion that, standing as it does, the statement could not be a legal basis for prosecution. The statement implies the emergence of sabotage in the 'official' programme and the expectancy that further time would have been available to complete preparations. It is well to remember too the earlier statement attributed to the same leader that "cutting of telegraph and telephone wires was probably part of the programmes."

All these examples I have given are of a character, connecting methods of a violent nature with a programme, though may be not entirely specific in its details, emanating from Gandhi and the Working Committee. I do not include the numerous examples which could be cited of local Congressmen all over the country giving their own ideas of the same character almost immediately after the arrests. All this evidence might well be connected up in an observation from the source report from Nagpur dated 12th August 1942.

I hardly think it a matter for surprise if an official instruction emanating from Congress, as undoubtedly the 12-point programme was, did not contain anything that would directly incite violence; and even the addition is left obscure enough to permit argument towards a non-violent interpretation. But the emphasis on every man being a leader, the initiative to be taken according to one's own lights, and the call for all to join, would make it a safe and effective measure to pass on the violent method by word of mouth as the general and necessary accompaniment for a successful movement.

References

1. The individual *satyagraha* or civil disobedience was started by Gandhi on 17th October, 1940 as a protest against the British denial of right of freedom to speech to Indians to preach against war and India's participation in it. He did not like to embarrass Britain which was then engaged in a life and death struggle against the Axis Powers by launching a mass movement and chose to vindicate this right by what later came to be known as "Individual *Satyagraha*". Under this movement Gandhi alone was to decide who should offer *satyagraha.* Vinoba Bhave was the first person to be selected by him to offer *satyagraha.* Vinoba Bhave was arrested and was followed by Jawaharlal Nehru and Vallabhbhai Patel.
2. Acharya J.B. Kripalani (b. 1888): General Secretary, Indian National Congress 1934-40; President, 1946-47; Member Constituent Assembly 1946-50; resigned from Congress in 1951.
3. P.C. Joshi (b. 1907): Secretary, Communist Party of India.
4. A.G. Tandulkar: A political worker of Bombay, arrested in 1942 and detained in Central Prison, Nasik Road.

5. Mira Behn (or Ben): disciple of Mahatma Gandhi, originally Miss Madeline Slade, daughter of Admiral Sir Edmond Slade; joined Gandhi's Ashram in 1925. Viceroy Linlithgow wrote to Amery (Secretary of State) on 8th June 1942 about the activities of Mira Behn in Orissa "information from other sources suggest that Gandhi is paying a good deal of attention to the use to which he can turn women agents in connection with the possible campaign of his . . . There were also signs that he was working for him not only Mira Ben but other ladies in other parts of the country, more particularly Assam, Bengal and Orissa—Manserigh N.(Ed.), *The Transfer of Power (1942-47),* Volume II, p. 192.
6. Their activities came to the notice of the governments of the various provinces and the Viceroy. There are frequent references to them in Manserigh, N.(Ed.), *The Transfer of Power,* Volumes II and III.
7. Mridula Sarabhai (1911-74): Follower of Gandhi; daughter of Ambalal Sarabhai, prominent merchant and industrialist, Ahmedabad.
8. Sucheta Kripalani (1908-74): wife of Archarya Kripalani, sometime Lecturer, Banaras Hindu University; Member, Constituent Assembly; Member, Congress Working Committee; Member, Lok Sabha 1951-62; Chief Minister of UP 1963-67.
9. Kanji Dwarka Das: Home Rule League Member; Labour Superintendent in E.D. Sassoon Mills, Bombay; author.
10. This was published in *Harijan* dated 29th June 1942. Extracts from the Report have been omitted.
11. Hiralal Mahadev Desai: Private Secretary to Mahatma Gandhi; died on 15th August 1942 in detention in Aga Khan Palace in Poona; author of some books including the biography of Maulana Azad.
12. Lal Bahadur Shastri (1904-1966): Prominent Congress leader, later Home Minister, Central Government; Prime Minister of India after Nehru; died in Tashkent in 1966.
13. *Harijan* dated 12th July 1942. Please see relevant portion in Extracts from *Harijan.*
14. *Ibid.*
15. See relevant portion in extracts from *Harijan.*
16. *Ibid.*
17. Ram Nandan Misra: b. 1905. Prominent Congress Socialist leader of Bihar; took active part in the 'Quit India' movement of 1942; arrested in August 1942; escaped from Bhagalpur jail and worked underground till his re-arrest in February 1943. Retired from politics 1952; leading wife of an ascetic.
18. Krishan Gopal Dutt: (1899-1957) Prominent Congress worker of Punjab; belonged to Sialkot, now in West Pakistan. Minister, East Punjab, 1948.
19. Rajinder Nath: Congress worker of Batala in Punjab; son of Gauri Shankar Khatri.
20. Dr. Gopi Chand Bhargava: (1889-1966) Congress leader of Punjab; elected to Punjab Legislative Assembly in 1931 and again in 1946; Chief Minister of Punjab 1947-51.
21. R.S. Ruikar: (1895-1954) Labour leader of Bombay; President, Nagpur Textile Labour Union; Leader Forward Bloc, President Hind Mazdoor Sabha, 1948.
22. H.K. Bose: Forward Bloc leader.
23. Prem Dutt Paliwal : Revolutionary leader of UP.
24. Dattatraya Balkrishna alias Kaka Kalelkar: Congress leader of Bombay, close associate of Mahatma Gandhi; Member, Rajya Sabha 1952-64; Educationist, Journalist and Literateur.
25. Kedar Nath Sahgal: A well-known Congress leader of Punjab; imprisoned several times for his nationalistic activities; took a vow to wear black clothes till the achievement of independence.
26. Gopi Nath Bardoloi: Premier of Assam (1938-39); Chief Minister of Assam in 1945.
27. Satyamurti: Member, Indian Legislative Assembly for Madras; Member of All-India Congress Committee.
28. Dr. Tungamma: Political worker of Bombay.

17

Road to Partition

I

Ramgarh Congress Session

The Congress Ministries resigned and the 'Deliverance Day' was over. The main issue that agitated public mind was the controversy over the acceptance or refusal of the Congress demand for a Constituent Assembly. The possibility of civil disobedience was time and again referred to as a means to enforce the Congress demand. But Gandhi dismissed it as inopportune.[1] Jinnah, on the other hand, pressed for a concise statement on behalf of the British Government that the Act of 1935 would go lock, stock and barrel and that the entire scheme of Constitutional reform would be scrutinised *de novo* in the light of the experience gained from the working of the Congress ministries for a period of two years. Meanwhile, the Congress concluded its session at Ramgarh on 20th March and the All India Muslim League at Lahore the days after both pulling in different directions. While the former trying to back its demand for *independence, democracy and national unity by a threat of civil disobedience, the latter demanding for a separate sovereign state for the Indian Muslims who are to be treated not as a minority as hitherto but as a nation, separate and distinct from the Hindus.*

The Ramgarh Congress resolution regarded Britain's war against Germany as being waged 'fundamentally for imperialist ends and for the preservation and strengthening of her empire' and directed Congressmen and those under Congress influence not to help in the prosecution of the War, which might lead to the perpetuation and strengthening of British imperialism in India. Communal harmony was to be sought through no other agency except a Constituent Assembly where the rights of all recognised minorities were to be settled by settlement between the elected representatives of the various majority and minority communities or, if necessary, by negotiation. The proposed Constituent Assembly was, however, not to frame any Constitution except on the basis of 'independence, democracy and national unity'. The resolution, in fact, not only pushed aside all attempts to divide India or to split up her nationhood, but rejected to 'admit the right of the rulers of Indian States or of foreign vested interests to come in the way of Indian freedom'. Lastly, the Congress session recommended a resort to civil disobedience[2] and authorised the All India Congress Committee and, if necessary, the Working Committee, to initiate steps to secure the implementation of the resolution.'

Meanwhile, the international war situation began to change rapidly. With the war losing its aggressive character, the defence of India was getting closely linked with the defence of Britain. The Congress President, Maulana Azad, immediately convened an emergency session of the Congress Working Committee at Delhi on 3rd July to consider the Viceroy's proposals made to Gandhi at Simla. After the five-day session concluded on 7th July, the Working Committee unequivocally passed a resolution requesting the British Government, in return for full cooperation, to make 'an unequivocal declaration granting total Independence to India' and by way of giving effect to it, to initiate immediate steps to constitute 'a provisional National Government' at the Centre. Jinnah, however, stated this resolution as an expression of the Congress determination to dictate terms to the British by the institution of its own *Raj* to which the Muslim League stood strongly opposed. Nehru, as the spokesman for the Working Committee, was a little more vocal in his support of the resolution. He said that as his people were not prepared for complete non-violence and as the only alternative left was slavery, he would adopt violence rather than submit to slavery. Moreover, he would not support the idea, unlike Gandhi, that the Congress should influence policies and decisions by remaining outside. Rajagopalachari, the mover of the resolution, also concentrated on the immediate formation of the National Government as a must to the Congress' full participation in the prosecution of the war. Sardar Patel also promised the 'full and hearty cooperation' of the Congress if the British Government accepted its demands.[3]

In the circumstances, the Viceroy issued a statement the famous August offer on 8th August 1940 wherein, it was briefly stated: (a) Though the differences which prevented national unity remained unbridged, the expansion of the Governor-General's Council and the forming of an advisory war council should no longer be postponed, (b) In view of the doubts as to whether the position of minorities would be broadly safeguarded in any future constitutional change, the British Government re-affirmed its desire that full importance should be given to minority opinion, (c) Subject to the fulfilment of their obligations an allusion to such issues as defence, minority rights, the treaties with the States, and the position of the Secretary of State's services the British Government converged in the Indian desire that the framing of the new Constitution should be 'primarily the responsibility of Indians themselves, and should originate from Indian conceptions of the social, economic and political structure of Indian life'. (d) Constitutional issues could not be settled at a 'moment when the commonwealth is engaged in a struggle for existence'; but after the war a representative Indian body should be formed to frame the new Constitution, and in the meantime the British Government would welcome and assist any efforts to come to an agreement as to the form and operation of this Constitution-making body and as to the principles of the Constitution itself, and (e) In the interval, the British Government expected that all parties and communities would co-operate in India's war-effort, and by thus pave the way for India's attainment of free and equal partnership in the British Commonwealth.

Congress against August Offer

The Congress, however, rejected the August offer mainly because their demand for a national government had not been conceded. In war time there was no question of converting the Executive Council into a national government. Lord Linlithgow was unmoved on this issue and so was His Majesty's Government. Had the Congress joined the Viceroy's executive council and with Congress ministries coming back into power in the provinces, the political situation would have changed broadly to the advantage of the Congress. Once the Congress rejected the offer, the Viceroy was in no mood to carry on any further parleys with it.[4]

The Viceroy's declaration of 8th August 1940 described by its apologists as one more Magna Carta generously granted to India, made it clear to the people of this country that they should expect nothing by way of transfer of power during the war years.

The League cordially welcomed the declaration at the meeting of its Working Committee held on 2nd September 1940. It characterised the declaration of the Viceroy and the Secretary of State as 'a considerable progressive advance towards the approach of the point of view and the stand taken by the League on behalf of the Muslim India regarding the problem of the future Constitution of India.

Thus, while the Muslim League had every reason to support and put forward the scheme of Partition; even the non-party leaders, noted for their eminence and temperate outlook, made undeterred attempts to break the national stalemate but without success. Meanwhile, the Bombay Conference made two recommendations: one for the duration of the war and another for the future. As for the future, the conference pointed out that the British Government should make a declaration, simultaneously with the reconstruction of the government, that 'within a specified time limit after the conclusion of the war, India will enjoy the same measure of freedom as will be enjoyed by Britain and dominions'.

Japan's unexpected attack on Pearl Harbour and her thumping victories in the Far East leading to the surrender of Singapore on 15th February 1942 vastly changed the war scenario. The United States of America could no longer remain a passive onlooker of the massive turn of events especially after the fall of Pearl Harbour. Her entry into the war not only ensured the victory of the Allied cause but also gave it a new ideological content. President Roosevelt had strong views on the issue of India's freedom. Apart from America, China also demanded that Britain should withdraw from India. Bowing to the immense pressure, the British Government decided to send Stafford Cripps to India with an offer which he probably knew would be rejected by Indian opinion. In fact, the Cripps Mission represented an adroit attempt to delude world opinion into the belief that political stalemate was inherent in the Indian situation.

Seen from any point of view, the Cripps offer did not suggest any change of heart on the part of the British Government concerning the future disposition of this country.

The principle of self-determination which was mentioned in the provision providing for non-accession of states was circumscribed in such a way that it posed a strong threat to India's future as a united nation. The Congress leaders felt that the scheme smacked of separation while the real and immediate problems of socio-economic amelioration of the country would recede into the background. Any proposal to split India into parts was a painful possibility to contemplate.

Over and above, the British offer had limitations and it came too late to save the situation. Cripps nevertheless considered it justified to blame the Indian leaders for the failure of the mission. Further his criticism of the Congress for seeking American support to influence the course of negotiations was clearly denied by Nehru and others. Such adroit attempts to malign India's case before the bar of world public opinion ended in total failure. On this occasion, Cripps exhibited remarkable stubbornness and insensitiveness combined with a lack of depth in his understanding of the Indian problem, notwithstanding his assertion to the contrary.[5] It was, indeed, ironic that a man who possessed intense socialist convictions and had come as Churchill's emissary—that stubborn champion of the status quo—ended up as the devil's advocate.

The rejection of the Cripps offer by the Congress served Jinnah's purpose admirably. It was this fact which instigated Jinnah to assert confidently that he would realise his goal earlier than what he had anticipated and that there would be no greater happiness for him than to see Pakistan established during his lifetime. On the other hand, by recalling its ministries in 1939, the Congress allowed itself to be outwitted both by the government and by the Muslim League. By rejecting the Cripps offer in 1942 and by choosing to proceed alone, it made the dominance of Jinnah and the subsequent submission to his extravagant demands inevitable.[6] It is also said that if the proposals placed by the Cripps Mission in 1942 had been accepted by Indian National Congress, the partition of India could have been avoided.[7]

Failure of Cripps Mission

The failure of the Cripps Mission provoked a wave of anger and bitter disappointment both in Congress camp and in the country. Gandhi and the Congress leaders were confident that Britain which had refused to resile from her position even in spite of potential danger to India's security, would never leave this country of her own accord. The critical war situation and threat of Japanese invasion lent weight to their distrust. They argued among themselves that if the Britishers were not prepared to part with power even when they are in peril, how could they be expected to do so after the war when their position would be stronger.

Under these circumstances, Gandhi hit upon the idea of 'orderly and timely British withdrawal from India'. Non-Congress leaders opposed it and argued that in view of the critical war situation any mass movement would be 'ill conceived and inopportune'.[8] But to Gandhi critical nature of war situation seemed to make it the need of the hour. Previous British withdrawal from Malaya and Burma had destroyed his faith in British capacity to defend India. Many Congress leaders, especially Nehru[9] and Azad[10] did not agree with Gandhiji initially but 'the logic of facts overwhelmed' them and they had to admit that 'Passivity on our part at this moment and hour of peril would be suicidal'.[11]

The idea of 'quit India' was first aired by Gandhiji in the beginning of April 1942 in a letter to Alexander and A. Harrison, which contained inter alia; "My firm opinion is that the British should leave India now in an orderly manner and not run the risk that they did in Singapore, Malaya and Burma. The act would mean courage of a high order, confession of human limitations and right doing by India".[12] In June he modified his stand to a certain extent by telling Louis Fischer that "Britain, America and other countries too, can keep their armies here and use Indian territory as a base for military operations".[13] On 14th July, the Congress Working Committee met in Wardha and accepted the concept of quit India[14] with three objects in views: (a) to remove all foreign domination over India, (b) to check "the frustration and widespread increase of ill-will against Britain and a growing satisfaction at the success of Japanese armies, with its danger of "Passive acceptance of aggression; "to build up resistance to any aggression or invasion of India by the Japanese or any foreign power." (c) to achieve communal unity by the removal of the foreign power whose long record has been to pursue relentlessly the policy of divide and rule." The removal of the foreign power would be followed by the formation of "a provisional government representative of all important sections of the people of India".

According to Michael Brecher, the quit India movement had several long range consequences of serious importance. For almost three years the Congress was outlawed, its leaders in prison, its funds seized and its organisation virtually destroyed. In the political vacuum thus created, the Muslim League was able to build a mass Party by appealing successfully to religious emotions and genuine Muslim fears. Between 1942 and 1945, the League increased its membership to *two million with the result that by the end of the war it was able to put forward a strong claim to Pakistan.* The Congress was to pay clearly for its "quit India" resolution. Unwillingly it helped to pave the way *for Pakistan.*[15] Almost unwittingly they became willing tools of British imperial interests and played into the hands of the Muslim League which took full advantage to advance its communal goals.[16] How important for the Congress was the acceptance of its basic conditions before it joined the allies is indicated by the refusal of the Congress Working Committee to accept Gandhi's initial advice that the Congress should confine itself to extending only moral support to Britain on war issue and that it should do so without any conditions. Since at least 1936 if not 1927 when it had passed a resolution against Fascist aggression, the Congress had been formulating its position regarding the war issue. It was based on a pragmatic appreciation of the possibility to utilise, in the event of war, the British need for India's support to hasten the country's march towards Independence. Idealism was added to pragmatism to advance the argument that only a free country could fight enthusiastically for the freedom of others.

II

While the Muslim League was putting in its best possible effort not to resolve political stalemate and was continuing its objectionable propaganda against the Congress, the British politicians found it hard to close the chapter of political negotiations with Indian leaders. The National movement of 1942 made a deep impact and probably convinced the British Government that the retention of India for long would not be possible. In fact, the Congress had fully demonstrated the underlying potentialities of Indian nationalism and during the period of war British commitments to free India had been plentiful for efforts were made to placate Indian and world opinion. It is true that in 1945 the desire to transfer power to Indians was not strong or else the Simla Conference would not have failed so miserably.

The aftermath of Lord Wavell's visit to England to consult the Cabinet was favourable and on 14th June 1945 he was able to broadcast 'the new proposals to resolve the Indian deadlock'. These proposals were commonly known as the Wavell Plan, after his name. Lord Wavell declared that he would invite Indian leaders to discuss with him for the formation of a new executive council 'more representative of organised political opinion'. Though it would work within the frameworks of the Act of 1935, it was to be entirely an Indian Council. The portfolio of external affairs, which till then was held by the Viceroy, was to be entrusted on an Indian, to the extent of the interests of British India. A British High Commissioner in India was also to be appointed 'to represent great Britain's commercial and other such interests in India'. Though the Council represented by the Viceroy was to function within the limits of the present Constitution, yet the Viceroy promised that his constitutional powers of control would not be exerted unreasonably. Moreover, the interim arrangements would 'in no way prejudice the final constitutional settlements'.[18]

The Viceroy further announced that he would invite for a conference the existing and the former provincial Premiers, the ordinary leaders and the deputy leaders of the Congress and the Muslim League in the Central Assembly, the leaders of the Congress and the Muslim League parties in the Council of States, and also the leaders of the Nationalist Party and the European group in the Assembly. Mr. Gandhi and Jinnah as representatives of the two chief political parties, Rao Bahadur N. Shiva Raj to represent the Scheduled Caste while Master Tara Singh as a representative of the Sikhs. The proposed conference was to commence its proceedings on 25th June 1945 at Simla[19] and hence, went down in the annals of history as the Simla Conference. It was meanwhile declared that the conference would, apart from other things, discuss the time for fresh elections for the Central and Provincial Legislatures.[20]

Whatever good impression the offer might have created at first was dispelled by Amery's statement in the House of Commons on the same day. The Secretary of State asserted that equal representation would be given to the Muslims and the caste Hindus in the reconstituted council. He further said that the temporary arrangements would in no way affect the future disposition of the country. It was, however, impossible for Amery to displease Mr. Jinnah.

Nevertheless the conference was commenced on 25th June 1945 and the representatives of all parties attended it. The Viceroy agreed to Mahatma Gandhi's view that Maulana Azad (and not he) should represent the Congress while he himself would be available at Simla during the conference for advice.[21] But it was apparent from the outset that the deliberation would lead to no settlement. Earlier Gandhi had cautioned Wavell that he would "quite unconsciously but equally surely, defeat the purpose of the conference if parity between caste Hindus and Muslims is unalterable." Maulana Azad who led the Congress delegation showed utmost keenness to ensure the success of the deliberations. On 29th June 1945 it was considered desirable to adjourn the Simla Conference, as Maulana Azad said, "to enable the parties to come to terms."[22] This agreement could not, however, be arrived at due to the ruthless attitude of the League Leader, Mr. Jinnah, who in conformity with the League ideals, insisted on its recognition of being the only representative of Mussalmans. He claimed the right of the League (or himself) to nominate all Muslims to the Executive Council, which the Viceroy found impossible to concede. This signalled the death warrant of the Simla Conference and when the adjourned conference met on 14th July, the Viceroy announced its breakdown.

The Congress was evidently not responsible for the unexpected failure of the Simla Conference. In fact, the undefendable position taken by Jinnah was believed to be responsible for the failure of the conference. The Viceroy demanded a list of candidates from each of the parties, from whom selections for the Executive Council was to be made. But the Muslim League declined to respond, whereupon the Viceroy wishing to avert the failure of his plan made his provisional selection, which was disapproved by Jinnah. What disgusted Jinnah was that the Congress list contained Muslim names which, in turn, offended the League's claim of being the sole representative of Mussalmans. Maulana Azad clarified that the Muslim League claimed the sole right to nominate all the Muslim representatives on the new Executive Council. This claim was untenable and unsustainable. The Congress was not a Hindu body. It could not wipe out history of fifty years.[23]

Both the British Government and the Viceroy were equally responsible for the failure of the conference. The collapse of the Simla Conference took after the close of elections in Britain. Jinnah's sudden change of front coincided with the termination of British elections. Statements made by Jinnah and his known and unknown hangers-on began to be prominently featured in Anglo-Indian Newspapers.[24] The failure of the Simla Conference indicated, in broadest terms possible, that the League's veto in the determination of national issues was finally accepted. The Viceroy was hostile to it in the beginning. "It was only towards the end, that is, after the rumour of that mysterious telegram that Jinnah jumped up and stoutly demanded that he must be acknowledged as the sole representative of the Muslims, that he would not concede a single seat to a non-Leaguer and that the League representatives must have the right to veto any decision of the Council if they considered that such decisions went against what they would define as Muslim interest".[25]

The simple fact is that the British Government was not sincere about its offer. A fortnight after the Simla failure, Nehru was informed from London that the Wavell offer was "maintained in being as part of election necessities. Also that the final termination of the talks by Wavell, without taking the obvious course of forming a Government without Jinnah, was dictated from here."[26] Gandhi summed up the situation with sheer conciseness when he was told that Wavell's attempt to break the deadlock was sincere: "An honest attempt should have ended honestly."

Besides even at that stage, Jinnah was not such an invincible hero of his community as to invest his veto with lethal authority. In the provinces where Muslims enjoyed majority, there was no League ministry. Had the Viceroy stood firm and not yielded to Jinnah's *truculence*, the unionist party would have continued its dominance in the politics in the Punjab and this would have certainly avoided the partition of India. Had the Viceroy formed the new Executive Council even without the League, an all-community political Government would have been in power for the duration of the war and for sometime afterwards, which would have changed substantially the political history of India. Nehru observed that by allowing the League to 'obstruct a settlement out of wilfulness', the British Government shared the responsibility with the League for the failure of the conference.

The withdrawal of the Wavell plan was a signal triumph for Mr. Jinnah and it came particularly at a time when the fortunes of the Muslim League were none too sound. It weakened the status of those Muslims who opposed the League and many Muslims who had been so far remained passive now jumped into the League's bandwagon. Notable among those who changed their political ideology and were welcomed "like lost sheep returning to their fold 'was Abdul Qaiyum Khan who had not only been an ardent Congressmen, but the Deputy Leader of the Congress Party in the Central Assembly."[27]

Soon after Lord Wavell was summoned to London for urgent discussions on the 'Indian problem'. On his return to India, he issued a new policy statement. "His Majesty's Government are determined to do their utmost to promote along with the leaders of Indian opinion the early realisation of full self-Government for India."

The Congress accepted in principle to participate in the elections, though it had few reservations about the Declaration. The apparent omission of any reference to 'independence' was a huge disappointment to the nationalists and the proposals were characterised as 'vague, inadequate and unsatisfactory'. The Congress election manifesto was so extensively conceived that it had something for everybody. It assured equal rights for all without discrimination on the basis of race, creed or sex and a 'free democratic state with fundamental rights guaranteed in the Constitution'. To alleviate Muslim fears, the manifesto proclaimed its faith in a federal Constitution 'with autonomy for its Constituent parts and minimum list of common and essential federal subjects'.

The Muslim League contested the elections on the issue of Hindu domination in a United India and the imperative necessity for a separate Muslim homeland, in the form of Pakistan. The easily excitable and ignorant masses who could be incited to commit any excesses in the name of religion, were sedulously fed with the fear that the Hindus would absolutely enslave them if they opted to remain in a united India. Besides serving such heady wine to them, the organisers of the League propaganda did not raise protests about adopting strong arm methods to ensure the electoral victory of their party.

The election results were most dramatic. The Congress enjoyed an overwhelming success in the general Constituencies, the Hindu Mahasabha and other opposition candidates preferring in most instances to withdraw rather than risk defeat. The Muslim League secured every Muslim seat, the nationalist Muslims forfeiting their deposits in many instances.

All other groups had faded into insignificance thereby leaving only the Congress and the League as two powerhouses. As a matter of fact, the electoral victory of the League was sweeping. The League had never before secured a majority in Bengal, the Punjab or Sind. In Bengal, the League won more than 90 per cent of the Muslim seats while the Congress victory in the general seats was equally impressive. It got smashing success in Punjab also. But its success had no reflection on the stream of nationalism in the country since it fought its electoral battles in communal Constituencies. Nevertheless, Jinnah had every reasons to rejoice at the results. He told the British Parliamentary delegation which arrived in India on 5th January 1946 that he would accept no arrangement, temporary or permanent, except on his own terms. Thus, after the elections, Jinnah appeared in a much stronger position to demand Pakistan.

The British intention to do something concrete became evident by Prime Minister Attlee's speech of the 15th March delivered in the House of Commons. "We are mindful of the rights of the minorities and the minorities should be able to live free from fear.

On the other hand, we cannot allow a minority to place veto on the advance of a majority."[28] This announcement made by the British Prime Minister aroused hopes in the Congress circles. Sardar Patel observed: "For the first time in recent years, the British Government have changed their attitude regarding minorities. The Congress has always been for the protection of legitimate rights of the minorities but during the war, the British Government adopted an attitude of 'do nothing', until an agreement had been reached between the Muslim League and the Congress and at the same time encouraged the Muslim League to adopt an abstractive attitude by making impossible demands, thus providing the League with the power of Veto, which it effectively exercised throughout the period of the war. I am glad that the British Prime Minister has now made it clear that no minority will be allowed to stop the progress of the majority. His declaration refers only to the Muslim League. "The Congress will meet the legitimate demands of the minorities and provide them with all reasonable safeguards, but it cannot concede the impossible demand for the partition of India—the Pakistan demand of Mr. Jinnah".[29] On the other hand, it drew passive response from Mr. Jinnah whose demand of separate Pakistan had blinded him to see reason. He went on accusing Mahatma Gandhi and the Congress for 'spoiling the atmosphere for negotiations with the British Cabinet Mission'.[30]

All this happened prior to the arrival of the mission in India. The Cabinet Mission reached Delhi on 24th March 1946 and on 25th March 1946 Pethic-Lawrence made the following declarations: "We have come with only one fixed intention and that is to play our full part as representing His Majesty's Government in helping Indians to achieve their independence. Beyond that we have open minds and are not committed to any particular views. But that does not mean we come in hesitant or indecisive frame of mind."[31]

As the diplomacy with the Cabinet Mission got under way, it became clear that the main tussle was between the Congress and the League. For the first time, Jinnah had been brought to the negotiating table and was made to spell out his terms. In one important respect, the condition had of course changed. The breach between the Congress and the Government which had given Jinnah his favourable bargaining position was closing. Sir Stafford Cripps had declared in July 1945, 'to hold up the attainment of self-government in India, any more than it would be right to force the majority provinces into a new constitutional arrangement'.[32] The Cabinet Mission told Mr. Jinnah that if he wanted a separate and fully independent sovereign state, he would have to be contended with the smaller Pakistan offered to him by Gandhi in 1944, for, in the Mission's view, there was no justification for including those districts of the Punjab and of Assam and Bengal in which the population was predominantly non-Muslim.[33] The Cabinet Mission also tried to ruin Jinnah's case for the partition of India by arguing that, apart from providing no acceptable solution for the communal unrest, there were 'weighty administrative, economic and military considerations' against it.[34]

The Tripartite conference of Simla, like its predecessor in 1945, failed due to the implacable position taken up by Jinnah. In his letter dated 8th May 1946 to Pethic-Lawrence, Jinnah among other things, expressed the League's inability to admit 'a single Constitution-making body'.[35] The League memorandum of 19 May 1946 demanded among many other things, the establishment of the Pakistan Federation and party of representation between the two groups of provinces in the Union Government. Conflicts over communal issues in the process of Constitution-making were claimed to be decided by the Constitution-making body belonging to the Hindu provinces and the Pakistan group voting separately.[36] This meant, in effect, the vesting of the power of veto in the League in matters of communal conflicts. In view of these and many other impossible demands of similar character, the Tripartite conference was fore-doomed to failure.

It was, therefore, natural for the Cabinet Mission to make its own proposal. It offered its own proposals in two stages. On 16th May, 1946 it put forth a long-range plan which had proposals for a constitutional settlement.[37] Addressing a Press Conference, Stafford Cripps made it clear that negotiations on the statement of the Cabinet Mission would not be allowed.[38] In fact, the outright rejection of the Pakistan by Cabinet Mission proposals was its positive feature, though the provision for provinces to opt out their groups was a concession in favour of the principle of self-determination and was calculated to pacify the Muslim League in its demand for Pakistan. As a matter of fact, the Cabinet Mission proposal was basically a complicated and purposely vague' proposals which offered the League the temptation of securing a bigger Pakistan. Not unnaturally, both the Congress and the League showed interest in the proposals of the Cabinet Mission and then shied away from them.

The core of the matter, however, lay in the Viceregal proposals put to the Congress President and Pandit Nehru regarding 'the formation of Interim Government on the basis of parity between the Congress and the League'. These demands of the Congress were too heavy and were intended to pacify Jinnah. To these, the Congress Working Committee was badly opposed.[39] The discussion with regard to provisional Government on an agreed basis of coalition failed.

The Congress Working Committee took serious exception to the list for its embodied principles against the Congress ideology. Among others, equality was maintained and Congress Muslims were excluded from it. They disclosed the important fact that the Cabinet Mission and the Viceroy yielded, to a great extent, to the League leaders' threats. Under such circumstances, the Congress Working Committee refused to accept proposals for the formation of an interim government contained in the statement of 16th June 1946. It, in fact, decided on 25th June 'to join the proposed Constituent Assembly, with a view to framing the Constitution of a free, united and democratic India'.[40]

The Congress Working Committee in its resolution on 25th June 1946 accepted long-term Cabinet Mission plan. In the final decision, Vallabhbhai Patel's influence probably appeared dominant, but he was able to carry with him his colleagues in the Working Committee including Nehru. The AICC met at Bombay on 7th July 1946 where Nehru took charge of the Congress Presidency from Maulana Abul Kalam Azad and delivered a speech which has been labelled as a 'serious tactical blunder'[41] and even an act of direct sabotage of the Cabinet Mission plan. This speech is alleged to have ruined the Cabinet Mission plan, and the last hope of preserving the unity of the subcontinent. The charge is based on some of the remarks made by Nehru but at the same time without reference to the context in which he spoke. A number of critics, however, had cast doubts on the status and power of the Constituent Assembly, which was to be convened by the Government and could exist only on its sufferance. It was this criticism that Nehru attempted to answer in his speech of 7th July. He boldly refuted the charge that the Constituent Assembly would be a 'sham', or a nursing game at which Indian politicians would play while the British Government supervised them. On the basis of this he declared that no 'dictation' from the British Government would be tolerated.

Three days later, on 10th July, Nehru covered the same ground at a Press Conference in Bombay.[42] Here again, while highlighting the sovereign character of the Constituent Assembly, he affirmed that the Congress was all set to make a success of the Constitutional mechanism outlined by the Cabinet Mission.

Apparently, Nehru had no intention to repudiate the framework of the Cabinet Mission plan. All the available evidence indeed exposes his anxiety to arrive at a satisfactory solution of the minority problem and of Indo-British relations after the withdrawal of the British power.

His ideas on the functioning of Assembly were given in his broadcast on 7th September 1946 after the formation of the interim Government. In this he said, "There has been much heated argument about sections and groupings in the Constituent Assembly. We are perfectly prepared to, and have accepted, the position of formation of groups . . . . We do not look upon the Constituent Assembly as an arena for conflict or the forcible imposition of one's viewpoint on another. We seek agreed and integrated solutions with the largest measure of goodwill behind them. We shall go to Constituent Assembly with the fixed determination of binding a common basis for agreement on all controversial issues. It may well be that when we meet and face common tasks, our present difficulties will fade away."[43]

Besides, Nehru's assertions on this occasion revealed remarkable political insight. None could deny the fact that the option given to autonomous provinces like Frontier and Assam to go out of their respective groups was no better than Hobson's choice. Nehru's reference to the need for a strong centre gave indications of the future as this issue had loomed large in the history of independent India and Pakistan. Apart from this, his statement was a hard-headed recall to realities, rather than a patent error of political judgement.

In the resolution which the Muslim League passed on 29th July, cancelling its acceptance of the Cabinet Mission plan, it asserted that "of the major parties, the Muslim League alone has accepted the statements of 16th May, and 25th acceding to the spirit and letter of the proposals embodied therein'. One of the reasons stated in this resolution for the acceptance of the Cabinet Mission plan was that League found in it 'the basis and foundation of Pakistan which are inherent in Mission plan by virtue of the compulsory grouping of six Muslim provinces in Section B and C.' The resolution further went on to affirm that the Muslim League agreed 'to cooperate with the Constitution-making machinery mentioned in the scheme outlined by the Mission in the hope that it would ultimately result in the establishment of completely sovereign Pakistan'.[44]

Clearly, the League did not consider the Cabinet Mission plan, with its three-tier structure, as a last compromise between the Congress ideal of a strong and united India and the League objective of two separate sovereign states. On the contrary, the

League did not try to conceal its hopes and plans that the Cabinet Mission plan would be a stepping stone to an independent Pakistan.

As for 'groups of provinces', Jinnah told his Council, that they should have powers on all subjects barring defence, communications and foreign affairs. So far as defence was concerned, it would remain in the control of the British till the new Constitution was enforced. The Cabinet Mission plan was thus to be made a preclude to Pakistan in two days. Firstly, the 'grouping' of provinces in the east and the west was to be made compulsory, maximum powers were to be conferred on the 'groups', and provincial autonomy was practically to cease to exist. Secondly, the Central Government was to be made as weak as possible by the narrowest interpretation of its functions and by denying it any right for taxation. A Central Government which lived on receiving governmental grants had no say in trade, industry, communications (except for defence) and was composed of representatives of opposing units in its executive and Legislature, could scarcely be expected to prevent the secession of the League's groups of provinces in the North-west and east.[45]

Meanwhile, the Congress had no intention of letting the League get away with Pakistan of its own conception with six provinces, by disguising them as groups of provinces initially. This was the background of the opposition by Gandhi. Nehru, Patel and indeed the entire Congress leadership to the compulsory assembling of provinces. This opposition could have been softened if Jinnah had taken initiatives to assure the Hindus of Assam and West Bengal, the Congress Muslims of NWFP and the Sikhs of the Punjab that grouping of provinces was a purposeful and constructive association of neighbouring provinces for mutual advantage, and that it would not involve coercion of minorities. By failing to give this assurance, Jinnah sealed the fate of the grouping scheme and also that of the Cabinet Mission plan: it is true he thus made sure of Pakistan, but it was to be a Pakistan minus East Punjab, West Bengal and the major portion of Assam.

After the rejection of the Cabinet Mission plan by the Muslim League, events moved faster. The Congress Working Committee which met at Wardha (8 to 13th August 1946) passed a resolution reaffirming its acceptance of the Cabinet Mission plan. Nehru went to see Jinnah with a view to finding an agreement with the League so that it could participate in the Government. But Jinnah declined to cooperate in the formation of the interim government.

The decision of Mr. Jinnah to declare 16th August 1946 as 'Direct Action Day' led to a disastrous chain of events which engulfed the sub-continent in virtual civil war for the next eighteen months.[46] Mr. Suhrawardy, the Premier of Bengal, announced that 16th August would be a general holiday in Calcutta for both Muslims and Hindus which drew protest from Hindu members of the Provincial Legislature. He declared that 'Bloodshed and disorder are not necessarily evil in themselves, if resorted to for a noble cause. Among Muslims today, no cause is dearer or nobler than Pakistan'.

The stage was thus set for the demonstration which was to split India in two.[47] On 16th August 1946 the League observed its 'Direct Action Day' marked by utter hooliganism in Calcutta resulting in 90 deaths and 900 injured'.[48] The total toll of 'Communal Carnage' in Calcutta was 15,000 dead and wounded. The atrocities committed, surpassed even medieaval barbarism. This was followed by the Noakhali riots in the wake of Calcutta atrocities and brought untold misery on the Hindus. The Indian National Congress was however constrained to adopt resolution to condemn the acts of bestiality, committed by members of the League, and Mahatma Gandhi toured through Noakhali to the great annoyance of the Muslim community.

The communal riots which began from Calcutta with the observance of the 'Direct Action Day' spread from Calcutta to East Bengal, from East Bengal to Bihar and from Bihar to Punjab. Unfortunately the League leaders reacted to the communal riots with a political rather than a human bias. Jinnah blamed the riots on 'Gandhi, the Viceroy and British'. Each communal outbreak was highlighted as further endorsement of the two nation theory and of the inevitability of the partition of the country.

Shocked by the Calcutta riots, the Viceroy Lord Wavell decided to bring the Muslim League into the interim government where the League members functioned from the outset as an opposition bloc. Jinnah too, in the meantime, realised that by keeping out the League from the interim government, Nehru had allowed the Congress to acquire a prestigious position which might end in the League's isolation and drive it into a policy of sterile opposition, an administration which had the support of the British.

Jinnah accordingly sent out a 'feeler' to the British Government and in early October entered into separate negotiations with the Viceroy, putting a number of demands as a condition for the League's entry into the Government. There was nothing essentially unique in his demands and he had to be content with five representatives as against six for the Congress. Nehru was also involved in discussion with Jinnah and letters were exchanged between the two. He refuted all of Jinnah's demands except one. This concerned Congress and Nehru's willingness to concede the argument that "the Muslim League was the authoritative representative organisation of an overwhelming majority of the Muslims of India provided that for identical reasons the League recognises the Congress as the authoritative organisation representing all non-Muslims and such Muslims as have thrown in their lot with the Congress."[49]

The League's cooperation did not come forth so far as the Constituent Assembly was concerned. When its first meeting was held in the Constitutional Hall, New Delhi on 9th December 1946, the League members were apparent by their absence and 'the Congress effort to get the Muslim League to cooperate in the work of Constitution-making had failed'.[50] In the second session of the Constituent Assembly which began on 20th January 1947, 'the members of the Muslim League were absent again'.[51] The outcome of the whole affair was that the League did not take part in the Constituent Assembly even in spite of the repeated appeal of the Congress leaders and the Viceroy.[52]

In the circumstances, there seemed to be no respite from the difficult situation. At this juncture, Attlee came out with an invitation to the Viceroy, representatives of the Congress, and the League and one Sikh for parleys in London with a view to harmonising the conflict between the Congress and the League. The London talk ended in total deadlock and failed in their objective of securing the participation and cooperation of the League in the Constituent Assembly. At the conclusion of the talks, the British Cabinet raised a statement on the issues at dispute. The bone of contention was on the procedure for groups—whether decisions of the groups should be taken group-wise or province-wise. The Congress urged to accept this position as it would instigate the League to participate in the Constituent Assembly. As a concession, the Congress was ready to refer the issue to the Federal Court but this was not acceptable to the British Government and the League.

The significant portions of the 6th December 1946 statement was the concluding paragraph which indicated a drastic turnaround of British policy. "There has never been any prospect of success for the Constituent Assembly except upon the basis of an agreed procedure. Should a Constituent Assembly in which a large section of the Indian population had not been represented (i.e., the Muslim League), His Majesty's Government could not, of course, contemplate as the Congress have stated a Constitution upon any unwilling parts of the country.[53] This policy statement in effect provided a green signal for the League to persist in its goal of Pakistan. Nehru was shocked by this sudden turn of events."

On the other hand, Mr. Jinnah hailed the 6th December statement, disapproved the proposed reference of the grouping provisions to the Federal Court by the Congress and advocated a separate Constituent Assembly for Pakistan. The conflict on the grouping question was brought to an end. But politically the situation might have been different if this battle was not fought at all. The Congress fought doggedly and embraced defeat gracefully. In recommending AICC resolution, Nehru frankly stated the position: "The main question before them was how to keep the Constituent Assembly alive and extract from it the greatest possible good for the country. By accepting the statement of 6th December we would leave the door open for the League to enter and put forward their point of view. If we did not accept that statement, it would give an opportunity to the British Government to change or withdraw their earlier statement of 16th May 1946 with the result that the Constituent Assembly might be changed radically." The League Working Committee met at Karachi on 31st January 1947 and adopted an aggressively offensive resolution. Even the *London Times* otherwise friendly to the League was surprised. It observed on 4th February 1947 that "it was highly preposterous for the Karachi meeting to call upon the British Government for a declaration that the Cabinet Mission's plan had failed and to demand the dissolution of the Constituent Assembly."

References

1. *The Indian Annual Register,* 1939, Vol. II, pp. 40-45.
2. Nehru, *The Discovery of India,* p. 440.
3. *Ibid.* II, pp. 10-11.
4. V.P. Menon, *op. cit.,* p. 97.
5. Nehru, *op. cit.,* p. 496.
6. V.B. Kulkarni, *op. cit.,* p. 175; V. T. Patil, *op. cit.,* p. 143.
7. Pendrel Moon, *op. cit.,* pp. 26-27.
8. Amba Prasad, *The Indian Revolt of 1942,* p. 97.
9. J.L. Nehru, *The Discovery of India,* pp. 480-85.
10. Maulana Azad, *op. cit.,* pp. 73-74.
11. Nehru's speech on Tilak Day Celebration, Allahabad, p. 204.
12. D.G. Tendulkar, *Mahatma,* Vol. II, p. 92.
13. *Ibid.,* p. 117.

14. *The Indian Review,* dated August 1942, p. 424.
15. Michael Brecher, *op. cit.,* p. 294.
16. V.T. Patil, *op. cit.,* p. 144.
17. Allah Bux letter to the Viceroy, 26th September 1942, pp. 74-76.
18. *The Indian Review,* dated July 1945, p. 394: The Wavell Plan.
19. *Ibid.,* p. 395.
20. *Ibid.*
21. *Ibid.,* p. 408 : Diary of the month.
22. *Ibid.,* August, 1945, p. 453.
23. *Ibid.,* p. 453.
24. *The Modern Review,* dated August 1945, p. 64.
25. *Ibid.,* p. 65.
26. Pyarelal, *Mahatma Gandhi, The Last Phase,* p. 138.
27. V.P. Menon, *The Transfer of Power in India,* p. 166.
28. *Ibid.,* p. 43.
29. *Ibid.,* p. 44.
30. *Ibid.*
31. *Ibid.,* p. 45.
32. Gwyer and Appadorai, *op. cit.,* Vol. II, p. 566.
33. *Ibid.,* p. 578.
34. *Ibid.,* p. 579.
35. The Cabinet Mission in India, compiled by Anil Chandra Banerjee, Lecturer in History, Calcutta University and Dakshina Ranjan Bose, News Editor, *The Jugantar,* Calcutta, p. 59.
36. *Ibid.*
37. *The Indian Review,* dated May 1946, p. 247.
38. *Ibid.,* June 1946, p. 339.
39. *Indian National Congress Report of the General Secretaries,* March 1940—October 1946, pp. 78-79.
40. *Ibid.,* p. 82.
41. Michael Brecher, *Nehru, A Political Biography,* p. 317.
42. *Bombay Chronicle,* 11th July 1946.
43. Dorothy Norman, *Nehru: The First Sixty Years,* Vol. II, p. 251.
44. Gwyer and Appadorai, *op. cit.,* Vol. II, p. 601.
45. For Muslim League's conception of the functions and the resources of the Central Government, see the "Terms of the offer made by the Muslim League as a basis of agreement 12th May, 1946", reproduced in Gwyer and Appadorai, *op. cit.,* Vol. II, p. 573-74.
46. V.P. Menon, *op. cit.,* pp. 280-84.
47. *Ibid.,* p. 178.
48. *Dawn,* dated 6th April 1946, p. 1.
49. The text of the Nehru-Jinnah correspondence and Jinnah-Wavell correspondence are to be found in the *'The Indian Annual Register,* Vol. II, 1947, pp. 265-69 and 273-75 respectively.
50. *Indian National Congress Report of the General Secretaries,* November 1946—December 1948, p. 8.
51. *Indian Review,* dated February 1947, p. 81.
52. *Ibid.,* March 1947, p. 144.
53. The text of the 6th December declaration is to be found in *The Times* (London), 7th December 1946.

18

Freedom and the Partition of the Subcontinent

The Constituent Assembly question was yet to be solved. The British Government found the situation grave and desperate. Then came the famous statement of Prime Minister, Clement Attlee in the House of Commons[1] and of Lord Pethic-Lawrence, the Secretary of State for India in the House of Lords on 20 February 1947, in the course of which they observed, 'His Majesty's Government desire to hand over their responsibility to authorities established by a Constitution approved by all parties in India in accordance with the Cabinet Mission's plan, but unfortunately there is at present no clear prospect that such a Constitution and such authorities will emerge. The present state of uncertainty is fraught with danger and cannot be indefinitely prolonged. His Majesty's government wish to make it clear that it is this definite intention to take the necessary steps to effect the transference of power into responsible Indian hands by a date not later than June 1948'. It was a very significant pronouncement. It fixed a particular date when power would definitely be handed over to Indians. But it caused an unhealthy reaction in the Muslim League which redoubled its effort to secure Pakistan. The League's presence in the Punjab, the frontier and Assam was not very well felt and only Bengal and Sind were practically under the League's clout. Hence, Bengali Muslims were encouraged to migrate to Assam so as to increase its Muslim population. When the Assam Government stopped migration, the League raised the cry of 'Islam in danger'.[2] It was well observed, 'The Muslim League used the February statement not for settling with the Congress peacefully and cooperatively but for creating conditions by coercion and intimidation in which certain decisions could be made in its favour.'

At such, the League followed double tactics of (a) launching Civil Disobedience movement in provinces where Muslim presence was inadequate and of (b) manoeuvring communal riots to compel the Congress to accept its demand of Pakistan. The League was tactful enough to misrepresent the movement as non-communal in character and Chaudhuri Khaliquzzaman urged the Muslims, Tribals, Scheduled Castes and the Manipuris to join the struggle.[3] Chaudhuri Khaliquzzaman, for example, said, 'Assam is sure to be in Pakistan. So it is not true that the Muslim League is fighting to establish Pakistan in Assam'. He also added, "The League's fight is not against any particular community but it is against a certain policy of the Congress Government."[4]

While troubles were, thus, created in Assam and the NWFP, the Punjab was also not spared. The League's claim and capability to form government in the Punjab were stressed by Mumtaz Daultana. He claimed that the League enjoyed an absolute majority in the Punjab Legislature and, as such, it was its constitutional right to form a ministry.[5] In fact, the February statement of the British Government made the League anxious about its future position in Punjab. The League believed that resort to extra-Constitutional methods alone would immediately bring the situation in its favour. Agitation against the Government took place here, as in the NWFP and Assam.

On the other hand, Nehru publicly announced the British Government's decision as 'wise and courageous'.[6] The Congress Working Committee met on 5th March to consider the British Government's statement of 20th February. The Committee repeated its acceptance of the Cabinet Mission plan and the interpretation of it by the British Government; it welcomed the decision of a number of states to join the Constituent Assembly, and asked the elected Muslim League members to take their seats. The resolution declared that the Constituent Assembly was a voluntary body so that the Constitution framed by it would apply only to those areas which accepted it; in the same manner, no province or part of a province which desired to join the Indian union could be prevented from doing so. It appealed to all parties and groups to shun violent and coercive methods and to cooperate democratically and peacefully in the making of a Constitution.[7]

On 9th March 1947, Nehru wrote to Lord Wavell that it was the intention of the Congress to approach the Muslim League for a joint meeting to consider the situation. If unfortunately, these were not possible, then the Congress would try to lay down a course of action which would avoid friction and conflict. It was with this object in view that they had sought and had also suggested the division of the Punjab into two parts. This principle would, of course, apply to Bengal also.

Mountbatten Assuming Office

Lord Wavell was replaced by Lord Mountbatten who took charge of the Indian administration on 24th March. Gandhi called on him on 31st March and explained his political convictions to the new Viceroy. He astonished Mountbatten by suggesting that Jinnah should be called upon to run the Indian administration. He did not bother even if the whole country was converted into Pakistan, 'provided it was done by appeal to reason and not under threat of violence'. He had complete confidence in the impartiality of Mountbatten.

Lord Mountbatten was determined to find a solution of the Indian problem with the least possible delay. He also at first tried for a solution on the basis of a united India but when he found that the League demanded the creation of Pakistan, he began to explore the possibility of a solution on that basis. The situation had changed dramatically within a few years. At the time of the Cripps Mission in 1942, Congress was hostile to partition. Even when the Cabinet Mission arrived in India in 1946, the Congress leaders were unanimous to preserve the unity of India. But in March 1947, the situation turned totally different. Jinnah was now confident that with a little more pressure he would win his point. Its attitude seemed to be that while united India was certainly desirable, immediate independence of the major part of India was preferable to a postponement to the independence of the entire India.

Mountbatten was a man of quick decisions. Once he realised that the Congress was more likely to yield than the League, he began thinking in terms of dividing the country. Nehru, for instance, in a public speech on 20th April declared: 'The Muslim League can have Pakistan, if they wish to have it, but on the condition that they do not take away other parts of India which do not wish to join Pakistan.'[8] But perhaps the more authoritative pronouncement was made by Dr. Rajendra Prasad, President of the Constituent Assembly, when the Assembly met on 28th April: 'While we have accepted the Cabinet Mission's statement of 16th May 1946 which contemplated a union of the different provinces and states within the country, it may be that the union may not comprise all provinces. If that unfortunately comes to pass, we shall have to content with a Constitution for a part of it. In that case, we can and should insist that one principle will apply to all parts of the country and no Constitution will be forced upon any unwilling part of it. This may mean not only the division of India, but a division of some provinces. For this we must be prepared and the Assembly may have to draw up a Constitution based on such a division.'

Jinnah issued a statement that the proposal for the partition of Bengal and the Punjab was 'a sinister move actuated by spite and bitterness'. He asserted that the principle underlying the Muslim demand for Pakistan was that the Muslims should have a national state in their homelands comprising of the six provinces of the Punjab, the NWFP, Sind, Baluchistan, Bengal and Assam. If the Punjab and Bengal were partitioned, all the other provinces would have to be divided in a similar way. He suggested that an exchange of population would sooner or later have to take place and that this could be effectively carried out by the respective governments in Pakistan and Hindustan. He then demanded the division of defence and forces and stressed that the states of Pakistan and Hindustan should be made absolutely free, independent and sovereign.

The Hindu and the Sikh legislators of the Punjab and the non-Muslim members of the Central Assembly and Constituent Assembly from that province met in New Delhi and passed a resolution that the only solution of the political problem of the Punjab lay in a just and equitable division of the province, and also that the non-Muslim population must be assured of such territories and assets as they were entitled to according to their numbers and stake in the province. On the other side, taking their cue from Jinnah, the local bodies of the Muslim League in the United Provinces and Bombay started to demand the right of self-determination for the Muslims in certain areas in those provinces.

The communal tension in the country was thus steadily worsening. As such, Lord Mountbatten felt that if the procedure for the transfer of power was not finalised quickly, there was a possibility that at least in some parts of the country there would be no authority to whom power could be transferred. But the first partition plan which Mountbatten's staff produced in May 1947 according to the instructions of the British Cabinet was so defective that Nehru angrily rejected it.[9]

Nehru rightly pointed out to Mountbatten, the plan 'would encourage disruptive tendencies everywhere and chaos and weakness'.[10] In fact, the inevitable results of the proposals would be to invite the Balkanisation of India; to provoke certain civil conflict and add to riots and disorder: to weaken the central authority, which alone could prevent the growing chaos, and to demoralise the army, the police and the central services. Jinnah fought hard against another feature of the plan, namely, the proposed split of Bengal and the Punjab, but ultimately reconciled himself to the inevitable.

Almost as a consolation prize he managed to have the predominantly Muslim district of Sylhet in Assam for Pakistan.

Nehru not only violently rejected the first partition plan but on the advice of Sardar Patel and V.P. Menon threw a temptation to Mountbatten that India would be willing to accept dominion status and appoint him as Governor-General. The move worked and Mountbatten got the feeling that the Congress was not as hostile to the British as the Tories in London had imagined. Mountbatten thereupon prepared along with V.P. Menon—a distinguished Indian civil servant who appears to have played a crucial role[11]—a new plan on the basis of partition which is known as the 3rd June or the Mountbatten Plan. It provided for the transfer of power to India and Pakistan on the basis of dominion status without hampering constitutional continuity. Members of Bengal and Punjab Assemblies were given the right to decide whether their respective provinces were also to be partitioned on a communal basis. The NWFP deserved special mention because of its geographical location and although two of its three representatives were already attending the existing Constituent Assembly, it was settled to give the province an opportunity to reconsider its position. Nevertheless, the AICC approved the Mountbatten Plan at its meeting held on 15th June 1947.

Opposition to the resolution came mostly from Nationalist Muslims, members of the Hindu minorities in the proposed Pakistan Provinces and also among the topmost leaders. Only Purushottamdas Tandon stood out against the partition. In an impassioned speech, he said that the decision of the Working Committee was a revelation of weakness and that it arose out of a sense of despair. Accepting the 3rd June Plan would benefit neither the Hindus nor the Muslims, he was ready to suffer the British rule a little longer rather than pay this heavy price. He said that the Nehru Government had been scared by the League. Nehru asserted that there was no question of any surrender to the Muslim League. Sardar Patel said that, looking at the Cabinet Mission's proposals considering his experience in the Interim Government during the past nine months, he did not feel sorry that the statement of 16th May had gone. Had they accepted it, the whole of India would have gone the Pakistan way.

Congress Agrees to Partition

In agreeing to the partition of India, Congress leaders chose the lesser evil. Partition was definitely bad, but the alternatives to partition in 1947 were even worse. Continued slavery, civil war, anarchy and the fragmentation of India—these were the only alternatives to partition in 1947. India was at long last free. The unity of at least two-thirds of India had been preserved. Some Congress leaders hoped that partition would be transitory and that it might even clear the way to real reunion. 'The division', asserted Maulana Azad, 'is only on the map of the country and not in the hearts of the people, and it is going to be a short-lived partition'.[12] Nehru remarked: 'The united India that we have laboured for was not one of compulsion and coercion but a free and willing association of free people. It may be that in this way we shall reach that united India sooner than otherwise and then she will have a stronger and more secure foundation.[13] Doubts and apprehensions about the future were pressed by certain other Congress leaders but these were inundated in the intense agony and ecstasy of the hour. The reunion was merely a dream and later on even the State of Pakistan was divided into two States—Pakistan and Bangladesh.

It is important to mention that the decision in favour of Partition was not that Patel and Nehru alone; it was backed by the Working Committee and in the AICC. e hundred fifty seven voted in favour of it and only fifteen against it. It was a nful decision taken with a heavy heart but there seemed to be no alternative to it that time. The immediate problem that Nehru saw was 'to arrest the swift drift to archy and chaos'. Realising this, the Congress leaders began to think in terms of rtition of the country from the beginning of the year 1947. Thus, by March 1947, e Congress leadership had been sobered by its experience in the Interim overnment as well as by the increasing lawlessness in the country. A Modus Vivendi ith the League appeared not remote but impossible. In the twilight of the British npire in India, some of the Indian princes were nursing new ambitions. The princes f Western and Central India, under the inspiration of some of the larger states, specially Bhopal, were thinking in terms of Leagues of princes. It was the trickery y the ruler of Baster, a small state in Central India with the Nizam of Hyderabad which finally convinced Patel that it was imperative to secure immediate British withdrawal even if it meant acceptance of the partition of India.

The acceptance of Partition has been staunchly criticised as inconsistent keeping in mind the best interest of the country; as contrary to the professions of the Congress; as a humiliating surrender to the British and the League. According to Maulana Azad, it was an unnecessary and unprepared step because 'the Cabinet Mission plan was the best solution from every point of view. It preserved the unity of India and gave every community an opportunity to function with freedom and honour'.

It would be interesting to know why Nehru finally accepted partition. Nehru did not like the idea of partition but he could see no other alternative. It was not a perfect solution. It is considered that it was the only solution which had any chance of being accepted by all political parties and of ensuring a fairly equitable deal for all minorities. Even if it was accepted as necessary, the condition had changed drastically in the first half of the twentieth century when Hindu-Muslim relations were patterned on a basis of perennial conflict and crisis.

Nehru and Patel were two prominent Congressmen who took the last decision to accept partition on the understanding that 'by conceding Pakistan to Mr. Jinnah they would hear no more about him and eliminate his nuisance value. Nehru admitted that partition was by nature wrong and a potent evil, but his experience with the conduct of the League in the interim government left him with no hopes of joint action and joint responsibility. Faced with a stalemate in the functioning of the Government, Nehru could not see any other way as situation were inevitably heading towards Partition. Nehru was considerably influenced by Mountbatten's advice that the Congress had agreed to a weak centre only in order to accommodate the viewpoint of the League. Accordingly provinces were to be given full autonomy, but in a country with such a diversities in language, community and culture, a weak centre was bound to encourage fissiparous tendencies. Nehru had a feeling that even if India got freedom and remained undivided, it would be a weak India with too much power concentrated in the provinces. A composite India would have been beset with myriad problems and constant disintegrating pulls.

Besides Nehru had a hidden fear that if Congress rejected the Mountbatten Plan,

PART—II

19

Congress Under Nehru
(Post-Independence Period)

On the eve of Independence, India still suffered from acute disparities rising out of a society with various strata. The chaotic conditions of partition had created innumerable problems. There was also an acute food shortage. Although 80 per cent of India's population were engaged in agriculture, the country had to spend more than Rs. 100 crore yearly for importing food.

While confronting the challenge posed in the post-Independence years, Prime Minister Nehru and the Congress were only too aware of the basic urges behind the national liberation struggle—the urge to eradicate poverty and to build a new India on egalitarian principles. The INC had promised many things before the Independence and when it took over the administration of the country as the undisputed leader of the nation, it was faced with the task all that they had been preaching thus far. There were two options open to them, i.e., either to proceed on purely capitalist lines or follow the socialist model. Since the Congress had been advocating socialist politics, everyone was looking to it to bring about a new order. They realised that had they opted for the capitalist model then the conditions of the majority of the peasants would have remained the same and only the small landowning class—in whose hands all the assets and power were in any case concentrated—would be the only ones to benefit. As the Congress was likely to be the spokesman of the masses, it could ill afford to take recourse to such measures. The integration of the country was important to the Congress but equally important was to find a commonly acceptable way to tackle the myriad of problems. To maintain the harmony, unity and integrity of the nation was what they told they were interested in. But in reality the survival and leadership of the party was what they were working for, but without making it too obvious. The socialist policy became accessible at a time when the Congress was on the horns of this dilemma. The entire decision-making of the Congress, subsequently, must be understood in view of this.

The INC which was a primarily middle class organisation, with a very strong conservative wing, no doubt must have found extremely difficult to keep the balance between the demands of the vested interests and the poverty stricken masses. As a result, these words and policies sought to appease the masses while their actions worked in the interest of the business lobby.

Nehru had many a time asserted that the prime task of the national movement was to end all forms of exploitation which politically implied independence and dissolution of the British connection and economically it meant putting an end to all class privileges and vested interests and the ultimate establishment of socialism. In his famous 'Tryst with Destiny' speech, Nehru had explained the socio-economic aims and objectives of independent India in the following words: "The service of India means the service of the millions who suffer. It means the ending of poverty and ignorance and disease and inequality of opportunity. The ambition of the greatest men of our time has been to wipe every tear from every eye. They may be beyond us, but as long as there are tears and sufferings, so long our work will not be over. And so we have to labour and to work hard to give reality to our dreams."

On the one hand, the Congress claimed to be the spokesman of the masses, but on the other, it was also managed by the business community in the urban areas and the landowners in the rural areas. During the national movement, this had not surfaced out properly because of the more urgent problem of attaining freedom. After Independence, the Congress had taken on a tremendous responsibility and in order to achieve its goals, it had to change its class composition. The establishment of a socialist state could not be achieved by the Congress with its existing class composition. The Congress which had undergone changes in its class composition during the movements of 1921, 1931 and 1942 still lacked the base for building up a socialistic state. There was the absence of 'a class based party organisation' among the peasantry, all of which proved to be major hindrances in the adoption of socialist goals and programmes.

It is a fact, however, that ever since its formation, the Congress had been taking help from the business community. Nehru had in 1945, strongly denied that the business community financed the Congress and stated that the Congress carried on almost entirely on petty subscriptions and also that the 'normal' work was financed by the membership fees primarily. Gandhi himself had never been against the assistance given to the party by the industrialists. All this coupled with the fact that the majority of the Congress leadership (the conservative wing) gave them support, not only inspired the business community, but also installed them in the party. No doubt, their links with the party were indirect. The business group favoured rapid development with maximum government assistance and protection of industry and with a minimum of government control. Although many efforts were made to bring about a socialist society, steps were also taken to promote and boost Indian business through protective tariffs, financial aid, tax concessions and *giving loans to new industrial investments.* Efforts at eliminating any bottlenecks that emerge in private sector were also continuously made. The attempt was to bring socialism through legislation. It is however also a fact that the whole planning effort in India almost inevitably bolstered business organisation basically with regards to transport facilities, new materials or licensing of new capital issues. In the rural areas, the landlords exerted a similar influence on the Congress party. As a result of this, two contradictory tendencies became firmly established in the Congress. While on the one hand, the national party executive continuously accorded superficial support to socialist principles of state ownership, regulations, curbing any form of concentration in the economy, on the other hand, the national Congress government continued to pursue liberal economic policies and incentives to private investment. On this issue, both Nehru and Patel were in complete agreement with each other. It revealed that the differences of opinion between the two were not so extensive, after all, especially where the basic things were concerned. The influence of the business group on Congress policy-making is, therefore, apparent, and in view of this it is not difficult to understand why Congress move towards socialist policies was of a subdued nature.

The Congress party organisation and its parliamentary wing were complementary to each other in many respects and together they shaped the socialist policy of the Congress. There was a close interaction between the government and the party, since party men were also in government. The possibility of split between party and government policy was remote, although certain amount of 'healthy' conflict and confrontation was not ruled out. The party's role was, therefore, very important and whatever policy was formulated was reflected in some form in the government policies. There was normally a broad agreement and perhaps a proper example of how the general strategies for the Indian economic planning was evolved over a period.

Patel—The Icon with Conservative Traits

By 1946, the conservative stalwart of the Congress, Patel, had grown very powerful in the party and neither Gandhi nor Nehru were the only important power wielders in the Congress. Patel was, however, believed to be an important lieutenant of Gandhi especially in the years of freedom struggle. He had also played a very striking role in the building of the local and state party units. Patel, who was the treasurer of the Congress was strongly opposed to the socialists and virtually dictated terms to the various wings of the party. In fact, after Gandhi's death in January 1948, Patel was successful in bringing about a change in the party constitution which prohibited the continuation of organised groups within the Congress. Between 1947 and 1950, therefore, it was Patel, the then Deputy Prime Minister, who seemed to exert a great deal of influence in the party.

As Nehru was far more acceptable to the widely differing groups in the Congress he became the Prime Minister. Nehru's constant effort had been to dislocate the conservative's stronghold in the party and capture power for himself. However, he could get this opportunity only towards the end of 1949 and in 1950, especially after Patel's death. Nehru initially did not accept the membership of the CWC and he along with some of his colleagues kept away. But later, they joined the said committee on a rather unimpressive ground and finally after Patel's death, Nehru could establish his supreme hold over the party. This showed that strategy was far more important than ideology.

Patel shared most of the pivotal responsibilities with Nehru in the functions of the government and also in the shaping of policies. Nehru, on the other hand, was impatient of any restrictions put on him and insisted that the Prime Minister had to be "more responsible than any one else'.[1] The Congress shaped its policies including its economic policy in such a milieu—the constant tug of war left an everlasting imprint on the socialist policy of the Congress.

Preface to Congress accepting Socialism as a Policy

By 1954, the term socialism was being more frequently and openly used at the party and the government level. In his Presidential address in January 1954, Nehru spoke about the rural development and other problems of development. He said, "Our strength lies not merely in the cities but much more so in the countryside where thousands of millions of our people dwell... we cannot remove it by some magic but we can gradually put an end to it by proper planning and hard work. Where nationalisation is obviously beneficial, we should not hesitate. Indeed, we have built up already a large number of magnificent state owned undertakings and their number is growing. We must remember that the complicated problems of any country are not solved by a blind attempt to copy some other. The USA is a great and highly industrialised country—are we to introduce their methods and techniques in our underdeveloped economy? Or are we to copy the Russian method regardless of their applicability here? We have to face the problem of a heavily populated and underdeveloped country which is trying to make good in a democratic and peaceful way."

The new principles and directions of social and economic policies were settled by late 1954. As a result of Nehru's initiative, the problem of framing an economic development strategy was subsequently considered from a dual perspective.

The business community continued to make their demands about forming a people-friendly government. The FICCI at its 27th annual session adopted a resolution on unemployment and economic development and appreciated what had been done by the government for industrial and general economic development of the country. They felt that the rate of progress was rather disappointing and, therefore, suggested various measures so as to create the proper climate in which private enterprise may freely function. Besides, they urged the government to remove the numerous obstacles which stood in the way of industrial growth and their further expansion.

Nehru towards the later part of 1954, expressed the desire for resigning from Congress Presidentship. He had more or less achieved what he had wanted, i.e., to gaining the supreme position and command over the party and of shaping the policies of the party according to his principles and ideas. The Congress found a comparatively unknown figure—U.N. Dhebar to succeed Nehru—perhaps with the hope of keeping him as a mere figurehead. High ranking officials of the Congress party, Parliament, the Minister for Food and Agriculture, the Planning Commission and others had visited China who were becoming increasingly interested in China's economic programme. Both Nehru and Mahalanobis also visited China and were convinced that 'China provided a better model of development for India than the advanced western countries.' Nehru also found one of the most important and impressive things that is happening in China is the rapid growth of agricultural and industrial cooperatives.

It was around November 1954, that Nehru explicitly and openly stated a socialist state was what he had in mind. While addressing NDC Nehru observed that the picture he had in his mind was absolutely a socialistic picture of society. He emphasised, however, that there was plenty of room for the private enterprise, provided it was implemented as per aim. While stating it 'immoral' to base society purely on the acquisitive principle, the Prime Minister said he had no such intentions of doing away with private enterprises. At the meeting of the Congress Parliamentary party too, Nehru explaining the government's economic policy asserted that India's goal was a socialistic economy. He further characterised the criticism of the economic policy of the government made by the PSP as unrealistic. When the Congress talked of socialism the PSP seemed to resent it, Nehru stated, 'as if socialism is their copy right.'[2]

Meanwhile, the Lok Sabha on 22nd December 1954 set its seal of approval for the country's economy to be progressively modelled on a socialistic pattern of society. The House accepted an amendment moved by Congress members. The amendment stated, 'This House having considered the economic situation in India and the policies of the government... considered that: (i) the policy of the government is in harmony with the policy statement of 1948; (ii) the object of our economic policies should be a socialistic pattern of society; and (iii) towards this end the pulse of economic activity in general and industrial development in particular should be stepped up to the maximum extent possible.'[3]

Although the Congress commitment to socialism was welcome throughout the country, it created a rift among the Gandhians. The most orthodox warned that the Congress commitment was a radical departure which might cause further defections. The 1954 parliamentary resolution on socialistic pattern contributed to a certain amount of uneasiness amongst the business community, but the ministers of the time hastened to reassure them. In other words, though progressive economic policies were accepted, attempts to fix ceilings on land holdings and the distribution of excess land with meagre compensation raised a number of controversies. All said and done, by this time, the firm control of Nehru over the party, the disappearance of opposing members in the party, were important features that were fairly well established. The government resolution set the ground and paved the way to the 1955 Avadi resolution of the INC.

The Big Business and the Party Stratagem

During that time, in the FICCI meeting, the business lobby expressed their reactions and demands in the manner typical of them. They stated that "the Committee of FICCI have been following with great interest the discussions both in Parliament and outside on government's economic policy in recent weeks. The Committee have always been of the view that "in a country as large as ours with economic problems, too numerous and complex, there is plenty of constructive work to do both in the private and public sectors." It further stated that the "pressing problems are a challenge which both the state and the people must take up. Greater productivity is pre-requisites for a stable democracy and for sustained economic development. As the Prime Minister has rightly pointed out in the course of the economic policy debate in Parliament recently, what we are aiming at is production and employment." The above assertion of the FICCI shows the success of Congress leaders in sustaining the confidence of the business lobby, the vested interests. They even went to the extent of suggesting that when there were so many things to be done, and when the total resources available in the country were far from affluent the only positive approach was to see how best they could achieve the desired results. In conclusion, the Committee emphasised that the task of strengthening India should be regarded as one large scale enterprise in which both the State and the people cooperate and wherever possible, both the public and private sectors should work together and expand. The resolution did not betray any nervousness over the reference to a 'socialistic pattern of society' in the resolution passed by the Lok Sabha.

Nehruvian Policy

Nehru, in the message to the souvenir on the eve of the Avadi session expressed hope that the session would be a landmark in the country's history as well as the Congress history and hoped that it will give a lead which will work well for the country and bring all people of goodwill to the task of building up a new India. 'Every Congress session,' he said, 'was important in its own way, we are passing through an important stage in India's journey onward and are facing problems of great magnitude both internationally and in the domestic field. In foreign affairs, India has played a notable part which has added to our responsibilities. But ultimately it is our position in India itself that counts.' Recalling all the problems in the economic and social front, the country had faced, Nehru stated that it is very creditable that India had been able to achieve to some extent. He made repeated references to the Second Plan, revealing his anxieties regarding the acceptance of the Plan. Nehru criticised the activities of the CPI and said it was impracticable for anyone in this country progress in the line of the CPI.

How important the Socialistic slogan was from the point of view of elections, was revealed when, at Vijayawada, Nehru had said the task of achieving a socialist welfare state was a tremendous one and they had to work very hard for it. Nehru while addressing an election meeting there said that neither he nor the party were afraid of communism (and thereby exposing his nervous fear of the communists) and that they do not oppose communism as such.

Speaking on the eve of the Avadi session, Nehru pointed out how the Congress had always stood in the past for the common welfare of the people, especially the poorer sections and how Gandhi had identified himself with the poorest in the country. He further went on to say that the Congress stands for broad socialism. He also stated that the means Gandhi had taught to achieve these objectives would be adhered to. If these words, these objectives, would not win over the masses, what would we have? Nehru even very astutely said that the Congress may clarify the objectives in the present session, but it will not mean a departure from its creed. He also asserted that it is not necessary to aim injuring others or to spread the spirit of hatred and violence.

In another resolution of economic policy, the Steering Committee explained 'a socialistic pattern of society as envisazing the State' instituting and operating large-scale schemes providing of services such as power, transport, etc., having overall control of resources, social purposes and trends and preventing evils of anarchic industrial development by maintenance of strategic controls.[4] They emphasised that the public sector should play an increasingly significant role in the establishment of basic industries and the Committee also stated that there was necessity for the private sector, and accorded them a 'definite place' in our economy at present. Therefore, the stress on mixed economy continued, helping to keep every side happy. It is also interesting to note that the terms 'socialist' and 'socialistic' occurred alternately in the two resolutions adopted by the Committee. While the first resolution declared that the objective is to be a 'socialistic pattern of society', the second said 'the national aim is a welfare state and a socialist economy.' The Subjects Committee discussed the issue after the Steering Committee had passed the resolutions. It adopted unanimously the economic policy resolution moved by Nehru.[5] Although several amendments were moved during the debate, surprisingly they were all withdrawn later. Speaking on the occasion, Nehru stated that they were trying to make India a welfare state by putting an end to the private sector. He reiterated with greater emphasis most of his earlier suggestions like greater production through an integrated system considering the whole of India as a national sector, nationalisation, abolition of *zamindari,* speedy progress and the like. He, however, never failed to point out how even in China the whole process would take time. No doubt, Nehru wanted to play a dominant role in world politics and, therefore, could not afford to let China overshadow India.

R. Venkataraman seconded the resolution and said that although some might be critical of it because it did not lay down a set remedy, it was not their aim to hoodwink people with prescriptions which might lead them nowhere though they might sound attractive. He also asserted that it was on the basis of the experiences of the First Five Year Plan that the economic policy had been drafted. Another Congressman from Tamil Nadu, supporting the resolution said that read together with the resolution on 'socialistic pattern of society', adopted earlier, they were in effect, establishing 'a charter of economic liberty and salvation for the country.'[6]

Such statements only drove home the point that Nehru had full control of the party activities and its incumbents and his position and policy decisions was accepted by the majority of the Congressmen with almost loyalty. The resolution was supported by Congressmen from various quarters with minimum differences of opinion. The Congress Subjects Committee finally unanimously passed the resolution. Other senior and close aides of Nehru repeated much of the same things. Maulana Azad, for example, said[7] that the term 'socialistic pattern of society' was used with a definite purpose, i.e., not to tie the country down to any particular dogma or doctrine and that India should endeavour to build up a society befitting her own qualities and suited to her own requirements. He also stated that the resolution was only a restatement of what the Congress had been declaring from time to time. The Maulana too did not spare the Socialists and asserted that they had mixed up the end with the means and were pursuing dogmas with ridiculous fanaticism. Nationalisation, he said, was only a means to an end. He further stated that the Congress did not wish to tie itself down to any doctrinnaire theories and miss the target in the bargain. He also reassured the people that the Congress was in no way digressing from its old path. He discussed how the world was divided into two blocs—the capitalist and the socialist and that the professed aim of both was that society should be duly set up so that people may benefit from it. The real thing, however, according to him was the distribution of wealth. The Congress, he stated fully supported the point of view that the private sector should receive governmental assistance to increase production and said that they would stick to the 1948 policy strictly in which the private sector has been assigned a very clear role.

The Subjects Committee of the Congress also passed a resolution on land reforms urging the government to take every possible step to secure reasonable stability in the price level of agricultural commodities and stressing the need for giving adequate credit facilities to the rural areas. The Resolution[8] was moved by Nanda, Minister for Planning and was seconded by S.N. Aggarwal. Nanda also took the opportunity to declare that it would be incorrect to think that the resolution defining the economic goal of the Congress as the establishment of a socialist society, would only be a dead letter. The Congress had been solely inspired by socialist aspirations and with this it has taken the first practical step towards the achievement of that ideal. Nanda also hoped that the resolution would go a long way in ameliorating the condition of the agricultural people. It had been urged by more than one speaker that the principle of ceiling on land holdings should be extended to convert other forms of income as well. Nanda fully agreed with this proposition and went on to say that social justice was something indivisible and all sectors of the population must be dealt with without further discrimination. He, however, pointed out that a beginning had to be made from a certain stage and that it was considered wise to commence from a sector where changes might not adversely affect the means of production and create the very problem which it was intended to resolve.

At the 60th[9] session held at Avadi, it was Nehru who moved the resolution on socialistic pattern of society. In his rather impressive speech, Nehru further stated that it was not merely a vision and an aspiration rather it was a pledge which everyone must take to meet the challenging future. He said that everything from then onwards would be governed by the ideal of a socialistic society. Meanwhile, it can be seen from some Reports from the Avadi session that the implications of the resolution had not been properly understood by the more thoughtful sections of the Congress and that the leadership was accused of speaking in riddles and being quite vague. It was Nehru with his towering personality and charismatic appeal who was more or less in control of the entire show at Avadi. All this is only an indication of the fact that apart from these at the apex of the Congress organisation, the rest of the party men, failed to play any significant role in the decision-making process of the party. In fact, it seemed as if the whole session hinged on one personality—Nehru. Critics point out that if the purpose of the session was to discuss the issues before the people and associate them with the decisions arrived at, that was not at all evident during the session.

Even the labour organisations like INTUC gave their endorsement and approval to the Congress policy without any large-scale amendment.[10] Their resolution said that if the plan is to lead the nation towards its declared aim of a socialistic pattern of society it should provide everyone in the country particularly in the villages with the means of decent livelihood, adequate clothing, shelter, etc. It also stated that the Government of India policy to establish a socialistic pattern of society was a landmark in the history of peaceful revolutions which aimed at social and economic freedom through sheer peaceful democratic means. They even stated that the decision of the government to amend the Constitution was indicative of the fact that the determination of the government to remove the main hindrances in the path of progressive realisation of this policy. They pledged full support to the Government of India policy in this respect.

The Socialists outside the Congress opined that the Congress resolution was a mere eyewash. The Congress, they said, should be completely wiped out of reactionary elements and fully reorganised if it wants to establish a socialist state. Narendra Deva pointed out that "the very fact that not a single member of the Congress parliamentary party stood up in opposition to the resolution sponsored by the Prime Minister showed that the whole atmosphere was unreal."[11] Socialists welcomed the change, for, according to them it was an indication of the growing strength of democratic socialism. As the *National Herald*'s editorial put it "it might not mean socialism but to talk socialism is better than not to talk it. It will help people to think socialism."

The much-needed facelift of the Congress had come to fruition through the Avadi resolution. The decision-makers took the basic features of the Resolution and blended in the 1957 election Manifesto—with the hope of winning the elections with a thumping majority. The manifesto said "the basic objective of the Congress it must be repeated are democracy and socialism and the methods have to be peaceful... caste and class have no place in the socialist order that is envisaged by the Congress."[12] The third plan also made special references to this policy, "the accent of the socialist pattern of society on the attainment of opportunity for all... economic policy and institutional changes have to be planned in a manner that would secure economic advance along democratic and egalitarian lines."[13] The victory of the Congress in the general elections proved the fact that the purpose of the Avadi resolution had already been served.

First Non-Congress Government in Kerala

Shastri's motives were rarely questioned, except obliquely, that too only by a few leaders of the Congress party itself, who apparently felt that they had better claims to the two high offices of state he held one after the other. They did not think that Shastri's apparent silence entitled him to inherit the mantle of the awesome Govind Ballabh Pant, and even less deservedly the august office that Jawaharlal Nehru had held. Indeed, these disappointed aspirants seemed to doubt even the genuineness of Shastri's meekness; they felt that behind the outward appearance of meekness there was a cold and calculated pursuit of political ambition. But the opposition parties, including the socialists, though having difference of opinion with some of his policies and decisions, did not generally doubt Shastri's good faith—until he dealt with the critical political division in the coalition Ministry in Kerala, under the Praja Socialist Party (PSP) leader, Pattom Thanu Pillai.

The Congress had a strength of 66 in a House of 127 while the PSP had just 17 members. Pattom Thanu Pillai of the PSP had become Chief Minister because he was a political leader of long standing, going back to the period before the merger (with the Indian Union) of the princely States of Travancore and Cochin. Far from realising his limitations as the leader of the much weaker allies in the coalition, he was disposed to disregard the sensitivities of his Congress colleagues, with the result that personal wrath gave a sharp edge to the frustrated political ambition of R. Shankar, the leader of the Congress.

Shastri asked the civil servants accompanying him to explore whether there was anything seriously wrong in the manner in which the Ministry had been conducting official business; and after closely studying the Rules of Business, it was reported that the Kerala rules entrusted far more power to the Chief Minister than the rules in the States generally. The explanation for the substantial difference, it appeared, was that the rules in Kerala had been framed by the earlier leftist ministry led by E.M.S. Namboodiripad, and were tailored to fit the then current concept of leadership in a communist government.

The PSP accused Shastri of Machiavellian conduct, of having unethically instigated Pillai to resign his Chief Ministership and to accept a governorship without consulting the party to which he belonged. They considered it an act of political seduction, and considered that Shastri had been utterly unscrupulous in acting the way he did without taking the PSP leaders into confidence. The question may be asked why Shastri did not come out with the facts when he was attacked. Obviously, Shastri could never have done so without betraying the confidence Pillai had reposed in him; and Shastri was a person who would accept staunch criticism himself rather than expose another person to it.

It was necessary to mention the details of Thanu Pillai's case in the interest of a true record of what happened, and also to remove an unjustified stain on Shastri's character.

References

1. *Fourth Year of Freedom,* 1950-51, INC, New Delhi.
2. *The Hindu,* 10 November 1954.
3. *The Hindu,* 3 December 1954.
4. See Harekrishna Mehtab, *Call to Action,* Friends Prakashan, 1963.
5. *Ibid.,* 20 January 1952.
6. *Ibid.*
7. *Ibid.*
8. *Ibid.,* 21 January 1955.
9. *Ibid.,* 22 January 1955.
10. *Ibid.,* 3 January 1955.
11. *Ibid.*
12. Election Manifesto, 1957, AICC, New Delhi.
13. See, V.N. Gadgil, *Government from Inside,* Meenakshi Prakashan, Meerut, 1969, p. 167.

20

Indo-China War

Under the Prime Ministership of Nehru, till halfway through his tenure as Home Minister, Shastri's energies had been devoted to internal affairs; to manifold problems of national integration; to sensitive developments that had occurred in some of the States, such as the issue of language in Assam and the rift in the coalition in Kerala. But by the autumn of 1962, the growing threat of aggression by the People's Republic of China had begun to loom large in the nation's consciousness, thereby pushing into the background other problems. As was to be expected, this change was fully reflected in the priorities and pre-occupations of Shastri. An external threat gives rise to several problems within the sphere of the Home Ministry, and Shastri was something more than the Home Minister; he was an influential member of the Cabinet, known for his sagacious judgement.

During the critical autumn and winter months of 1962-63, when the nation experienced the traumatic experience of external aggression and humiliation caused by the reverses which India's armed forces suffered, Shastri was acutely conscious of his responsibilities. At no time since Independence had the country faced such political and security crises. For the first time in its long history, India had to face hostility developing into an invention across the Himalayan ranges. The government and people of Assam felt that they had been let down by the Union Government and there was a sense of panic and disorganisation in some north Assam areas.

Shastri had not taken any special interest in defence. But he had plenty of commonsense and a deep insight into the psychology, strengths and weaknesses of our people. He stated before leaving for Assam that he had suggested to Nehru that the plan to deploy some 50,000 troops, with heavy artillery and armour, at the foot-hills and adjoining plains, and give battle to the Chinese there. Nehru had replied that Shastri would be in a better position to discuss these suggestions after a visit to Assam. In the light of what happened during the next four weeks, Shastri must have regretted that his views had not been accepted.

The Chinese advance into NEFA (now Arunachal Pradesh) had created apprehension in the areas on the north of the Brahmaputra. Members of the Assam Cabinet had a long meeting with Shastri, at which they expressed their anxieties particularly about Chinese air strikes, for which they thought our civil defence arrangements were wholly outdated.

Shastri was greatly impressed by the professionalism and confident leadership which Lt-Gen. Harbaksh Singh performed. So Shastri left Tezpur with a change in his view that under Harbaksh Singh's leadership our forces would be able to prevent the further onslaught of Chinese troops. This assurance, however, did not last. On reaching Calcutta we learnt that Lt-Gen. Kaul was returning to resume command of the Corps, and that Harbaksh Singh was being given command of another Corps. Rumours were circulating that he had returned to Delhi because of loss of courage.

Shastri returned to Delhi in a depressed mood, but since it was reported that Kaul had already left for Tezpur he did not appear to think he could approach the Prime Minister with a request to change his decision. One felt on a certain occasion that Shastri had gone too far in his reverential attitude towards Nehru, formed after a visit to Gauhati and the corps headquarters; that Lt-Gen. Harbaksh Singh was the right person to deal with the critical situation. The aftermath of Nehru's ill-advised decision, which Shastri ought to have questioned, proved detrimental to national interests and even to Nehru's own prestige.

The events of the next few weeks are well-known military history. It is beyond the scope of the present undertaking to recapitulate those facts or comment on the causes. However, in looking at the way Shastri dealt with situations during those critical tension packed weeks, it must be recorded that he remained cool and composed, and dealt with issues that arose in a practical way, carrying with him the cooperation of all concerned.

An emergency was proclaimed under Article 352 of the Constitution and certain special powers were assumed and used. Shastri's firm view was that a person should not be detained merely because he belonged to a particular party. So Shastri's decision was to approve of the detention of only those members of that party, and others, who had generally supported the Chinese assault secretly and were suspected to be supporting anti-national intentions.

As reports of the Chinese advance in Ladakh and, more particularly, NEFA started coming in during the first part of November, the matter of replacing General Thapar as Chief of Army Staff began to be considered at the highest levels of Government. The name of Lt-Gen. Choudhary was mentioned as his possible successor. There was a suspicion in certain high quarters that Choudhary would not be fully loyal to the civil government, and might attempt a coup d'état. At the final stage of consideration Shastri supported Choudhary's appointment; as Home Minister he was in the best position to judge from intelligence reports Choudhary's intentions.

There was another instance which showed that Shastri was a quintessential Gandhian, and that related to his ultimate respect for truth. Bertrand Russell, writing about the Sino-Indian conflict, had expressed the view that India was more to blame than China. There was a strong demand in Parliament to ban the book, and Shastri asked us in the Home Ministry to go into the question and report our conclusions to him.

Through that period of distress and confusion created by military defeat, local civil disorganisation, recriminations, the expression of outrage against the Government in Parliament, and a change of Defence Ministers and Chief of Army Staff, Shastri remained seemingly unmoved. He was not constitutionally placid; he was, in fact, a highly sensitive person. But he rarely exposed his feelings; restraint and patience were part of his innate dignity, which could stand the test of adversity. There is a well documented example of his preserving his dignity and composure even in personal bereavement. In 1942 he had come out on unconditional parole for fifteen days to visit a daughter suffering from typhoid. The child died the day he reached her; but soon after performing the last obsequies, he returned to prison without even meeting the grieving members of his family. Perhaps the same sort of spiritual sustenance and acceptance was there when facing a national misfortune.

As reports about the fighting in NEFA came in, the question was raised as to why our forces had not taken any prisoners, while China had taken quite a few. Shastri put this question pointedly to some officers in the Ministry.

Highly disturbing reports of panic, disorganisation and demoralisation in Assam caused deep concern to the Prime Minister in Delhi. With the virtual collapse of IV Corps and the complete loss of morale and confidence of the Corps Commander, Lt-Gen. B.M. Kaul, there was uncertainty about the further advance of Chinese forces on the north side of the Brahmaputra. Shastri, who had been keeping close touch with the developments, was asked by the Prime Minister to visit Assam to study the situation, and help in steadying things.

Peking Radio had announced that a ceasefire would begin the following midnight. The announcement had been monitored by our agencies at the Delhi and other radio stations at about 3 a.m. It may be recalled that even before his visit to Assam on 26 October, Shastri had suggested to Nehru that our forces should mass in great strength below the foot-hills, where the Chinese could not have the resources to fight effectively. Whatever political criticism there may have been of allowing the Chinese to occupy some Indian territory without any resistance, India would then have been saved from the humiliation of military collapse in NEFA and its political fallout.

Despite the Chinese declaration of a ceasefire, an apprehension of further assaults continued and there was great bitterness against the Government of India for issuing instructions to withdraw the civil administration. We proceeded to Tezpur to find Lt-Gen. Kaul in a completely demoralised state. He said that the Indian army had faced disgrace and that it was incapable of making any stand not only in North Assam but anywhere in the State.

With uncertainty about China's further aggressions, national security continued to be under threat till the end of 1963. Defence preparations had in fact, though not by public acknowledgement, taken precedence over the paramount importance so far attached to economic and social development. There was also a subtle reorientation of India's outlook in international relations. Even apart from his profound respect for Nehru, Shastri would not have thought of doubting Nehru's views regarding international affairs. It was generally accepted that Nehru understood world affairs best—that is, until the Chinese invasion. Nehru with all his vision and wisdom, had not proved infallible.

Election

In its Election Manifesto for the second general elections in free India in 1957, the Congress had earlier explained its stand in relation to Reorganisation of States. It said, 'During the past year or more, the question of the reorganisation of the States gave rise to much controversy and even conflicts. Such questions, involving languages and a new distribution of provincial areas have often roused strong passions in other countries also. But after full discussion and consultation, the States were reorganised and a new map of India took shape. However, it was admitted that the feeling of provincial separateness was even then strong and had to be combated. It emphasised that the revolution in India could only be completed when the political revolution was followed by an economic as well as a social revolution. The resounding victory in 1957 vindicated the Congress stand. It secured more seats than the last election in 1952. The percentage of votes polled by the Congress also showed an improvement from 45.0 per cent to 47.7 per cent in 1957. In the Election Manifesto for the 1962 elections, the Congress Party harped upon the achievements of the first two Five Year Plans and talked about the third Five Year Plan in the same strain. It appealed to the masses to vote it to power so that the road to progress might be maintained. The Congress party secured majority of the seats than the other parties.

Consequent to the State Reorganisation Act, 1956, when the political map of India was drastically redrawn, the constituencies were also delimited in 1956. The process of change started just before the general election of 1957, saw its fruition in 1962; by that time the constitutional distinction between Part A, Part B and Part C States was abolished and two types of units, namely, States and Union Territories remained.

In the State assemblies, the Congress Party had secured a fairly high percentage of votes in 1962 in all States, viz. Andhra Pradesh, Assam, Bihar, Gujarat, Madhya Pradesh, Madras, Maharashtra, Mysore, Punjab, Rajasthan, Uttar Pradesh, West Bengal, but in Kerala and Orissa it did not fare well. It had improved its position in Andhra Pradesh where it fared badly in 1957 elections. During the intervening period elections took place in Kerala in 1960 where the Communists came to power in 1957. They had substantially increased the popular votes in comparison to 1957 elections; but the Congress joined hands with other opposition parties to keep out the Communists. It had mustered 94 out of 127 seats in the Kerala assembly. Subsequently in the third general elections of 1962, the Communists again regained absolute majority and the Congress was reduced to a minority. In the Lok Sabha also, the CPI increased their representation from 27 to 29.

The Praja Socialist Party had fared badly even in 1957 general elections. Acharya Narendra Deva's death in 1956 had delivered a blow to the party. Dr. Ram Manohar Lohia left the PSP in order to revive the old Socialist Party but he could not forge unity in the party. In the 1962 elections, the Socialist Party and the PSP both fared badly. In the Lok Sabha, their representation declined from 19 to 12. After the elections, the PSP expelled Asoka Mehta who joined the Congress Cabinet at the Centre in defiance to the party's directive. The grooming of the Socialist, Praja Socialist and the Communist parties to democratic process was a personal triumph for Pandit Nehru who regarded himself as a democratic Socialist. It was, on the other hand, a vindication of the Congress objectives set from time to time during 1952 and 1962. The Third Plan launched in 1961 had more ambitious targets and aimed at making India self-sustaining in national economy. It was decided by the party that the mixed system of economy was to continue and planning was to be democratic and not totalitarian.

However, the implementation of the Third Five Year Plan (1960-61—1965-66) was criticised from several angles. Even K. Brahmanand Reddi argued that 'Planning is either not necessary or has created a good deal of hardship . . . that in the name of planning the Union Government and the Planning Commission have made imperceptible inroads into the autonomy of States.) Acharya J.B. Kripalani launched his criticism when he said, "Russia had dictatorship first and planning afterwards. We will have planning first and dictatorship following in its wake." In spite of such criticisms, the Congress forged ahead and extended an invitation to the progressive elements to join it. At the Nagpur session adoption of the New Agrarian Pattern led to the formation of the Swatantra party. There were two proposals which aroused the active hostility of the Swatantra party, one relating to co-operative farming and the other to the imposition of ceiling on land. However, it contested the elections as a multi-state party with Star as its symbol even in 1967.

Towards Nationalisation

The Congress Election Manifesto of 1957 had clearly stated that "The Congress welcomes the nationalisation of the State Bank as well as Life Insurance. This is another step towards the socialist pattern and it gives a greater measure of strategical control for planning and other purposes of the State". At the Amritsar session of the Congress in February 1956, an official resolution had clarified the position in this respect. The 'socialist pattern' was replaced by 'socialism' as the guiding principle of the party. The President took pride in stating that the elimination of the princely order, the abolition of *Zamindari,* nationalisation of the Imperial Bank of India, and other reforms were deliberate measures towards socialism. The establishing of the State Trading Corporation to equate the prices of indigenous and imported cement and to apply the same to other commodities was a useful instrument of state trading to control the prices and ensure proper distribution. This initiated the concept of State monopoly of either internal or external trade in particular commodities, if the exigencies of the situation so demanded. In order to meet the shortage of food, the Government of India negotiated a large scale deal with the USA for the import of foodgrains under Public Law 480 (PL-480). India had not to pay for that in foreign currency.

In 1956, the Government of India decided to nationalise Life Insurance. The major considerations which led to this drastic step lay in the mismanagement of these concerns by private agencies or individuals, embezzlement and misuse of public money and speculation in shares. It was accepted alround that expansion of Insurance had been achieved at the expense of integrity. The Haridas Mundhra affair attracted so much attention that a one-man enquiry commission headed by M.C. Chagla, Chief Justice of Bombay High Court, enquired into the whole affair. Justice Chagla did not find any corrupt motive but found error of judgment in the use of public funds. Consequently. T.T. Krishnamachari had to resign. This showed the high standard of efficacy in the parliamentary democracy of the weapon of interpellation. Although the Minister of Finance disclaimed responsibility, yet he had to go. This was acclaimed as an example of democratic functioning. The Government of India accepted the Commissions' findings. The Congress vindicted its policies by removing many of the malpractices prevailing then. Establishment of the Life Insurance Corporation of India with zonal offices removed many of the evils prevailing in private insurance companies. Such control on General Insurance was also enforced by Insurance (Amendment) Act, 1968, which came into force on 1st April 1969.

The nationalisation of the Imperial Bank of India and Life Insurance had been preceded by the take over of country's air transport services under the Air Corporation

Act of 1953. The Reserve Bank of India was established as a Government concern. In his speech at a public meeting at Bangalore, February 6, 1962 Pandit Nehru explained the policy of the Congress towards socialist democracy. According to him India was to advance along the particular path of democracy with a large measure of socialism—not doctrinaire socialism but practical, pragmatic socialism—which was to fit in with the thinking of India and with the demands of India. However, in spite of all the explanations offered by Pandit Nehru, a number of Congress leaders felt that the government should go slow with nationalisation. They thought that this process was beset with grave dangers, such as lack of country's financial resources, stagnation in the productive capacity and want of adequate experienced personnel. So the Congress party tried to achieve the targets of socialism by allowing the Plans to operate in a capitalist framework of economy. It had to change the Indian society which was complex, full of contradictions, incongruities and diversities. The social structure was descrepid, stratified, multi-class, multi-religious, multi-caste and multi-lingual. The regional variations, especially in the areas covered by erstwhile Indian Princely States, were appalling. No wonder with this background the policies followed by the Congress party till 1962 could not effect fundamental changes in socio-economic structure. In the private sector, it could not check the growth of monopoly and private capitalism. In public sector, it could not ensure proper benefits to the workers.

In the agricultural sector, although the recommendations made by the Agrarian Reforms Committee appointed by Dr. Rajendra Prasad in December 1947, continued to guide the Congress ministries in legislating for abolition of *zamindari,* but the agriculture labour could not be protected. The old *zamindars* and *jagirdars* were replaced by new rich peasant class often termed as new *Kulaks* and these ingratiated themselves in the party hierarchy. Due to heavy compensation awarded and opportunity to invest in urban property, the former intermediaries could improve their position in 1962 and thereafter. So, on the one hand, impression arose that the Congress party had failed to advance the cause of the poor. On the other hand, the rightists decided to capture the party, to protect the interest of the capitalists and the haves. So, after the general elections of the 1962, confrontation between the two wings of the Congress, i.e., the Rightists and the Leftists became inevitable. At the sixty-seventh session of the INC at Patna, in January 1962 differences came to the surface.

After independence, workers' participation in public enterprises was advocated. The Industrial Policy Resolution of 1956 pleaded for progressive association of workers in the common task of industrial development and urged the public sector to set an example in this regard. As a result Joint Management Councils (JMCs) were set up and were entrusted with the responsibility of matters of administrative importance. By 1958 three Central Government undertakings and nine controlled by authorities in the States had moved in that direction. Pandit Nehru stressed the need of strengthening the economic position speedily. He said that the Five Year Plan had been presenting with a dynamic concept of India's social and economic changes. The Congress party continued to highlight the importance of participative management for increased production and industrial peace in its election manifestos.

Right from the beginning in the post-Independence era, alarming growth of corruption had worried the top leadership of the Congress. Control or decontrol, the evil continued and there were all round complaints that the high dignitaries of State and influential leaders in the party were busy amassing wealth or currying favours. The enormous finances mobilised under the Five Year Plans whetted appetite for becoming rich overnight. The mounting election expenses and the problem of meeting them either directly or indirectly forced the ministers to connive at corruption. Suggestions were made by MPs for the eradication of the roots of corruption. Nehru in the course of his addresses to the party members emphasised the need for the exposure of acts of corruption, purity in public life and setting an example of well-disciplined life. This ideal was preached and prescribed for public leaders as well as public servants. As the Congress from the very beginning was not an entirely homogeneous organisation, its own members operated as restraining influence on the Congress party as a whole. The several Committees set up by the Indian parliament and, in particular, the Public Accounts Committee, not only criticised audit irregularities but also drew attention to waste and corruption in administration and thus acted as a democratic check on the power of the government. The right of interpellation led at times to the setting up of inquiry commissions or investigation bodies whose findings had far-reaching consequences.

But as the Congress had deviated from its basic principles it began to lose its hold on the people. When the AICC met at Poona on 4th and 5th June 1960, the Congress President N. Sanjiva Reddy admitted in his opening remarks that organisational work had suffered in some places due to lack of harmony among Congress workers. The achievements of democracy and socialism placed before the country could not be realised. He, however, remarked that the Poona session of the AICC would mainly consider constitutional matters raised by K. Hanumanthayya and Humayun Kabir and the sub-committee of the Congress Party in Parliament.

Pandit Nehru remarked that the idea of bringing about an integrated leadership through the merger of the two offices, namely, the leader of the Congress Party and the President of the Congress was absolutely wrong. By doing so, the Congress would lose its essential character. However, he deprecated enlistment of bogus membership and advocated action against such persons. He insisted that the Working Committee should be a nominated body. He was for retention of four-anna membership. Membership fee could be raised to one rupee per member. At the close of the discussion, the Congress President placed before the AICC the proposal of K. Hanumanthayya that the one-third of the members of the Working Committee should be elected by the AICC. But even that was lost, there were 78 in favour and 148 against. Six members remained neutral.

The proceedings of the AICC meeting held at Poona were confirmed at the next AICC meet at Raipur on October 29 and 30, 1960. The Annual Report for the year 1960 recorded that 1960 was a year for active work. The main organisational elections were over by the end of 1959. The year 1961 was also a year of intense activity for the Congress organisation.

Kamraj Plan

From January 1962 to January 1964, the period was indeed most eventful in the history of the Congress since independence. The Elections of 1962 had disclosed certain weaknesses. Prominent among them were group rivalries and lure for power, which were mainly responsible for the decrease in the Congress voters' strength. At its October meeting at New Delhi, the Congress Working Committee viewed with great concern the crisis that had arisen by the invasion of India by China. It called upon every citizen to do his or her duty with redoubled vigour and efficiency. At its subsequent meeting in November it decided that "every active member of the Congress should put in some work daily to contribute his mite for winning the war". The Committee also decided to issue a directive on Economic Mobilisation for defence and the role of the people to all the PCCs and the Chief Ministers of the States.

The trends revealed in the 1962 General Elections were treated with seriousness and their rectification was sought through a Plan which came to be known as Kamraj Plan. By this plan the senior Congressmen who were holding ministerial offices were to step down and engage themselves in full time organisational work. Pandit Nehru was also very anxious to reinvigorate the Congress as the same was losing its dynamism. So when, in this context Kamraj, the then Chief Minister of Madras proposed that he and some other Chief Ministers might resign and devote themselves to party work, the idea was welcomed all round. It is not clear whether this was exclusively Kamraj's own idea or he was acting as the instrument of others. The Prime Minister denied that he had inspired the Kamraj Plan, but he welcomed it, as it suited him at various levels.

The AICC meeting held at New Delhi, on August 9 and 10, 1963 discussed the Kamraj Plan, with a view to strengthen the organisation. According to the President, D. Sanjivaiya, said, "The main theme of the proposal was that experienced Congressmen should come out leaving their ministerial posts and take up organisational work. There was general agreement over this suggestion in the Working Committee."

In moving the resolution on behalf of the Congress Working Committee, Kamraj said that even Pandit Nehru had told him that he (Nehru) should also leave the Government and lead the organisation; but to this he was told that "if he stepped down from the Prime Ministership then a worse situation might be created in the country". Although Pandit Nehru entertained the idea to the end, the Working Committee came to an unanimous decision that "it would be disastrous for the country if Pandit Nehru was allowed to step down from the Prime Ministership." When the resolution was passed Pandit Nehru spoke on the same and said that the consequences of that were far-reaching. He emphasised the importance of discipline.

When the AICC met again at Jaipur, on November 3-4, 1963 it was admitted that the Kamraj Plan had enthused the rank and file of Congressmen and workers. It also proved that India's millions had confidence and faith in Pandit Nehru's leadership. Initiating the discussion on the resolution Morarji Desai said: "The—fatal tendency—of clinging to power had also set in among some individuals", so everybody welcomed the Kamraj Plan. But Morarji Desai discounted the rumours that the Kamraj Plan was the outcome of the existence of 'left' and 'right' in the Party and that it was designed as a conspiracy to overthrow the Prime Minister. He suggested that there should be some rule that no one should remain in office for more than 5 or 10 years. Frequent consultations between the organisational and parliamentary wings of the Party were essential. B. Patnaik seconded the proposal. But when the plan was actually implemented misgivings arose in the mind of Morarji Desai. He has recorded in his

The Story of My Life that when 'Jawaharlalji went to Hyderabad soon after the plan was first mooted, there he discussed it with Shri Kamraj and with Shri C. Subramanium. Nobody had told me anything about these discussions. *I suspected some hidden purpose in them…*'

All the ministers were asked to resign before the Working Committee meeting. When the matter was discussed by him with Pandit Nehru, he told him; "I am not at all unwilling to give up office. On the contrary, I am quite happy about it." The next day when the Working Committee met, Pandit Nehru gave his decision, according to which Morarji Desai, Lal Bahadur Shastri, Jagjivan Ram, S.K. Patil, Gopala Reddy were relieved from the Central Cabinet. Among the Chief Ministers, Kamraj from Tamil Nadu, Mandloi from Madhya Pradesh, B.N. Jha from Bihar and C.B. Gupta from UP had to go. According to Dr. S. Gopal, Pandit Nehru "used the opportunity to send out many of these either reputed to be inefficient or rumoured to be corrupt or known to disagree with him on basic policies . . . . The Finance Minister, Morarji Desai, in particular, Nehru wished to see out of office."

Explaining the objectives of the resolution on Kamraj Plan, Pandit Nehru said at the meeting of the AICC, at New Delhi on August 9 and 10 that "by the resignation of top ranking Congressmen the people should realise the importance of the organisation and the organisational work." According to his address to the Congress Parliamentary Party, 12 August 1963, "Doing a rather odd thing in a dramatic way would not change the whole surface of the world or reverse major trends in India, but it would wake people out of their slumber, make them think, get them out of ruts and generally held to create an atmosphere in which the right impulses were encouraged." Consequently it checked the spreading lust for office and patronage. It tended to strengthen the organisation to some extent.

According to some of its critics, the Kamraj Plan weakened the Central Government. It also weakened the basis of Pandit Nehru's way of running the Congress Party. It led to unnecessary bickerings in some of the States. In his memoirs Morarji Desai has gone to the extent of saying that "Lal Bahadurji (name) was also included in the plan, but there was an understanding that he would be taken back in the Cabinet after three or four months"; and it soon became clear "that he (Pandit Nehru) wanted Indiraji to succeed him." At the November meeting of the AICC, on November 3-4, 1963 Pandit Nehru paid handsome tributes to Kamraj, former Chief Minister of Madras, for coming forward with a plan which had given a jolt to the Congress as well as to the administration. "His name has got engraved in the history of India", he said. And he secured Kamraj's election as the President of the Congress to see its implementation.

As a follow up, a number of high-level Committees were set up such as the Organisational Affairs Committee, Constitution Sub-Committee to suggest amendments to the Constitution and a Committee to enquire into the charges against Congressmen including the ministers. The Parliamentary Board was enlarged and the Disciplinary Action Committee had started functioning. But the sad and sudden demise of the Prime Minister, Pandit Nehru on 27 May 1964 became the most tragic event that overtook the country after independence. The nation was left bereft and a gloom was cast through the length and breadth of the country. Many became apprehensive about the future of the Congress. But as the Annual Report for the year 1964 recorded : "All these fears and suspicions were dispelled and the leadership rose to the occasion and proved to the people of this country and the world outside that Nehru had not worked in vain."

The Working Committee authorised the President to convene a meeting of the Congress Party in Parliament and to elect a leader on the basis of consensus of opinion. Consequently in June 1964, under the presidentship of K. Kamraj, Lal Bahadur Shastri's name was proposed by G.L. Nanda and seconded by Morarji Desai. So Shastri was declared elected and became the Prime Minister. As mentioned by the Annual Report, Kamraj's leadership at the crucial time of the nation as also of the Indian National Congress proved to be beacon light for all.

As provided in Article XXVI (A) of the Congress Constitution, the Working Committee set up the Central Parliamentary Board. And in terms of the recommendation of the Organisational Affairs Committee, dated 13th September 1962 Co-ordination Committees were constituted in various Pradeshes for closer coordination between the organisational wing and the parliamentary wing. Rules had been framed for admission of non-Congress legislators to Congress Legislature parties and directive issued on collection of funds by ministers and Congressmen. As authorised by the Working Committee, the Congress President, K. Kamraj appointed a Disciplinary Action Committee with five members and General Secretary, Incharge Organisation as sixth member. The Congress organisation was all set to meet the exigencies of the new situation.

The basic constitution of the Congress had remained more or less the same after Jaipur session in December 1948. Major amendments were effected at the Bhubaneshwar Session of the Congress. The main objective clause of Article I of the Constitution was amended with a view to 'the establishment in India by peaceful and constitutional means of a Socialist State based on Parliamentary Democracy.'

Besides this another change was brought about by replacing Mandal Congress Committees by Block Congress Committees which were to be formed by the latter half of 1965. Certain other minor amendments were also affected to Article XI of the Constitution which related to the formation of District and Pradesh Congress Committees. A Mandal Committee, the lowest unit under the then existing Constitution of the Congress was abolished and replaced by a Block Committee. In urban areas where there were no blocks. Ward Committees were to be formed, areas having a population of 10 lakhs and above were allowed to have PCCs.

In this way, the Indian National Congress even after the death of Pandit Nehru emerged as one of the biggest anti-imperialist force in the world. It successfully waged heroic post-independence struggle in the cause of unity, external defence and the establishment of a just socio-economic order within the framework of democratic institutions. *Freedom was firmly consolidated and challenges after independence successfully met.* Eighteen months after Pandit Nehru's passing away, when his daughter assumed the reins of government in the country, the Indian National Congress was poised to take the country towards the goal of Democratic Socialism, so dear to Pandit Nehru and the people of Free India.

21

Lal Bahadur Shastri: The Quintessential Gandhian

The Assam Language Problem

A movement to make Assamese the official language of Assam had taken a violent turn around the middle of June 1961, with the State witnessing what was till then the worst rioting in its recent history. Bengali-speakers were at the receiving end and the nature and extent of the attacks were such that they evoked anguished reactions from Pant and Nehru. In his speech in Parliament, Pant warned that the disturbances raised issues of terrifying magnitude and of paramount importance to the country's future. Nehru asked, 'Do we only have a superficial covering of nationalism and is it bursting open?' The Assam happenings, he went on to say, had done one good thing: they had brought the 'skeleton of narrow nationalism out of our mental cupboard'.

Tension between Bengali and Assamese speaking people had long existed and while there was an acute sense of insecurity among Bengali community in the Brahmaputra valley, a separatist feeling was developing and there was a strong agitation in the Bengali dominated Cachar district. Visits by some Central Ministers and a visit by Members of Parliament had not led to any marked improvement and, in fact, violent demonstrations had taken place in Cachar, which led to firing by the police and several casualties. It was against this background that Shastri, who had succeeded Pant as the Home Minister, visited Assam, probably at the instance of Nehru. However, it was not easy to make a new start with a reasonable prospect of settling the language dispute to the satisfaction of all the three components of the State's population: the Assamese-speaking majority, the Bengali-speaking minority and the tribal inhabitants of the Garo, Khasi and Mizo Hill districts, who had accepted English as the language of education and administration. Pant, with all his authority had, on a visit to Shillong in October 1960, recommended the adoption of Assamese and Hindi as official languages of the State. A Bill embodying provisions with some refinement of the above formula had been introduced in the State legislature, but the tribal leaders and Bengali-speakers not only opposed it, but raised their protest through the resignation of the Tribal Affairs Minister, Williamson Sangma and two Mizo members holding public offices. Members from the Cachar district had also stood against the impending enactment. The Bill had, nevertheless, been passed in October 1960; but as mentioned earlier, tension prevailed and there had been serious incidents in Cachar. Large-scale demonstrations by Bengali-speakers and the tribal people were imminent in Shillong and there was apprehension that these might lead to violence. Against this background and the prevailing tension, the question was whether Shastri, new to the office of Home Minister, would be able to do something to ease the tension and restore peace for a while. It was to be in a sense the first major test of his political sagacity.

Shastri held back his own conclusions till the end of the discussion. But once a formula had been worked out under his guidance he put it to the Chief Minister, Chaliha, and asked whether he considered it fair and workable. Chaliha was a person who thought deeply and expressed his views unhurriedly. But as soon as he said that the formula was both fair and practicable, Shastri spoke in an entirely different tone. All the soft, explanatory style had gone; he was firm and unequivocal: Chaliha by that time got the formula through. To the latter's reasonable caution that he would have to put it to his Cabinet, Shastri's reply was that, if his Cabinet did not agree, Chaliha should step down; this, Shastri seemed to suggest, was a political and constitutional imperative. Nehru and Patel, however, had often taken vital decisions in anticipation of the approval of the Congress organisation and with the confidence that the organisation would stand by their decision.

All that remained was to make the decision public and Shastri was not prepared to take any chances with those concerned of making use of an interval to go back on their commitments. So he had drafted a statement immediately and after getting it approved by Chaliha and Choudhary, he had it released to the press. This was the first, but not the last occasion, when people witnessed the soft-spoken, tentative, and supposedly hesitating Shastri transformed into a person of the utmost firmness in decision and unequivocal in expressing it.

Shastri was deeply moved and distressed by the gruesome firing at Silchar in which a number of people were killed. The firing had been ordered by a very senior police officer, who was himself a Bengali-speaker, as were those killed and injured. But Shastri's abhorrence from bloodshed, and in particular from violence by state agencies, was too profound for him to go into what he would have considered nuances of administrative exigencies. His intuitive feeling was that the firing could and should have been averted. He visited the injured in hospital including the policemen who sustained injuries in the names of the demonstrating mob. He insisted on the Assam Government ordering an enquiry by a judge. As it turned out, the result of the enquiry confirmed Shastri's intuitive assessment. On returning to Shillong, Shastri found the Governor, a General of the Indian army, who had retired from the post of Chief of Staff of the army, visibly shaken by an expected demonstration in Shillong by Bengali-speakers and tribal people. Shastri, who had not expected a General of the Army to be so worried, took the prospect coolly and was happy when the demonstration passed off peacefully. He had succeeded in lessening the tension by the way he had conducted the talks and the atmosphere of conciliation and goodwill he had created.

The language arrangement worked out by Shastri bore the impression of his personality and reflected his deep conviction that in a democracy, and particularly in a society such as Assam's with its marked linguistic and cultural diversities, the prime necessity was a reconciliation of apparently conflicting interests. In the development of Assamese sub-nationalism, the Assamese language had become the prime instrument of self-assertion and the symbol of Assamese identity. On the other side, both in matter of language and culture, Cachar district had an understandable Bengali personality, with nearly 90 per cent of its population of over two million being speakers of Bengali language, which was the language of education in schools and the language used in the courts. The Shastri formula recognised Assamese political sensitivity and the advisability of maintaining the situation of Assam under control by recognising the position of Assamese as the sole official language of the State but providing with legislative sanction for the use of Bengali in Cachar district for various official purposes and for its use in addition to Assamese in communications from the State government to Cachar. The arrangement thus harmonised the interests and sensitivities of both sides.

Shastri's success in dealing with the language problem in Assam was widely acclaimed. Nehru expressed his relief and happiness to Shastri by remarking that he had only hoped Shastri would work out a truce, whereas Shastri had in fact brought about a settlement. This was indeed true, as was found years later. Cachar had other problems with the Government of Assam and Assamese-speaking people but not on the question of the official language—at least not till 1981.

National Integration

The disturbance in Assam resulting from the cleavage on the language issue, the demand of the Sikhs for a separate Punjabi-speaking State, and the language question becoming a central issue in the separatist, even secessionist, politics of Tamil Nadu, indicate that the questions which appeared to have been settled by the Constitution, and the reorganisation of States in the mid-1950s, had by the early 1960s thrown up issues, and increase in demands, which needed to be attended to urgently. In addition to language and regional questions, Hindu-Muslim riots which had broken out in some districts of Madhya Pradesh early in 1961 showed that the relations between the two communities were still very much volatile. Altogether, the relatively placid flow of public life appeared to be coming to an end and Shastri started his Home Ministership facing the challenges which these unwanted developments presented. Prime Minister Nehru's high sensitivity towards these disturbing portents and his absolute faith in Shastri were valuable assets with which Shastri began his tenure as Home Minister.

The National Integration Conference held from the last days of September to the beginning of October 1961 was indeed a historic event. The most eminent Indians in all walks of life like politics, scholarship, science and letters, the learned professions, social service, business and industry—a total of about 130 distinguished persons, met under the chairmanship of the Prime Minister to realise the situation and contribute their experience and wisdom towards promoting national integration. This was the first and last time after the enactment of our Constitution that such a mammoth gathering of the country's 'great and good' applied their minds to the nation's problems and jointly sought solutions to them. The Conference set out, with general agreement, a code of conduct for political parties which provided that no party shall indulge in any activity which would intensify existing differences or create mutual hatred; that every political party would ensure that there was no instigation to violence and that if despite this there was an outbreak of violence, it would be categorically condemned. There was more in the same vein in the code, and as the statement issued at the end of the Conference said, 'This unique Conference itself was an act of faith in ourselves and our people, and our ability to cooperate with one another.'

At the Chief Ministers' conference in August 1962, it was decided based on a report of the Chief Minister of Tamil Nadu on the separatist activities of the Dravid Munnetra Kazhagam (DMK), and some other political groups in south India, that such activities by any individual or organisation should be made a penal offence. Shastri wrote to Nehru that such a law could be passed only after an amendment of clause (2) of Article 19 of the Constitution as it would permit restrictions on freedom of speech and expression for the sovereignty and integrity of India. He accordingly proposed an amendment of Article 19. Nehru replied that the matter was not important or urgent enough for action. Shastri was not convinced and as desired by him the question was raised at a meeting of the Committee on National Integration and Regionalism.

Shastri, in fact, believed wholeheartedly that the solution to disaffection or a violent secessionist movement in any part of India had to be sought through talks carried on with sympathy, understanding and perseverance. As Home Minister he supported the amendment of the Constitution to confer statehood on Nagaland. As sections of Nagas continued violent activities even after Nagaland came into being, Shastri as Prime Minister had to take the final decision on the question of suspension of military operations there in September 1964.

Article 343 of the Constitution had laid down that the official language of the Union shall be Hindi. The real issue in 1965 was not Hindi becoming the official language of the Union, but that the period of fifteen years for which English was required to be used under the same article for all the purposes. The use of English was to be continued in accordance with the law passed in 1963, but it was the primacy of Hindi over English which had been the sole official language of the Central Government for nearly a hundred years, that created resentment and a general feeling of discrimination in the non-Hindi States.

Shastri's whole attitude on the language issue was based on his principle that democracy required rule by person and consent; there should be no sense of accuracy among those in authority, and if necessary he was prepared to re-open the question of the official language. The country's larger interests, unity, and connection among people residing in different parts of the country and speaking different languages were of over-riding importance to him.

Death at Tashkent

Shastri was an exceptionally sensitive person who was deeply hurt by any discourteous behaviour, improper pressure, or unjust criticism; and yet he was determined not to show any anger. He had an innate revulsion of dishonest or unclean conduct by people in public life or in government, and yet he refrained from expressing his real feelings of indignation. Not only did he suppress a natural reaction, but he covered it with an unruffled, even amiable expression. Above all, he was a true Gandhian, who abhorred war or even coercive methods in administration. Yet his duties as Home Minister demanded the use of coercive crime and disorder. Both war and government, particularly in a period of distress or turbulence, wear out men, and Shastri had to handle both. Rarely, if ever, in our brief history as a free nation was there such a bunching of grave problems in so short a period.

The circumstances of Shastri's death at Tashkent were explained in a statement in Parliament more than twenty-five years ago and the report of the group of physicians, including Shastri's Indian physician, Dr. Chugh, was placed on the table of the House. After this, there should not have been any doubt that Shastri had died of a sudden, severe heart attack. But some in India needlessly look for conspiracy behind major occurrences, including the death of a national leader.

Shastri had his first heart attack in 1959 and a second one in June 1964 just after he had been sworn in as Prime Minister. The distinguished cardiologist who was looking after him told that if Shastri had another heart attack it would be fatal; and thus he had advised Shastri to take certain essential precautions, such as having an hour's rest after lunch and about eight hours' sleep and to maintain a nutritious diet. As already noted, Shastri did not follow the advice. He seemed to feel that it was far more important for him to do full justice to his responsibilities as Prime Minister than seek to preserve his health.

22

The Indo-Pak War, 1965

The Indians launched a major attack on September 6 across the international border towards Lahore, lying fifty miles from India. A second offensive began next day against Sialkot, an important railway and road centre, fifty miles to the north.

...neither side was capable of fully exploiting a major offensive while simultaneously resisting the outflanking attacks of the opponent. In the Akhnur area and on the Lahore front this situation apparently resulted in a military draw.

There are indications that the Indians were stopped at Sialkot by Pakistani defences which were assembled with relative speed.

On 3 September the UN Secretary-General, U. Thant, reported to the Security Council that he had not

> obtained from the Government of Pakistan any assurance that the Cease-Fire and the CFL will be respected henceforth or that efforts would be exerted to restore conditions to normal along that line. I did receive assurance... that India would act with restraint to any retaliatory acts and will respect the Cease-Fire Agreement and the CFL if Pakistan does likewise.

India's priority was the Akhnur area. It was essential to relieve Pakistani pressure in that sector. If the Pakistanis had cut the road leading to Indian-administered Kashmir and established a defensive position of even modest dimensions, it would have been difficult to dislodge them. Had the Pakistanis managed to advance only another ten miles, matters might have been critical for India. The Indians, however, and contingency plans for an attack in Punjab 'based on the hypothesis that Pakistan would have the initiative in launching an attack in Kashmir with possible diversionary attacks in other sectors'.

India's Concern

Although India's immediate concern was to prevent Pakistan severing the link with the north, the aim of their advance into 'West' Punjab was clear: to defeat the Pakistani army. On 6 September at 0530 their forces crossed the border towards Lahore; on the night of 7-8 September the advance began in the Sialkot sector. The main battlefields were to the south and east of these cities.

The 15 Indian Division advance towards Lahore from Amritsar was led by 54 bridge, made up of 3 Jat, 15 Dogra and 13 Punjab infantry battalions. The advance was slowed by intense Pakistani artillery fire directed by forward observers that whose accuracy was assisted by prominent concrete pillars among the border. These had been positioned over the years by survey units for just this eventually. 3 Jat pushed ahead and crossed the bridge over the BRBD canal at about 1000 PST on 6 September but were repulsed by 3 Baluch in fierce fighting around the Bata shoe factory and withdrew to the area of Dograi on the east bank, followed up by 3 Baluch which had about 50 men trapped on the west of the canal when Pakistani sappers blew up the bridge (and most others) during the night of 6-7. Throughout the day, the PAF conducted ground attack missions on elements of 15 Division with considerable effect, thus lessening the pressure on 10 Div's forward localities.

Claims that the area of Burki and Nurpur/Hudiara (half-way between the border and the BRBD Canal) was strongly defended appear incorrect. If an examination is made of units available to the Pakistan Army on 6-10 September, and where they were in other sectors according to Indian and independent sources, it can be calculated that the Burki-Nurpur area was not well-defended—to the point, indeed, of indicating poor planning. There were, however, about a dozen pill-boxes camouflaged to resemble huts, each occupied by three-men heavy machine-gun teams, and the area was mined.

It appears that the advance towards Lahore via Burki was indeed slowed by Pakistani troops and Rangers in the Nurpur-Hudiara area and along the axis to the canal at Burki, but that their numbers were not as large as claimed by some commentators, although there was a strong Pakistani artillery presence in the shape of two regiments, one each of field and medium guns, and a battery of 8-inch heavy guns. Nurpur-Hudiara could be seen from specially-constructed observation posts in Burki and artillery observers directed fire on the advance to the rear and flanks. The reason for the advance being slow is probably that forward troops were hesitant about pressing on through or around the opposition, not realising that the area was so lightly defended. In difficult country with poor observation, as in the flatlands around Burki, it is not possible to assess immediately what size of force might be blocking an advance.

The Pakistani thrust was reasonably well-planned but the machinery and expertise of higher command were not effective enough for it to be successful. In his examination of the operation in his *Memoirs*, Lt.-Gen. Gul Hassan explains not only, 'Why the Counter-Offensive Failed,' but states that, 'The tale of the [1st] Armoured Division was decidedly heart rending... After the 1965 War I met many officers who expressed disappointment that this division had let the side down.

Dera Baba Nanak

The significance of the battles around Jassar and Dera Baba Nanak is that, had either side been able to secure the bridge and bring up anti-aircraft guns to neutralise air attacks, it would have been possible to induct a comparatively large force (perhaps an armoured brigade group) into the territory of the other. This might have affected the battles around Lahore and Sialkot by encouraging withdrawal of troops to counter a thrust, but it is unlikely there would have been any great difference to the outcome of the war. An Indian commentator claimed that the Pakistani advance was intended 'at striking at Gurdaspur and the vital road and rail centre of Pathankot,' while Gulzar Ahmed states the advance was a feint to draw Indian troops away from more important areas. It seems the Indians attacked simply because capture of the bridge would have been a bonus, permitting a wider front and keeping the Pakistanis off-balance, and the Pakistanis responded in the best fashion possible at the time. For the Pakistan army the action was important in that it highlighted deficiencies in command and control.

The Indians attacked on the night of 5-6 September and achieved a lodgement in the Pakistani salient on the east bank of the Ravi at about first light on the 6th. Concurrently, 4FF drove out Indian troops occupying the western salient. Accounts of the battle thereafter are conflicting but it appears that, following Indian occupation of the west end of the bridge on 6 September, the Pakistanis thrust east across the bridge on the 7th. This caused a withdrawal of Indian troops that might have become a rout but for the courage and leadership of Lt.-Col. Chajju Ram, who rallied his men to counter-attack, forcing back the Pakistanis who then demolished the western span of the bridge, leaving some hundreds of troops on the far bank of the river. Ram was awarded the *Vir Chakra*, the medal for gallantry. The commander of 15 (Pakistani) Division was replaced at midday on 7 September, and it was rumoured that an Indian general (perhaps the commander of 26th Inf. Div.) was court-martialled.

Diplomacy and Politics

The UN Secretary-General, U. Thant, visited India and Pakistan from 9-15 September but failed to persuade the leaders of either country to declare an unconditional ceasefire. He went first to Pakistan but was obviously poorly briefed. If he expected the Pakistanis to accept any sort of compromise on 11 September (he flew to Delhi on the 12th), the death anniversary of the Quaid-i-Azam, Mohammad Ali Jinnah, he was mistaken. In reply to U. Thant's request, Ayub insisted that an agreement for a ceasefire must include an arrangement for settlement of the Kashmir dispute. In his turn Prime Minister Shastri replied that India 'shall not agree to any disposition which will leave the door open for further infiltration,' which, as he must have known, was an impossible condition—just as Ayub could hardly have counted on India agreeing to discussion of Kashmir. Negotiations continued in New York, as the Soviets, Americans, French, and British were apprehensive about China entering the war. On 16 September, the Chinese sent the Indians a belligerent Note indicating, among other things, support for Pakistan.

In the north, two battalions of India's 26 Division crossed the border astride the Jammu-Sialkot road at about midnight on 7 September. They quickly overcame the outposts of the Sutlej Rangers (light scouting forces) but were brought to a halt by 101 Brigade and the weight of Pakistan's artillery. According to Manekar (1967) and Johri, the approaches to Sialkot 'bristled with pill-boxes, bunkers and gun emplacements,' the latter including 'three field and one medium artillery regiments, one heavy battery and one heavy mortar regiment.' A concentration of this number of guns and mortars would cover an area of about 500 metres by 150 metres in which the weight of shells and mortar bombs from one round of fire from each equipment would be approximately two tonnes. Not only this, but the artillery was well-handled and 'some senior Indian army officers who had served in World War II likened the scale of Pakistani artillery fire to heavy concentrations in the latter stages of that war. While this is not borne out by inspection of battlefields it does indicate that Pakistan artillery fire was substantial and effective.'

The Pakistanis had three armoured regiments and three infantry battalions—a mixture of units from 1 Armoured Division and 24 Infantry Brigade. India had two armoured brigades each of two tank regiments and an infantry battalion. Forces of about equal strength had met in battle and one had been made to retreat. Unfortunately for Pakistan, it had insufficient armour immediately available to strike a quick blow that would have destroyed the Indian armour which was, naturally, in some disarray. Even Indian commentators acknowledge that 1 Armoured Brigade was 'hit... hard in the rib' because it 'dashed forward somewhat rashly....' (Verghese).

Both sides used the comparative lull to regroup. The Indians rapidly regained balance and probed forward, while the Pakistanis brought up as many reinforcements as they could to match the preponderance of Indian armour, which was also being augmented. It was a desperate time for the Pakistanis. They well knew that India had large resources on which to call, which almost every unit on the Pakistani Order of Battle was already committed to the fight. 11th Cavalry arrived from Chhamb along with 10 Infantry Brigade (14 Punjab and 6FF) not a minute too early to join in defending the area against the Indian assault that began at first light on 11 September.

On the night of 15-16 September, the Indians again tried to outflank the main Pakistani force, this time by pressing west to Jassoran, three miles due west of Chawinda, across the railway line, then south to cut off Chawinda from the rear. Once the village was isolated, the Indians considered it would fall. At first the advance went well, with Jassoran being occupied at about 1100 on the 16th by 8 Garhwal Rifles supported by a squadron of 2nd Poona Horse. The infantry then turned south and managed to take the village of Buttar Dograndi, but their armour was engaged so heavily by Pakistani anti-tank weapons that it could not advance further. The battalion held out until 17 September, when it was forced to withdraw to Jassoran. It had been impossible to reinforce the unit in order to continue the advance, but neither could the Pakistanis bring in enough force to mount a counter-attack. Furthermore, the Pakistani artillery was running short of ammunition. By mid-September the daily allocation of 155mm ammunition was five rounds per gun, about ninety seconds' fire at the 'intense' rate. Ammunition for the Pattons was also limited. The US embargo on supply of military *material* to its SEATO ally was taking effect, but in spite of this the Pakistanis fought magnificently in the Chawinda battles. This is not to denigrate the bravery of the Indians; but the Pakistanis were heavily outnumbered, short of ammunition, and subject to increasing international pressure that it found more difficult to counter than the Indians, who were more skilful in selling their points of view to the international media.

In spite of ammunition shortages and tank casualties, the Pakistanis regrouped yet again, and on 18-19 September cleared the area west of Chawinda, around the railway line, but did not manage to fully retake the station at Alhar, the north side of which remained in Indian hands until the ceasefire. The Pakistanis planned Operation *Wind Up* for 19-20 September with the aim of outflanking the Indians and penetrating west to cut them off. Weather forced postponement to 21-22 September, but the operation was then cancelled.

The war ended on 23 September. Both countries' economies were badly affected and their defence forces had suffered severe blows. There was no winner, but important military lessons had been learned.

23

Towards Democratic Socialism

The year that passed between the Durgapur session of the Indian National Congress from January 9-10, 1965 and the Jaipur session from February 10-12 witnessed another tragedy, which shook and shocked the country, i.e., the sad and sudden death of the Prime Minister, Lal Bahadur Shastri at Tashkent on January 11, 1965. At that time Indira Gandhi was holding the portfolio of Information and Broadcasting. During her short tenure of office, the Home Ministry by issuing an order to enforce the deadline for making Hindi, the official language of the country by 1965 enraged the South so much that violent riots broke out in Madras City. Indira Gandhi courageously flew to Madras and tried her best to pacify the agitators.

Besides, the country witnessed the worst food crisis and the unprovoked aggression by Pakistani army by an attack on India. Though Lal Bahadur Shastri faced the situation courageously by counteracting the aggression, yet the intervention or mediation efforts by USSR, which resulted in Tashkent Pact, deprived the country of the services of Lal Bahadur Shastri. When as a result of consensus arrived at by the then Congress President Kamaraj, Indira Gandhi was elected as leader of the Congress Parliamentary Party. She said on January 19, 1966, 'I have always considered myself a *desh sevika* (servant of the nation) even as my father regarded himself as the first servant of the nation. I also consider myself a servant of the party and the great people of this country.' But soon after assuming power she was faced by worst type of language agitation which had taken a violent turn following the decision by the Government of India that Hindi would come into force as the 'Official Language' of the Union with effect from January 26, 1965 according to the provisions of the Constitution of India. The Working Committee, in order to allay the fears of the States in the South, recommended 'complete and unfettered freedom' to every State to continue to transact its own business in the languages of its choice, which may be the regional language, Hindi or English. The Hindi States were free to correspond with the Central Government in English. English was to continue as *associate language*. No change was to be made in these arrangements without the consent of the States. The Government of India was to take steps to amend the Official Languages Act of 1963 in order to give effect to the assurances given by Pandit Nehru and all the recommendations made by the Working Committee. During 1965-66, the Congress Working Committee was seized of the possible danger of differences degenerating with acute discussions. So the resolution on *Organisational Solidarity* passed at the Bangalore Session in July 1965 laid down a code for the Congressmen and an appeal was also made to all to close their ranks. The Congress President made indefatigable efforts to bring about greater understanding between groups of Congressmen.'

Indira Gandhi's election as leader of the Congress Parliamentary Party on January 19, was a welcome surprise to most of the partymen. Other contenders for the high office were Gulzarilal Nanda, acting Prime Minister; Y.B. Chavan, Defence Minister and Morarji Desai. Intense excitement preceded the fateful meeting. According to some, "The provincial chieftains, headed by Kamraj had secretly decided to get her nominated for the post. The Chief Ministers had blessed the move. These weighty endorsements guaranteed her victory." Besides Kamraj, Atulya Ghosh of the West Bengal Congress and D.P. Mishra, the then Chief Minister of Madhya Pradesh emerged as staunch supporters of Indira Gandhi. D.P. Mishra discounted the reports that the Chief Minister had been pressurised; and asserted that the members of his State met freely and were requested by him to vote freely. According to Morarji Desai, Kamraj was prejudiced against him ever since 1964 and won over Jagjivan Ram also by promising him a Ministership in the new Cabinet. He did not consider Indira Gandhi to be suitable for the office of Prime Ministership so persisted to contest for the high office in spite of pressure from several directions to pull out. When at last he said, "I do not want to refer to the elections, which is now over, because one should not go into any post-mortem. It does not help us. But I hope and pray that in future, at any rate, the atmosphere of fearlessness will be cultivated in the party and in the country, because this party has the greatest responsibility in the matter of creating fearlessness in the country."

On the fateful day when the ballots cast in secret were counted, Indira Gandhi secured 355 and Morarji Desai 169. There were only 2 invalid votes. So Indira Gandhi became Prime Minister of India on January 24, 1966, when she was sworn in before President Radhakrishnan in Rashtrapati Bhawan. Indira Gandhi also sought the cooperation of all sections of Indians, irrespective of caste and creed. In the sphere of foreign policy she pledged to fully implement the Tashkent Declaration in its letter and spirit. She also pledged to fight the war against poverty, disease and ignorance. She said, "We have promises to keep with our people—of work, food, clothing and shelter, health and education. The weaker and underprivileged sections of our people—all those who require special measures of social security—have always been and will remain uppermost in my mind." Speaking to a crowded press conference on January 19, she said: "I do not regard myself as a woman in regard to the job. In the Indian Constitution all citizens are equal regardless of sex, religion, State or any other division. Therefore, I am just an Indian citizen and the first servant of the land."

The Congress party had a tradition of service and a record of achievement of which the people of India were proud. And the Party sought the mandate of the nation for a social order based on freedom and justice which would ensure that every individual had the means and opportunities for a full life and was enabled to make his maximum contribution to the service of the nation.

Besides approving the Election Manifesto the Jaipur session in 1966 adopted the new Constitution of the Congress; as well as Rules of the Indian National Congress. The session also considered the resolution adopted by the Working Committee on Democratic Socialism, which contained the famous Ten-point Programme, viz.

1. Social control of the banking institution—necessary steps were to be taken to implement that.

2. Nationalisation of general insurance—steps were to be taken to bring that under public sector.
3. Commodity-wise progress in State-trading in imports and exports—a phased programme for their take over was to be formulated.
4. State trading in foodgrains—national policy of food distribution was to be worked out: for this purpose Food Corporation of India and co-operative agencies were to be utilised.
5. Expansion of Co-operatives.
6. Implementation of the Monopolies Commission Report—and steps to be taken to curb monopolies and concentration of economic power.
7. Provision of minimum needs to the community—steps were to be taken for provision of minimum needs to the entire community and promulgation of a Socialist Charter for children.
8. Unearned increments in urban land values—limitations were to be imposed on urban income and property.
9. Improvement in the implementation of laws for tenancy reforms. Credit was to be made available to the agricultural labour. Minimum wage legislation was to be effectively imposed.
10. Privileges of Princes: Privileges other than privy purses, which were incongruous to the concept and practice of democracy were to be examined and removed.

Hardly a year had elapsed since Indira Gandhi had taken over as Prime Minister on January 24, due to the sudden demise of Lal Bahadur Shastri, in January 1966; and she had to face the parliamentary elections to the Fourth Lok Sabha. In the general elections the basic issues, socio-economic and political, were the same as under Nehru and Shastri. There was only difference of opinion regarding relationship between the organisation wing and the government leadership.

The Leadership Issue

The leadership issue was no doubt settled by the Congress Parliamentary Party, when it met on March 12, 1967. Indira Gandhi was elected as Prime Minister and Morarji Desai as the Deputy Prime Minister. But the sharp differences on policies and programmes highlighted in the Election Manifesto for the fourth general elections came to the fore after the results were out. According to the critics, they were responsible for the reduced majority, on the other hand, the protagonists of socio-economic reforms attributed that to tardy implementation of socialistic programmes. Party's declaration that a dynamic and growing public sector was an important tool for the socialist transformation of society, that the nationalisation of Life Insurance and the Imperial Bank of India were important landmarks in the growth of public sector, and that the plans in India would have to assign an increasingly important role to the public sector. According to the manifesto, there was compelling need to impose limitations on urban income and property. Indira Gandhi focussed the economic issues as the cause of disunity and thus differed from Morarji Desai.

Although certain fundamental policies had been settled by the Congress ever since Karachi Resolution, acute differences arose on questions of policy of nationalisation of Banks, imposition of ceiling on urban property; reduction in monopolistic control; and over-concentration of economic power by big industrial houses. Dissentient voices were vociferously raised at the crucial meeting of the AICC at Delhi in June 1967. The focus was primarily on the reduced majority of the Congress party in the Lok Sabha, wherein it had secured only 279 seats in a house of 520 members. Election results in as many as seven of the States of the Union were equally disturbing.

The AICC session took great pains to analyse the causes of the reverses in 1967 elections; and majority felt that the setback was not due to radical policies but due to tardiness in the implementation of such policies. The setback to Congress in State assemblies resulted in the formation of coalition governments known variously as United Front or SVD (Samyukta Vidhayak Dal) governments and a period of instability resulted. In Madras, PEPSU, Rajasthan, Travancore, the Congress candidates fared badly. But the worst was to come when, even in States of Uttar Pradesh, Bihar and West Bengal, large-scale defection took place. However, Indira Gandhi remained unnerved and regarded that too as "... A significant development". She said, "Democracy implies choice. Choice involves alternatives. It is a healthy sign that alternatives are emerging and competing ..."

Indira Gandhi's fighting spirit had been aroused and she was ready to part company with the Old Guard. However, intermediaries had persuaded Morarji Desai to join as Deputy Prime Minister. This compromise did not last long. On the other hand, a section of the Congressmen, known as "YOUNG TURKS" led by Krishna Kant, Chandra Sekhar, Madhu Limaye and others called upon the old guard, the then Congress President, Nijalingappa, Morarji Desai, S.K. Patil, N. Sanjiva Reddy to step down and not retard the progress of the country towards socialism. They had outlived their utility, had exhausted their energies and so deserved to step down to save democracy. A signature campaign was launched to force the President of the Congress resign. Chandra Sekhar even accused Morarji Desai of favouring certain firms with which Kantilal Desai, his son, was connected.

In her speech at the meeting of the National Development Council at New Delhi on March 21, 1970, Indira Gandhi declared that plans were indispensable for the mobilisation of the resources of the country. She remarked that the plan cannot obviously be perfect—no plan could be, more specially with the difficulties faced by a developing country. According to her if the Plan was needed when there was one political party in power in the Centre and in the States, there was greater need of the Plan when the country had different political parties.

With the death of the serving President, Dr. Zakir Hussain, on the 3rd May, 1969, the political atmosphere in the country became very acute, tense and exciting. In the words of S.P. Sen-Verma, "This controversy brought to the surface the simmering discontent which was accumulating in the Indian National Congress and this led to the Great Schism in the Indian National Congress to which there was hardly any parallel in the history of political parties in the world. Perhaps, the only case, which came near this Great Divide was the Great Schism in the Whig Party in Great Britain in the year 1796."

When the Congress Parliamentary Board met at Bangalore to choose the party candidate for Union President, the stage was set for the final showdown. Indira Gandhi scented the danger and fired her missile from New Delhi in the shape of a note to the

Committee on Economic Policy in which she had 'jotted down a few stray thoughts in a hurry' for the Committee's consideration. The Note dated New Delhi, July 8, 1969 was a follow up of the Congress MPs Note on Economic Policies—An Outline for National Economic Policies, dated New Delhi, July 1969, and Draft Resolution on Economic Policy prepared by C. Subramaniam and Sadiq Ali, New Delhi, July 8, 1969. In order to cater to the needs of the weaker sections, minorities and underprivileged, whose cause had been championed by the Congress, she listed a number of measures to be implemented. They included the Ten-points already listed and approved at the Bangalore session, but this note acted as a red-rag to the Syndicate, Nationalisation of banks was opposed by Morarji Desai tooth and nail, and he made that a personal issue. As long as he was Finance Minister, he was not prepared to allow that. The note acted as an apple of discord in the Working Committee which met on July 10 and August 25, 1969, as the majority sided with Indira Gandhi, including Kamraj, Chavan, Fakhrudin Ali Ahmad, Jagjivan Ram and D. Sanjivayya. However, due to the role of Y.B. Chavan as peace maker, the Prime Minister's note was referred to the Central and State Governments. But the selection of Sanjiva Reddy vitiated the move for compromise. The schism became a reality and the Great Divide took place, when new Working Committee met at 1, Safdarjung Road on November 23, 1969, under the presidentship of C. Subramaniam.

Indira Gandhi thought that the mode of selection of candidate for Presidentship by the Parliamentary Board was wrong. When it was rumoured that his candidature was a step in the direction of her removal, she confided to the press, by telling the partymen why she was opposed to nomination of Sanjiva Reddy. She said it was against the spirit, if not the letter, of the Constitution, and the principles of democracy to involve the Speaker in a political issue. She decided to act.

On 16 July, 1969 she decided to change the portfolio of Morarji Desai and take over the Finance Ministry herself. Desai resigned on the same day. On July 21, Indira Gandhi made a statement in Parliament on Desai's resignation.

Banks Nationalised

On 19 July, fourteen major Banks were nationalised. Indira Gandhi in her broadcast to the nation announced that presidential decree had been issued to that effect. She claimed that it would enable the government to provide credit to the small farmers, petty manufacturers and to backward regions. By giving the government political control of the banking system, the measure would curb the malpractices of big business. It was not aimed to starve the private sector of funds. Savings would be mobilised for productive investment according to the Plan priorities. She asserted, 'An institution, such as the banking system, which touches—and should touch—the lives of millions, has necessarily to be inspired by a large social purpose and had to subserve national priorities and objectives.' She continued to assert, 'That is also why we nationalised, more than a decade ago, the life insurance business and the State Bank or the Imperial Bank as it was then called.'

At Delhi besides nationalisation of the banks followed the abolition of the Privy Purses of the Princes and appointment of a judicial commission on 28 August 1969 to inquire into the alleged irregularities by the Birla group of industries. Polarisation between the different groups of leading Congressmen in Bengal and Tamil Nadu precipitated a crisis in the hierarchy of the party. With the resignation of Subramaniam from the presidentship of the Tamil Nadu Congress, Nijalingappa was set to remove him from Congress Working Committee. In their last minute effort to avert parting of ways Indira Gandhi, Chavan, Jagjivan Ram, Fakhruddin Ali Ahmad, Uma Shankar Dixit, and Subramanian wrote a joint letter to Nijalingappa, requesting him not to "aggravate the situation and make the implementation of the unity resolution more difficult." On 18 October, several leaders signed a requisition requesting the Congress Working Committee to convene a session of the AICC as early as possible to facilitate the election of a new party president before the end of 1969. On the 31st October, a rival Congress Working Committee meeting took place at Indira Gandhi's residence at New Delhi and the November 1 meeting was boycotted. In a resolution adopted by the ten Members of the Congress Working Committee held under the Chairmanship of Indira Gandhi on November 1, Nijalingappa was called upon to retrieve the situation.

Indira Gandhi asserted that the Congress stood for democracy, secularism, socialism and non-alignment in international relations. These objectives from time to time have been confirmed by the various policy-making units of the organisation, like the Working Committee or the AICC or the delegates' session. Shankar Dayal Sharma in his article on 'Indira Gandhi and the Congress', said that what happened at the Bangalore session of the AICC in 1969 and previously at Faridabad, was only a continuation of the policies and programmes laid down by the Congress at the Karachi session of 1931 and Jaipur session in 1948. So, in his words, "In retrospect it would seem the 1969 split in the Congress was a blessing in disguise. It marked a watershed in the history of the Congress. The Party regained its lost soul and identity and it freed itself from bossism and Right reaction. The Congress was reborn, and it recaptured its hold among the masses."

Election Manifestos—1971-72

In the 1971 Election Manifesto it was admitted that 'as a result of certain judicial pronouncements, it has become impossible to effectively implement some of the Directive Principles of our Constitution. It incorporated the five points, implementation of which was emphasised at the Bombay session, viz.:

(i) a limit on holdings of urban property;
(ii) resorting to Parliament the authority to amend the section of the Constitution on fundamental rights which the Supreme Court of India had vetoed; (Article—31)
(iii) funnelling key imports through State-owned commercial undertakings, like State Trading Corporation;
(iv) imposition of curbs on monopolies and restrictive business practices; and
(v) priority to agriculture in framing national plans for development and fiscal policy.

It was clearly stated that land reforms and the provision of irrigation along with other inputs to the small farmer must be accompanied by a thrust to end social discrimination on grounds of caste or religion. In order to achieve these reforms, a complete reconstruction of the socio-economic base of the party and the elimination of the then existing power blocks in it was necessary. Clearance for such radical changes had been given by the Bombay session, wherein Ten-point programme was approved.

About 500 members of the old AICC had attended the session, thereby confirming that the requisitionist' Congress was the real one. The new Congress claimed that "the rebirth of the Congress symbolises our commitment to democracy and socialism. The Congress party is clear in its mind of the party's goal—Socialism."

In short, the Congress election manifesto was a "Twelve-point programme for progress." It asked for a clear mandate from the people "to continue the advance to socialism through the democratic process and devise an administrative system capable of speedy implementation." The Congress made its socio-economic policies and their implementation for the welfare of the people an important issue for the fresh mandate from the people in the Fifth General Elections in 1971. The two-word expression *Garibi Hatao* and *Arthik Swaraj* found special mention in the manifesto released in January. The party was committed to 'defend secularism and safeguard the interests of the minorities and the weaker sections of the community, particularly the Scheduled Castes, Scheduled Tribes, and the backwards sections so that they may attain equality of status and opportunity and fraternity, assuring the dignity of the individual."

The manifesto promised to enlarge the role of public sector, improve its performance, the private sector was also to be allowed to play its part in the country's economy. However, concentration of economic power and wealth was to be curbed and in order to fulfil the pledges, the Constitution would be amended 'as may be necessary'.

The landslide victory in 1971 Lok Sabha Elections, the victory in the War against Pakistan and liberation of Bangladesh were followed by 1972 elections which were held in most of the States. In the second election manifesto, the Congress appealed to the people to give the country a stable government, harmony between the Centre and the States. However, the objective remained the same, viz., socialism to be realised through democratic means. In her whirlwind tour of the States, Indira Gandhi asserted that if people voted for Congress, its strong and stable governments could effectively fight poverty. *Garibi Hatao* emerged as one of the catching slogans. She said, "If the *Garibi Hatao* programme is to succeed, there should be such governments in States which were committed to its implementation."

Indira Gandhi continued the consolidation of territories and accordingly four new States were created, bringing the overall total to 21. The new States were Himachal Pradesh, Manipur, Maghalaya and Tripura. The new autonomous regions under the Central Government were also created in the North-Eastern region, viz., Arunachal and Mizoram. A regional Council to coordinate the economic and social plans was also created. In the words of Prime Minister, the primary purpose of the Council was "the development of the region for greater human welfare."

Then followed the three constitutional amendments, viz., 24th, 25th and 26th which revolutionised the Indian polity. The 24th amendment gave back to Parliament and the Indian people the sovereign right to change the Constitution and amend the fundamental rights listed therein. It was proclaimed by the Prime Minister as a historical measure, as the same represented an important step in the further democratisation of society. The 25th amendment removed another hurdle in the way of nationalisation process which related to award of compensation for nationalised properties based on market value or just compensation. Such payment could not be challenged in a court of law. It sought to avoid time-consuming legal wrangles resulting from the take over of large agricultural holdings and monopolistic industrial concerns.

The 26th amendment enabled the government to abolish the privy purses and feudal privileges of the princes and withdrew recognition of their princely status. Although savings on this account were only about Rs. 50 million a year, but the psychological impact on the common man was superb. It acted as a major factor in tilting the votes for Congress candidates.

The election manifesto spelt out the programme in detail. In addition to the three Constitutional amendments, it included nationalisation of general insurance, self-sufficiency in grain production, special programmes to provide gainful employment, especially for the weaker sections of society. Self-reliance was on the top of the list. The manifesto, however, clarified: 'While we shall not deny ourselves such friendly assistance as will enable us to strengthen critical sectors of the economy, we shall redraw out economic programmes and mobilise our material and intellectual resources as to be able to do without foreign aid.' Progress towards self-reliance was to be accompanied by greater efforts to reduce social and economic inequalities. Land reforms were still a priority. Non-alignment was the keynote of the foreign policy to be pursued. The Treaty of Friendship, Cooperation, and Peace signed in Dacca on March 19 was to serve as a guide to the Indian Ocean countries in ordering their relations with each other. Thus, all the factors favoured a Congress victory. The Congress Working Committee meeting held at New Delhi on 11 May 1972 expressed satisfaction at the results of the General Election to various State Assemblies.

The Fifth General Election to the Legislative Assemblies of 18 States, Union Territories and the Metropolitan Council of Delhi were held during the first quarter of 1972. No general elections to constitute new Legislative Assemblies were held in the States of Kerala, Orissa, Tamil Nadu, Uttar Pradesh and Nagaland. All the results were declared by 28th April 1972 and the new Assemblies were summoned to meet thereafter.

Victory for Congress

Election results party-wise in 1972 were as under:

Party	*Seats contested*	*Seats won*	*Percentage of seats won*
Congress	2,529	1,927	70.77
Congress (O)	870	89	3.27
Jana Sangh	1,233	104	3.82
Swatantra	307	16	0.59
CPI	330	112	4.11
CPI(M)	467	34	1.25
SP	659	57	2.10
Other State Parties	456	114	4.18
Independents and Others	5,177	270	9.91
Total	12,028	2,723	100.00

The Congress Party won a massive victory in these elections. It secured majorities in all the States and Union Territories with the exception of Manipur, Meghalaya and

Goa. The Syndicate in this election put together could get only 89 seats. The Jana Sangh also badly mauled. The Swatantra Party was completely disintegrated. It could get only 16 seats. The CPI which secured 112 seats, comparatively fared better. The Socialists Party in spite of merger of PSP and SSP could get only 57 seats. The Congress won 70.77 per cent of the seats.

The fifth Lok Sabha constituted on March 15, 1971 continued functioning upto January 17, 1977; it had the largest lease of life, due to two extensions under Article 85 of the Constitution. Due to extension its term would have ended in March 1978, but it was dissolved earlier in January 1977, when on the advice of Prime Minister, the Rashtrapati ordered fresh elections. Polling was scheduled to take place in March.

During its longest lease of life, the Lok Sabha took up consideration of about 50 government and 23 private members' bills, introduced with the object of fulfilling the promises made by the Congress party to ensure socio-economic reforms and establishment of a just society. According to the Election Manifesto of 1971, the Congress party had pledged itself to the ownership and control of the material resources of the community in such a way as to subserve the common good. It accepted the dominant role of the public sector and so took over General Insurance, and greater state control of industries where substantial funds were required. But for successful implementation of industrial policy objectives, the Government sought cooperation of the private sector. Indira Gandhi in her inaugural speech to the 44th annual session of the Federation of Indian Chamber of Commerce and Industry (FICCI) held at New Delhi immediately after the Lok Sabha elections said, 'Many of the crucial decisions which shape our economy are taken in the private sector. If these decisions go awry, it is the economy, which has to bear the consequences. This is why we are so anxious for a proper understanding between the government and the private sector.'

24

Indira Gandhi and Congress Party

A Party Leader

The Congress, born as a loosely organised body of delegates representing manifold interests, underwent a sea of changes under the leadership of Indira Gandhi. With the passage of time, this organisation acquired certain unique features.

Indira Gandhi made certain major alterations in most of these characteristics. Before she assumed the leadership of the party, the organisation enjoyed a monopoly of power. The reason for this dominance of the Congress was that it excelled party character in the form of national movement for India's independence and also because of its 'Aristotlian character'.[1] The result had been the emergence of a party of consensus which functioned through a vast network of groups which provided the chief competitive mechanism of the Indian system.[2] Thus, the Congress was pluralistic in character which made it more representative, it was flexible as well which made it sustain internal competition.

The umbrella character of the Congress with its vast patronage after Independence and its increasing social base resulted in the growth of the Congress into a dominant party, though the opposition parties from 1952 onwards managed to win more votes than the Congress party in all the parliamentary and assembly elections.[3]

The Congress had the advantage of having a highly structured national-level organisation with effective and strong state units. In the pre-independence period, the promotion in the party was based on sacrifice and service. Dissent was tolerated and dissenters managed to get away with. As a result, in some States, local leaders were becoming powerful but at the national level, Jawaharlal Nehru concentrated power in his own hands since he was leading both the party and government. This situation, however, could not last long. After the Chinese War, it began to change and contributed to the decline in the prestige of Jawaharlal Nehru as well as of the Congress.

Indira Gandhi and Her Relations with the Congress Party

When Indira Gandhi succeeded Lal Bahadur Shastri, the choice of successor had proved difficult due to a lack of consensus in the party and because 'the politics of unanimity had given way to the politics of over conflict'.[4] The setting of this succession proved to be 'one of drama, poignant and historic . . .',[5] because the death of Jawaharlal Nehru and the process of succession had resulted in the emergence of a collective leadership in the Congress and decision-making process based on consensus. The situation had become more difficult after the sudden demise of Lal Bahadur Shastri because, firstly, Kamaraj Nadar was not as strong as he was before. Secondly, the Syndicate[6] had lost its cohesion and had acted indecisively. Thirdly, there was no other leader who could command a wider support as compared to Shastri. And finally, the pressure of unanimity was not as huge as at the time of Nehru's death.[7]

Kamraj: the Kingmaker

The important role played by Kamraj Nadar in the election of the two former Prime Ministers had invested the party president with great power. He had manoeuvred the support of the majority of the state Chief Ministers who were already in support of Indira Gandhi, Indira Gandhi on her part was aware of the reluctance of the Syndicate and the support of the Chief Ministers. Until the 1967 general election, Indira Gandhi was considered as a 'stop-gap arrangement'. At this stage, 'the inevitable difference in outlook did not prevent the Congress president and the Prime Minister from acting in harmony'.[8] But soon, Indira Gandhi became aware of the design of the Syndicate and started building up an image of her own among the masses and a base for herself in the party.[9] This gradually led to a struggle for supremacy between the 'king-maker' and the 'king',[10] which revived the old conflict between the government and the organisation.

In 1966, for about six months, the relations between the party president and the Prime Minister were cordial. At this stage, the powerful Syndicate had continued to function through the party president, the state party bigwigs and the Old Guard within the Cabinet[11] and Indira Gandhi had to depend on bureaucrats and few trusted members of the kitchen-cabinet.[12]

The real conflict came to light when Indira Gandhi, without consulting the party and its president, devalued the Indian currency on 5 June 1966.[13] This action was criticised by Kamraj Nadar. Morarji Desai, T.T.K. Krishnamachari, V.K. Krishna Menon and Dr. Ram Subhag Singh lambasted this decision. Even in Parliament, the Congress MPs stood against this action as vehemently as the Opposition.

In dealing with the party organisation also, Indira Gandhi had become assertive and self-confident even before the 1967 election as was evident from her pronouncement her 'uncontested' position among the masses[14] and the 'country being above the party'.[15] At this stage she told her advisers to evolve 'a long strategy, taking advantage of the positive aspects of the Kamraj Nadar leadership and to establish channels of communication with party organs especially the AICC and the CWC to fortify her position through a process of consultation, mandate and endorsement'.[16] But she continued to disregard her colleagues in the Working Committee and also dropped the idea of evolving a collective leadership.

Indira Gandhi had also, by that time, realised that "her mass appeal was her strongest weapon, making her a valuable election symbol for Congress candidates and she was learning how to use it".[17] In her public speeches she combined an aristocratic refinement with populism and maternal common sense,[18] which worked for her soaring popularity among the masses. To the marginal victory of the Congress in Parliament,[19] Indira Gandhi made the major contribution. It was a victory to her art of electioneering and political proficiency.

The result of the 1967 election changed the position of Indira Gandhi to a great extent in relation to her position in the party and the government. Though she got herself re-elected as Prime Minister, the party bosses sought 'to clip Indira Gandhi's wings'.[20] Morarji Desai was pressed to get inducted as an alternative centre of power in the central cabinet.[21] But this time she was not prepared to exchange the tutelage of

Kamraj Nadar for that of Morarji Desai, she made it sure by the formation of her cabinet that she kept on her counsel.

The manner of formation and the composition of the new cabinet reflected Indira Gandhi's growing independence and the increasing weakness of the Syndicate.[22] She inducted those she trusted into the cabinet and rewarded those who supported her in the party.[23] The organisational leadership had been entirely bypassed in the formation of the cabinet.[24]

The Congress had contested the election on the slogan 'one country, one team'[25] and claimed that only the Congress could maintain stability in the country. It had nothing positive to offer and failed even to formulate the Five Year Plan. It entirely had to depend upon the past record because its present record was only rising prices, increasing unemployment and growing corruption, favouritism, nepotism and inefficiency in the administration. All these factors contributed to the downfall of the Congress.

Morarji Desai and his hangers-on maintained that the party bigwigs who had chosen Indira Gandhi had been rejected by the electorate and that her government's policies had made the party unpopular. So her leadership was to be blamed for the fiasco.[26] On the other hand, Indira Gandhi and her followers argued that the Congress reverses were the result of the party's organisational weakness.[27] So, at the Delhi AICC session in June 1967, Indira Gandhi attacked the party organisation for the enrolment of bogus membership.

In 1967, Indira Gandhi further tried to consolidate her position in the party at the time of the election of the Congress president. She did not want Kamraj Nadar elected for the third term and wanted herself to be in the saddle of the party.[28] A day before the nomination, she manipulated[29] to get S. Nijalingappa accepted. Though it was a compromise, Indira Gandhi succeeded in deterring the re-election of Kamraj Nadar. She emerged as a shrewd politician who had mastered the art of political manoeuvre to keep the troublesome rivals at bay.

The struggle for leadership after Shastri's death had eventually broken the party asunder and had contributed to its failure in 1967. "From then on the 'Umbrella Party System' was it, ruins, and the party system became more fragmented, open and competitive. Dramatic swings of fortune in Delhi and unstable coalitions in the states followed".[30]

The period from 1966 onwards was a crucial phase not only in the intra-party relations but also in the party-government relationship.[31] The Prime Minister was no longer ready to work as per the guidance of the organisational leaders, and they, on the other hand, were not prepared to surrender their power. Whereas Indira Gandhi had thought that she might exert more influence in organisational matters than S. Nijalingappa, the latter had adopted the line that "the Prime Minister and her cabinet were answerable to the CWC".[32] At the next Congress session at Hyderabad in 1968, Mrs. Gandhi again found herself isolated and outmanoeuvred which made it apparent that unless she had a provincial or an organisational balance in the party, she could not have her say.[33] Her isolation made her to expose the party bosses and used C. Subramaniam and Young Turks for the purpose.[34] In return, the Congress bosses started discussing the need of her being removed from the office of Prime Minister.[35]

Even before the Faridabad Congress session, the ideological difference had begun to surface out in the Press. On 19 April 1969, S. Nijalingappa stated that C. Subramaniam's 'programme for socialist action'[36] could not be the principle of the party's new economic strategy and it could not be discussed as an official document at Faridabad. The Congress Forum for Socialist Action became active and it stressed the need for the restoration of democratic functioning of the organisation and also for stimulating Congress Committees at all levels to end bossism. Change was sought in the Congress constitution to make it a cadre-based party.

The Congress assembled at Faridabad for its annual session in April 1969, where two rival viewpoints emerged on virtually every issue whether political, economic or organisational. The tone was set by S. Nijalingappa's controversial presidential address. The Congress president, in his address staunchly criticised the poor performance of the public sector, stressed the need for greater encouragement to private enterprise and lambasted the Young Turks for their lack of party discipline.[37] Indira Gandhi asserted that 'there must be more and more investment in the public sector'.[38] She further stressed the need for greater state control and lashed out the weakness of the Congress organisation and its failure to support government policies.[39]

Indira Gandhi had come to believe that the loyalty of the next President of India was a threat her prospects of remaining Prime Minister. She already had received reports about a conspiracy to install Sanjiva Reddy as President with the purpose of removing her from office and thereby electing Morarji Desai as the next Prime Minister.[40] The Bangalore AICC session provided an opportunity for her to project a populist image in the on-going tussle with the 'reactionary' Syndicate and win public support. The Congress Working Committee was taken by surprise when they received Indira Gandhi's note on economic policy. Though they did not give too much importance to it, there were initial reactions because of the influence of the Young Turks on the Prime Minister's note.[41]

The party stalwarts were put on the defensive as it was a departure from the policy adopted at Jabalpur. The note also indicated the wide rift between Morarji Desai and her.[42]

However, the nomination of Sanjiva Reddy as the party candidate was decided which represented a blow to Indira Gandhi which 'reopened the whole question of the Prime Minister's position inside the party'.[43] She took it as a threat to her authority and characterised the Board's action in forcing a candidate that she opposed as an insult 'to my views and attitudes and my social and foreign policies'.[44]

On 16 July, Indira Gandhi announced to the Press her decision to discharge Morarji Desai of the portfolio of Finance Minister.[45] Strategically, the time was ripe for her plans. The ground-breaking announcement of the government to nationalise fourteen major banks through a Presidential ordinance followed.

The results of the Presidential election revealed that Indira Gandhi's 'free-vote' strategy had finally worked. V.V. Giri defeated Sanjiva Reddy, though by a narrow margin of 1,650 votes.[46] The victory of V.V. Giri was, in other words, Indira Gandhi's victory[47] and her success mobilising just enough votes for V.V. Giri was 'nothing short of a political coup executed with the professional finish, leaving her opponents far behind'.[48] She soon realised that she had to work much harder in order to consolidate her control over the party organisation.

In the ultimate analysis, what comes out clearly is that Indira Gandhi's rise to fame as a leader of the party was "the result of a masterminded political operation'[49] leading to the split which made a clean sweep of every other factor in the Congress party's power structure which counted in the making of a Prime Minister.[50] The split, however, failed to bring about the polarisation of political elements[51] on grounds of ideology. She took a wrong decision here and was compelled to continue on it throughout her political leadership. As a result, the Congress party from then onwards became her convenient and serviceable tool. She continued this Machiavellian politics throughout her political career.[52]

The split brought three inestimable benefits[53] to Indira Gandhi. Firstly, it gave her the new socialistic appeal and people believed that it was the conservative elements in the party who were thwarting her growth.

Secondly, she achieved a personal status which she would not have gained otherwise because of her past track record as Prime Minister. With this split, she had asserted strongly against the stalwarts of the Syndicate and emerged as the most dominant single personality at the time of the election a year later.

Thirdly, after the split, the Left parties, like the CPI and the Praja Socialist Party treated her as a friend worth having[54] and this helped Indira Gandhi later to electoral alliance with them.

But in the context of Indian politics, the Congress split ushered in a new era. The superficial unity of the Congress appeared and the system of one-party dominance had come to an end.[55] With this, the intra-party democracy within the Congress also ended and the battle for supremacy, which had started in 1966, came to a conclusive end with the split of 1969 and Indira Gandhi emerged as unanimous leader both of the government and the party,[56] as the single locus of power from where all initiatives emanated.

Runaway Success

The domination of the Syndicate runaway success during this phase (1970-1977) was substituted by the domination of Indira Gandhi. She set this by changing the function and power structure of the Congress to some extent similar to that of the Nehru era. The age-old conflict between the government and the party was resolved under the supremacy of Indira Gandhi after the split. She emerged as the nerve centre of power controlling both in a more masterly fashion than Jawaharlal Nehru.[57]

In the very first session of the new Congress at Bombay it was decided to involve the cadres in carrying out the 10-point programme and popularising it throughout the country. The need for 'internal party democracy as opposed to bossism'[58] was also stressed.

Still, Indira Gandhi was depending heavily on the left, especially the CPI and CPI (M)[59] for support. To satisfy this section and the Congress Forum for Socialist Action, she chose to strike at the privy purses and found an easy victim in the princes. The abolition of prince's privileges and privy purses was one of the items in the 10-point programme.[60] A bill to this effect was passed by the Lok Sabha in September 1970 but it was defeated in the Rajya Sabha by one vote. This provided Indira Gandhi another chance to prove before the people how her progress towards socialism was being obstructed by the conservative elements among the judiciary.

The split of 1969 had provided a great opportunity for Indira Gandhi to rebuild the Congress. Its character underwent a sea change after that, though not in the right direction. It ceased to be a political movement or instrument which could withstand any political challenge. Gradually, the party lost its political character[61] and became transformed from a democratic mass movement into a movement serving an individual and obeying her whims.

In fact, in the final analysis, the 1971 parliamentary election was a plebiscite partly because Indira Gandhi was appealing for support to overpower opposition to her government's programme and partly because the opposition parties choosed her as a prime target.[62] Consequently, the sweeping victory in the election became the personal victory of Indira Gandhi.

Meanwhile, since April 1971, Indira Gandhi's attention was turned towards Pakistan's atrocities in East Bengal (now Bangladesh). In the name of reorganisation of the party, a resolution was passed to enrol new members and Jagjivan Ram was replaced by D. Sanjivayya.[63] The strategy for state assembly elections was also discussed during the session. But soon after this, the focus of activities of the government shifted from national to international scene culminated ultimately in Indo-Pak War of December 1971 and the birth of Bangladesh.

No local issues were put in the elections because the Congress had the advantage of the towering personality of Indira Gandhi as it emerged after the Bangladesh War. As expected, the Congress came out victorious in 14 states, including West Bengal, the stronghold of the CPI (M). Thus, these elections extended Indira Gandhi's unchallenged authority to the states as well. Apparently, the 'Indira wave' rebuilt the pattern of one-party dominance at the centre and in the states. From 1972 to 1977, the political system of India was transformed from the Westminster model to that of prime ministerial model and the Congress as a dominant party was superseded by Indira Gandhi's personal power. The old party structure, a well-built organization with a high degree of loyalty of its workers, was no more existing. Indira Gandhi had promised to build a more purposeful, cohesive and committed party after the split. And even later, her style of leadership did not prove conducive to the growth of autonomous grass-root structures which were important for giving vitality and direction to the party.

Indira Gandhi introduced three major changes[64] in the structure of the Congress. Firstly, she formed a new decision-making pyramid in which the power of the party and government became centralised with the Prime Minister. Secondly, she reformed the federal character of the party and government by strengthening their unitary tendencies. Thirdly, she tried to change the support base of the Congress through new and arbitrary standards of recruitment.

After the 1971 victory, Indira Gandhi became so powerful that the High Command was virtually reduced to a rubber stamp and there was no likelihood of a clash between the two.[65] So much so that Congress president D.K. Barooah went to saying, "Indira is India and India is Indira." This indicated that in policy matters, the ultimate decision was taken by Indira Gandhi herself rather than the party president.[66]

After 1972, the party committees and offices were filled by appointment rather than election. "This severely impeded the flow of information and diverse opinion through the organisation to decision-makers who were increasingly concentrated at the top. Indira Gandhi also largely abandoned the distribution of patronage, which had been the life blood of the old machine and many of its skilled personnel and selected people of dubious competence as political managers on the basis of their loyalty to her".[67] Party elections were postponed year after year without any apparent reason.[68] Consequently, the representative federal character of the party was further eroded.

By 1972, Indira Gandhi had consolidated her position in the party as well as government. The forum members became very vocal in their criticism of Indira Gandhi's leadership,[69] which annoyed her and made it difficult for the forum to get things done in her name. This became an important reason behind the decline in their influence. Secondly, the forum itself split into two, the moderates and the radicals, which affected its strength within the party. Thirdly, the creation of another forum called the Nehru Forum,[70] proved a further setback to the influence of the Socialist Forum.

In fact, this forum came on the scene when Sanjay Gandhi started taking active interest in politics and started playing a role in the Congress party. It was a reactionary forum formed to counter the Socialist counterpart. It was meant to check the growth of progressive ideology and influence inside the Congress.[71] Some Congress people close to Indira Gandhi during this period perceived that these forums were the creation of Indira Gandhi. Analysing the existing state of affairs in the Congress, Romesh Thapar wrote: 'Indira Gandhi is not unware that the party is being infiltrated by all manner of rightists and leftists who do not have any respect for Congress aims and methods. The Socialist Action Forum, the Nehru Forum, the Backward Classes Forum have certainly helped to expose this aspect of the chaotic organisational state of the ruling party'.[72] These forums were building all-India networks with enormous funds available to them. Thus, they posed 'a dangerous threat to the normal disciplines within which a party leadership functions'.[73]

After the 1969 split, the Congress under the able leadership of Indira Gandhi lost much of its character of consensus and inclined towards that of confrontation which also changed its group support among the voters.[74] Many of the traditional voters tilted towards the opposition and only power-seekers stuck to the party in power. Indira Gandhi had dimmed the distinction between the party and government. As a result, the Congress party could not perform to its potential in working as a linkage between the government and the people. This led to the spontaneous outbreak of violence and protests against the ineffective Congress governments in Bihar and Gujarat. This was later converted into a mass movement under Jai Prakash Narayan.

Under the emergency, the power and influence of the chief ministers further declined,[75] and the control of the states by the central government further consolidated. President's rule[76] was proclaimed in Tamil Nadu on 31 January 1976 and later in Gujarat on 12 March 1976. On 28 March, President's rule was extended to Pondicherry. Orissa Chief Minister Nandini Satpathy was forced to resign and the President's rule was imposed in the state on 16 December.

Sanjay Gandhi became a member[77] of the executive committee of the Youth Congress in December 1975. He was treated next to the Prime Minister in terms of power.[78] His importance attained new heights when his 5-point programme was made the official programme of the party and treated at par with 20-point programme of Indira Gandhi.[79]

Meanwhile, apart from absolute control over the Congress organisation, Indira Gandhi also controlled the constitutional hierarchy of India, such as, the Parliament, cabinet bureaucracy, judiciary and President. She also amended the Constitution to make this control lasting. After the Congress split, Indira Gandhi had begun to place her personally-trusted people at the higher levels and to select bureaucrats based on their 'commitment'. During the emergency 'the new genre of committed bureaucrats' acquired great dictatorial power and behaved in a ruthless manner which further brought disrepute to the Congress.

Observers had often been misled to give a unique interpretation that during the last years of her leadership, Indira Gandhi increasingly began to bank on the new political institutions which had been assuming shape since 1971 due to the centralisation of authority.[80] During the emergency, these institutions increased in importance such as *centralized intelligence organisations*. These were directly under the control of the Prime Minister to keep 'dossiers on government opponents, or critics within the governing Congress party, journalists, businessmen and bureaucrats'.[81] In the past decade, under Indira Gandhi, the Central Reserve Police Force, Border Security Force, Central Industrial Security Force and Home Guards[82] were consolidated after being expanded.

Indira Gandhi became the Prime Minister at a time when the Congress was a well-knit organisation, a party based on intra-party democracy where decisions were taken by consensus and even dissent allowed. But following the 1969 split, a process of personalisation and centralisation of power began and the process struck at the very roots of the organisation which had previously been the support structure of the regime.

The decay in the Congress led to regionalism in politics. The trend towards vertical centralisation combined with horizontal centralisation destabilised all the 'major institutions of the system namely, Parliament, Congress party and local bodies, as well as the large network of voluntary associations and secondary group that accounted for the articulation of demands and gave strength to the democratic process'.[83]

Thus, in March 1977, Indira Gandhi left the legacy of confrontational approaches by personalised and group-leadership alongside continued erosion of cohesion. Over the years, the Congress party had developed a very strange and undemocratic mystique.[84]

The Indian National Congress, during the national struggle, was a mass movement fighting for a single cause. In 1947, it began to lose its character and Mahatma Gandhi advised that the Congress should be converted into a social movement rather than a political party. Jawaharlal Nehru, the first Prime Minister, with his mass appeal and towering status managed to lead the party. But even then the organisation began to shrink. The period of Lal Bahadur Shastri was too short for bringing any vital change in the organisation.

Under the leadership of Indira Gandhi, the Congress began to adopt a different stand. She also realised the need for a change in its structure, functioning and policies. She coined catchy slogans heightened the expectations of the people. Consequently, the new Congress got an absolute majority both at the centre and in the states. Thus, Indira Gandhi gave an electoral popularity to the Congress. Yet, its mass base began to shrink. The centralisation of power eroded the democratic process in the party. Sycophancy, factionalism and corruption paid dividends. Patronage increased all levels and dissidence was crushed. By 1977, the organisation was virtually reduced to an election machine based on the charisma of a single leader. There was no scope left for party-building. During the Emergency she lost her charisma and credibility. The party, too, was severely mauled in the election of 1977.

Strategies and Tactics

For prolonged stay and perpetuation in power, leaders usually employ considerable fore-thought and planning. Competent leaders usually take into consideration the difference between approach and a particular tactical action. Their activities are manoeuvred according to a particular situation. While explaining the term 'strategy', Wriggins observes, "The term strategy suggests more advanced planning and rational calculation of means to ends than may be entirely accurate in a field where 'feel' and improvisation play such an important role."[85]

Strategy is distinguished from its related term 'tactics'. While tactics refers to the localised hostilities that occur where opponents are in contact, strategy refers to the basic character of strength that constitute the entire conduct of a campaign or a war. In simple words, one can say that tactics is fighting and strategy is planning where and how to fight.

As is clear from the above definitions that the strategy and tactics are made to attain certain objectives. Indira Gandhi had the political objective of self-perpetuating and remaining in power and she had adopted the political strategy and tactics for this objective. To promote her objective, she had very successfully managed to utilise the traditional base of the Indian National Congress—the rural base, particularly the Scheduled Castes and the minorities.

Indira Gandhi had two objectives: one was real while the other fake. After analysing her leadership and achievements, one can easily draw the conclusion that her real objective in the beginning was to assume more and more power than to consolidate it. Her fake objective was to build secular, socialist, democratic and strong united India. The objective remained merely a slogan and could not be implemented in action. Thus, at the time of her death, India had a fractured democracy, fake secularism and rise of big business and monopolies.

To achieve her real objective, she had changed her tactics but not the strategy. The major policy of her strategy was to rule the country from a centrist position but with a leftist trust as she told an audience in Washington in 1966. She was more a pragmatist than an ideologue. She had said at a meeting of Congress workers: 'My father was a saint but I am a practical politician'.

Indira Gandhi had fashioned her grand strategy from a number of political strategies to remain in power and pursue additional purposes. This blending of strategies resulted from the way she perceived her political resources in relation to her goals, how she came to power, her own personal qualities, political organisation and political resources available to her, widely accepted rules of game, and her opponents and their threat to dislodge her. She had developed her own theory of strategy taking all these factors into account and many more. The second strategy followed by Indira Gandhi was to carry on and increase the struggle for power continuously, the use of relevant policies and by advance preparation of the machinery and personnel to implement those policies. The third pivotal part of her strategy is the policy of ambivalence, which makes others indulge in a perpetual guessing game. She depended for support on the Congress and opposition at the same time. She could also patch up temporarily with her rivals for tactical reasons. The political leadership of Indira Gandhi as identified by Wriggins can be examined on the basis of eight standard categories of strategy:

I. Projection of Personality

The projection of the personality of Indira Gandhi started from the very beginning, which later on became converted into a personality cult. Prior to the 1967 election, she travelled 15,000 miles and spoke at 160 public meetings. Precisely enough, this was her strength and she demonstrated this time and again in spite of the fact that she was often heckled in public meetings, such as in Jaipur.

In her visual projection, she was very choosy about her dress, speech, mood, movement and actions so as to reflect the desired mood and occasion. On her trip to Punjab, she spoke one or two sentences in Punjabi and referred to herself as the mother-in-law of the region. In Gujarat, she used to project herself as the daughter-in-law of state since Feroze, her husband, was from there. In her visits to Meghalaya, Manipur, Nagaland, Shimla she expressed her wish to live in the hills. These projections obviously aroused the sentiments and emotions of the local people and won their support for her.

II. Building an Organisation

Another important strategy to centralise power is to build an organisation through which the leader enjoys the support to be in power and the strength and infrastructure for implementing the policies and solving problems. When Indira Gandhi assumed leadership, the Congress was in the process of downfall and had merely become an electioneering machinery and an organisation of power-seekers.

In the 1967 Lok Sabha election, the Congress lost its dominance both at the centre and in the states. At this stage, the party needed a major revitalisation. So, in 1967, the Congress lost its mass support. Thus, after the election, the Congress leadership decided to reorganise the party and for this purpose they chalked out a 10-point programme.

After 1971, she ignored the party and directly established her contact with the masses. In this process, she concentrated all the power of a giant organisation, that once led India to freedom in her own hands.

III. Promoting an Ideology

Indira Gandhi was not an ideologue but a pragmatic politician. She was interested in promoting an ideology because she neither had the inclination nor the knowledge required for theoretical speculation necessary for building an ideology. After 1967, she understood that the masses needed a radical change. In 1969, through nationalisation of fourteen banks and later by abolition of privy purses, she had taken the wind out of the sail of the leftists and also downgraded the Syndicate at one stroke.

In 1971, she coined the slogan of *Garibi Hatao* and called for the socialistic pattern of society. In 1975-76, she inserted the word 'socialism' in the Preamble but never clearly defined it. During her leadership, monopoly houses and big business increased their capital with the collusion of her party people.

IV. Rewarding the Faithful and the Susceptible

No political leader has been successful without devoting considerable ingenuity and resources to rewarding the faithful and withholding advantages from the opponents. Modern theorists, however, believe that mostly men aspire for personal safety, income and defence and successful leaders usually manipulate these aspirations and grant or withhold the advantage arising out of them to promote their own political position. Like any other successful leader, this formed an ingredient of Indira Gandhi's political strategy. Hers was a grand mixture of Kautilya's famous policy of *sama, dama, danda* and *bheda* and Machiavelli's expediency.

V. Intimidating the Opposition and Wavering the Ally

This strategy has been popularly linked with Machiavellian statecraft and Mrs. Indira Gandhi was believed to have taken a page out of *The Prince* to work out the strategies in practice. In Kautilyan terms, it represents the use of *danda*, i.e., the use of force (or punishment). Intimidation is meant to create obedience, to overawe by threat of serious sanctions or deprivations. These methods are used to force conformity to the will of the leadership. Indira Gandhi had used intimidatory methods against her political opponents as well as associates. When Jagjivan Ram and Bahuguna left her party in February 1977, they said that the Cabinet ministers and important leaders were under police surveillance.

The police and bureaucracy were the major instruments of intimidation and persons in the saddle of these departments were chosen on the basis of personal loyalties. In spite of the fact that intimidation was repugnant, the ruling class used this method to its advantage. This method could also be used to check violence, disunity and destruction but Indira Gandhi did not use intimidation effectively for these purposes. She used it for her own self-preservation and political advantage. Intimidation provoked antagonism and led to reprisals during the Emergency. To get the right information, the Prime Minister had to depend on the intelligence and her courtiers. It resulted in widespread discontent and ultimately led to her defeat in 1977.

VI. Uplifting the Economy

The Congress was committed to the development of India's economy for the benefit of the people and for building up a prosperous future. But this could also be used to enhance not only material benefits to the ruling class but also to improve its status. Economic development strategy was thus a tool in Indira Gandhi's hands to perpetuate her power design. During the 1971 election compaign, her electoral message promised both stability to the propertied classes and immediate reforms to the poor. She won the election mainly banking on the slogan of *Garibi Hatao* which inflated the aspirations of the people who believed that there was a leader who could solve their problems.

From time to time, Indira Gandhi had talked of land reforms but in 1972 she abandoned them under the pretext that the state chief ministers were not prepared to implement the programme. So she expressed helplessness. But there was no respite to people's misery, degradation and destitution. There was serious fall in agricultural output and massive budget deficits which led to extraordinary price rise.

By 1974, the economic condition had worsened further due to shortages, indiscipline, huge budget deficits, black-money adversely affecting money supply, unemployment, and massive price rise. This process also affected the popularity Indira Gandhi had gained during the Bangladesh war. At this stage, Emergency was imposed. It was conceived and justified as a tool to restore the economy and production. The Emergency was projected as a boon for Indian economy. It was claimed that prices had started to decline and inflation was reversed. However, from March 1976, prices again began to rise despite the tightening of Emergency through constitutional amendments.

VII. Political Participation

From 1967 onwards Indira Gandhi took a stance of leftism not only to garner the support of the new strata but also to discredit the old guard. In 1971, she identified herself with the masses, especially with the poor, with the slogan of *Garibi Hatao*. On the other hand, she made very well-thought-out electoral campaigns. Maneka Gandhi described her election strategy: "Just before the elections she attacked the minorities, engineered riots, communal incidents, and then came in the guise of a saviour . . . in comparison to the opposition, the Congress has always been made out to be the saviour of minorities".

With the elections of 1971 and 1972, Indira Gandhi had inflated the expectations of the people which she could not fulfil. By 1974, people were left disillusioned and the country demoralised. The opposition parties unitedly resorted to agitation methods from 1974 to 1977.

VIII. Use of Foreign Policy

It is considered that domestic politics affects foreign policy and vice-versa. In the beginning, Indira Gandhi literally followed the policy of her predecessors and she was 'more a prisoner of her political legacy than its driving force'.

But in 1969, she had taken the risk of splitting the party so as to get rid of the old guard and from that time onwards she had shown a will and determination which was reflected in her foreign policy. When she became the Prime Minister India's relations with its neighbours were by no means good. She tried to improve relations with them until 1976 when 'the balance of power in the region had changed in favour of India.'

For many years after the Bangladesh War, internal problems were given the backseat. People also allowed this because the war had restored their national pride and prestige after the 1962 humiliation. Many foreign policy activities promoted the stature of the political leader at home. The addresses of Indira Gandhi at world conferences bettered her stature and made her a natural leader of Asian and African countries and this helped her to gain control and more power at home.

Overall View of Strategies and Techniques

As already stated, strategies are used to attain certain objectives and Indira Gandhi's objectives were to retain power. Her main aim was to increase power in her own hands and for this she used a double strategy of 'limited clash' and 'static balance'.

Indira Gandhi revealed her powerful strategy in the very first operation of making a clean sweep of every other element in the party's power structure which counted in the making of a Prime Minister. It was a masterminded political operation, a mixture of various stratagems.

Though her overall strategy was entirely anti-ideology and she never believed in any defined ideology, she successfully projected the split of 1969 on ideological grounds. In this process, she sought the support from both the rich and the poor. The rich supported her for stability and the poor for her slogans.

Due to internal contradictions in her political approach, she was not able to take a firm political stand and relied more on tactics. Like Elizabeth I, Indira Gandhi, as a woman ruler, was able to satisfy all factions that she was not too near to anyone in particular and could enjoy a long tenure and could survive the initial stages of uncertainty.

Even in her tactical moves, Indira Gandhi showed a calculated show of indecisiveness when it suited her purpose. In her tactics, there was "no impulsive, irrational jumping into the foray" but "well-thoughtout action executed with a coolness". In her scheme of politics, it was only a means to an end and not an end in itself. She was largely guided by her political intuition and survival instinct.

During her course of leadership, Indira Gandhi had developed a skill in understanding the psychology of the masses and accordingly she coined the new phrases and slogans. Sometimes it was socialism (*Garibi Hatao*) and sometimes it was secularism (communal danger) while at other times it was unity and integrity of the nation.

In the final analysis, a leader can have only two strategies to consolidate supreme power. The first strategy is to try to narrow down and finally to monopolise power by use of force or terror. The other is to appeal for more popular support, thereby implying a broadening of participation. Indira Gandhi used the first strategy more during the process of monopolising power. But she occasionally used the other and even tried to appeal for more popular support. Her strategy and tactics were mainly offensive and aggressive, but at the same time, also populist in their content and effect.

Return to Power

On 14th January 1980, Indira Gandhi became Prime Minister for the third time and formed Congress government. The Assemblies in States, where majority of Lok Sabha seats were lost by the party in power in the State, were dissolved and the elections were called. In these elections the Congress emerged with the absolute majority and formed governments. In order to boost up the organisation from January 16 to December 29, 1980 as many as 22 circulars were issued by the AICC headquarters. They covered wide ranging organisational matters. Besides that immediately after assuming reins of office Indira Gandhi set in right earnest to put the economy in proper shape. A new 20-Point programme was announced on 14th January 1982 and AICC circulars were issued thereafter by Dr. Rajendra Kumari Bajpai and G.K. Moopanar, General Secretary to all PCCs, TCCs and centrally supported DCCs as well as all convenors of Pradesh Congress Mahila Front. Dr. Shankar Dayal Sharma was appointed as Convenor of the Implementation Cell at the AICC level to monitor the publicity and accelerate the process of implementation of the programme. Besides this, a Time Table was set for organisation elections, beginning with enrolment drive from 5 October 1982. Even Time-table was laid down for election of Congress President. Consequently with the organisational set up gearing up, the implementation of the new programme started yielding visible improvement of the conditions of the very poor. Popularity of the Congress began to increase.

In the International field also Indira Gandhi renewed her efforts for world peace, lessening of tensions, and encouragement to disarmament and creation of a new world economic order. She assumed leadership of Non-Aligned Movement and decided to host the seventh NAM session in Delhi. The session was a crowning success so much so that the President of the Session requested Indira Gandhi to bring together the leaders of USA and USSR. In accordance with the decision of the Seventh NAM Indira Gandhi called, as such, all world leaders in New York at the time of the UN Session to discuss various issues. The response to such a move was encouraging.

As a result of these two international meet, the prestige of India went up very high in the world affairs. India once again became a centre of world politics, a country working for peace and faster development of the third world countries. She was called a champion of the Third World and one of the greatest statesman of this century as the world community expressed its outrage at her assassination. "Her death is a great loss not only for the people of India, the non-aligned movement and the Commonwealth, but also for humanity as a whole", said the General Assembly President, Mr. Pairl Liausaka of Zambia. He said, "Indira Gandhi was born in one of the cradels of the concepts and practice of non-alignment. The daughter of one of the founders of the non-aligned movement, she herself worked tirelessly to help nurture the movement in an international environment . . ."

On 23 November 1983, Indira Gandhi addressed the Commonwealth Heads of Government meeting at Vigyan Bhawan in New Delhi. She drew attention to apartheid in South Africa and the militarisation of the Indian Ocean, which, according to UN Declaration made in 1971 was to be declared a 'Zone of Peace'. In spite of the Ocean bristling with fleets, bases and command structures outside powers, she expressed the hope that before the next meeting of Commonwealth Heads of Government in 1985 (at Bahama), the UN Declaration on the Indian Ocean as a Zone of Peace would be implemented. In the end she said, "The Commonwealth itself was born out of dialogues and in the belief that human and international problems can and should be resolved through goodwill. The Commonwealth spirit asks us to rededicate ourselves to peace and development through dialogue."

In the field of international sports too, Indira Gandhi got ninth Asian Games staged in New Delhi and won laurels from all people and all countries. Successes in science, India entering space, in the field of oceanography and expeditions to Antarctica were other achievements of the Congress Government under the dynamic leadership of Indira Gandhi. The AICC session held at Bombay on October 20 and 21, 1983 also placed on record its appreciation of the Ninth Asian Games held in Delhi. The event had enthused country's young people and evoked their deep emotional involvement.

During 1980-83 the Indian National Congress was revitalised with vigour. This process gained a new momentum with the appointment of Rajiv Gandhi as General Secretary.

The Congress since then has taken various steps for training programmes, e.g., Seva Dal for which camps had been organised all over the country. Similarly training camps for NSUI were also organised. Attempts were made to make almost every frontal organisation active and spread out to different States. In her presidential address to the seventy-seventh session at Calcutta, December 29 and 30, 1983 Indira Gandhi

Editor and his family with Shri Rajiv Gandhi, Prime Minister of India, 1985.

Editor's family function attended by Smt. Indira Gandhi.

Editor congratulates President Shanker Dayal Sharma on his birthday.

Smt. Indira Gandhi felicitates on Editor's daughter's marriage ceremony, 1978.

said, "... The Congress is the world's largest democratic party but it is and has always been more than a political party. It is mass democratic movement of vast proportions. In and through the Congress, millions of people from all parts of our country have transcended differences of caste, religion, language and economic or educational background." In short, the session projected that the Congress ideology had withstood the test of time. It has kept evolving in tune with changing circumstances. It has always had a special place for women, the minorities, the Scheduled Castes, the Scheduled Tribes and all other disadvantaged sections. Accordingly, it was the historic duty of the Congress to carry forward the unfinished social revolution, the removal of the old and new obstacles to social equality and the need to fight regional, communal, extremist and near-secessionist agitations and organisations at home as well as the international forces of destabilisation which were receiving help from domestic elements.

References

1. See, L.P. Singh, "Political Development and Political Decay in India", *Pacific Affairs,* Vol. 44, No. 1, Spring, 1971, p. 66.
2. See, Kothari, n. 1, pp. 1162-63.
3. The non-Congress parties secured more votes than the Congress. For Lok Sabha, it was 55 per cent in 1952, 55.2 in 1957, 55.3 in 1962 and 62 in 1967. Same was seen in relation to state assembly elections where the opposition parties secured 58 per cent votes in 1952, 55 in 1957, 56.3 in 1962 and 60 in 1967.
4. It was evident from the fact that the committee which was formed by the CWC to choose a unanimous successor of Shastri never met. See Michael Brecher, *Nehru's Mantle: The Policy of Succession,* Frederic A. Praege, New York, 1966, pp. 205-06.
5. Brecher, n. 10, p. 190.
6. The 'Syndicate' was born in October 1963 at Tirupati in Andhra Pradesh. It consisted of Atulya Ghosh, Sanjiva Reddy, S. Nijalingappa, S.K. Patil and Kamraj. This group played a leading role in deciding the succcessor of Nehru and later the successor of Lal Bahadur Shastri. They became assertive and influential after Nehru's death. Kamraj was its leader. They did not like Morarji for his assertiveness and faddist nature. Also see, G. Lakshman Rao, "The Background of the Recent Crisis in the Indian Congress Party', *The Australian Quarterly,* Vol. 42, No. 1, March 1970, pp. 44-46.
7. See, Stanley A. Kochanek, *Congress Party of India: The Dynamics of One Party Democracy,* Princeton University Press, Princeton, 1968, p. 97.
8. Kochanek, n. 15, p. 10.
9. At the time of her election, S. Nijalingappa and S.K. Patil had warned Kamraj Nadar that she would one day turn against them all but he did not agree. Later on Kamraj Nadar himself said, "I was proved wrong; she wanted all power for herself and allowed nobody to come anywhere near her.' See, Kuldip Nayar, *India After Nehru, op. cit.,* p. 66.
10. See, Sahni, n. 17, p. 482, who observed that "the king-maker" would soon lose favour with "the king".
11. See Rajni Kothari, "The Congress System on Trial", *Asian Survey,* Vol. 7, No. 2, February 1967, p. 86.
12. See, *Mainstream,* Republic Day Special, 1967, p. 19.
13. See, for details, Michael Brecher, "India's Devaluation of 1966: Linkage Politics and Crisis Decision-making", *British Journal of International Studies,* Vol. 3, No. 1, April 1977, pp. 1-25.
14. When asked about her differences with the Congress president on 25 December 1966, she confidently declared: "Here is a question of whom the party wants and whom the people want." My position among the people is uncontested." See, *Times of India,* 26 December, 1966.

15. She adopted this strategy to bypass the party and project herself as a national leader.
16. *Mainstream*, Republic Day Special, 1967, p. 19.
17. *Ibid.*
18. See, for details, *ibid.*, pp. 170-72.
19. The Congress got 275 seats out of 520 in the Parliament and polled 39.57 per cent of valid votes. It lost in eight State Assemblies (Kerala, Madras, Punjab, Haryana, UP, Rajasthan, Bihar, Orissa, West Bengal and the Union Territory of Delhi). Even the Congress president lost the election alongwith other stalwarts of the party and central and state ministers. See for details, Norman D. Palmer, "India's Fourth General Election", *Asian Survey,* Vol. 7, No. 5, May 1967, pp. 275-91.
20. See, M.P. Singh, *Split in the Predominant Party,* Abhinav Publications, Delhi, 1981, p. 53.
21. C.S. Pandit, n. 33, p. 27. The induction of Morarji Desai into the cabinet as the Deputy Prime Minister was the result of a compromise formula reached by the Congress party leaders to avoid a contest for leadership. Initially, Indira Gandhi was reluctant to accept Morarji as No. 2 with the home portfolio and Morarji was reluctant to accept anything except this. Ultimately, as a compromise to keep unity and consensus, Indira Gandhi accepted Morarji as No. 2 but gave him the finance portfolio. Morarji told that he accepted it because, "she came to my house and I did not go to her and in the interest of the party I accepted it". (App. C).
22. Even before this election, the Syndicate had been looked upon as men who wielded power and influence not because of their idealism but because they controlled the organisational machinery of the ruling party in a number of states. They had used their power in the making and unmaking of cabinets both at the centre and in states. After the defeat in the election, they had virtually no say in the formation of the 1967 cabinet.
23. See *IRD,* Vol. 13, No. 4, April 1967, pp. 2-4.
24. The organisation leadership of the Congress was not consulted and even Kamraj was shown the list only a shortwhile before it was due to be submitted to the President. See Masani, *op. cit.,* pp. 175-6. Also see, Kochanek, *op. cit.,* p. 413.
25. The slogan was coined by Indira Gandhi at the Ernakulam session of the AICC in September 1966.
26. See Masani, *op. cit.* p. 173.
27. See, *The Indian Nation,* Patna, 8 May 1967.
28. See, Durga Das, n. 17, p. 406 and also Kochanek, *op. cit.,* p. 413.
29. At midnight, Indira Gandhi called a meeting of the Congress Working Committee to which Kamraj was not invited. She persuaded Nijalingappa to accept the nomination. Kamraj disapproved this action but ultimately endorsed it. After the withdrawal of other candidates, S. Nijalingappa was elected unanimously. See *Hindustan Times,* 1 December 1967. See also *Motherland,* 16 February 1971.
30. Judith M. Brown, *Modern India: The Origins of an Asian Democracy,* Oxford University Press, Delhi, 1984, p. 359. Also see, Inder Malhotra, "Congress Credibility Sadly Eroded", *Statesman,* 11 April 1969.
31. The party faced a great crisis in March 1969 over the inclusion of the Raja of Ramgarh in the Bihar cabinet. C. Subramaniam resigned from the CWC on this issue. The Young Turks also levelled charges against Morarji Desai. See, for details, *The Hindu,* 10 March 1969; *Free Press Journal,* Bombay, 11 March 1969; *The Searchlight,* Patna, 10 March 1969 and *Times of India,* 11 March 1969.
32. Uunnikrishnan, n. 11, p. 289.
33. See for details, Masani, *op. cit.,* pp. 187-88.
34. It is evident from facts that Morarji Desai was charged by Chandra Shekhar of giving concessions to the Birlas. It was alleged that Indira Gandhi was behind the 'Young Turks' and allowed them full say. See, for details, S. Swaminathan, "Deepening Crisis in the Congress Command", *Free Press Journal,* 12 March 1969.
35. See, Kuldip Nayar, *India: The Critical Years,* Vikas, Delhi, 1971, p. 26.
36. See, *Sunday Standard,* 20 April 1969.
37. See, for details, The Text of S. Nijalingappa's address, *National Herald,* 28 April, 1969. It is

notable that "the Congress president did not mention Socialism anywhere in his 6,000 words address but Indira Gandhi repeated several times in the course of her two speeches that the Congress party was committed to establish a socialistic pattern of society and any move to dampen the expectation of the people would be fraught with danger." *Hindustan Times,* 28 April 1969.

38. *Ibid.*
39. *Ibid.*
40. See, Unnikrishnan, n. 17, p. 303.
41. See, for details, Basant Chatterjee, *Congress Splits,* S. Chand & Co. Delhi, 1971, p. 111. S.K. Patil said, "Any snap decision on nationalisation would dislocate the credit structure and disrupt the economy".
42. See for details, Rao. n. 41, pp. 96-98; and also Chatterjee, n. 90, 112-13.
43. *The Statesman,* 13 July, 1969.
44. *Ibid.*
45. See the text of the letter in A.M. Zaidi, *The Great Upheaval: 1969-72,* Orientalia, India, 1972, pp. 92-93.
46. He got 420,077 votes as against 405,527 secured by Sanjiva Reddy. See, Nayar, *op. cit.,* p. 46.
47. The vote analysis showed that the large majority of Congress MPs and MLAs voted for Sanjiva Reddy and V.V. Giri won with the minority of Congress votes in combination with those of diverse opposition parties. See, Zaidi, n. 97, p. 491 and also Nayar, *op. cit.,* p. 46.
48. S. Nihal Singh, *Statesman,* 23 August 1969.
49. J.D. Sethi, *India's Static Power Structure,* Vikas, Delhi, 1969, pp. 53-56.
50. See, for details, Joseph Lelyveld, "India: Crisis in . . . the steel in this woman explains why she is winning in the present political tug of war. Her opponents just do not have that kind of nerve. She is a great political gambler; I cannot think of anybody anywhere who compares with her in this particular aspect." *Ibid.,* p. 24.
51. A Hariharan, "A Place of Progress", *Far Eastern Economic Review,* 10 October 1970, p. 20.
52. *Ibid.*
53. See, Pran Chopra, "Congress in Fifth General Elections (Patron Client Relationship)", *World Today,* May 1971, pp. 185-92.
54. See, V.R. Rajamani, "Mrs Gandhi and Communists", *Hindu,* 8 January 1970 and also, Peter Hess, "Indira Gandhi and the Communists", *Swiss Review of World Affairs,* Vol. 1, No. 11, February 1970, pp. 15-16.
55. See, Robert L. Hardgrave, "The Congress in India—Crisis and Split", *Asian Survey,* Vol. 10, No. 3, March 1970, pp. 256-62.
56. Initially she had thought of becoming the party president but due to some reasons abandoned that idea and chose such people for the party offices who remained personally loyal to her and depended for their office on the support of Indira Gandhi.
57. Though the methods through which Indira Gandhi had reached the position of unchallenged supremacy were different to the political practices of the Nehru era. See, J.D. Sethi, *India in Crisis,* Vikas, Delhi, 1975, p. 89.
58. This was the main theme of the opening remarks of the new President Jagjivan Ram. See, Indian National Congress 73rd Plenary Session, Bombay 26-29 December 1969, *Presidential address by Jagjivan Ram.* 28 December 1969, New Delhi, p. 6. Also see, *Indian Recorder and Digest (IRD),* Vol. 16, No. 1, January 1970, pp. 10-11.
59. See, for details, Sumanta Bannerjee, "Congress (R), CPI and CPI (M)", *Economic and Political Weekly,* Vol. 5, No. 45, 7 November 1970, pp. 1804-07.
60. The other important point was the "ceiling on land" which she left for the heads of state governments and did not touch it because it could possibly harm her support base greatly. The programme had been adopted by the AICC in June 1967.
61. K.P. Unnikrishnan, in the interview (App. C).
62. See, B.D. Graham, "Congress as a Rally: An Image of Leadership'. *South Review,* Vol. 6, No. 2, January 1972, p. 121 and for a detailed analysis of the 1971 parliamentary election, see,

Marcus F. Franda, "Thoughts on the Indian Elections", *Asia,* New York, No. 20, Winter, 1970-71, pp. 1-8.

63. In fact, Jagjivan Ram was replaced because he had become a popular mass leader and Indira Gandhi wanted a pliable Congress president without a base in the masses and D. Sanjivyya was found suitable for the purpose. Even earlier, at the Bombay session, after the split, she wanted to make him the party president but the move was scuttled by Brahmanand Reddy and she had to choose Jagjivan Ram and later the Congress Working Committee was again constituted without any major change except that Dinesh Singh and Raghuramaiah were dropped. This showed that there was no chance in the composition and structure of this decision-making body even after the split.
64. Kochanek calls them three major characteristics of the new political process created by Indira Gandhi. *Ibid.*
65. See, Sarla Malik, *The Prime Minister of India: Powers and Functions,* Chinta Prakashan, Pilani, 1984, pp. 221-2.
66. *Hindustan Times,* 11 March 1977. Poorvi Mukherji, one of the general secretaries, provided the logic thus, "A leader has to lead, not be lead by others". *Ibid.* A.R. Antulay, the extent of advocating the complete subordination of the organisation wing to the Prime Minister. See, *The Statesman.* 18 December 1976.
67. Manor, n. 15, p. 28.
68. See, *Indian Express,* 20 October 1974.
69. See, J.C. Johari, "Young Turks and the Radicalisation of the Congress," *Indian Journal of Political Science,* to feel that the growing influence of the Socialist Forum was bringing the communist and Soviet influence in the Congress. They considered it a front organisation of the Communist Party of India. See, Satindra Singh, *Communists in Congress,* D.K. Publishing House, Delhi, 1973, p. xxii.
70. The Nehru Forum was created in August 1972 by a group of Congressmen led by Uma Shankar Dixit. Its prominent members were S.D. Sharma, Jagjivan Ram, Y.B. Chavan, Kamlapati Tripathi, C. Subramaniam, T.A. Pai, etc.
71. Chandrajit Yadav (App. C).
72. Romesh Thapar, 'Who Rules the Ruling Party?", *Economic and Political Weekly,* 7 April, 1973, p. 654. According to Hariharan, "Even the big 1969 split notwithstanding, there are leftists, centrists and rightists in Mrs. Gandhi's Party, all pulling in different directions." A. Hariharan, "Stormy Congress", *Far Eastern Economic Review (FEER),* 30 July, 1973, p. 17.
73. *Ibid.*
74. See, Graves, n. 76, pp. 866-71.
75. Amit Roy, "Why Mrs. Gandhi Lost", *Round Table,* No. 266, April 1977, pp. 161-67.
76. See, Madhu Limaye, "The Record of Mrs. Gandhi's Government" *Everyman's,* 2 March, 1975. See also Ajit Bhattacharjee, "Misuse of President's Rule : Waning Confidence in Democracy", *Times of India,* 16 July 1973.
77. After the Congress defeat in 1977, it was disclosed that Sanjay Gandhi was never a member of the Congress but Barooah declined it in his interview. Indira Gandhi also kept saying that she was not grooming Sanjay Gandhi for Prime Minister nor was he interested in any high office. *Ibid.,* p. 165.
78. See, Denzel Peiris, "The Rise of Sanjay Gandhi", *FEER,* Vol. 92, 21 May 1976.
79. Kothari. n. 74, p. 24.
80. Manor, n. 15, pp. 31-33.
81. Weiner, n. 74, p. 898.
82. Gerard Viseatelle, writing about India under the Emergency observed, "Since 1969, Mrs. Gandhi got rid of the Congress 'old guard', the police machinery has been considerably strengthened. Intelligence gathering has developed so well that India now has a "central" agency, the Research and Analysis Wing, resembling the CIA but of much more modest proportion. It is run by a 'Kashmiri Brahmin' and supervised by Mrs. Gandhi herself." *The Guardian,* 30 August 1975. There developed almost a coterie of Kashmiri Brahmins such as P.N. Haksar, D.P. Dhar, Kao, T.N. Kaul, B.K. Nehru, etc.

83. Kothari, n. 74, p. 24.
84. Romesh Thapar, "Congress—Undemocratic Mystique", *Economic and Political Weekly, 1975,* p. 745.
85. W. Howard Wriggins, *The Ruler's Imperative,* Columbia University Press, New York and London, 1969, p. 92.

25

Congress and Congressism in Indian Politics

Party Leadership

At each level of the party, the Congress has its executive organ which constitutes its leadership. At the Block/Town or Ward level there is the Block/Ward/Town Congress Committee; at the district level there is the District Congress Committee (DCC) under the District Congress chief; at the state level, there is the Pradesh Congress Committee (PCC) headed by the Pradesh Congress chief; at the national level, there is the All India Congress Committee (AICC) headed by the Congress President. The AICC had its working committee the Congress Working Committee (CWC). The other two adjacent organs of the Congress Working Committee are the Congress Parliamentary Board (CPB) and the Central Election Committee (CEC). These committees and their chiefs constitute the organisational leadership.[1]

A Block/Town/Ward Congress Committee is constituted provided there are at least 25 active members residing in the area. Such a committee encompasses an area having a population of about 60,000 people. Its members consist of (a) those elected by the primary members of the Congress of the area at the rate of one per 2,000 population, and (b) members of the DCC who reside in or have been elected from the area to the DCC.[2]

A District Congress Committee encompasses an area prescribed by the Pradesh Congress Committee. It consists of: (a) two members elected by the active members of the Block/Town/Ward; (b) presidents of Block/Town/Ward Congress Committees; (c) ex-Presidents of the District Congress Committees who have completed their full term (normally two years) and are active members; (d) members of the Pradesh Congress Committee who belong to the district; (e) members of the Congress legislature party both in the state and at the Centre; (f) leaders of the Congress party in the local bodies; (g) members co-opted by the executive of the DCC from special elements not represented duly in the DCC; and (h) representatives of organisations or institutions working in the area.[3] Each District Congress Committee or each Block/Town/Ward had its own president and administrative organ.

A Pradesh Congress Committee covers the area of a state or union territory. The PCC functions, ordinarily, through the DCCs. It has its own constitution which has not to be inconsistent with that of the Congress and before it is enacted, the prior approval of the CWC is essential. It has to submit to the CWC an annual report of the work done by the Congress in the Pradesh including audited balance-sheet of the accounts.[4] In case any PCC fails to deliver in accordance with the constitution or in accordance with the directives of the CWC, the latter is empowered to suspend the PCC and form an ad hoc Committee to continue the Congress work in the Pradesh.[5] Each PCC has its president and administrative organ.

The AICC which is the national committee of the Congress consists of one-eighth of the PCC members elected proportionately from each province, president of the Congress, ex-Presidents of the Congress, presidents of the PCCs, leader of the Congress Legislature Party in Parliament, leaders of the State Congress Legislatures, 15 members to be elected from the Parliament's Congress Legislature party, members co-opted from special elements not adequately represented and representatives of the organisations and institutions working in the country.

The president of the Congress is elected by the delegates consisting of all members of the PCCs for two years.[6] In case the election of the president is found impossible as a result of the procedure laid down in Article XVIII (a to g), the AICC is convened by the CWC which elects the president.[7] The Congress president presides over the Congress session and he enjoys all the powers of the CWC when it is not in session.[8]

The Congress Working Committee comprises of 20 members. Of these, seven are elected by the AICC and the rest are appointed by the president. It is the highest executive authority of the Congress and therefore possesses powers to implement the policies and programmes laid down by the Congress and by the AICC to which it is accountable.[9] Among its other powers, mention may be made to: (i) framing rules for the proper working of the organisation; (ii) issuing instructions to the lower units; (iii) controlling, directing and supervising all PCCs and other subordinate bodies; and (iv) taking disciplinary action against a committee other than the AICC.[10]

The two other special committees, at the national level, are the Congress Parliamentary Board and the Central Election Committee. The Congress Working Committee is empowered to find a Congress Parliamentary Board which consists of the Congress president and seven other members. The Congress Parliamentary Board, headed by the Congress president, directs and co-ordinates the parliamentary activities of the Legislature Congress parties with the power of framing rules in this connection.[11] The Central Election Committee consists of the members of the Congress Parliamentary Board, the leader of the Congress party in the Parliament and five other members elected by the AICC. This Committee makes the final selection of the candidates for the state and Central legislature and conducts party's election campaigns.[12]

The Congress Working Committee, as the chief executive organ of the Congress, has served the organisation by building and guiding it. As the aims and objectives of the Congress increased and as its base broadened, the Congress Working Committee came in for more importance both in the pre-independence and post-independence periods. It has been empowered with the powers of implementing all the policies and programmes of the Congress, directing and controlling all the lower party units and invoking sanctions for breach of party discipline.[13]

As intra-party rivalries were more and more coming to light the Congress Working Committee has spent a major part of its time in maintaining party unity and in preventing rift within the Congress. This has led the Congress Working Committee to lay down broad policy for the organisation, to establish mediating mechanism and, if necessary, to intervene in the affairs of the subordinate Congress bodies.

Factionalism destabilises any political party, though Brass believes that it has an integrative function of recruiting new groups into the Congress. What the Congress Working Committee has in the initial decades done, is that it has tried consistently to reduce the disintegrative efforts by adopting procedures and policies to control internal factional conflict. It has attempted to frame rules with regard to the scrutiny of members enrolled and the maintenance of the permanent register is a testimony of that. One manifestation has been the repeated revision of the party's constitution. But document tinkering notwithstanding the experience of the twenty years suggests that any reasonable procedural machinery works well in states where factionalism rarely has a presence. The task of the Working Committee throughout the first two decades has been to reduce factionalism and protect the majority groups suffering at the hands of opposing factions.

As a sub-committee of the Congress Working Committee, the Congress Parliamentary Board attempted to co-ordinate the party-government relationship at the state level. The task of the Congress Parliamentary Board was easier as far as the factional rivalries at the state level remained within the reach of conciliation. It refers to the other two, the first being the factional, factors affecting the normal pattern of operation so far as the conflict between the parliamentary and organisational wings is concerned. If factionalism enlarged the dominion of the Congress Parliamentary Board, the journey from limited action in the tussle between the organisational and legislative wings during the first few years of independence provided help the adoption of procedures by the Congress Parliamentary Board for resolving the conflicts between the party and governmental wings. The causes of the conflict between the party and the parliamentary wings made the task of the Congress Parliamentary Board more complicated and more complex.

The very setting up of the Congress Parliamentary Board in 1936 meant the creation of an institution to co-ordinate and guide the activities of the state ministries. Hence, the Congress Parliamentary Board was created to co-ordinate the work of the various ministries in the states. With the advent of freedom and with the change in the character of the Congress from a nationalist movement to a ruling political party[14] and with the entry of the careerists in the Congress to make use of political and governmental power for their own sake, numerous problems arose at the state and national levels. As factional competition increased, so increased the rivalries and so changed the role of the Congress Parliamentary Board from a mere co-ordinator to an umpire. By 1960s, the Congress Parliamentary Board was less to co-ordinate and more to arbitrate; intra-state problems were more visible than the inter-state ones. Attempts were made to provide guidelines so that there were fewer conflicts between the party and the legislative wings at the state levels.[15]

Factionalism guided the task of the Congress Parliamentary Board during the final years of Nehru and Lal Bahadur Shastri and until the first major split of 1969. In states where the party was divided into factions and groups, the Congress Parliamentary Board set down general principles for the election of the Chief Minister so as to maintain unity in the party and stability in the government; in states where one faction was dominant, the Congress Parliamentary Board attempted to prevent a contest and got unanimous election with the representation of the minority party group in the cabinet.

Decision-making Process

That the Indian National Congress has been able to govern the country during the significant period since independence speaks much of its credentials. It governs because it has successfully led the nationalist movement from the front. It governs because it alone has been able to provide the people a government. Weiner says, "Few other nationalist movements have been so successfully transformed into political parties… It (India) is a rare new nation which has succeeded in developing political parties able to provide stable and effective government in a competitive environment."[16]

Experience shows that the Congress has been an organisation more at the top rather at the bottom. This suggests that the Congress is what its leaders are. During the last years of India's liberation, the Congress was able to achieve independence largely due to the united leadership at the top.

During the transitional period of 1947-51, the party-government relationship touched nearly the breaking point, party insisting on its supremacy over the government and the Congress Presidents, Kripalani and Tandon, trying to surpass Nehru while the parliamentary wing attempting to emphasise on the new role of the Congress and the accountability of the Congress Parliamentary Party towards the Parliament. With Nehru assuming the charge of the Congress presidency, the party-government relations entered a phase of real co-ordination where the parliamentary wing and the organisational wing merged into one and the process of decision-making at the Congress Working Committee level was smooth.

The third phase, beginning with the last days of Nehru till the eve of the 1967 elections, witnessed the return of those days when the organisational wing began prevailing over the parliamentary wing. This is evident from the selection of Shastri (1964) and Mrs. Indira Gandhi (1966) as Prime Ministers, largely through the efforts of Kamraj, the Congress president, and his close followers in the party. The years between 1967-69 were years of conflicts between the party and the government when Mrs. Indira Gandhi fought the survival battle in which the Syndicate dominated Congress attempted to oust her.[17] The future was on her side and the elections of 1971, following the split of 1969, brought her in power both in the government and in the party. From here began the Congress as the Congress of the party President. Party matters received low priority and party organs at the Centre, state and district levels either fell into disuse or were made to work in tune with the lines adopted by the party leader. The deinstitutionalisation of the Congress was complete after the 1978 split. The Janata government did break this; for a brief period between 1977-78, but its rule, or say its misrule hastened the re-emergence of Mrs. Indira Gandhi to power again in 1980 and till the time of her assassination in 1984.

The so-called 'umbrella' image of the Congress had in the past, and has in the present, and probably, would in the future make the organisation, as Morris-Jones feels rightly, "the party of generous shelter, mixed social base and very broad goals."[18] These were the days of the neglect of the party and its various institutions from where the party had never recovered. Morris-Jones further writes, "If the repair of the machine was, therefore, hardly Nehru's subject, his own occupation of the party's presidency in a sense made the job less urgent; . . . Preferring on most matters to avoid nettle-grasping decisions and relying on his capacity to reconcile diverse positions he discouraged the party from making too explicit the choices before it."[19] Such a tradition continued with Mrs. Indira Gandhi and Rajiv Gandhi except between the period when Mrs. Indira Gandhi was out of power. As Mrs. Gandhi strengthened her position after the 1969 and 1978 splits, greater concentration of power relating to decision-making revolved around the Prime Minister (government) who happened to be the Congress president (party). A major development in the Indian politics after the 1969 split and later, with greater magnitude, after the 1978 split in the Congress was the emergence of personalised politics. The rise of the Janata coalition was as quick as was its fall. The fall of the Janata government assured the re-emergence of the Indira Congress and return to personalised politics and personalised party system. The country elected a leader who was firmly in command of her party and whose appeal cuts across all the great divides in the Indian community—religious, social, linguistic and regional. In personalised party system, the leaders of the party "vociferously declared their unflinching loyalty to the Prime Minister and the party president Smt. Indira Gandhi and after her, Rajiv Gandhi. All of them swear that they faithfully want to implement her policies."

Within the framework of the personalised party system, it is from the top that a party is organised. This means that all the organisational posts are filled by persons appointed directly by the party president. The decisions are made at the Congress' president level (or say at the Prime Minister's level) and all the other party bodies become merely the supporting committees. The Congress seems to have been deinstitutionalised while the leadership is institutionalised. A single person's popularity makes all the differences in electoral support. Notwithstanding the occasional talks of party elections by Rajiv Gandhi, the institutionalised leadership of Mrs. Indira Gandhi and Rajiv Gandhi had much in common.

The Indian National Congress: Organisational Issues

Like any other political party, the Indian National Congress, formed in 1885, had its own constitution, its own methods of recruiting its members, both primary and active, its own norms of electing its delegates to the bodies at higher levels, its own procedure of selecting its own president. Like any other political party, the Congress (the short name of the Indian National Congress) too experienced splits and rifts ever since the Surat split of 1907. Being an umbrella party, the Congress could save itself from numerous possible divisions. In the beginning, the Congress was known more because of Hume than because of the party itself. Whenever there came a time when the Congress was led by a lesser known leader, the party became insignificant. That is why the Congress period has been rightly characterised as the Gandhian era (between 1917 and 1948), or the Nehruvian Congress of the period between 1948 and 1964, or the Indira Congress, following the 1969 split.

Before independence, the Congress had lesser problems of organisation as well as of leadership, for it was the goal that guided the Congressmen and Congresswomen. As leadership was commonly regarded as a crown of thorns, fewer people came forward. To be a leader of the Congress meant inviting the wrath of the British authorities. He who dared to accept the leadership retained it as long as he wanted and in the process became the favourite in the eyes of the people especially of the British India and the enemy of the British Government. Mahatma Gandhi became the leader following his launching of the Non-Cooperation Movement in 1920 and kept on maintaining his leadership until his assassination in 1948.

The Congress was not intended to be a party of the governors and rulers, at least Gandhiji never wanted it to be the party of the administrators. He wished it to turn itself into a party of the servants of the people, Lok Sevak Sangh, as he would describe it. The Congress, according to Gandhiji's thought, would get itself dissolved and the task of ruling the country would be left to the newly-politically oriented class organisation. But that was not to be so. It became the uncrowned ruler during the initial twenty years after independence. For most part, Nehru became the real ruler, holding the office of the Prime Minister and also the post of the President of the Congress party himself or to the one chosen by him. During the first twenty years, in particular, the Congress had its say both at the centre and also in the states. Socialism, secularism, non-alignment, democracy had already become its objectives. Nehru was the uncrowned king; the Congress was the ruling party, the dominant one, the system had become, as Rajni Kothari had once said, the Congress one.

On the organisational structure, the Congress retained its federal structure as provided by the amended Constitution of the Indian National Congress in 1920. At the top stood the president of the Congress party followed by the All India Congress Committee (AICC) consisting of delegates from the Pradesh Congress Committees (PCCs).

Below each Pradesh Congress Committee, there were to be the District Congress Committees. There were a total of 422 DCCs in 1969. In each District Congress Committee, there were to be Block Committees, one Committee for 60,000 population. And below every Block Committee, there were Mandal Congress Committees, some informal organisations, abolished by the Kamraj Plan.

The Congress Working Committee (CWC) was also the highest executive organ of the party, consisting of 21 members including the president. The vacancies falling vacant owing to the resignation of the elected members of the CWC are filled by the nominations by the president. During the post-independence years, the CWC became the decision-making body.

The Congress Working Committee was accountable to the All India Congress Committee (AICC). The AICC has power to lay down guidelines for the party. Yet the Central Party Executive and the State Party chiefs too exerted considerable influence in party and state matters. The Parliamentary Board played an important role in shaping the governmental policies.

During the times of Jawaharlal Nehru, the Congress party functioned in a federal manner; there used to be elections, annual sessions, discussions and debates, though the dominance of Nehru was always there. After the death of Nehru and during the tenure of Lal Bahadur Shastri and during the early period of Indira Gandhi as the Prime Minister, the functioning of the Congress was more or less decentralised, the politics of dominance was replaced by the politics of consensus. It was only after 1969 and until 1977 that Mrs. Gandhi became the undisputed leader of the Congress, defeating the syndicate or what was then known as the organisational group and putting herself in the Congress saddle. The defeat of the Congress and Smt. Indira Gandhi during the 1977 Lok Sabha elections and the subsequent split, the Congress became the Indira Congress. After the failure of the Janata government, the Congress, now the Indira Congress, became the ruling Congress, its leader emerging as the most powerful leader of both the party and the nation until she was assassinated in 1984. Rajiv Gandhi, as the successor of her mother, began with a clean image and attempted to depersonalise power by widening the circle of consultation in matters relating to administration. Like his grandfather, Rajiv too was unable to concentrate on party and organisational matters, though he would make occasional remarks at organisational elections which were not held for almost two decades. Rajiv started like his grandfather but ended like his mother, embracing even the death the way his mother had embraced. Rajiv was assassinated in 1991, though he had made promise to democratise the Congress. P.V. Narasimha Rao fulfilled the promise and got the elections of the party done almost after two-and-a-half decades. As a Prime Minister, he tried to have democracy in the party as well as in the government.

Factionalism has been and in fact is always a characteristic of the Congress party. The Congress party has been an umbrella party and as such has not demonstrated any systematic political orientation on political matters at any point of time. The result has been infightings and intra-party divisions.

During the most part, especially between 1947 and 1967, there has been one dominant party system, in the form of multi-party system under which the Congress played the dominant role. It was a system under which the Congress internalised the political competition which was possible because there had existed a number of factions owing their origins to numerous diversities but finding their due disciplined expression in one form or the other. After Nehru's death, factionalism appeared forcefully. Shastri survived it through his politics of conciliation and consensus. Indira Gandhi worked with it unwillingly for some time, but following the split in 1969, formed her own Congress and managed factional infightings herself. Before her towering personality and during the period between 1969 and 1977 first and between 1980 and 1984; factionalism got subdued.

The Congress, due to the nature of its organisation has always been a party of various factions. Rajiv began, following the assassination of his mother, hesitatingly, but soon controlled the numerous factions and became the leader. He kept ruling the party until his own assassination in 1991.

With the passage of time every organisation suffers decay. Attempts are thus made to arrest the decay and efforts of revitalisation are put into operation. This is true about the Congress party. The numerous amendments made in the Constitution of the Indian National Congress aptly demonstrate that changes are made to keep the party in pace with the changing times. At times, even 'operation' or 'surgery' is also suggested.

The result of the 1967 elections were, for the Congress, unsatisfactory. This led to serious discussion on how cohesion could be restored, how membership could be mobilised and how new blood could be activised. The debates and discussions at the annual Congress sessions accelerated rifts leading ultimately to the famous split of 1969. With this split, numerous shades of Congress emerged at the Centre and at the state levels. The results of the Lok Sabha in 1971 brought Smt. Indira Gandhi not only back to power but she became the undisputed leader of the party; her Congress became the real Congress. Personalisation of power remained in force until her assassination and that of Rajiv Gandhi, though signs of collective and consensus politics were seen for a brief time when Rajiv got the power initially or during the brief spell of the non-Congress rule at the Centre. P.V. Narasimha Rao's efforts of revitalising the party and holding organisational elections of the party in 1992 were equally commendable.

During the earlier months of 1992, elections to the PCCs were held. PCCs were composed and preparations were afoot for the Tirupati session of the Congress. Complimenting the Congress family, Rao, the Congress President had said, "The organisational elections have revived our party and given us a new plan. I pay my tribute to the thousands of Congressmen and Congresswomen who made them a success and the hundreds who bore the responsibility of conducting them. The elections have refuted the charge that our party had been converted into self-perpetuating power groups. Regardless of these charges, we live by our own lights. The Indian National Congress is the largest democratic party in the world; it will continue to remain so."[20] This statement of P.V. Narasimha Rao shows that the conducting of the organisational elections was not a smooth affair, but at the same time, the statement also demonstrates that the Congress had tremendous faith in democracy and that it has clung to democratic norms of life.

The elections to the PCCs levels were not smooth. Factionalism was seen almost in each state. The rival groups fought for the office of the party chief in each state. Some of the examples were of factional fighting between Somen Mitra and P.R. Dasmunshi in West Bengal, between Dr. Jagannath Mishra and Siddeshwar Prasad in Bihar, between Shivajiro Patil Nilangekar and Shivajirao Deshmukh in Maharashtra, between Sudhir Ranjan Majumdar and Radhika Ranjan Gupta in Tripura, between Birendra Singh and Dharampal Malik in Haryana. There were factional fightings also in Rajasthan, Himachal Pradesh and Uttar Pradesh.

Power has been a factor responsible for uniting the Congressmen and it has been a factor for bringing about split and conflict among them as well. Factionalism has been a characteristic of Congress ethos. The Tirupati session was attended by about nine hundred and fifty delegates chosen from the numerous PCCs, "The break-up of delegates from different states was; Andhra Pradesh (81), Assam (21), Arunachal Pradesh (9), Bihar (93), Delhi (13), Goa (5), Gujarat (35), Haryana (18), Himachal Pradesh (12), Jammu & Kashmir (13 old members as there were no elections in the state), Karnataka (42), Kerala (36), Madhya Pradesh (74), Maharashtra (72), Manipur (11), Meghalaya (10), Mizoram (7), Nagaland (9), Orissa (43), Punjab (21), Rajasthan (36), Sikkim (5), Tamil Nadu (6), Tripura (9), Uttar Pradesh (144), West Bengal (52). The Union territories of Nicobar, Chandigarh, Dadra & Nagar Haveli, Daman, Diu, Lakshadweep sent two members each while Pondicherry sent 3 members as delegates to the AICC."[21]

At the Tirupati session, 48 candidates were in the race for their positions in the Congress Working Committee. Of these ten were elected. Those who were elected on the Congress Working Committee were Arjun Singh, Jitendra Prasad, A.K. Anthony, Sharad Pawar, R.K. Dhawan, Gulam Nabi Azad, Balram Jakhar, Rajesh Pilot, Ahmed Patel, and Vijay Bhaskar Reddy.

The factional infightings were quite visible even in the election of the Congress Working Committee, reflecting, thus, the factionalism prevailing in the PCCs. The same story got repeated itself at Tirupati as well. Even the geographical representation was not fully covered in the CWC. The Congress President had to ask for the resignation of a section of CWC members so as to reconstitute the CWC in the most representative manner.

The organisational issue had not been resolved so far as the Congress is concerned. Organisational elections had been held after a period of over two decades, but they were neither free nor fair. In fact, voting got intervened at numerous places and at numerous times. The election norms were flouted and the procedures relating to elections were put to mockery. The announcement of the party election by the late Congress president, Rajiv Gandhi, on the eve of centenary celebrations surprised most of the Congress members. Further, amendment in Congress Constitution in July 1990 made the matter worse. The membership drive resulted in duplicity and in bogus membership.[22]

A significant development witnessed during the 1992 organisational elections was that though new faces appeared at the District Congress Committees' levels, yet the leadership at that level largely remained unchanged. The statusquists continued to dominate the PCCs. As many as 30 PCCs chiefs attended the session at the Tirupati. Out of these, 10 have either retained or got back after a very short interval. Thus, "the power brokers could not be removed; lower units could not come close to the power. New entrants remained marginal in strength."[23] Though the democratisation of the Congress could hardly be achieved, yet the Herculean task of holding the organisational election was over. What had been done is that the step had been taken. A beginning has been made.

Objectives of Congress

The Indian National Congress, as the mass political party, had been an organisation not only of mass character but also of mass objectives. The character of the party has dictated the objectives and programmes of the party. Regarding the national character of the Congress, Nehru had said, way back in 1930, "If the Congress is looked upon from the Right and Left points of views, it might be said that there is a small Rightist fringe, a left minority, and a huge intermediate group or groups which approximate to Left-Centre. The Gandhian group would be considered to belong to this intermediate Left-Centre group. Politically the Congress is overwhelmingly Left; socially, it has leftist leanings, but is predominantly Centre. In matters affecting the peasantry it is pro-peasant."[24] Morris-Jones expressed nearly in the same way when he had said, "Congress long ago learned that it had to be an Aristotelian party, a party of the middle way, if it was to survive and succeed. And the Congress political leader became moulded as a man of the Centre, normally permitting himself the luxury of only a shade of emphasis on one side or the other . . . Also the political centre of India and of Congress has on many matters, such as planning, an inherent left bias. Further, Congress like the British Labour party, can perhaps be more easily led from slightly left of its own centre than from slightly right."[25]

A centrist party like the Congress was, by nature, supposed to "articulate the interests of diverse segments and strata of the population, whether they be landless labourers, *adivasis, harijans,* middle classes, peasants, landlords, or urban capitalists."[26]

Within the broad framework of its programme relating to parliamentary democracy, socialistic and secular state, and peaceful co-existence, the Congress passed on from election to election, stressing on some minor issues concerning modernisation and economic development. From the time, the Congress chose to liberate India from the British colonial rule, its tasks increased year after year. Gandhiji saw in the Congress an apostle of national liberation[27] and Nehru, the destiny of future India.[28]

During the years of freedom movement, the Congress devoted itself with the objective of attaining independence for the country. Then, during those years when Gandhiji took over the charge of the Congress, national freedom was its chief aim.[29] And yet, during those years, the Congress had set before itself a long agenda of social and economic reforms. To that extent, the post-independence Congress programme may be considered as an extension of its pre-independent objectives. It will be difficult for anyone to deny that the pre-independence Congress ideology has done nothing less than to provide the foundation to the edifice of post-independence Congress ideology.

Congress like 'democracy', 'socialism', 'secularism', 'non-alignment and international co-operation' appeared in the various election programmes of the Congress but with varying degrees of importance and emphasis. Though a brief study of each such concept has to be made for understanding the premises on which the present programme of the Congress rests, yet the Congress programme of the 1970s and 1980s would be taken into consideration for the purpose of this study.

Congress and Democracy

From its initial years, the Congress had followed the Western type of democracy. Such a democracy was the emphasis on popular participation in the affairs of the society through the system of parliamentary representation based on universal adult franchise exercised through periodic elections. In its early years, the Congress, dominated by the English-educated middle classes, had set its eyes on the representative institutions. During the period covering nearly first twenty years, the Congress made several representations and sent numerous deputations to the authorities in India. The Act of 1892 gave very little by introducing limited elective system, yet it instigated hopes in the Congress for greater and larger representative institution in the coming days. The rise of the militant nationalists and with them the demand of *Swaraj* advanced the cause of representative institutions. The Indian Councils Act, 1909, or what is called the Morley-Minto reforms extended the elective system though partially, and the Congress believed that the eventual establishment of a parliamentary government in India was not a distant dream. The Montegu-Chelmsford reforms or the Government of India Act, 1919, extending the elective system still further and liberalising the legislative councils of India, made the Congress sure that the future India was going to be a parliamentary democracy. Throughout the Gandhian period, though the emphasis was more on nationalism and social reforms than on the form of government, still the Gandhian Congress "generally assumed, and often proclaimed, that the aim of Indian political endeavour was the establishment of a parliamentary form of government." Persuasion is the chief essence of democracy and Gandhiji was one who believed in it. Even if there was a touch of magic in his (Gandhiji's) persuasiveness, there was also considerable proportion of reasoning and reasonableness. The other Congressmen of the Gandhian era saw in democracy not only its political aspect but also its social and economic aspects as well. The Government of India Act, 1935 further extended the scope of parliamentary democracy by introducing full provincial autonomy in the British Indian provinces so as to establish in India a responsible government. The World War II provided the Congress an opportunity in pressurising the British Government to withdraw from India. The end of hostilities and the subsequent Cabinet Mission paved the way for the eventual withdrawal of the Britishers. The Constituent Assembly, formed under the proposals of the Cabinet Mission Plan of 1946, in its 'Objective Resolution' chose political democracy in India based on universal adult franchise. The Constitution of India, accordingly, provided for a parliamentary system in which the executive is responsible to the legislature which is chosen by the people on the basis of universal adult franchise.

Though it is difficult to define democracy, it is more difficult to practise it. Democracy means, at the same time, freedom, peoples' participation in political affairs, periodic elections, universal adult franchise, rule of law, independent press, social and economic equality, decentralisation, constitutionalism and the like. When one emphasises on one of these, one speaks a part of democracy and not the whole of it. The Congress has committed itself to democratic order and hence had/has spoken in favour of the above at one time or the other.

There was a time when with the Congress, democracy meant end of the British rule. "For the vast millions of our countrymen," the Congress Election Manifesto of 1937 declared, "the problem of achieving national independence has become an urgent one, for only independence can give us the power to solve our economic and social problems and end the exploitation of our masses."[30] The election manifesto of 1952[31] recalled the Congress' objective of establishing in India co-operative commonwealth based on equality of opportunity and of political, economic and social rights.[32] In the 1957 election manifesto of the Congress, it pledged itself for democracy.[33] As years passed by, emphasis came to be laid on the social aspect of democracy. The election manifesto of the Congress in 1967 declared, "In proclaiming democracy as our way of life we emphasise not only on its central concept of political equality but also its equalitarian implications in social and economic fields."[34] The thrust of the manifesto was on the combination of democracy and socialism. The 1977-manifesto of the Congress complimented itself for establishing in India a democratic state, saying, "The record of the Indian National Congress in the years of freedom has been steadily to enlarge the power of the people. Democratic institutions have been built and nurtured. In the policy and decision making process, the voice of the people has been made supreme."[35] When the Assemblies Elections were held in some states in 1983, the Congress manifesto affirmed, "We are firmly committed to democracy not because it is an instrument of power but because it is the basic perquisite for the unity and progress of the country."[36] The 1984 Lok Sabha elections saw in the Congress manifesto glimpses of almost all the significance of democracy. It stated, "The Congress (I) is the standard bearer of democratic values." It will:

Preserve the unity and integrity of India.

Defend democracy against all attempts to subvert it through violence and through movements which weaken the confidence of the people.

Uphold the freedom of the press and the independence of the judiciary.

Strengthen the rule of law.

Enhance the capability of our institutions to secure the rights of the weaker sections.

During those days when Nehru held the leadership of the Congress and the country, the form of democracy which evolved can be termed as the consensual democracy. With Nehru and Shastri disappearing from the scene, the consensual democracy gradually gave way to the populist type of democracy, as Mrs. Indira Gandhi came to establish herself as the sole leader of the Congress and the government. The trend of populist democracy continued till her assassination in 1984.

By and large, the Congress, ever since the days of Gandhiji, had become more of a political party of the leaders than of the rank and file. The success of the Congress party, as a ruling political party in the post-independence period, especially until 1964, can be attributed to the towering personality of Nehru who had embodied the Congress in his own person.[37] Describing the Congress as the only party capable of ruling the country, Nehru was convinced that the future of India was dependent on Congress' remaining in power.[38] The Congress, during the Nehruvian years was tolerant towards the opposition because it was well-aware that the latter was weak. Notwithstanding the dominating personality of Nehru, the Congress followed the rules of the consensual democracy both in policies and electioneering by compromising the varying views in the party.

With Indira Gandhi establishing herself as the leader of the country, there appeared a type of democracy which was more personalised and more populist than that of the Nehruvian days. She, like her father, possessed a remarkable capacity of getting people behind her. The slogans like *Garibi Hatao* won her the 1971 elections and 'Government that Works' brought her back to power in 1980. Her 20-Point Programme and the other populist measures introduced a kind of democracy in which it was reduced to competitive electoral victory. Within the sphere of sharing power, Mrs. Gandhi, unlike her father, did not allow any opposition. Thus, the attempts were made to use Article 356 against the non-Congress ministries in the states. Within the party, no leader or group of leaders was allowed to challenge the authority of Mrs. Gandhi. The consensual democracy gave way to patrimonial democracy during the days of Mrs. Gandhi. The Congress was reduced to one-man's show as was the government itself.

Indeed, the conditions as exist in the country in Rajiv Gandhi's times were different than those which existed in Mrs. Indira Gandhi's times. Rao too believed in consensual democracy partly because of his compulsion and largely because of choice and long training. But his unrelenting attitude towards some of the partymen raised suspicion on his democratic temper. Similar was his treatment with Non-Congress Governments in states and non-confirmists within the party.

Congress and Socialism

Another characteristic feature of the Congress' programme, basically in economic field, can be termed in one word as socialism. Gandhiji, after having given the Congress the character of a mass party, had paved the way for the economic programme of the Congress. If then the eradication of poverty, rural upliftment, welfare of the backward classes had figured in Congress programme, it is not to say that Gandhiji was a Marxist or that the Congress believed in Marxist ideology. As the Congress was concerned primarily with the overthrow of the British rule in India, it has not addressed itself to any particular economic ideology, though it was aware of the rural backwardness, industrial neglect and poverty of the Indians. It was in the Karachi Congress session of 1931 that the Congress felt that the welfare of the people demanded economic reforms in the society. By and large, the Congress remained a political party of the Centre or at the most, the party of the left or the Centre.

Before one attempts to examine the socialistic policies of the Congress, it is important to state that those policies under the leadership of Nehru, Mrs. Indira Gandhi and Rajiv Gandhi had not the same flavour of socialism. Nehru was temperamentally, if not ideologically, a socialist. Mrs. Indira Gandhi too supported socialism, but more with a view to woo the poorer sections of the Indian society. Her attempts to derecognise the princes and thereby abolish privy purses, bank nationalisation, progressive take over of export and import trade, *Garibi Hatao* campaign, 20-points programme, etc., hardly produced socialism. Rajiv Gandhi's commitment to socialism required time, but it was one in which 'everyone must get richer.'

The Congress' acceptance of the type of socialism was, and is, subject to the taking of country towards the type of equality necessary in a democracy. In fact, democracy could not be substantial without socialism nor could socialism be real without democracy. But to make both of them real what was necessary, said Indira Gandhi, was not mere slogans but a determination to work hard and make sacrifices. The Congress under the leadership of Rajiv Gandhi retained the same policies.

The Congress' concept of socialism lacks the doctrinaire fervour. It was "workable via media between capitalism and socialism which had been free from defects of either and also had been in accordance with the genius of the people." Now, socialism in Congress Programme became a thing of the past and capitalism—a proposed and accepted agenda for the future.

Social Creed of the Congress

The traditional Indian society suffered from various social evils as it came into the British contact during the 18th-19th centuries. The issue of social reforms weighed much with the socio-religious reform movements in the 19th century. The Brahmo Samaj movement, the Arya Samaj movement, the Prarthana Samaj spirit, and the ideals of the Ramakrishna Mission and the Theosophical Society aimed at social and cultural revival. In the social sphere, there began awareness and subsequent movements of caste reform or caste abolition, equal rights for women, campaign against child marriage and a ban on widow remarriage, a crusade against social and legal inequalities. The social and religious movements and the leaders leading such movements were convinced that the new Indian society could "politically, culturally, and economically develop only on the basis of liberal principles such as the recognition of individual liberty, freedom of unfettered expression of human personality, and social equality."

The early Congress, mostly of the moderate era, sought to demand social reforms along with the political reforms under the support of the British rule. The extremist-nationalist leaders preferred political *swaraj* to the reforms in the Indian society. The Gandhian Congress had a blend of both the political *swaraj* and social reforms together during 1920—1947.

The independent India found itself amidst numerous social problems particularly the communal-religious, lingual and those others relating to the conditions of Scheduled Castes, Scheduled Tribes, women and the youth. The social objectives of the Congress, thus, relate to the solution of these social problems (the Congress) pledges to wipe out untouchability and promises to give special attention to educational and economic interest of Harijans, tribals and backward classes. It promises to give protection to linguistic, religious and cultural minorities and to provide facilities for education in the mother tongue.'

Congress and the Foreign Policy

Even during the days of dependence, the Congress was able to formulate and articulate its views on the foreign affairs mostly due to the efforts of Jawaharlal Nehru. Nehru was not only the chief exponent of the Congress foreign policy but also the ambassador at large of the Indian National Congress. "He was the first of the important Indian leaders who placed India on the world map by taking a keen interest in the world affairs at large and broadened the Indian mind by posing the local problem in a world setting." "His vision went beyond his own nation," Saleem Kidwai writes, "and embraced the entire human race. By virtue of being the Prime Minister of India, the largest democracy in the world, Nehru was able to make a significant contribution to the theory and practice of international affairs."

The Congress foreign policy, shaped and practised largely by Nehru, the later Prime Ministers only following him, can be summed up in Nehru's version, "In the sphere of foreign relations India will follow an independent policy, keeping away from the power politics of groups aligned against one another. She will uphold the principle of freedom for dependent people and will oppose racial discrimination wherever it may occur. She will work with other peace-loving nations for international co-operation and goodwill without exploitation of one nation by another.' 'It is an independent policy in the sense that it is determined solely by factors which influence India's national and international interests. It is a non-aligned policy in the sense that it has no link with any power bloc. It is not escapism in the sense that it attempts to build a world free of wars. It is not isolationism in the sense that it endeavours utmost participation in the world's affairs and a spirit of co-operation and goodwill among various nations of the world. It is a policy which builds a world of peace, co-operation and goodwill, a world without wars, without fears and without exploitation.

Nehru had firmly laid down the foundations of Congress' as well as India's foreign policy which, in one word, can be termed as 'non-alignment'. It is non-alignment against the very concept of war and in favour of peace. It is non-alignment against imperialism and racial discrimination as well and in favour of a peaceful, mutually-dependent and free world.

A glance of the various election manifestoes of the Congress too express the fundamentals of India's foreign policy.

The 1971-election manifesto of the Congress states, 'The Congress pledged to uphold the principles of non-alignment and freedom from military blocs . . . . the

Congress would continue to develop and consolidate friendly relations with all countries and more especially with her neighbours.' The 1977-election manifesto of the Congress stated that the Congress "will continue the policy of non-alignment, which has kept India out of military blocs, preserved her independence and integrity and has allowed her to judge international issues on their merits. This policy, which has been reaffirmed by the Fifth Summit of Non-aligned Countries, has made a significant contribution to the cause of world peace, progress and stability." The 1980-election manifesto of the Congress stated, "On the basis of sovereign equality, mutual respect and non-interference in internal affairs, Congress will maintain and strengthen friendly relations with all countries. Congress will . . . . adhere firmly to the policy of Jawaharlal Nehru." The 1984-election manifesto of the Congress reiterates its firm resolve to pursue "the policy of non-alignment, peace, co-operation and friendship."

Thus, the basic theories of the Congress foreign policy, as formulated by Jawaharlal Nehru, had been non-alignment, peace, enlightened self-interest and maintaining friendly relations with all nations of the world.

Over the years, the Congress foreign policy has remained the same as it was during the times of Jawaharlal Nehru. The vital characteristic of the foreign policy of the Congress can be summed up as:

(i) The Congress is opposed to the use of force in international relations;
(ii) It is opposed to the interference in the internal affairs of sovereign states;
(iii) It favours total elimination of nuclear weapons as the only sure guarantee against their use;
(iv) It stands firmly for maintaining friendly relations with all countries of the world based on mutuality of interest and Panchsheel;
(v) It strives to improve relations with India's neighbours, especially Pakistan, China, Nepal, Bhutan, Bangladesh, Sri Lanka and Myanmar;
(vi) It believes that any discrimination on grounds of race is an anathema and is against all human values, feeling all forms of apartheid against world opinion and the UNO resolutions;
(vii) It wishes to strengthen the efforts of the UNO in maintaining world peace and security; and
(viii) It demands India to play a more dynamic, useful, positive and unifying role in international affairs, particularly in narrowing the gap between the developed and the developing countries and in ensuring enduring peace and equitably distributed prosperity in the world.

References

1. Constitution of the Indian National Congress as adopted in 1967.
2. Article IX of the Constitution of Indian National Congress.
3. *Ibid.*, Article X.
4. Article XI (C) of the Constitution of Indian National Congress.
5. Article XI (D) of the Constitution of Indian National Congress.
6. Kochanek, n. 19, p. 451.
7. Article XVIII (H) of the Constitution of Indian National Congress.
8. Article XVIII (i) of the Constitution of Indian National Congress.
9. Article XIX (C) of the Constitution of Indian National Congress.

10. Article XIX (F) of the Constitution of Indian National Congress.
11. Article XXVI (A) of the Constitution of Indian National Congress.
12. Article XXVI (B) of the Constitution of Indian National Congress.
13. See V.R. Rao, *Development of the Congress Constitution,* New Delhi, AICC, 1958, p. 115.
14. K. Hanumanthayya, *Report of the Congress Constitution,* New Delhi, AICC, 1960, p. 26.
15. *Report of the General Secretary, January-December 1964,* New Delhi, AICC, 1965, pp. 42-43.
16. Weiner, n. 2, pp. 2-3.
17. Zareer Masani, *Indira Gandhi, A Biography,* New York, Thomas Crowell, 1976, pp. 142-79.
18. W.H. Morris-Jones, "Dominance and Dissent: Their Interrelations in the Indian Party System", in Rodney Barker (ed.), *Studies in Opposition,* London, The Macmillan Press Ltd., 1971, p. 294.
19. *Ibid.,* p. 297.
20. Presidential address, Tirupati Plenary Session, AICC, 1992, p. 1.
21. List of Delegates released by AICC and quoted in Ramesh Kumar's Organisational Elections : An Assessment, *Link,* May 17, 1992, p. 12.
22. *Ibid.,* p. 13.
23. *Ibid.*
24. Jawaharlal Nehru, *The Unity of India: Collected Writings—1937-40,* London, Lindsay Drumond, 1948, pp. 121-22.
25. W.H. Morris-Jones, *The Government and Politics of India,* Bombay, B.I. Publications, 1974, p. 172.
26. V.M. Sirsikar and L. Fernandes, *Indian Political Parties,* Meerut, Meenakshi Prakashan, 1984, p. 162.
27. Mahatma Gandhi, *India of My Dreams,* Bombay: Kitab Mahal, 1956, p. 28.
28. "The Congress is the Country and the Country is the Congress," Quoted by Morris-Jones, n. 2, p. 89.
29. See K.P. Karunakaran, "Obsolete Ideologies", *Seminar,* Vol. 124, December 1969, pp. 23-24.
30. See A.M. Zaidi (ed.), *Promises to Keep: A Study of the Election Manifestos of Indian National Congress 1937-85,* New Delhi, Indian Institute of Applied Political Research, 1986, p. 17.
31. See, *Ibid.* p. 25. Also see the Congress Manifesto of 1945-46.
32. *Ibid.,* p. 34. See Congress Election Manifesto of 1952.
33. *Ibid.,* p. 48. See Congress Election Manifesto of 1957.
34. *Ibid.,* p. 80, See Congress Election Manifesto of 1967.
35. *Ibid.,* p. 163, See Congress Election Manifesto of 1980.
36. See, *Ibid.,* p. 210. Also see Congress Election Manifesto of 1984.
37. Bhagwan D. Dua, "Indian Congress Dominance Revisited", in Paul R. Brass and Francis Robinson (eds.), *The Indian National Congress and Indian Society, 1885-1985,* Delhi, Chanakya Publications, 1987, p. 357.
38. Lucian W. Pye, "Party Systems and National Development in Asia", in Joseph LaPalombara and Myron Weiner (eds.), *Political Parties and Political Development,* New Jersey, Princeton University Press, 1969, pp. 384-85.

26

Congress and Rajiv Gandhi

Economic Developments

India, over the years, has achieved a distinguished position in different sectors of our economy. In 1964, Indian economy recorded a marked growth in the GNP and a slow-down in the rate of inflation. Under the leadership of Rajiv Gandhi, the nation entered an era with greater flexibility to face new challenges. His government concentrated on urgent tasks on the economic front not only to consolidate the gains of the period that ended but also to set the pace of development in the seventh 5-year plan, commencing from 1 April, 1985.

The new government showed commitment in increasing the economic resources and providing priority in handling policy matters. Rajiv Gandhi came out in support of boosting economy in the field of electronics, telecommunications and computers.

In regard to government policy about taxation and duties, Rajiv Gandhi clarified that the government was looking at them for quite some time. It came out with a fully new package for the electronics industry.

Rajiv Gandhi's concern has all along been about the time and speed to put the nation on the track of development. In a speech, he addressed by saying, "You will find this government moving faster than you are moving. The problem will not be with government constraints or government restrictions or the time taken by it." These were not mere assurances because they reflected a positive and dynamic approach to increase the pace of development. The declaration of the prime minister was followed by a programme of quick actions.

Another area which attracted his attention is telecommunication system. Ever since the beginning of his taking over as the head of the government he pointed out, "We have been looking at this sector and I think in the coming policies . . . you will find that we tried within our resource-constraint to do something for telecommunications. We are already looking at the licensing policy. It will take some time to get to you. But on most of it, action has been taken pre-empting your thoughts."

In a policy statement, the Prime Minister proposed in March 1985 a new strategy for technology upgradation saying that the government would work on certain areas leaving others to the private sector. He said that the government would come up with a programme for the purpose.

Rajiv Gandhi always echoed confidence in India's potentiality to move ahead quite rapidly. He always advised the concerned people in the sphere of Indian economy not only to understand India better but to understand Indian systems, people, policies and will to learn from the people and to learn to do better.

The Prime Minister concentrated on the preparation of seventh Five-Year Plan with a promise of establishing a strong foundation for future growth. The basic trust at the time of preparation of the plan was for growth with equality and social justice, which had always been the basis of development strategy since independence.

Another sector has been the contribution of foreign business participation in the national development. Referring to the question of foreign participation, the Prime Minister added:

> This is a very difficult question because there are so many areas that we have opened up. But without spending time on the non-essential areas, really the basic infrastructure areas are where we need most help, which is energy, whether it is power of fossil energy, communications and transport and agriculture, agricultural technology right from the development of biotechnology required for seeds to other larger technologies required for maximum output in production. These are the really core areas where we look for more help.

A major step in the realisation of socialist path was an effective participation of workers in the management of factories. Rajiv Gandhi had taken various steps for workers' participation in the organised sector of our economy. Apart from it, a blueprint was also prepared to see that the workers, in the course of time, take over managerial functions in big institutions. In addition, provisions were also made for ensuring safety of workers. The Bhopal tragedy was a big eye-opener in this regard. The question of safety of workers needed multidimensional measures to ensure that the tragedies of this nature were averted. The Prime Minister, emphasising the need for safety measures, said:

> On our part, we are taking steps to see that all safety rules and regulations are fully enforced. Everyone should know where the danger is likely to arise and how they can face it and guard themselves against the danger.

The conditions of the bonded labour were most distressing. They were virtually living like slaves and denied all opportunities of their development. Some voluntary organisations even tried to exploit their conditions in order to get political wealth of it. They least bothered to improve their conditions. In spite of various measures taken by the government, the people were still suffering in the web of bonded labour. Rajiv Gandhi expressed his deep anguish over their plight and said:

> Some steps have been taken to that end to free the bonded labour, but now we have to ensure that after their freedom they are able to move ahead on their own, by providing them with resources through banks or otherwise. It is not enough that the bonds are freed. They must be rehabilitated and equipped to make progress.

The Government of India had taken many steps and there was a comprehensive plan of action connecting this programme with education, planning and other social reforms. The mass media had come out to play its role in educating people. These steps had been taken at the initiative of the Prime Minister so that our country is in a position to answer the growing needs of our society.

India is generally categorised as one of richest countries in terms of its natural resources. The capacity of India to exploit these resources is the essence of our economic development.

Rajiv Gandhi's insight into the problem, his keenness to look into the minutest aspects and his ability to adjust in every situation has prompted him not to leave the sources unexploited. Speaking on use of water resources and environmental protection he said:

> We somehow do not seem to feel that water is a resource and that not having water can be a problem. May be we get it too easily. But this is not going to last for too long. Our demands are going to increase. We must ensure that weather-patterns are not changed because of cutting of forests, because of our changing the whole geography of a region. We must see that all the water is collected, is monitored, is used at every stage. We have to see how we can modify our agriculture to suit the water that is available. It is not necessary to grow rice in the driest areas of the country. We have to adjust our cropping patterns, the seasons in which we can use the water. Finally we have to see how we can re-use the water.

It is an established fact that aimless development leads nowhere. Development has to be accompanied by equity and social justice and by removal of social barriers that hindered the growth of the weak and the poor. Rajiv Gandhi had often pointed out that equity, social justice and removal of social barriers were the bases of socialism. The draft Seventh plan had adequately reflected these features. The anti-poverty schemes, which form the core of the 20-Point Programme, had been expanded and restructured to give maximum assistance to those who were below the poverty line.

Socio-cultural Aspects of Development

The modern social scientists have endeavoured to look into the concept of development in the present-day changing world. Such an outlook is not only apposite for the development of the economic sector but is also equally important for meaningful social transformation, which is one of the most difficult tasks. The change envisages a challenge to the old attitude and introduces new ones, for instance, the idea of equality was gaining hold in India at a time when the old hierarchies of society certified groups were on a decline. The element of induction of technology, social mobility to urbanisation, industrialisation, etc., have posed new challenge to be faced with and certain caution and care.

The most crucial thing is to plan and manage the development of diverse sections of our society with an element of justice and equality. This task at the outset needs restructuring and proper functioning of required institutions. Being conscious of this fact, Rajiv Gandhi had pointed out on 19 March, 1985:

> We are today a democracy because we have established institutions, we have nurtured these institutions and we have strengthened them. And if our society is to progress, it can only progress on the basis of strong institutions. None of them trying to pull down the other but each of them trying to build up the other institution.

He also had made it clear that democracy would survive if there was social justice.

Progress without social justice carries no weight. Indian society as a whole must be confident of getting it as a means of their progress and development.

Youth Welfare

In terms of social engineering, there is great responsibility on the shoulders of the youth. The Prime Minister himself being young had become a dynamic force to inspire the younger generation to help transform our society into a vibrant and meaningful institution of change. He had been drawing the attention of the youth towards the existing global situation, tensions within the society and the responsibility of the youth to strengthen unity and integrity of India by rising above considerations of caste, religion, regional and linguistic differences.

He cautioned the youth:

> India has gone through its first phase of development, now we start the second phase. We must evaluate what we have achieved. We must identify the mistakes we have made, because it is only then that we can correct them and we can move ahead. We have to build the strength of our youth. In present day India, almost 71 per cent of our population is below 35. India is a young country and India looks ahead to the next century. If we work from today towards making India a progressive and strong country we shall be ready in the next 10 or 15 years. We have to build not just in the traditional ways in which we have been building. They have kept us occupied in procedures, tied us to very heavy overheads, which we cannot afford to carry any more.

It may be easy to fix targets but these targets, particularly in the areas of social change are hard to realise. The realisation necessitates planned and joint efforts. The most noteworthy element in present day effort is that the youthful Prime Minister has prepared a complete blue-print of a balanced and phased programme of social development. There is no doubt that a disciplined nation can accelerate the pace of development and achieve desired results.

Child Welfare

Another area that needed attention was child welfare. The children must be provided with excellent conditions for development of their personality and character. Ignoring the care of children would mean ignoring the future of India.

On an occasion, Rajiv Gandhi expressing serious concern about child labour said:

> Child labour is another very serious area for us to consider and it is not something that we can just pretend, does not exist or legislate away. Again the economic standing, the social standing has to be such that we come out of this as fast as possible. And during that period we should try and see what we can do to make it easiest for the children to see that they get education, they get proper care, they are not exploited and they are not used in areas which spoil their eyesights, their limbs or make them handicapped in any way.

Women's Contribution to Society

For building a new India, the women have to play a vital role in the society. Rajiv

Gandhi while inaugurating the Conference of Non-aligned and other developing countries on the 'Role of Women in Development,' on 10 April 1985 had drawn the attention of the people towards this crucial point by saying:

> The role of women in developing countries is very crucial to the rate at which a country develops and in many ways is an indicator as to how well the country is developing.

He pleaded that Indian people had a tradition of waging war against imperialism, colonialism, racism or in other words against all forms of discrimination and domination. India had always stood for equitable social and economic order and the fight for the rights of women forms a part of it. On the role of women, he said:

> Women are the social conscience of a country. They hold our societies together. In developing countries women have been active in all fields and specially they have risen to prominent places in the political field. But, unfortunately, at the lower level we have not been able to give them enough freedom of movement, enough help to rise above the discriminations that they are faced with which have built up over thousands of years of a male-dominated society.

Rajiv Gandhi while praising women's contribution to society further added:

> Women's contribution to humanity throughout history today, whether it is in the work place, in society or in home, has been no less than anybody else's. Still today, women do not get adequate opportunity in education, in employment. We realise that one of the key factors is education. And as a first step, we have made education free for girls upto the High School stage in India. We will take other such steps to see that women are able to develop in India. In India, women will be equal partners in building our nation.
>
> As a group women are the largest underprivileged group in the world. And we must fight to remove this disparity. But it is really at the grassroots, at the daily-level that the discrimination must be removed. It is the fight up to lower rung of the ladder that has to be made easier and we hope that this conference will contribute towards this struggle.

Education Policy

Education plays an important part in national development. Since Independence, education got priority in our various developmental programmes. However, the system of education could not undergo a drastic change. Rajiv Gandhi lost no opportunity to address himself to this issue. In the Convocation address at Lucknow University on 23 March 1985, he spoke on different aspects of education and pointed out that the government was busy in reviewing the educational system in the country.

Highlighting the role of teachers, he emphasised that excellence in education would originate from the teachers. If we were in a position to achieve excellence, most of our problems could be solved. Education must be reoriented to suit the growing needs of our society. This is possible by developing skills so that India could emerge as a highly developed nation.

On 18 April 1985, the Parliament was informed that the new Education Policy had been formulated. The new policy aimed at encouraging positive values, strengthening national integration, facilitating study of science and technology, establishing a connection between education and employment, promoting spirit of cooperation and sense of equality and equity as a way of life. The policy was also to contemplate that adult education was taken up as a people's movement.

Education, for Rajiv Gandhi, was a continuous process of understanding. It was a question of attitude, a way of thinking. The new education policy envisaged planning for a realistic vocational education as a part of higher education. Vocationalisation should be viewed in a broader perspective with its linkages. In his address to the Conference of the State Education Ministers on 29 August 1985, Rajiv Gandhi said:

> You have raised the question of finances. I have been discussing this point with the Planning Commission and I am very glad to be able to tell you that we have managed to squeeze out Rs. 1,500 crore over and above what was allocated originally for human resource development. A very large chunk of this, I am sure, will go to education.

Issues relating to literacy and skill improvement, brain drain, need for excellence, national and moral values, developing an Indian mind, further utilisation of funds, etc., had been taken up by Rajiv Gandhi as question of national importance. A national debate on the role of education was never taken up so seriously before as it was done during this period. The new Education Policy linked education with growth and development. There was emphasis on vocationalisation, technical skills, computers, new technology, manpower planning and delinking of degrees from jobs. It envisaged education as an integral part of nation's drive towards economic modernisation and industrialisation, rather than as an instrument for achieving mere social cohesion. The apparent objective seemed to be taking education as an 'economic investment'.

It was essential to explore new resources of revenue. The industry and the professional bodies who used trained manpower coming from higher education must be made to share a part of the burden on higher education. The industry should also be involved in framing and conducting vocational courses and there should be tax concessions on contribution to education as in the United States.

Another reforms should have been in the area of expansion of higher education. There had been a tremendous growth in higher education. In 1950-51, the number of students attending 695 colleges affiliated to 27 universities was 3.62 lakh. In 1983-84, the number of students had gone up to 33.6 lakh while the number of colleges and universities increased to 5,246 and 140 respectively.

The higher education scenario presents a weak system, variation of standards, infiltration of politics, stream of unemployed graduates and many more. The reforms needed should be linked with improved mechanism and sense of planning where centre and states should have joint education policy. According to an UNESCO survey of developing nations in Asia and the Pacific region, India had the lowest rate of literacy growth at that time which was similar to countries like Afghanistan, Bangladesh and Pakistan. On the other hand, countries like Korea, Singapore and even Maldives had attained a literacy rate of 80 per cent or more than that. The literacy rate since independence had definitely improved but the gaps in regard to male and female education, rural-urban high-low cost education have to be carefully planned. Studies and related researches had shown that a nexus was existing between illiteracy on the one hand and the problems of poverty, widespread epidemic and communicable diseases, malnutrition of children, low life expectancy and low economic earnings on the other. Rajiv Gandhi had rightly taken up education in the context of the supportive and facilitative role education can play to help fulfil the basic needs of our people.

Eradication of Poverty

One of the major areas of concern for Rajiv Gandhi had been the problem of poverty. He specifically mentioned in his address to the Special Session of the ILO in Geneva on 17 June 1985:

> Poverty alleviation is the core of our strategy for development. It is not only a function of growth but also requires conscious state intervention. But in the ultimate analysis, it is faster growth that provides us the means of intervention. We have been able to mount anti-poverty programmes precisely because we had struggled hard to build the foundation of a self-reliant and dynamic economy. Workers in India can look forward to greater opportunities of contributing to progress and sharing in it. We are creating a policy environment conducive to faster growth, to the infusion of modern technology and to higher productivity. This has been a process of evolution. Policy changes were initiated in the early eighties. We are integrating them in a framework consistent with our philosophy of planning. And we are accelerating their pace to galvanise the vast productive forces of our society for the welfare of the poorest sections.

The issue of eradication of poverty was taken up by the Congress Party on a war footing during the Prime Ministership of Mrs. Indira Gandhi. Rajiv Gandhi had reaffirmed that commitment to eliminate poverty. This question was raised by the Congress during the centenary celebrations. While moving the resolution, it had been pointed out that there would be no deviation from the socialistic policies and the public sector would be further strengthened.

The anti-poverty programme was the kingpin of Seventh Plan. Spelling out the development strategy it was pointed out that modern agriculture would be taken to all agro-climate zones and to all strata of population. The 20-point programme had been implemented with improved efficiency and utmost dedication. Inviting the Congressmen to participate in developmental efforts, the resolution affirmed that the 20-point programme was a challenge to the administrator and the political worker alike. The resolution said that the country had completed the first phase of industrial revolution but it would have to be consolidated and give a further momentum with a view to eradicating poverty.

27

Administrative Reforms during Rajiv Administration

The credibility of government, particularly in a democratic set up, depends largely on two organised sectors, the civil service and the party in power. India is the largest democracy in the world. The complex and delicate issues are to be tackled largely by the government and the party in power with the cooperation of the people. Over the years, in spite of satisfactory rate of progress in different walks of life, much remains to be done.

Rajiv Gandhi was conscious of his responsibility and had been tonning up administration and the party. The administration had to act as an instrument of change in the society according to the wishes of the people reflected through their representatives in the legislature. In his first broadcast to the nation, Rajiv Gandhi had spelt out priorities which the new Government would give. He said:

> Administrative reforms are crucial for social and economic transformation. It is for this reason that I decided to take under my own charge the Department of Personnel and Administrative Reforms. A full scale review of administrative organisation, policies and procedures is in progress. I have asked that the decision-making processes should be decentralised along with enforcement of accountability. Rules and procedures will be drastically simplified to speed up decision-making. Results will take precedence over procedures.
>
> I have directed all concerned agencies to ensure that citizens get prompt and courteous service from government departments and agencies. An effective machinery for redressal of public grievances will be set up in offices with large public dealings. Action will be taken to raise the morale of public service. We shall prevent extraneous interference in the normal functioning of public service. We must create a new administrative culture for service of the masses. Training of civil servants of all categories will be restructured to develop competence and commitment to the basic values of our society.

An administration not fully committed to the welfare of the people would contribute nothing either to solve the problems or to enhance the credibility of the government in public. Within a short span of time. Rajiv Gandhi had introduced far reaching changes in the administration. He had created a full ministry of Science and Technology and had also implemented Sarin Committee's recommendations about bifurcation of the department of Posts and Telegraph. A new ministry of Environment and Forest had also been created with two separate departments, one for Environment and the other for Forests and Wildlife.

These efforts were aimed at closer cooperation between scientific research and development and also for upgradation of technology for better utilisation of non-conventional sources of energy. Departmental reorganisation in the Defence Ministry has also been affected. Department of Defence, Department of Defence Production and Supplies, and Department of Defence Research and Development have been created.

Rajiv Gandhi had very clear views regarding the role of administration. He said:

> India has faced a number of challenges and has shown that the system, when clothed with authority and made accountable, can produce as good results as anywhere else in the world. Administration is the point where government meets the people. A spirit of friendliness and courtesy must permeate the civil services.
>
> We have been working on several projects but they have yet to be implemented. We really have no time. All we have been able to accomplish is to set the bureaucracy moving and working. The ministries also are at their jobs seriously attending to different portfolios and problems.

On 4 July 1985 the Prime Minister had said that the government was set on fighting corruption with all the strength it could muster. He told a joint conference of the CBI and state anti-corruption officers that they should concentrate on big shots and see that they were punished. The basic strategy in fighting corruption was: prevention, proper detection and seeing that the proper punishment was awarded where due.

He further stressed the need for training in service. He was in favour of a system where at least once a year, everyone got together at all levels so that there was interaction and the difficulties faced in one region, the methods worked out to solve the problems, could be fed to others. He also stressed the need for refresher courses once a year for about a week where these exchanges could take place.

Rajiv Gandhi is believed to have devoted a good deal of time and thought to finalise 101-page Presidential order defining the composition and functions of various union ministries and departments. An effort had been made of combining accountability with autonomy.

Rajiv Gandhi deserves full credit for taking a prompt initiative in order to curb defection malpractices that had reduced Indian politics to a farce—from value-based to money-based. It is no more a secret that like any other saleable commodity, the price tag had got attached to those legislators who were willing to change sides.

Anti-Defection Bill provided the first major breakthrough in checking the country's political corruption that has been growing systematically ever since *Aya Rams* and *Gaya Rams* emerged as new villains of Indian politics.

Intervening in the debate on Anti-Defection Bill, Rajiv Gandhi said in the Lok Sabha on January 30, 1985:

> Anti-Defection Bill has been pending for a very long time. I think it was first mentioned almost seven years ago. We have taken it up as one of our first major tasks because we felt that this is an area where public life needs cleaning up. As

> rightly promised during the debate on the Presidential address, our government has the political will to implement what we promise. We also have promised that we will carry the opposition with us. And I am happy to say that we carried almost all the opposition with us. There are one or two exceptions.

Intervening in another debate on Anti-Defection Bill, Prime Minister had said on the following day in Rajya Sabha: 'Yesterday, on the 30th January, we had all gone to Gandhiji's Samadhi to pay our respects and homage. On Gandhiji's Samadhi in very large letters are written what Gandhiji called seven social sins. This Bills cover new ground in our country's history. There may be shortcomings in this. There will still be differences of opinion. But after spending a long time with leaders from all sections of both Houses we have produced a paper which, I think, meets the requirements of every opinion within these two Houses. The Bill for the first time recognises a political party as an entity. It recognises the factual position on the ground that you win your seat on the ticket of a political party.

On 14 October 1985, while speaking at the India League, London, the Prime Minister said:

> The Congress is to Indian politics what the Ganga is to our cultural mainstream. It has attracted the allegiance of all religions and all economic classes. The existence of a mass part like the Congress gave the Indian Republic its broad base, its reach and its durability. I can tell you that India and Congress will ensure that the country moves ahead faster and faster to fulfil the programmes of alleviation of poverty, speedier economic growth and modernisation of technology.

Rajiv Gandhi was critical of lack of discipline in his partymen and speaking on the occasion of the Congress Centenary Celebrations in Bombay, he warned:

> We obey no discipline, no rule, follow no principle of public morality, display no sense of social awareness, show no concern for the public welfare. Corruption is not only tolerated but even regarded as the hallmark of leadership. The brokers of power and influence, who dispense patronage to convert a mass movement into a feudal oligarchy, are reducing the Congress organisation to a shell from which the spirit of sacrifice has been emptied.

Rajiv Gandhi was determined to make Congress effective in playing its role to make India vibrant, strong and dynamic in all spheres. He had the political will to bring India to the 21st century.

28

Congress and P.V. Narasimha Rao

Leadership and the Dynamic Consensus

It was No. 10 Janapath, P.V. Narasimha Rao was waiting to see Rajiv Gandhi after Parliament had been dissolved and elections to the Lok Sabha announced on March 13, 1991 following the withdrawal of Congress support to Chandra Shekhar's Government. Meanwhile, it was not known what plans Mr. Rajiv Gandhi had at that time for Mr. Rao. It was believed he would not contest the Lok Sabha election. But that was not to be. The first phase of elections showed that the Congress fared badly in Uttar Pradesh and Bihar. As P.V. was to say later, the forces responsible for the assassination of Mr. Gandhi might have felt threatened by the prospect of his return to power. The gruesome assassination was a great personal shock for Mr. Rao, and a great personal loss.

The leadership mantle ultimately fell on Mr. Rao. He was elected the Congress party president by Working Committee on May 29, 1991. Mr. Rao told the Working Committee soon after his election as party president that the stakes were high for the country. "What India needs most of all now is a strong and stable government that can protect the unity of the present and nourish the vision of the future."[1] As for the National Front, he saw it as an "opportunistic conglomeration" that had accepted casteism as its creed for political ends.

After the electoral results were announced in which the Congress party failed to secure a clear majority, and after he was elected leader of the Congress Parliamentary Party and then became the Prime Minister on June 21, 1991, he sought the cooperation of all the parties. In response to the vote of confidence he was asked to take within 30 days of assuming office, Mr. Rao said that "my style of functioning is to be one of consensus . . . I will not ride roughshod, the Congress party would not ride roughshod over others and we would like to create areas of agreement".[2]

The four major and difficult issues that confronted Mr. Rao as the Prime Minister were to ensure a stable government though his party did not have a majority, to restore the national economy, normalise the situation in the strife-torn border states of Punjab, Assam and Kashmir and to set the course of foreign policy in the new radically changed international situation.

The success that P.V. had achieved at the Centre as the Prime Minister, unlike the frustrations he underwent as the Chief Minister of Andhra Pradesh two decades earlier was due to various factors. As has been shown by Prof. Prasanna Kumar,[3] the four political factors of region, caste, faction and party had worked against Mr. Rao in the state. The same factors operating at the national level had helped to sustain him as the Prime Minister.

At the state level, in the leadership changes in Andhra Pradesh, Karnataka and Maharashtra, P.V. retained the decisive initiative in his hands as the various factions in the state party units failed to agree on the new leaders. So what was Mr. Narasimha Rao's weakness at the state level, in not having his own groups, became his strength at the Centre.

Beyond these factors, leadership at the national level calls for other attributes. These can be identified as charisma or the lack of it, the ability to build a consensus around one's political status a grasp of the international situation and its bearing on domestic developments. Charisma is another factor which is difficult to define. It is some kind of a personal magnetism that a leader exerts over his supporters which even renders them blind to all his faults. Jawaharlal Nehru and Indira Gandhi were charismatic personalities. Mr. Narasimha Rao cannot by any stretch of the imagination said to be a charismatic personality. He has admitted as much often, as at Tirupati, at Bombay and in other places as when he said he was not Nehru or Indira Gandhi, but was there to follow their inspiration.

For Mr. Rao, the ideological confusion and political antagonism within the rival camp appeared to provide convenient ground to push through his objectives. First he obtained the support of the BJP to major economic liberalisations in 1991, the BJP abstained in crucial votes in the Lok Sabha on motions against the Government. He told Parliament that there was no question of jettisoning the public sector. He asserted quoting Nehru, that the public sector was interested even originally on becoming efficient and profit-making and that it was all that was being emphasised now.

Apart from the conceptualisation of 'continuity in charge' as the mainstay of Congress policies, P.V. had taken the precaution to slow the pace of reforms while sticking to the basic concept of the policies. For example, when there was strong opposition from the farmers' lobby, including in his party, to the withdrawal of fertiliser subsidy, he first formed a committee to decide the extent of the cut to be imposed and consequent increase in the prices of fertilisers to be permitted.

Later, when his government faced a grave challenge on the motion of thanks to the President's address, at the commencing of the Budget Session in March 1992 with the BJP and all other opposition parties seemingly coming together, Mr. Rao as a matter of caution, took active interest in seeking the support of a section of the Telugu Desam party which broke away from the parent organisation.

An ideological conflict between the Congress and the BJP on the communal issue was inevitable from then on. The Congress leaders knew that the BJP formed the governments in the four northern states of Uttar Pradesh, Madhya Pradesh, Rajasthan and Himachal Pradesh on the strength of its parochial movement to build the Ram Temple at the disputed Babri Masjid.

Despite his strong ideological differences with the BJP, Mr. Rao went on to settle the Ayodhya dispute amicably through negotiations.

The Left parties and other non-BJP opposition rallied round the Congress as the RSS and VHP were banned and the BJP governments of Madhya Pradesh, Himachal Pradesh and Rajasthan were dismissed and the three state assemblies were also dissolved. The BJP moved a no-confidence motion against the government in Parliament which was defeated on December 21, 1992 by 334 votes to 106. The Left voted in favour of the Congress while the Janata Dal and others abstained. This was in contrast to the close vote earlier in July.

The communal divisions in the country, however, assumed gigantic proportion. Communal riots broke out in Ahmedabad, Bombay, Bhopal and a few other cities in the north as well as in the south. There was a fanatic outcry in Islamic countries and some Western governments were shocked. The Shiv Sena-sponsored riots in Bombay in February were followed by widespread bomb attacks organised by Islamic fundamentalists from abroad.

In the first three decades after Independence, India had strong political leadership at the Centre in Mr. Jawaharlal Nehru and Mrs. Indira Gandhi who fostered national interests and followed an independent policy. India drifted closer towards the Soviet Union following the 1971 war with Pakistan over Bangladesh when the US held out a threat by sending its aircraft carrier Enterprise to the Bay of Bengal. India followed it up by signing a Peace and Friendship Treaty with the Soviet Union that provided a blanket of security to India.

Mr. Narasimha Rao can consider himself fortunate for his Prime Ministership coincided with the *detente* between the Super Powers unlike the intense ideological as well as military conflict that characterised the first four decades after the Second World War when the Super Powers directly or indirectly intervened in the national politics of India and other developing countries.

The influence of big business house in national-level politics is considerable though it is not clearly definable as these forces operated from behind the scenes. The relationship between the political leaders in power and business leaders was generally forged in pusuit of mutual advantage.

The recent liberalisations in industrial licensing and other controls that the Rao government introduced has greatly reduced the scope for corruption and dependence of business houses on government. Yet the Government had enormous patronage at its command exercised through financial and fiscal controls. Mr. Rao himself had tried to keep a distance from any business house.

Meanwhile, Mr. Rao as president of the party had tried to revive the organisation which had remained totally disorganised and centralised since the split in 1969. No Congress plenary session, nor any election to various party bodies at any level had been held since 1972. For the first time after 20 years, Mr. Rao managed to constitute district and pradesh committees, and held the first plenary session of the Congress in twenty years at Tirupati in June 1992. He was the Prime Minister as well as party president for an year.

The Tirupati session also witnessed Mr. Rao launching a frontal attack on communalism and emphasising the need to explore constitutional measures to separate politics from religion. The Congress party was wanting to destabilise at the earlier the four BJP governments in the northern states that were established on the basis of its successful appeal to Hindu sentiments in the last elections. Congress leaders were aware that the "kar sewa" launched by the VHP to build a temple at the disputed mosque site at Ayodhya was fully supported by the BJP in view of the political gains it promised. The opportunity finally came when the disputed Babri Masjid was demolished on December 6 by the overzealous congregation and the BJP and VHP leaders did not make any attempt to prevent the demolition of the mosque. A ban was imposed on the RSS and its front organisations, the VHP and the Bajrang Dal. The dismissal and subsequent dissolution of the other three BJP governments and state assemblies followed.

In the post-Babri Masjid demolition era, the Central Government has acquired the disputed area including the masjid site and has referred to the Supreme Court under Article 143 of the Constitution, the issue whether a temple actually existed in the previous centuries at the demolished masjid premises.

In the initial stages, P.V. sided with the BJP as he could not get the Left and the Janata Dal agree on a consensus over the election of the Speaker of the Lok Sabha.

He tasted tremendous success in resolving the Punjab imbroglio. The Punjab situation was crying for a solution after nine years of unabated internecine killings. The violence in the state had been escalating ever since the Blue Star Operation in the Golden Temple. In spite of severe action launched by the Centre, the killings crossed the 3000 mark in 1991.

A two-pronged strategy was adopted to check terrorist activities in the state. While the state government was asked to concentrate on rounding up the ring leaders of the various terrorist groups, the Central Government settled with several countries extradition treaties and agreements of cooperation to curb terrorism. The efforts with the USA to get Pakistan declared a terrorist state were intensified. All these efforts yielded results. Though the total killings in the state in 1992 were at 2059, towards the month of January 1993, they came down to 20 including those of police personnel killed. That was, indeed, a dramatic improvement in the situation in the trouble torn state.

Like the settlement in Punjab, the Bodoland problem that had led to unabated violent agitations in Assam has also been successfully overcome through negotiations. An accord for the formation of a Bodoland Autonomous Council within the state of Assam was signed on February 20, 1992.

Among the state building activities, two measures taken by the Narasimha Rao government stand out. One is the passage of the *Panachyati Raj* legislation introducing mandatory elections to local bodies and making adequate provision for their funding. This was an important piece of legislation as local bodies in several states have been lying dormant and thoroughly neglected. The second important structural change in administration that P.V. had brought about is the introduction of the committee system in Parliament for the consideration of the Union budget. This was again a proposal that has been pending for several years.

In the area of nation building, the two most controversial issues that constantly confronted the Narasimha Rao government were the issue of reservations of backward castes and the dispute over the Babri Masjid. Both the issues were spillovers from the previous period and were rooted in divisive party politics. The issue of reservation in government jobs was already settled in the southern states and Maharashtra after prolonged agitations.

The compromise formula that was evolved by Mr. Narasimha Rao on the job reservation issue through personal negotiations with the leaders of the political parties was to enhance the total percentage of jobs to be reserved to 60 per cent and allot 10 per cent of that to the economically backward even among the other upper castes. But owing to the rejection by the Supreme Court of the move to raise the limit, the Narasimha Rao government implemented the reservation order with the condition that the creamy layer of privileged sections belonging to the backward classes had been identified and excluded.

References

1. *Op. cit.*
2. Rao, Narasimha, Collected Speeches.
3. See Part I, Chapter 4, this book.

29

Congress under Sita Ram Kesari

Born in a lower middle class family in Bihar, Sri Sitra Ram Kesari rose to the status of the Congress president, a significant position in the political hierarchy. While he was a school student, he began to feel that India under the colonial rule would never be able to make any kind of economic progress. So he showed much concern about the economically weaker sections of the society to which he also belonged.

Sita Ram Kesari was much inspired by the Gandhian movement which was anti-*Raj* and having deep impact on non-violence. He offered his services to Gandhiji and in this way he became a staunch Gandhian and a *satyagrahi* who was jailed several times.

Kesari's identification with Congress was very sincere as he began to organise the workers in his own region. Depending on discipline and hard work in the field, he could mobilise the people with the grassroot level. As a result, people pinned their faith in him and from district level worker, he ascended to the position of the all-India position.

While contesting for the Congress seat of Lok Sabha, he came into contact with Indira Gandhi, Rajiv Gandhi and Narasimha Rao. He was elevated to the position of the Union Minister, with the portfolio of Welfare.

Kesari through public address could impress thousands of people regarding the ideology of the Indian National Congress. He laid emphasis on use of khadi, promoting education for backward classes, developmental schemes in the villages following Gandhian philosophy.

With the dawn of new politics and emergence of newer political parties was a setback to the prospect of the Congress, particularly in the states of Uttar Pradesh and Bihar. The political situation assumed such a proportion that it went beyond the control for Sita Ram Kesari who by this point of time had become over-ambitious with much power in his hands.

The criticism in the inner circles as well as in the media had made it difficult for Sita Ram Kesari to control the political goings-on. The 'hawks' in the Congress wanted an immediate change and many of them even proposed the name of Sonia Gandhi who, at various occasions, showed her reluctance to assume the office of the Congress president, at last agreed when majority of the members of the CWC requested her to do so.

Sita Ram Kesari was immediately asked to vacate the office which he denied. His reluctance in this regard proved fatal for him as almost all the senior Congress members elected Sonia Gandhi as the party President. The 'insulting' exit of Sita Ram Kesari gradually made him a political non-entity as he could not enjoy the power which he had enjoyed for a few years.

30

Congress under Sonia Gandhi

Rajiv and Sonia

Rajiv was barely 18 when he arrived in England at Trinity College, Cambridge. He fell in love with a pretty Italian student Sonia who had also come to Britain to learn English. She was born in 1946 in a well-to-do Italian family.

Rajiv's interest in aviation had developed while he was studying in England. By 1967, Rajiv was deeply obsessed with flying. He soon got his commercial flying licence and became an honorary instructor at the Delhi Flying Club. Rajiv officially joined Indian Airlines as an apprentice on 5 July, 1968.

Rajiv and Sonia were engaged on 25 January, 1968. Recalled Smt. Vijayalakshmi Pandit in an interview with All India Radio in 1985; "I remember Indira telephoning me to ask if I was prepared for a mild shock? My reply was, 'obviously' we were all immune to shocks by now. She laughed and said: "Sit down, while I tell you, Rajiv is engaged to an Italian girl." I don't recall that as a shock, But I told Indira, "The news is going to shock a lot of our own pretty girls."

While drastic changes were taking place in Indian politics, Rajiv and Sonia smoothly settled down to domestic life. Rajiv was enjoying his job as pilot with Indian Airlines while Sonia shaped herself into the role of a typical Indian housewife. She started wearing *saris* and learning Hindi.

Rajiv spent twelve years (1968—1980) with Indian Airlines. This was the crucial period in the Indian political history. The government was facing array of challenges on all fronts.

Indira Gandhi revoked Emergency in early 1977 and called for general elections to seek a fresh mandate. As a reaction to the emergency, the Congress was washed out in the general elections in March 1977. Janata Dal was voted to power and Morarji Desai was subsequently sworn in as Prime Minister of India.

In the middle of 1979, unable to combat the infightings in his government, Prime Minister Morarji Desai stepped down and Chaudhary Charan Singh took over as the caretaker Prime Minister. Elections were called for in January 1980.

On 3 January, 1980 in a verdict, the Indian electorate voted Mrs. Gandhi's Congress (I) back to power.

Sanjay Gandhi died on June 23, 1980 in a plane crash. Indira Gandhi was stunned by Sanjay's death. Rajiv, of course, was deeply upset over Sanjay's death. After Sanjay's death, Mrs. Gandhi got much support from Rajiv and Sonia.

Rajiv Gandhi introduced a new style of electioneering. He would address the people thus, "I have come to meet you and know your problems and I have come to make friendship with you. This election you are contesting. It is yours and the victory that will be . . . will be yours."

Soon after Rajiv took over as the Prime Minister of India, a part of North India turned volatile. He felt seriously about the law and order situation which he realised with quick administrative decision. He advised the Chief Ministers to go back immediately to their respective states and keep a watch on law and order situation. He assured the people that the Government would safeguard the life and property of every citizen, irrespective of his caste, creed and religion.

Rajiv Gandhi created history by leading his party to an unprecedented victory in the Eighth Lok Sabha General Election, shattering all previous electoral records since Independence. At one stroke, the Congress achieved the double distinction of winning nearly four-fifths of the total Lok Sabha seats voted for and securing more than 50 per cent of the votes cast.

One of the principal challenges that Rajiv Gandhi had during his term of office was to establish his own charisma and political credibility vis-à-vis the population where 63 per cent of the population were illiterate.

I am deeply touched by the trust placed on me by the CWC. However, the tragedy that has befallen on my children does not make it possible for me to accept the presidentship of the party . . ."

This was told by Sonia in a statement made on May 23 following Rajiv Gandhi's assassination.

Mrs. Sonia Gandhi kept her promise and did not join politics for more than five years. But the dwindling and continually declining fortunes of the Congress Party under successive presidents and leadership after Rajiv's assassination in 1991 and the consequent loud clamour by Congressmen for succour and repeated requests to Sonia Gandhi to help save the Congress Party of Nehru and Gandhi.

So she obliged and entered politics because she could not see the sacrifices made by her family go in vain.

Sonia said while campaigning at Hanamkonda, Andhra Pradesh, January 1998. "After my husband's death, I suffered in silence as canards were spread. Now I won't keep quiet." Sonia said in Mathura on February 12, 1998.

While Mrs. Sonia Gandhi has resurrected the Congress, Mr. Ramakrishna Hegde had given the BJP the much-needed shot in the arm. Until Mrs. Gandhi decided to enter the political arena, Congressmen in Karnataka were a demoralised lot. Sitaram Kesri's actions had brought down the credibility of the party.

Congress rallies addressed by Sonia Gandhi had been attracting huge crowds. Her apology on the Babri Masjid issue seems to have had a fairly good impact on Muslims. She has applied the brakes on what was once perceived as the BJP's smooth run to victory and dealt a blow to the Dal plagued with desertions.

Meanwhile, Sonia had asked the electorate not to support the smaller (regional) parties in the Lok Sabha elections as they had a narrow and limited vision. Their politics was detrimental to the country, she cautioned and added that small parties had no programmes on poverty eradication, providing employment or developing basic facilities.

Without naming the BJP, she further alleged that some parties were indulging in politics based on religion. She even claimed that opponents of the Congress were exploiting the slogan of *swadeshi* which was coined during the fight against Britishers.

Mrs. Gandhi also lashed out at the United Front government for suspending the pro-poor economic reforms initiated by the Congress government.

She, in the meantime, addressed four election meetings in the constituencies of top party leaders Arjun Singh, Kamal Nath, Arif Beg and Ashutosh Dayal Sharma, son of former President, Shankar Dayal Sharma, at Hoshangabad, Chhindwara, Bhopal and Vidisha, respectively. In all the meetings, Mrs. Gandhi recalled the association of Jawaharlal Nehru, Indira Gandhi and Rajiv Gandhi with the state.

In Bhopal, a major part of her speech was devoted to the achievements of the Congress government in the state.

She also warned that the secular fabric of the country was in danger from vested interests in the garb of religion. "Religion means *dharma*, which in turn means love, peace and good faith. The Hindu religion has never opted for violence and all religions and sects lived together in India and conflicts among different religions results in pain and agony", she added.

Meanwhile, giving due regards to her campaign for the Congress throughout the country, then Congress president Sitaram Kesari had described Sonia Gandhi as a 'mass leader' and claimed that she alone could lead 'crores and crores of Indians'.

"I am merely the president of Congress organisation and not a mass leader, and even if I claim to be, it will be wrong (to call myself a mass leader)", Mr. Kesari told a public rally in presence of Sonia Gandhi.

"Whenever Congress got delinked from Nehru-Gandhi family, it was weakened," Mr. Kesari said, adding "Sonia, by her entry, has taken the country by storm".

An air of festivity started blowing at the AICC headquarters as soon as the news regarding Mrs. Sonia Gandhi's decision to take over as the Congress president trickled in. Euphoric party workers and leaders started dancing to the tune of drums and a brass band.

The volunteers of the Youth Congress and DPCC leaders and workers were present in numbers to add to the festivity of the occasion. Most of the senior leaders also came to the party office carrying garlands and colourful bouquets to greet Mrs. Gandhi. Mrs. Gandhi went to accept their greetings after attending the brief meeting of the reconvened CWC.

Plot to Kill Sonia Unearthed

Meanwhile, the Congress party claimed that a plot to assassinate Sonia Gandhi had been unearthed at Bilaspur in Madhya Pradesh, where an engineer, said to be an explosives expert, was found dead in mysterious circumstances. Party spokesperson Najma Heptullah claimed that the Madhya Pradesh police had confirmed the 'serious conspiracy' and was investigating the matter. She said the investigations by the security agencies into the mysterious death of the Tamil engineer A.R. Venkataraju alias A.R. Raju had led to the untangling of the plot to eliminate Sonia Gandhi at Shahdol or Bilaspur, the two places where she was scheduled to address rallies on February 25. Raju hailed from Coimbatore, she added. Mrs. Heptullah expressed concern over the conspiracy and demanded that the Centre be more vigilant and beef up Sonia Gandhi's security.

Sonia Steps into 'Gandhi' Mould

Meanwhile, with her rise to power, Congress president Sonia Gandhi stunned her partymen and those responsible for her security. She walked from her residence to the AICC headquarters next door with SPG commandos and her car on toe. In choosing to walk down to the party office she was only following the footsteps of her husband Rajiv Gandhi, an old-timer recalled. It may be recalled here that when Mr. Gandhi was out of office, between 1989 and until his assassination two years later, he used to reach the party office on foot using the wooden gate connecting 10, Janpath and 24, Akbar Road.

It had also been learnt that Mrs. Gandhi would like to conduct the affairs of the party very much like the way her husband did. She had, in fact, sought reports about the state and functioning of the party apparatus during her husband's tenure from party leaders who were office-bearers at that time.

In her first meeting with the AICC office-bearers Mrs. Gandhi directed that the AICC session, rescheduled to be held on April 6 at the Talkatora Stadium, would be without fanfare. An office-bearer said, "Mrs. Gandhi asked us to economise. She has forbidden us from indulging in anything ostentatious."

Sonia's Word Scotches Front's Efforts

Just before President K.R. Narayanan had formally decided to invite Bharatiya Janata Party (BJP) leader Atal Behari Vajpayee to form the next government, the United Front and its Left constituents gave up the attempts to forge a coalition with the Congress.

The fizzling out of the effort was apparent in the statement of the new Congress president Sonia Gandhi that owing to paucity of number her party would not stake its claim.

After the meeting, the erstwhile Tamil Maanila Congress chief G.K. Moopanar had said that the UF had 'virtually no role' left, since Mrs. Gandhi's point of view, had cast the seal on the matter and if conveyed to the president, would have also facilitated his choice.

Those who attended the meet included former Prime Minister H.D. Deva Gowda, Janata Dal leader S. Jaipal Reddy, Communist Party of India general secretary A.B. Bardhan and Janata Dal chief Sharad Yadav.

Meanwhile, Janata Dal supremo Sharad Yadav said, "Janata Dal has always been saying that the Front had secured mandate only to sit in the opposition as its strength had come down from 191 to a mere 100 in the 12th Lok Sabha". Asked to comment on some of UF constituents' suggestion for a Congress-led government to keep, he said this could be contemplated only if the Congress had shown any interest in this regard. "When the Congress itself had decided not to stake claim where was the question of the Front trying to forge such an alliance with just 100 MPs", he added.

Sonia Hesitates on CPP Post

Meanwhile, Sonia Gandhi was in a hesitant mood about accepting the leadership of the party's parliamentary wing also as Mrs. Gandhi did not want to convey the impression that the Gandhi family was out to 'grab' all party-related posts. But at the same time, she was not too sure if an election of the post would have helped in uniting the Congress.

Mrs. Gandhi had become the inevitable choice as the three contenders for the post. Sharad Pawar, Madhavrao Scindia and Rajesh Pilot had indicated they would only be in the race if she were to turn down the offer.

Meanwhile, Mrs. Gandhi launched an image-building exercise. She even resumed the practice of Janata Darshan at her residence and had begun meeting partymen throughout the day.

As an Opposition Leader

She is playing a constructive role in Indian politics. Her popularity among Indian masses at present, no doubt, projects Sonia Gandhi as the future prime minister of India.

Congress as a Political Force in Future

The Indian National Congress, the premier political party in the Indian subcontinent was founded in 1885 which later launched all-India mass movements under the leadership of Mahatma Gandhi. The Nehru era and the Indira Gandhi era comprised of a 35-year old period and the contribution of these two leaders is indeed significant enough. In 1990s when Rajiv Gandhi was no more on the national political scene and P.V. Narasimha Rao was appointed the Prime Minister of India, there cropped up several regional parties. Their political programme of socio-economic agenda or developmental scheme were almost the same. Thus, the regional leaders became critical of the Congress and its ideology.

Elections were held in the Hindi belt and Congress failed to perform better in UP, Rajasthan, Bihar and elsewhere. Some parties like Samajwadi Party, Bahujan Samaj Party, Janata Party, Samata Party, the Haryana Manch, Akali Party, the National Conference, the new political parties in the North-Eastern region and others became deep rooted in several regions where they claimed their monopoly of votes.

Meanwhile, stalwarts like Sharad Pawar and P.A. Sangama left the Congress on account of internal differences in the party. It was indeed a great setback to the political stature and future prospects of the Congress which came under a heavy cloud in western and eastern India.

Some senior Congress leaders however stuck to the party like a rock and showed much discipline in the organisation. In the Northern belt, the issue of Hindu-

Muslim unity was highlighted and a socio-economic programme was put forward for weaker sections of our society. As a result, it is found that there had been substantial progress of the party in Delhi, Rajasthan, Central India, western India as well as other regions of Indian subcontinent.

Above all, the Congress is a well-known party to the people of India as it has been a mass-based party for a period of more than a hundred years. People are well aware of the fact that this Party, under the leadership of Mahatma Gandhi, Pandit Nehru, Sardar Patel, Subhas Bose, Dr. Rajendra Prasad and several others had launched a long-drawn political party for the attainment of *Swaraj* for India. People residing in the far-flung areas representing different communities are familiar with its ideology and sense of secularism.

Though opposed by various forces at different levels, it is believed that the Congress would meet the opposition with confidence based on the support of the millions of people and will again emerge as a force to reckon with. The downward trend which it had to experience between 1995—2001 will no longer remain a glaring phenomena at the political stage of the Indian subcontinent.

Sonia Gandhi as the Inheritor of Nehru-Gandhi Legacy

Mrs. Sonia Gandhi is the sole inheritor of Nehru-Gandhi legacy. She attracts and enjoys spontaneous confidence and support of the people from all walks of life and different sections of our multilingual and multi ethenic society. During her tenure as president of the Congress Party and leader of the parliamentary party, Mrs. Sonia Gandhi has nurtured both the wings (organsational and parliamentary) to the extent of a mature and disciplined party once again. Her quick understanding of the assessment of the different state leaders and her decisiveness is helping the party to reorganise itself to the level of winning the confidence of the people of this country.

The Congress Party under her leadership has once again found out its moorings and slowly but certainly is being re-organised as the only party which is democratic and secular in its content and credentials and is true to its utterances and commitments. It is the only party which is wedded to the ideals of socialism, meant for the benefit of the weaker sections of the society. It is only Sonia Gandhi's Congress Party which wants *Liberalisation* and *Globalisation* to be adopted to this country's situation according to the ground realities and with a *human face,* meant to benefit the poor sections of our society.

Now, the day is not far off when the Congress under the leadership of Mrs Sonia Gandhi will again come to power at the Centre and will usher in an era of progress and development with peace and goodwill among all.

Index